VALUE ENGINEERING

A PRACTICAL APPROACH FOR OWNERS, DESIGNERS AND CONTRACTORS

VALUE ENGINEERING

A PRACTICAL APPROACH FOR OWNERS, DESIGNERS AND CONTRACTORS

LARRY W. ZIMMERMAN, P.E.
Certified Value Specialist

GLEN D. HART
Certified Value Specialist

CBS

CBS PUBLISHERS & DISTRIBUTORS PVT. LTD.

New Delhi • Bengaluru • Chennai • Kochi • Mumbai • Pune

ISBN : 978-81-239-1877-8

First Indian Edition : 1988

This edition has been reprinted in India by arrangement with
Van Nostrand Reinhold Company Inc., USA

Published by Satish Kumar Jain for
CBS Publishers & Distributors Pvt. Ltd.,
CBS Plaza, 4819/XI Prahlad Street, 24 Ansari Road, Daryaganj,
New Delhi - 110002, India. • Website: www.cbspd.com
e-mail: delhi@cbspd.com, cbspubs@airtelmail.in
Ph.: 23289259, 23266861, 23266867 • Fax: 011-23243014

Branches:

- ***Bengaluru:*** Seema House, 2975, 17th Cross, K.R. Road, Bansankari 2nd Stage, Bengaluru - 560070
  • Ph.: +91-80-26771678/79 • Fax: +91-80-26771680
  • E-mail: cbsbng@gmail.com, bangalore@cbspd.com
- ***Pune:*** Bhuruk Prestige, Sr. No. 52/12/2+1+3/2, Narhe, Haveli (Near Katraj-Dehu Road By-pass), Pune - 411041
  • Ph.: +91-20-64704058/59, 020-32392277 • E-mail: pune@cbspd.com
- ***Kochi:*** 36/14, Kalluvilakam, Lissie Hospital Road, Kochi - 682018, Kerala • Ph.: +91-484-4059061-65
  • Fax: +91-484-4059065 • E-mail: cochin@cbspd.com
- ***Chennai:*** 20, West Park Road, Shenoy Nagar, Chennai - 600030
  Ph.: +91-44-26260666, 26208620 • Fax: +91-44-42032115
  • E-mail: chennai@cbspd.com
- ***Mumbai:*** 83-C, Ist Floor, Dr. E. Moses Road, Worli, Mumbai-400 018, Maharashtra Ph.: +91-9833017933, 022-24902340/24902341
  • E-mail: mumbai@cbspd.com

Printed at :
Nikunj Print Process, Delhi

Preface

Spiraling construction costs and an ever-increasing tightening of money have fostered a need for controlling and managing costs. Federal agencies, through their various construction grants programs, have adopted Value Engineering as a means of stretching construction dollars and at the same time improving the performance and reliability of the end product. Constraints on spending, tightening of investment dollars and a desire to obtain the maximum value for each dollar spent have helped increase the acceptance of value engineering.

The initial success of value engineering on construction projects within the General Services Administration (GSA), and the Environmental Protection Agency (EPA) has brought about an awareness of the merits of value engineering by architects, engineers and contractors. Initially, VE studies were conducted under the direction of a Certified Value Specialist (CVS), an accredited professional value engineer certified by the Society of American Value Engineers (SAVE). Now, engineers and architects are conducting value studies and often run into pitfalls not readily apparent.

This book is a how-to-do-it book! Its purpose is to explain the ins and outs involved in conducting a value engineering study. The book is intended to express the practical rather than the theoretical aspects of value engineering. Many books have been written about value engineering as it relates to the manufacturing field with emphasis on the theory behind it. The authors have drawn freely from their experience in conducting value engineering seminars and studies in compiling the major contents of the book. Every attempt has been made to address the key elements of value engineering and to provide examples of actual case studies.

The authors have attempted to exclude material of a general nature that appears in many value engineering texts and instead have concentrated on value engineering as it relates to the construction industry. The key elements the authors wish to cover are the background of value engineering in the construction industry, the tool-kit of value engineering, managing and conducting a value engineering study, and an in-depth explanation of the value engineering job plan with successful examples of its results. Examples of actual value engineering cases provide the reader with a guide for applying value engineering in their own work. It is hoped that the examples and the accompanying written description will give the reader adequate comparison material to serve as a guide for his/her work.

During the past 22 years over 5000 people have attended value engineering seminars conducted by Glen Hart. These seminars included people from the fields of manufacturing, research, construction, procurement, purchasing, software, hardware and the like. Many of these people have encouraged Glen to summarize the contents of the VE seminar in book form. A large portion of this book is based on Glen's 22 years of experience conducting VE seminars and leading value programs. This material is augmented with technical data, cost control techniques, energy modeling, life-cycle costing models, and the management approach that the authors used in conducting value engineering studies in the construction field.

Much of the stimulus to write a text on value engineering has been generated by the results of the value engineering studies. Time and time again unnecessary life-cycle costs have been drastically reduced resulting in substantial savings to the owner. When comparing the savings for value engineering studies to the study costs, the results have been astonishing. Return on investment ratio (savings divided by cost of study) have ranged from as high as 485:1 to 2:1. Results of this nature applied throughout the construction industry are impressive. It is estimated that if 3 to 5 percent of the cost of construction were eliminated (within the realm of possibility with value engineering) the Environmental Protection Agency would be able to fund thousands of additional wastewater treatment construction projects as some projects cannot be funded due to a shortage of money.

It is the hope of the authors that the contents of the book will benefit managers, engineers, architects, contractors, developers, politicians and others responsible for ensuring that we receive the maximum value for our money and that teachers and students will find the book useful in their curriculums.

Early efforts at value engineering were directed toward the manufacturing field where a savings in a product would be magnified by the number of times the product was produced. Value engineering in construction came to the forefront in the 1960s when construction costs were changing faster than estimators could keep track of the fluctuating costs. The enormous amount of construction money expended and the potential for cost savings has thrust value engineering to the forefront of the industry.

The authors of the book have been fortunate to be involved in the development of many of the federal government's first endeavors into value engineering studies and to have conducted 40-hour value engineering workshops to train many of the architects and engineers in the field today. Many of the ideas and concepts expressed in the book are the result of experience gained from these individuals to whom we owe our thanks. In addition, the requirements for value engineering of federal construction projects has stimulated the challenge to our profession to maximize the value of our product.

Our thanks to Arthur Beard Engineers, Inc. and Smith Hinchman & Grylls Associates, Inc. and especially to the participants in value engineering workshops who have been helpful in providing much of the case history text material from studies conducted by the authors. Writing any book requires motivation and we thank our wives, June and Sue, and our colleagues for their support and ego-building during preparation of the manuscript. Our thanks goes out to all of you.

Larry W. Zimmerman, PE, CVS
Glen D. Hart, CVS

Contents

Preface v

1. Introduction and Background of Value Engineering 1

Definition of Value Engineering 2
All Designs Have Unnecessary Costs 5
The Reasons Poor Value Occurs 6
Background and History of Value Engineering 10

2. Habits; Roadblocks and Attitudes 19

Habit Ruts 20
Attitudes 23
The Attitude Screen 27
It Can't Be Done 29
The Power of a Positive Attitude 30
Realizing Our True Potential 31

3. The Value Engineering Job Plan 32

Introduction 32
The Inventive Process 32
Reasons for Using The Job Plan 32
The Job Plan 34

4. Function Analysis 60

Function and Its Role in Achieving Value 60
Criteria Used to Evaluate Value 62
Function: An Approach to Obtaining Value 63
Quantifying Function in Terms of Its Cost and Worth 67
Graphical Function Analysis 71
Evaluate by Comparison 71
Advantages of Function Analysis Approach 73
Functional Analysis Systems Technique (FAST Diagramming) 74

5. Creative Thinking 83

Introduction 83
Definition of Creative Thinking 84
Creative People 84
Characteristics of Creative People 87
Creative Processes (Toolkit of Creativity) 89
Psychological Basis of Creativity 91
What Stimulates Creativity? 93
What Stifles Creativity? 94
Conducting a Creative Session 97
Crux of Creative Thinking 98
The Creative Process 100
Creative Problem-Solving Techniques 100

6. Managing the Value Engineering Study 103

Why the Program Works 103
The Relationship Between Owner-Designer and Value Engineering Consultant 107
Who Influences the Cost of a Project? 109
Facility Life-Cycle Process 112
Who Influences the Cost of a Project? 121
When is the Owner Ready for Value Engineering? 121
Selecting a VE Consultant 123
Staffing and Structuring Teams for a VE Study 124
Conducting a VE Project Study 129

7. Cost Modeling 141

Cost Validation 142
Cost Estimating 142
Cost Models 144
Matrix Cost Model 144
Functional Cost Models 145
Uses of Project Models 147

8. Life-cycle Costing 150

Definition of Life-cycle Costing 150
Purpose and Implications of Life-cycle Costing 151
Economic Principles Used in Life-cycle Costing 152
Accounting for Escalation 152
Types of Life-cycle Costs 156
Using Life-cycle Costing as a Tool 160

9. Energy 173

Introduction 173
Energy Resources and Consumption 173
Energy Cost Escalation 176
Sources of Energy Supply 178
End Use of Energy 179
Energy Embodiment of Construction Materials 179

Transportation Systems 182
Water and Wastewater Treatment 185
Building and Energy Design 187
Factors Affecting Energy Consumption 190
Energy Models 193
Analyzing Building Energy Use 193
The Building as a Heat Body 196
Factors Impacting Energy Consumption 196
Key Factors Affecting Energy Consumption in Buildings 208
Impact of Maintenance on Energy Savings 212
Demand Charges for Electrical Energy 212
Energy Prospectus 213
Areas of Potential Energy Savings in Plant Design 213

10. Value Engineering Case Study No. 1: Wastewater Treatment Plant 216

Introduction 216
Treatment Plant Service Area 216
Project Requirements 217
Description of Project 217
Organization and Staffing of VE Teams 217
Description of VE Workshop 218
Information Phase 218
Creative Phase 221
Judgment Phase 221
Development Phase 221
Recommendation Phase 222

11. Value Engineering Case Study No. 2: Wastewater Treatment Plant 235

Project Requirements 235
Description of Project 236
Organizing and Staffing of VE Teams 237
Description of VE Workshop 238
The VE Workshop 239
Cost Model 239
Functional Analysis 241
Creative Phase 243
Judgment Phase 243
Development Phase 243
Recommendation Phase 243
Examples of Implemented VE Recommendations 248
Designer's Response 248

12. Value Engineering Case Study No. 3: Engineering Management Building 257

Building Requirements 258
Description of Project 258
VE Project Team 261
Description of VE Workshop 261
Examples of VE Recommendations 267

13. 40-hour VE Workshop Seminars 271

What do Participants Need to Bring to a 40-hour Workshop Seminar? 273

Bibliography 275

Index 277

VALUE ENGINEERING

A PRACTICAL APPROACH FOR OWNERS, DESIGNERS AND CONTRACTORS

1
Introduction and Background of Value Engineering

Saving money and, at the same time, providing better value, is a concept that everyone can support. The benefits of spreading our investment dollar, building more for less money, increasing efficiency and cutting down our dependency on energy-intensive buildings (high energy cost) and plant facilities need to be recognized today and pursued in the future.

People are interested in saving money. Everyone is looking for a sound investment with a high rate of return for their investment dollar. When the first value engineering study was conducted in the late 1940s, no one suspected that the savings would be so enormous and that the concept of value engineering would spread so rapidly. Return on investment (dollars saved per dollar spent) for manufactured products and construction projects have been remarkable. More on these returns later in this chapter.

In our constant battle to find a better way to fight inflation, the application of value engineering comes to the forefront. The value engineering program is a proven technique used to combat runaway costs. The program has been tried and proven for countless owners and manufacturers.

Several books have been written on the theory and technique of value engineering. Our book is intended to be a reference for people who will be doing value engineering, or to those people who would like to benefit from the cost savings potential that can be realized from its application. Its primary audience is composed of planners, engineers, architects, designers, operators and maintenance personnel who design and operate buildings and plant facilities, and owners, utility companies, developers, investors, contractors and private companies that must make the pivotal decisions affecting the total cost of their investments.

Construction areas are the main topics to be covered in this book. The application of value techniques with respect to the construction industry will be utilized. At this writing, the authors have participated in over 40 value engineering studies on buildings, highway projects and treatment facilities. In addition, Glen Hart, one of the authors, has led value engineering studies in over 100 manufacturing companies. Savings of over $50 for each dollar spent on value engineering were not uncommon. General Services Administration, the United States Environmental Protection Agency, Veterans

Administration, Federal Highway Administration, Department of Health, Education and Welfare and the Corps of Engineers all have requirements for the application of value engineering to their construction projects.

Figure 1-1 indicates the trend in costs of construction over the past 65 years. Costs remained relatively stable from about 1915 to 1940. From 1940 to 1948 the cost of construction doubled. It doubled again from 1948 to 1963, again from 1963 to 1973, and again from 1973 to 1979. Inflation alone will double the cost every 7 to 8 years. Value engineering helps curb this rapid rate of inflation.

This book is intended as a reference to teach how to conduct a value engineering study. We would like to share our experiences with our readers so that they may benefit from our experiences and learn the techniques we have used successfully.

DEFINITION OF VALUE ENGINEERING

Value engineering is a proven management technique using a systematized approach to seek out the best functional balance between the cost, reliability, and performance of a product or project. The program seeks to improve the management capability of people and to promote progressive change by identifying and removing unnecessary cost.

Value engineering has several techniques that serve as the tool kit of the value analyst. These techniques are identified in Table 1-1 as Key Elements of Value Engineering. Each of these areas are used in a value engineering study or are areas that must be addressed when conducting a project study.

Three terms have evolved in the value engineering field, each of which is used to describe methodology and procedure. Value programs have been described at different times as *Value Analysis, Value Engineering* and *Value Management*. When working in the field of value, all three terms will describe the application of value techniques (Table 1-2).

The systematic approach of value engineering is the Job Plan. The job plan is the road map for defining the required task, and determining the most economical combination of functions to achieve the task. The job plan also helps us to identify high cost areas in the design, i. e., items that are at a higher cost than on other similar facilities. Value engineering also uses the functional approach that makes it necessary for the designer to identify the real requirements of their project. In defining the project, the analyst uses two-word descriptions such as house personnel, transfer oil, convert energy, purify water, etc.

The Job Plan consists of five basic steps:

1. Information Phase
2. Creative Phase
3. Judgment Phase
4. Development Phase
5. Recommendation Phase

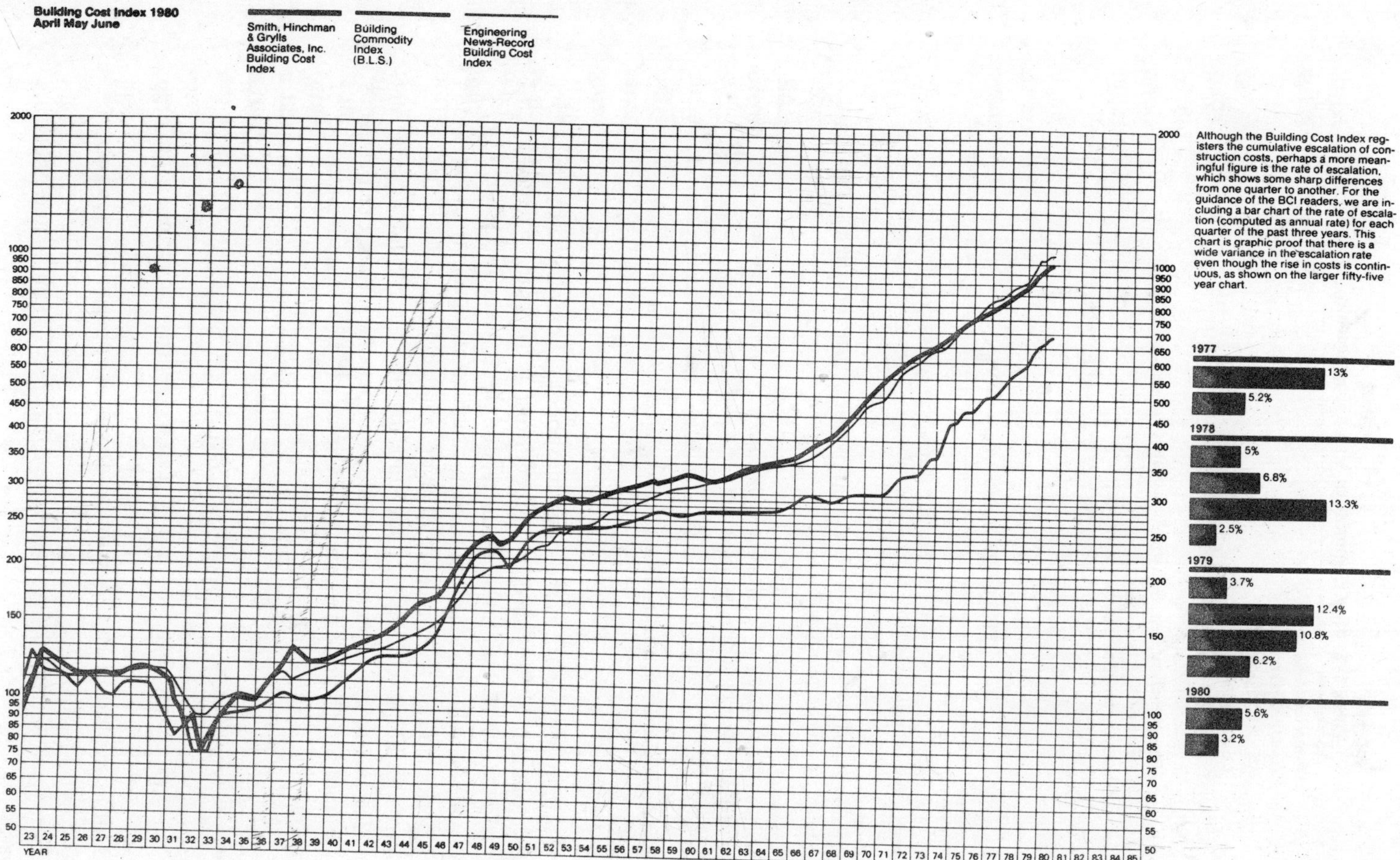

Figure 1-1. Construction Cost Index. (Courtesy of Smith Hinchman & Grylls Associates, Inc., Architects/Engineers/Planners).

Table 1-1. Key Elements of Value Engineering.

Key Elements
Function Analysis
Creative Thinking
VE Job Plan
Cost Models
Life Cycle Costing
Evaluation Matrix
Functional Analysis Systems Techniques
Cost and Worth
Habits, Roadblocks, and Attitudes
Managing the Owner/Designer/Value Consultant Relationship

Table 1-2. Value Programs.

Program	Description
Value Engineering	Describes a value study on a project or product that is being developed. It analyses the cost of the project as it is being designed.
Value Analysis	Describes a value study of a project or product that is already built or designed and analyzes the product to see if it can be improved.
Value Management*	Identifies the methodology and techniques used in value work, but does not distinguish between engineering of a building or facility and the analysis of a product. It is used to describe the entire field of value endeavors.

*Value Management was first used by the General Services Administration in 1974.

The job plan follows the same basic methodology employed by inventors in the development of new ideas and procedures. It forces them to go beyond their usual creative thresholds. Engineers, architects and contractors, for example would use value engineering to help generate new designs and methods of construction to remove unnecessary costs from projects.

It sometimes helps to have an understanding of "What Value Engineering is." The designer's first impression of value engineering is that it criticizes his design without involving engineering principles. A clearer understanding of value engineering is shown by the following list:

Value Engineering Is:

1. Systems Oriented—a formal job plan to identify and remove unnecessary costs.
2. Multidisciplined Team Approach—teams of experienced designers and VE consultants.
3. Life Cycle Oriented—examines the total cost of owning and operating a facility.
4. A Proven Management Technique.
5. Function Oriented—relates function required to the value received.

Value Engineering is Not:

1. Design Review—it is not intended to correct omissions made in design, nor to review calculations made by the designer.
2. A Cheapening Process—it does not cut cost by sacrificing needed reliability and performance.
3. A Requirement Done on All Designs—it is *not* a part of every designer's scheduled review, but a formal cost and function analysis.
4. Quality Control—it does more than review fail-safe reliability status of plant or product design.

While value engineering is none of the analyses mentioned above, it has benefits in many of these areas.

ALL DESIGNS HAVE UNNECESSARY COSTS

Another important factor is that all design projects have unnecessary costs designed into them. Studies invariably show that all designs have unnecessary cost regardless of how excellent the design team may be. It is impossible to bring together the innumerable details of a construction project with the best functional balance between cost, performance and reliability without a value engineering review. It is an elusive combination and almost impossible to reach in every detail. Even Thomas A. Edison's inventions were improved by lesser souls. Once the designer and owner are aware of this, it becomes easier for them to accept the fact that a VE study team will have ideas that will benefit the project. It should also be stated that the goal of the value consultant is similar to that of the designer—to ensure a design that meets the owner's required function at the most reasonable life-cycle cost.

We also point out that anyone conducting a value engineering study is doing an easier job than the original designer. Why? Because we are reviewing and not conceptualizing. The VE consultant is a Monday morning quarterback who reviews the Sunday game plan (his strength lies in hindsight and review). Everyone knows it is easier to quarterback on Monday morning than it is on the Saturday night or Sunday afternoon of the ballgame. A different set of circumstances faces the VE team because they sit down with plans and specifications that have been conceptualized to a certain point. Deductive reasoning is used to compare alternatives to the design. The designer uses inductive reasoning based on recall of past experience.

Designs of construction projects are complex. They require investment, experience and talented people. But, regardless of how capable or how overwhelmingly able a designer is, there will always be unnecessary cost hidden in his design. The very nature of construction design demands that countless variables be considered and pulled together by a certain date. The designer is under the gun to meet that due date and he must ensure that a viable, reliable plan is formulated. With that set of circumstances, the design grows and it

Table 1-3. Reasons Why Poor Value Occurs.

1. Lack of time
2. Lack of information
3. Lack of the idea
4. Misconceptions
5. Temporary circumstances that inadvertently become permanent
6. Habits
7. Attitudes
8. Politics
9. Lack of fee

takes form. Once the project is formed under the pressures of anxious effort, the designer becomes wed to the project as it is, and may be unable to review it for unnecessary cost. The VE team has an objective viewpoint, not having participated in the original design. In fact, one of the requirements of value engineering is that the team members cannot be involved in the original design. The value engineering team may not have the knowledge of the original designer on the project, but they can still improve it. Value engineering improves designs by viewing them from a parallel yet discrete viewpoint. It doesn't matter who designed the project. If the authors designed a project and someone else did a VE study, unnecessary cost would be found.

Unnecessary cost occurs in all designs and is an important point to consider in any relationship with the designer. He must understand that unnecessary costs in a design are not a reflection on his abilities as a professional, but rather a management problem that needs to be addressed.

THE REASONS POOR VALUE OCCURS

During a presentation to a design firm, the question was asked, "How can we manage our firm such that we will not need a value engineering study?" The reply was that although improvements can be made to the design, there is always unnecessary cost. The challenge is to keep these costs to a minimum.

There are many reasons why unnecessary costs, or poor value creep into designs. Although there are an endless number of reasons for poor value, the following reasons seem to recur most often (Table 1-3). This is evidenced in the 40-hour seminars taught by the authors. Not all of these reasons are attributable to the designer. Owners have an impact on value of a project because they establish the primary criteria of design and because they operate and maintain the final facilities. Contractors influence value by the quality of workmanship. Their skill in construction and the integrity of their product impacts the cost of the facility for years into the future. Regulatory agencies also impact the cost of a project by their laws, codes, standards and minimum design criteria. The cost of a project and its influence on value will be discussed in Chapter 7.

Lack of Time

We all know about that. Every architect and engineer, and every designer has a due date to deliver his final plans. If he does not deliver, his reputation suffers. The designer, also, has only a limited amount of time to make every possible cost comparison in order to achieve the most desirable degree of value. The lack of time is one reason unnecessary cost gets into a design. Imagine being told you have nine months to design a power plant or six months to design a $30 million wastewater treatment facility. The dramatic impact of time on increased construction costs is forcing tighter schedules and opens the way for added costs.

"I need more time to fine-tune this job!" wailed the engineer. Planning may take years to progress and evolve, but, when the design starts, it is expected immediately. But look at the bright side, that's why architects and engineers are hired—to accomplish the impossible!

Lack of Information

We live in an era of the technical explosion. New materials and products are constantly entering the market. It is impossible to become knowledgeable on all these changes. It is also difficult to accept all these new products until we are assured of their integrity.

An example is the use of nonmetallic chains on rectangular sedimentation tanks. A recommendation was made to change the specifications from metallic to nonmetallic. The savings in replacement cost was substantial. The engineer conducting a review of the VE recommendation had not realized that the savings in operation and maintenance was so substantial.

A building on the west coast had a rock veneer finish. The VE recommendation called for a slump block finish for almost half the price with an acceptable esteem value. The designer was unaware of the cost differential of the respective products. No designer can keep up with the technical explosion in all areas of design.

Lack of the Idea

No one can think of everything. Sometimes we just don't crystallize that ideal combination that is the best design. As designers, we have all looked at one of our projects and with 20/20 hindsight said, "I wish we had designed that a little differently." We did not have the idea at the time we prepared the design.

An example is the piping aboard ships, which are overhead, around bulkheads, and across the deck. When you put the ship up to 30 knots, the pipes vibrate with a terrific noise if they are not secure. The piping supports were being made with tailor-made fittings. The contractors used maleable clay, placed it up against a set of pipes to get an impression, then tailor-made a fitting to that exact impression. The fitting was then bolted to the overhead pipes or on the bulkhead. Somebody suggested using the metal strapping used to fasten packages and shipping crates. Why couldn't the metal strapping be placed around the pipes, attached to a support and then tightened? It would be a lot faster, less costly and just as effective. The savings was over $200,000 on one ship.

Misconceptions

All of us have honest misconceptions. Experience will sometimes give us an honest misconception because we were not exposed to subsequent development that would change the truth that we believe from our earlier experience. Our best efforts can end up being incorrect. In one instance, a designer was selecting materials for a gear shifter on a variable speed motor. The part was a fabricated piece costing $161. The designer knew that the part could be cast, but no one had actually checked out the casting because they thought it would fail. Deeper investigation by the VE team showed that a casting process existed that gave the required strength at a cost of $15. This part had been fabricated for over 10 years at a high cost because of an honest misconception. They believed that only a fabrication would be strong enough to endure in that application.

There is a need to ensure that we have chosen our design properly so that it is reliable and functional. We have to judge the facts when deciding whether to "stick to our convictions or be convicted by our stickiness." Paraphrase by R. Waldo Emerson.

Temporary Circumstances that Inadvertently Become Permanent

Time and again we are pressed for a decision. A temporary decision is made. We mean to get back to it later and make a change or we make a requirement for one project and it suddenly becomes a standard for all designs used by the company. This often happens in specifications. A floor loading rate is set at 100 pounds per square foot, or a lighting level is 150 footcandles. The designer means to recalibrate the specification when he gets more information, but he has to have something to put in there right away. This means that he sets the criteria high, where he knows it is safe, with the intention of returning to the problem when time allows. He never gets back to it so it goes in as a permanent requirement. It is a temporary circumstance that inadvertently becomes permanent and is a built-in unnecessary cost. It is a routine occurrence.

Habits

Everyone modestly considers themselves to be intelligent. Obviously, design engineers are very disciplined or they would not have achieved their degree or their current position. If you were asked whether you are primarily a creature of intelligence, a creature of habit, or a creature of emotion, how would you respond? Your answer would probably be intelligence, but that would not be true. Primarily, we are more creatures of habit. This is both good and bad. It is good in that it enables us to build skills and do things quickly and responsively. It is often bad on the design board when elements are repeated that should have been changed. The designer is following a habit solution that may have become obsolete, and habits are a big reason for unnecessary costs in a project. The temptation to use designs over and over again, simply because they worked once, is ominous. It worked on the last job, so let's slap it into this new job.

An example is an equipment building for a major utility company. They used the same basic building design whether the building was in New Orleans or Minnesota. It was the habit solution. The air-conditioning system was provided to maintain operating temperatures for equipment during hot weather in New Orleans, and provide the same function in Minnesota. An exhaust fan could be used in Minnesota to perform the same function. Habit solutions did not give true value in this case.

Attitudes

All of us realize that our attitudes sometimes get in the way of our reasoning. Even the best of us become defensive when analyzed by someone within our company or from outside. Let us compare two designers who are technically knowledgeable, experienced and hard working. One is flexible and open to compromise; the other is quite inflexible and rigid. The second engineer's inflexibility becomes apparent in his designs, his concepts and his ideas. Many times his uncompromising posture will inadvertently stifle his natural urge to broaden his creative base. Preconceptions can alienate us from reality and the new information we need.

Attitudes can make us obsolete. You have heard the expression, "Twenty-five years of experience tells me my design is good." How often is that one year of experience multiplied twenty-five times?

Politics

Politics are complex. There are many people to please and divergent forces involved. At times politics are beneficial and at other times they slow us down and steer us away from the best solution. Often the least costly alternative to a construction project may not be acceptable to the citizens in the surrounding geographic area. Take for instance the decision to construct a major landfill in the area of high-cost homes. Pressure is brought to bear on the planning agency through politics to move the site. The new site adds $1 million in cost to the taxpayers.

Control of grant funding is a controversial subject in many areas where the state or federal government pays for a portion of the project. Applications grants, funding requests, contract procurement regulations, plan review procedures, length of plan review, and the many reports involved in our projects today add extra dollars to our construction project costs.

Consider, also, the impact of having a major water resources contract stalled by disagreement over Congressional approval. Escalation cost of 1 to 1½ percent per month adds huge sums to the costs of projects. There is also the side of politics that protects our citizens from the indiscriminate pillage of our countryside and our natural resources.

One of the major impacts of politics is on the fluctuation in the investment dollars that allow development. A tight economy may tie up monetary resources and squelch construction. Construction costs may go down when this happens and go up when everyone has a backlog of jobs.

Lack of Fee

Not having the necessary funds to properly complete a design can materially affect the end product. Shortcuts taken to stay within schedule and within budget often add to the unnecessary costs in a design. Architectual and engineering firms are continually forced to lower their fees and profits. Costs of construction soar, but designer costs have remained relatively stable. Bidding for design contracts has forced the price of contracts down, forcing the designer to cut his costs to the point where he cannot make the comparisons necessary to obtain a cost effective job.

Design contracts represent 7 to 12 percent of construction cost and less than 3 percent of the total cost of owning and operating a facility. Lack of design fee is a small part of the project cost, but heavily influences the total life-cycle cost of the facility.

BACKGROUND AND HISTORY OF VALUE ENGINEERING

Early Development in the General Electric Company

It is important that the manner in which the value engineering program materialized, developed and evolved be understood. A person seldom can make a proper judgment about a technique unless he knows how it developed. Most people in the construction industry believe that value engineering is a new program still in its infancy. Value engineering, as applied to the construction field, has been used since the late 1960s or early 1970s.

Value engineering is not a new concept. Its origin dates back to World War II. The evolution of value engineering from its beginning in the manufacturing industry, into government procurement sections, and eventually into the construction industry, is an interesting story of success. However, the success was challenged at times by the reluctant designer. As in most success stories, progress overcomes resistance to change and the results are astounding.

The initial development of the value engineering concept was a product of the General Electric Company. The man responsible for the development of the value engineering program was Lawrence D. Miles, an electrical engineer with GE. Mr Miles was assigned to the purchasing department under the direction of vice-president, Harry Erlicher. Mr. Miles was a cost-conscious engineer who was often dissatisfied with the high cost of many of GE's projects.

As World War II broke out, material shortages were occurring. Miles and Erlicher noticed time and again that plants were faced with substantial material shortages and could not maintain a comfortable inventory. All types of steels, aluminum, copper, bronze, nickel and tin were committed to the war effort. Electrical components that once were plentiful were committed to strategic applications. To ameliorate the problem, production schedules for war matériel, aircraft, ships and other military needs were moved up and production rates were required to increase astronomically.

Being in the procurement field under wartime conditions must have been challenging. Imagine being responsible for manufacturing a product that had been produced easily in the past, but now must be redeveloped using different materials. The function remains the same, but the method of providing that function is now different. American industry overcame those adverse conditions with great success. One example is a pump rotor usually made of stainless steel for underwater use. Stainless steel was unavailable. The manufacturers searched for an alternative that would accomplish the same function. Spalding fiber was tried. Instead of costing $15 like the stainless steel, the spalding fiber pump rotor cost $5.00. It was more impervious to corrosive vapors, lasted longer and was one-third the cost of the original stainless steel. If this savings in cost with the same or improved job performance had happened only on rare occasions, it might have gone unnoticed. However, quite often, when the circumstances forced them to go to a different way, a different design, or a different material, they came up with superior performance with less cost. The reason for much of this previously unnecessary cost was that the designers had been in a rut. They believed the way they had been doing the job had to be the best because that was the way they had been doing it in the past. The underlying factor was that materials and designs were changed, but the function remained the same.

After the war, Erlicher and Miles were in agreement that there must be a mechanism to stimulate these progressive changes. Miles was made a GE Purchasing Agent in 1944 and applied the functional concept to purchasing. In 1947, Miles was assigned full time the task of reducing costs for General Electric's products. Efforts at cost reduction using the functional concept were noteworthy.

During the period of 1947 to 1952, Miles developed the functional concept as it relates to cost. It was recognized that people need to be pushed a bit, to be motivated beyond their normal habit solutions. Unnecessary cost should be identified and removed to stimulate progressive change even when materials and habit solutions are available. If a design has not changed in 18 years, the product is excellent or management has failed to improve it. Management needs to take the lead in order to bring out their employees' talents. Value analysis is one of the programs to improve the management of people.

As the program developed, other subjects were added to broaden the impact of cost reduction and to help stimulate the creative minds of designers, purchasing agents and sales engineers. Other subjects were added, such as creative thinking, evaluation of the basic function, habits and attitudes, roadblocks to change, new materials, new methods and new processes. As each project session was opened, a presentation was planned that either informed, motivated or reminded participants to think beyond their normal habit solutions. Many of the subjects were intended to perform all three of these functions.

At first, the functional approach was related to decreasing cost. However, other criteria also needed to be accounted for in the final analysis of the project. Was the product safe? Was it saleable to the public? Was it esthetically pleasing? The initial thrust of cost reduction was then expanded to evaluate the overall value of the product. The program developed by Miles was named *value analysis*. Its purpose was to analyze the cost required to achieve the required function without jeopardizing the reliability of the product. The first value analysis seminars at General Electric were conducted in 1952. It became clear that input on product value was needed from more than just the cost reduction group in GE. Valuable assistance was needed from all parts of the company that were involved in the production and sales of various products. To meet this need, a multidisciplinary team was organized to involve the key decisionmakers. The team concept was an instant success. The firmness of mind often called stubbornness was remedied by the team approach. Each department was immediately aware of their impact because of the team concept. In some cases, 60–80 percent of the cost of the project was removed. In other cases, 5–10 percent of the cost was removed. Though the magnitude of success varied, one thing was clear—the program was a success.

Larry Miles' program has spread to the other areas of industry and is an effective tool of management. He deserves the credit for developing the program that endures today, and will continue to grow in the future. This is the reason he is referred to as the "Father of Value Engineering."

The Spread of Value Analysis into Other Industries

For its first several years the value program was confined to the General Electric Company. Through technical papers, articles in journals, and word of mouth, GE's success in value analysis became known. The first major event that moved value analysis into other industries occurred in the early 1950s. A U.S. Navy Admiral was visiting the General Electric Company in Schenectady, New York and enjoying a tour of the huge turbine plant. The tour was conducted by GE vice-president, Glen Warren. The conversation, even in the early 1950s, turned to the high cost of defense. Glen Warren mentioned GE's value analysis program and spoke with some pride of its success in identifying and removing unnecessary cost in GE's products. He invited the admiral to send a representative to GE's next value analysis workshop to audit its possible application in the U.S. Navy. The Navy accepted the invitation and the representative returned to Washington and recommended the Navy initiate a value analysis program in the Navy shipyards.

In 1954 the Navy Bureau of Ships, a division of the Department of Defense, established a value program. The Navy did not call its program value analysis as GE's program had. GE's program was to take an existing product that was being manufactured and analyze it for unnecessary costs. The Navy felt it would be more prudent for their needs if they analyzed the engineering drawings before anything was built. It would not make sense to analyze a ship, a gun mount, or something like that after it had already been built. They thought the program should be applied at the engineering stage so they changed the name from value analysis to *value engineering*. The Navy's program showed excellent results and was a fine reflection on the Navy's management ability.

Following the Navy's lead, the U.S. Army and Air Force also launched a value engineering program. Representatives of the Army visited General Electric and started their value program shortly thereafter at the Watervliet Arsenal. The Army's results at Watervliet Arsenal were encouraging and soon nearly all ordnance commands and arsenals had value programs. The spread of value engineering was indicating that when owners tried the program, they usually implemented it on other projects.

Development of Incentive Clauses

The Armed Services were achieving good results using value analysis/value engineering (VA/VE) with their staff personnel. However, the resources and talents of the suppliers and contractors doing work for the government remained an untapped area for cost savings. The Department of Defense, at that time, was under the direction of Robert McNamara. He suggested that the Department of Defense should concentrate less on the allowable costs and more on the avoidable costs of Defense work. This was in relation to the cost of contracting for government services. He wanted attention directed at avoiding costs rather than on how much billing a supplier can get out of government. The value engineering program was given added emphasis.

As a part of this effort, the Department of Defense visited their suppliers and attempted to motivate them to launch value engineering programs in their companies to help reduce the Department of Defense costs. Success was embarrassingly moderate to nothing. The Department of Defense men visited the suppliers to inquire as to why the suppliers were so lacking in response. They sent out people from the Navy, Army and Air Force value engineering programs. The representatives questioned the suppliers: As a supplier, you have a big contract with us, $50 million, and we are sure you would like next year's contract. You must have ideas about identifying and removing unnecessary cost. We want to invite you to participate in our value engineering program. We want to ask you to make proposals to reduce the cost without degrading quality. This will improve the good will between you and us, and will put you in a better position for next year's contract. Do you think that is fair? They all agreed that it sounded reasonable.

The Department of Defense then waited for all these good ideas that they hoped for, but none came. They went back to the suppliers and noted that they had asked the suppliers to participate with vigor and enthusiasm in their value engineering program, but the suppliers were not responding. The Department of Defense representatives asked why? The suppliers indicated they had reservations about the concept.

The truth had come out. The Department of Defense suppliers said, Are you aware what happens to a big proposed savings by a supplier under the terms of the current contract? The suppliers gave an example of a $5 million savings that is investigated, tested, accepted, implemented and audited. Under the current contract terms the contract is reduced by $5 million and the supplier's profit is reduced proportionately. The result is the supplier is penalized rather than rewarded for proposing the idea that saves $5 million. The Department of Defense acknowledged that this was true and acquiesced to the thought that it should be changed.

Accordingly, in 1963, the Armed Services Procurement Regulation (ASPR) Committee added Article 17, Section I which made it mandatory that value engineering incentive provisions be included in all procurements exceeding $100,000, and value programs be included in certain contracts over $1 million. Defense Procurement Circular Number 11 went into effect in October of 1964 and allowed percentage sharing of contractor and supplier approved savings proposals. The change in policy was revolutionary in terms of procurement policy. With these sharing incentives in their contracts, many companies took advantage of the potential. As much as $20 million of extra profits as their contractual share of successful value engineering proposals were achieved by many firms. Hughes Tool Company, Aero-Jet General Corporation, General Dynamics, General Motors and General Electric Company are but a few of the firms to promote and push value engineering proposals because there was a big reward in doing so. It was a big incentive.

Value Engineering Society Founded

During the late fifties many of the major companies in the nation were interested in starting value programs of their own. There were many value practitioners in the government agencies and private industry seeking to reap the benefits of value analysis. Anytime a group of individuals is brought together with a common goal, progress may take place. These value analysts were looking for an identity—a place to exchange ideas. In 1958, the Electronic Industries Association (EIA) formed a committee on value engineering. The committee was headed by Admiral Mandelkorn (USN, retired). Admiral Mandelkorn had been with the Navy Bureau of Ships. Larry Miles later chaired the committees. The EIA committee scheduled a National Conference on Value Engineering in Pittsburgh. Glen Hart, co-author of this book, presented a paper illustrating examples of value engineering at General Electric Company. The first conference was attended by 300 people. Later that year at a conference held in Washington, D.C., the decision was made to form a society to perpetuate the field of value work. Those in attendance decided to call it the Society of Value Engineers (SVE). Someone noticed that the initials for the Society of Value Engineers were SVE and by inserting the word "American" into the title as the second word, the initials became SAVE. Hence, the title: Society of American Value Engineers was adopted with the descriptive acronym of SAVE. The society has grown to include 1500 members.

Foreign companies began attending the annual SAVE conferences. The Japanese began sending a yearly delegation. They now have their own society with more members than the United States. France, Italy, England, India, South Africa, West Germany, Australia and the Scandinavian countries are some of the nations with viable value engineering programs. Much of the success of SAVE is attributed to the members' belief in the theory and importance of value engineering.

Introduction into the Construction Field

As near as we can tell, value engineering was introduced into the construction industry between 1963 and 1965 when contractor sharing clauses were added to construction contracts.

In 1964, the Army Corps of Engineers began conducting value engineering workshops to train their staff in the application of value engineering. That same year, the Corps also started including incentive clauses in their contracts. The graph on Figure 1-2 illustrates cumulative savings realized by the Corps of Engineers' program. The Corps and the Navy have been two of the forerunners of value engineering in the construction industry.

The Bureau of Reclamation, a division of the Department of the Interior, began training their staff in 1965 and allowed contractor sharing clauses in 1966. As time passed, it became obvious that value engineering was having a great deal of success. The Senate Committee on Public Works held hearings on value engineering in 1967. Soon the National Aeronautics and Space Ad-

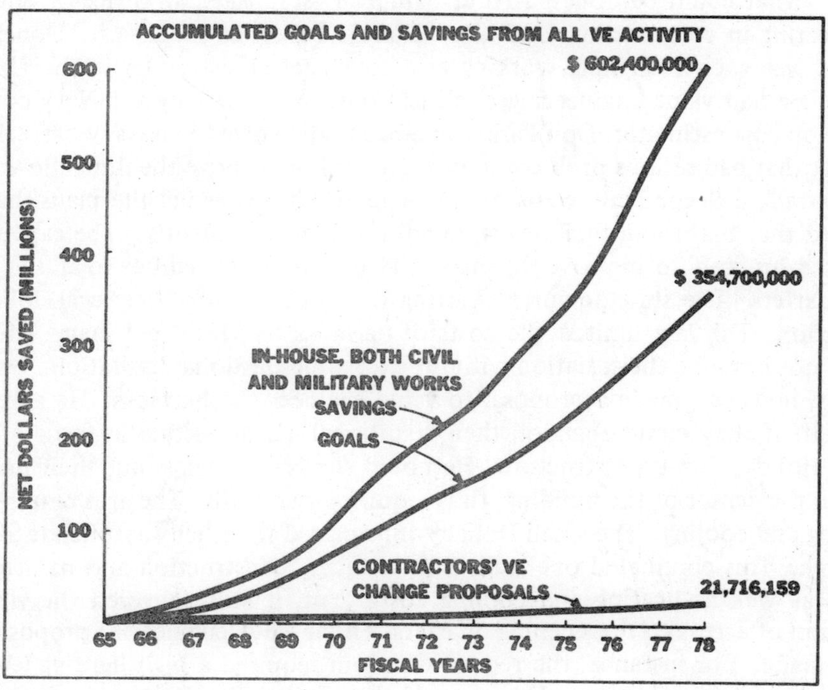

Figure 1-2. Value Engineering Progress Record. (Source: Value Engineering Progress Report, US Army Corps of Engineers, 1979.)

ministration (NASA), Office of Facilities began conducting training seminars and applying value engineering to their projects.

In 1970, the United States Congress endorsed contractor incentive clauses for the Department of Transportation and the General Services Administration (GSA), Public Building Service. That same year, GSA recommended the establishment of a value engineering program on their construction projects.

Up to this time, the thrust of value engineering was primarily centered around sharing clauses for construction contractors. While this effort resulted in savings to the government, it did *not* take advantage of the major savings available by using the function approach during the design phase. In reality, most contractor incentive savings were not generated using a function approach, but by the contractor's knowledge of cost cutting. The major savings of applying value engineering during design were not yet realized.

In the early 1970s construction management (CM) was being introduced. Many CM firms were advocating the use of value engineering during the design phase. You will recall that 1970–73 was a period of skyrocketing construction costs. It was not uncommon for contract bids to be 60–80 percent over the engineer's estimate. The time was right for the major thrust of value engineering into the construction sector.

Arthur Sampson was the General Services Administration Commissioner in 1972 in charge of GSA construction. He had a most difficult problem in trying to control construction costs. Far too many buildings were coming in over budget. The result was a continuous trip back to Congress for increased funds. What could be done? Arthur Sampson established an office of value engineering in construction, and hired Donald Parker to manage it. Donald Parker was a civil engineer working as a construction estimator in the U.S. Navy. He had value engineering qualifications. While serving as a Navy construction cost estimator, Don Parker had become involved in a Navy barracks project that had serious problems. First, the cost was above the limit allowed for barracks. Second, it seems a Navy captain, in reviewing the plans, had noticed that bathroom facilities were not located conveniently. The captain directed his staff to improve the proximity of restroom facilities to all sleeping quarters. The staff demurred, noting it was the fault of the legal dollar limitation. The law limited the costs of barracks to $1850 per man. They could not improve the situation without exceeding the dollar limitation. Don Parker, however, made a proposal to value engineer the barracks. He asked the staff if they could abandon their traditional barracks-style in favor of a small Holiday Inn-type structure. He noted the Navy always put their hallway in the center of the building, thus requiring two walls. The area required heating and cooling. The small Holiday Inns placed their hallway outside like a porch. This eliminated one wall, thus reducing construction and painting costs, as well as heating and cooling costs. Yet, it still delivered the vital function of access to the sleeping quarters. Other value engineering proposals were made. For instance, the recreation room required a high lighting level under Navy specifications. However, if they called it a living room, they could legally reduce the overall lighting level and provide task lighting where required. The changes resulted in a revised design within the $1850 per man limitation. Arthur Sampson hired Don Parker to manage his value engineering program.

In 1973, the General Services Administration, Public Building Services introduced the first value engineering service clauses requiring value engineering studies on their construction contracts.

To ensure that the principles of value engineering were used to their fullest, the GSA asked the Society of American Value Engineers to develop a certification program for value practitioners. The status of Certified Value Specialist (CVS) was established by SAVE as a standard recognizing competence in the field of value engineering.

With new requirements for value engineering at the General Services Administration, there became a need to educate architects, engineers, contractors and government administrators in value engineering. The National Capital Chapter of SAVE was interested in establishing a seminar on value engineering for the construction industry. The forty-hour workshop was sponsored jointly by the American Consulting Engineer's Council (ACEC) and the American Institute of Architects (AIA). Bud Brogan was the President of the National Capital Chapter at the time. He asked Glen D. Hart to participate in the first seminar. Glen was assisted by several representatives of government and private industry. The AIA/ACEC was approached about further workshops. They accepted and the next group of workshops were conducted by Glen Hart and Al Dell'Isola. Glen led the first 25 seminars for the AIA/ACEC.

The General Accounting Office of the federal government sent representatives to 40-hour value engineering workshops at five locations. They audited the program for possible application to the U.S. Environmental Protection Agencies (US/EPA) Construction Grants Program. The Congress' approval of Public Law 92-500 allocated $18 billion for construction of wastewater treatment facilities. The Government Accounting Office report entitled, "Need for Increased Use of Value Engineering, a Proven Cost Saving Technique in Federal Construction," judged that major cost savings could be realized with the application of value engineering to wastewater projects.

The US/EPA adopted a voluntary value engineering program by issuing Program Guidance Memorandum 45 in 1975. Value engineering was applied to projects that were offered for study by cities and design firms. The voluntary program produced significant results. Eight value engineering studies were completed under the voluntary program in 1975 and 1976. The results were a net savings of $18 million which amounted to a reduction of 4 percent of the construction cost in the projects studied. The VE fees for those studies totaled approximately $700,000. This equaled a 27 to 1 return for each dollar spent on VE. Through these initial VE studies, the US/EPA gained valuable information needed to expand their voluntary VE program into a mandatory one. The US/EPA program became mandatory in October

1976 by issuance of Program Guidance Memorandum 63, on wastewater treatment projects over $10 million in cost. It remained voluntary for pump stations and sewer lines and all projects less than $10 million. In the next two years, fiscal years 1977 and 1978, a total of 56 studies of wastewater projects were conducted with a resultant savings of $95 million or a reduction of 5 percent of the construction cost of the projects studied. The return on investment has averaged 12:1. As is apparent, the program has been a success. One boost to the US/EPA program came in 1976 when the SAVE and the US/EPA helped sponsor a conference on Value Engineering of Wastewater Treatment Plants. Glen Hart and Larry Zimmerman participated as panel members and speakers at the conference.

The Department of Transportation, Federal Highway Administration began training personnel for value engineering of transportation projects. This program, like the US/EPA program, started as a voluntary program in 1978. Contractor incentive clauses had previously been initiated in 1970. The guidelines establishing the voluntary program were published in the Federal Register in 1978.

One more category that must be mentioned is the private sector. It is not only government construction that endorses value engineering. For instance, in 1974, the Bell Telephone Company was faced with rising construction costs and no easy way to raise revenue to meet these increased costs. They adopted the value engineering program as a way to manage this problem and were delighted with the results. In some cases, they were able to reduce their building costs as much as $41 per square foot without compromising the required reliable function. Not only were they pleased with the results of identifying and removing unnecessary cost, but the program provided evidence of vigorous management effort to reduce costs in other areas to prevent the need to seek a rate increase. Bell Telephone now uses the cost model, a product of value engineering, as a tool to monitor their construction costs.

2
Habits, Roadblocks and Attitudes

Examination of the effect of habit on the cost of designs presents an interesting paradox. Often the force of habit allows the continued duplication of an old design, or the manufacturing process fails to utilize new and improved combinations. The benefit is in speedier formation of drawings through a quicker conceptualization. The benefits are immediate because by using habit solutions due dates are easier to meet. The penalties are often remote because the unnecessary cost that the habit solution often breeds does not occur until much later and is often unknown by the designer and the owner.

Also, when changes to habit solutions are considered there is the problem of attitude. Engineers and architects are subject to the same attitudes and habit ruts that narrow the path of their judgments as are the rest of the population.

Let's pause and look at some of our own habits for a moment. Take the four digits 9999 and arrange them to equal 100. The solution to this problem is well within our range of knowledge but not our habit solution. The solution, of course, is 99 and the fraction 9/9ths, which equals 100. No one can claim that this is not within their realm of knowledge. However, it is not within their realm of habit solution. It is not the combination that they are used to; therefore, only about one in ten arrive at that solution. Habit solutions are relied on and new alternatives are not explored when trying to arrive at a solution to the problem. This often occurs in the designs of projects. We pull out the old habit solution we are accustomed to using, and that becomes our design.

There is a book called, *The Dictionary of Thought*. It gives many of the greatest thoughts and quotations of the last 2000 years and arranges them by key words. Out of this book come some very pertinent ideas:

1. "The deepest law of human nature is habit, your mind is only an emergency instrument that you use when the habit can't take care of the situation."–Carlyle

2. "Habit works more constantly and with greater force than reason, which, when we have most need of, it is seldom fairly consulted and more rarely obeyed."–Locke

When you get up in the morning, your usual routine is regulated by habit. Almost everything you do is from habit. You fix your breakfast, take your shower and go through your normal routine. Then you get into your car and start to work; and the first thing you do is to go to your habit solution that has taught you how to operate a motor vehicle. The problem comes when you arrive at work and make your first or second decisions based on habit solutions rather than purposeful comparison of alternatives.

3. "Habit with many people is the test of truth."–Crabbe.

As an engineer or an architect, you arrive at your office and find you have a strict deadline to meet. The need to prepare a set of plans and specifications for a pump station is ominous. The deadline is coming up shortly, so you reach into your drawer of past projects and pull out the habit solution that worked previously. It seems that by the time you get to the end of the day, the majority of your decisions have been based on the habit solution. How often are alternatives explored before making decisions? *We are more creatures of habit than we are creatures of thought.*

4. "A child is a creature of impulse, and an adult is a creature of habit; the older we get, the more the grip of habit on our conduct."–G. B. Cheever

All of us are more or less slaves to habit. We first make our habits, and then they make us. Habits acquire a power over us. They enslave our will, and sometimes we cannot break loose.

It comes down to the fact that, "Habits are either the best of servants or the worst of masters."–Emmons

Why are habits important to us? The reason is: *Knowledge is fluid, always changing, always growing, very often requiring you to let go of a firmly held idea. Habit is just the opposite. Habit is rigid, unbending, unchanging, ungiving, unyielding, and naturally, because knowledge and habit are so diametrically opposed to each other, they often get in each other's way.* It happens again and again in our everyday life.

HABIT RUTS

Habit ruts are often the cause for stifling one's imagination. Relying on old solutions when changes are occurring around us often is the safest route, except that the competition will rapidly surpass you.

Do habit ruts explain the fact that:

1. It was slightly over 100 years ago that Alexander Graham Bell went to the owner of Western Telegraph Company and offered him the telephone for $25,000. The president of Western Telegraph said: "We already have a communication system. We don't need any talk over a wire. It's just a toy; it has no practical use." And he wouldn't pay the $25,000 for the telephone. Oftentimes people in very high places are confined in their thinking by their habits.

2. One of the inventors of the sewing machine was a poet and one a cabinet maker. The inventor of the cotton gin was a teacher, somebody who wasn't married to the procedure used in the cotton industry. It revolutionized the industry and made much of the South a wealthy commercial area before the Civil War.

3. The typesetting machine was invented by a watchmaker; again, someone not suited to a habit solution. Can we explain the fact that the peneumatic tire was invented by a veterinarian? Again, someone who was not tied to a rigid set of rules and guidelines. Oftentimes, what happens is that these individuals can sit back and use something objectively without the constraints of their habits. The veterinarian inventing the pneumatic tire was concerned with his son's safety while riding on cobble. He felt that he needed to make his bicycle lighter and easier to travel over the cobble surface. He had some surgical tubing and conceived the idea of wrapping the tubing around the tire and filling it with air. He showed it to a mechanic, a very experienced man, who looked at it and said: "Too unreliable; it will never work; forget the whole idea." And he showed it to another mechanic who said the same thing. Fortunately, the veterinarian proceeded with his new invention. This was the beginning of the pneumatic tire invented by John Dunlop, that we use today.

This brings up a very good question: Is experience always valuable? Never think for a second that experience is not very valuable. Experience is the way that we grow and develop. However, at the same time we are getting experience, we are often getting fixed habits. Habits become unbending and get in the way of our future development and growth. We need sensible ideas. However, if we allow our views to become too fixed and rigid, what we do is to put ourselves into a rut and do not consider the alternatives. Again, experience may be directing our pattern of life to the point that we lack flexibility.

Does this mean that habits are always bad? Of course not, habits are what we use to build basic skills. One of the best examples of the benefit of habit is reading. When we read regularly we find that our speed and our ability increases with the amount of reading. Two or three hundred words a minute is not an uncommon reading speed. When reading at four or five hundred words a minute the thoughts and meanings can be captured from the symbols at a glance. One doesn't have to think about the meaning of each word. Habits are used to digest this information from prior knowledge. Reading is a tremendous benefit in broadening our wealth of knowledge and the correct habits help us to improve it.

Consider now another benefit of habit. The benefit the Army gets from taking a recruit and training him to react over and over Later he may be placed in combat and need to react fast. He is normally scared to the point of great nervousness. His reactions will be from force of habit. This is a benefit.

Learning to type is another benefit of habit. When first learning to type, every key seems to be a chore to learn. Progress is very slow! But pretty soon we start relegating combinations to habit rather than trying to think where the letters are. Soon typing becomes like reading. Habits take over; speed goes up; more work gets done; production goes up. Modern factories and assembly lines couldn't run without the benefit of habit. Automobiles couldn't be operated without the benefit of habit. Remember the first time you drove an automobile? You had trouble working the clutch, the brakes and the gear shift efficiently. The first time you started the car, you put the key in the ignition and turned the switch—whoops!—the car stalls because the clutch was not disengaged. And then with the clutch pushed in, you started the engine, and started to let out the clutch, and the car stalled again. You forgot to give it enough gas to keep the car going. Then, once the car was going, you came to a stop sign. You forgot to push in the clutch, and the car stalled again. This dramatic situation is faced for the first several days while learning to drive a car. Then your habit skills build and the seemingly complex procedure that you are faced with becomes customary.

There are numerous examples of habits that are beneficial to us in operating our modern world. However, those same benefits, when it comes to the drafting board, often box us into fixed solutions that cause unnecessary costs. Habit solutions are pulled out of a drawer, and slapped onto the design board. That's the project used last year; it worked well for us then. Has anyone bothered to go back and check out how it might work for this particular application? In the course of our VE studies, many owners say that they have worked with engineers who have done several of their plants, and find that each design is the same for their plants and for other plants throughout the state. This is the reason why we pause and consider the subject of habit, because this is one area where extra costs creep into design. There are many areas where it is very beneficial to look at alternative solutions and to explore other means that might be more economical. In many areas, the habit solution may be an obsolete solution; it may have unnecessary combinations of costs and operating expense. It is the force of these circumstances that makes a VE study an improvement to the management of the project. There is a poem that sums up the whole subject of habit very nicely.

Path of the Calf

One day through the primeval wood,
   A calf walked home as good calves should;
But made a trail all bent askew,
   A crooked trail as all calves do.
Since then two hundred years have fled,
   And, I infer the calf is dead.
But still he left behind his trail,
   And thereby hangs my moral tale.

The trail was taken up next day
   By a lone dog that passed that way,
And then a wise bell-wether sheep
   Pursued the trail o'er vale and steep,
And drew the flock behind him too
   As good bell-wethers always do.

And from that day, o'er hill and glade,
   Through those old woods a path was made.
And thus, before men were aware,
   A city's crowded thoroughfare.
And soon, the central street was this,
   of a renowned metropolis.

And men two centuries and a half
    Trod in the footsteps of that calf.
Each day a hundred thousand route
    Followed the calf about.
And on his crooked journey went
    The traffic of a continent.

A hundred thousand men were led
    By a calf near three centuries dead.
They followed still his crooked way
    and lost one hundred years each day.

For thus such reverence is lent
    To well established precedent.

Excerpts from "The Path of the Calf,"
Samuel Foss, 1858–1911.

ATTITUDES

Attitudes support the continuation of existing habits and are susceptible to roadblocks. Attitudes play a big part in our decision-making process. Roadblocks are quite often expressions of our attitudes and cloud the true facts. They are roadblocks that are interjected to shade reality. They kill many good ideas before the ideas have a chance to develop. Reflecting on the Palm Springs Tramway in California, and the difficulty that Francis Crocker had in selling the community and the city fathers on the feasibility of building a tramway up the sheer cliffs of Chino Canyon contributes to our understanding of attitudes. Crocker was looked upon as a fanatic. A newspaperwoman called his dream "Crocker's Folly," but the youthful Francis Crocker in 1934 was not sidetracked and set out to prove his dream. Crocker believed a tram could be built similar to ones he remembered in his youth in Colorado used in mining. The tram could carry people to the top of the mountain range where the temperature would be as much as 40 degrees less than the hot desert floor of Palm Springs. He visualized the popular demand that could materialize. (Figure 2-1)

He and his wife made an exhaustive search on tramway construction and design. Crocker spent countless hours designing the tramway and tentatively chose a location for it's construction. Late in the 1930's, Russ Cone, a bridge engineer for San Francisco's Golden Gate Bridge came to the Desert Inn in Palm Springs for a vacation. He had heard about Crocker's dream to build a tramway and contacted an engineering colleague, who agreed to prepare an engineering study at a cost of $2400, which was all Crocker could afford. The study verified Crocker's location and that the project was feasible.

Soon thereafter, World War II broke out and stopped the project. After the war planning for the project moved ahead until the Korean War completely stopped it again. Later a bill supporting the project was twice passed by the California legislature but was vetoed by the Governor. Eventually, private investors financed the project and construction began in 1961. One Swiss

Figure 2-1. Chino Canyon Tramway.

expert offered this depressing prediction, "Construction of the tramway will take four years and at least three lives will be lost during it's construction." But what the expert did not consider was the innovation of a new workhorse, the helicopter. The helicopter carried men and material to the site and cut the time of construction from four years to two, with not one death or major accident.

Today the tramway means much to the economy of the desert resort. But like all great ideas, it had many, many setbacks and roadblocks before it became a reality.

The following is a list of a few of the roadblocks that people might throw up to the expression of new or different ideas for a project or design:

Table 2-1. Roadblocks to New or Different Ideas.

- IT NEEDS HIGHER APPROVAL.
- HE'S TOO AMBITIOUS FOR US.
- WE DID IT THIS WAY LAST TIME.
- IT TAKES TOO LONG TO LOOK INTO.
- THE DRAFTING ROOM DOESN'T LIKE CHANGES.
- THE CITY HAS PLENTY OF MONEY.
- WE CAN'T TELL THE CLIENT THAT WE CHANGED OUR DESIGN.
- WE HAVE NO PROBLEMS NOW–WHY CHANGE?
- IF YOU WANT A QUICK ANSWER–IT'S NO!
- THE BOSS ONLY LIKES ONE TYPE OF CONSTRUCTION.

Table 2-1. Roadblocks to New or Different Ideas. (Continued)

- IT DOESN'T AGREE WITH THE GUIDE SPECS.
- COST IS NOT REALLY IMPORTANT IN THIS CASE.
- IT'S AGAINST OUR POLICY.
- THAT'S THE WAY IT'S DONE HERE.
- IT WON'T WORK.
- TOO MUCH TROUBLE TO PHASE IN.
- WE TRIED THAT SCHEME TEN YEARS AGO; IT DIDN'T WORK THEN.
- WE HAVEN'T GOT TIME TO MAKE CHANGES.
- NOT A FAILURE IN 15 YEARS. WHY CHANGE?
- IT'S A GOVERNMENT JOB.
- SAFETY IS AT STAKE.
- THE FEDS PAY FOR 75% OF THE PROJECT.
- THE REGULATORY AGENCIES WILL TAKE TOO LONG TO REVIEW IT.
- MAINTENANCE CAN TAKE CARE OF IT LATER.
- OPERATIONS CAN HANDLE IT.

Sometimes these roadblocks are real, but very often they are only shadows, that stop the good idea as effectively as if they were real. Let's explore an example of the comment: "It won't work." An ordnance plant was making gun directors that cost $250,000 each. As the project was being developed, eight units reached the floor that would not assemble properly. The gears of the gun directors would not mesh. The manufactured product depended on tolerances as a part of production methods. Tolerances are set, hoping they will allow adequate clearances and prevent jamming of the mechanism. In such a situation, the tolerances will allow for the successful operation of the unit. The gun directors cost $250,000 each and the concern was obviously very intense. The vertical boring mill operators were informed that the gearing for the units would not mesh without binding. In order to make the gun directors operate properly, the tolerance must be tightened from 1/1000 to 1/2000. In this way, the problem could be corrected. The experienced boring mill operators said that this was impossible. The supervisors then got six apprentices who were totally new at the job. At the beginning of their eight-week training program, they were told that at the end of the program, they would be machining to the new tolerance and that this was common practice. The trainees were separated from the old experienced hands who would adversely affect their attitude. At the end of the program, over half of the participants had met the goal of the new tolerance and the problem was solved.

Attitudes are tough. They are very difficult to deal with and are even more difficult to change. Looking back in our past history, there are many good examples of the way people's attitudes usually work. It's interesting to reflect on these attitudes and to see how mankind's giant steps of progress were first perceived.

- *The cast-iron plow was invented in the United States in 1797.* This plow was really needed. The wooden plow, whenever it hit a rock, would break easily. A new blade had to be obtained every time the old one broke. The cast-iron plow was made. The response from farmers was *that cast iron poisoned the land and stimulated the growth of weeds.* For a long time they refused to use it.

- In Germany it was proven by experts that when a train traveled at the frightful speed of 15 miles per hour, blood would spurt from the travelers' noses, and that the passengers would suffocate when going through tunnels. Isn't it interesting to look at the phrase "proven by experts." It certainly was an attitude that was shadowed by preconceived notions.
- Men insisted that iron ships would not float; they would damage more than wooden ships when grounded; it was difficult to protect the iron bottom from rust, and the compass would be deflected to the point where it would be useless. They obviously had their own attitudes. Again, all those roadblocks were only shadows.
- In 1881, when the YWCA of New York announced typing lessons for women, vigorous protests were made on the grounds that the female constitution would break down under the strain.
- When patents were taken out for the steel-frame skyscraper in 1888, the "Architectural News" predicted that the expansion and contraction of iron would crack all the plaster, and that all that would be left would be the shell. When LeBaron Jenney first designed the steel-framed skyscraper, the Home Insurance Building in Chicago, he probably surmised, why make the walls load-bearing? Why can't we make a frame and hang everything from that frame? We can build faster, quicker, stronger, and possibly less costly. Jenney overcame these constraints and roadblocks through a new combination and revolutionized the construction industry.

When looking at these shadows and roadblocks to invention and creativity, we also think: Isn't it great that we are not this way anymore? Society is more openminded and progressive than these people that thwarted past ideas. We ask the reader to reflect a moment:

- How many of us have killed a good idea because we were guided by opinions rather than by facts?
- How many of us have killed a good idea because we had a preconceived notion as to the results of the solution?
- How many of us have killed a good idea because we could not break our habits?

We already know the answers. We've all probably killed new ideas unfairly. Prejudice influences our opinions and our attitudes. Everyone is prejudiced in some manner—for or against a material or a certain method of doing things. It depends on our experience and our background. The end result is that it is very difficult to conduct oneself free of prejudice.

Many times, the idea that is proposed is not rejected on its own merit. The concept is rejected without drawing fully on its meaning and what the basis for the new idea might be. We often don't let ideas develop to the point where they can be fully understood. Snap judgments are made on the initial statement of an idea or concept.

A primary concern of designers and contractors is with their past failures. When faced with an application similar to the past failure, the tendency is to unequivocally say NO, even though the experience is different from everyone else's. The response may not be representative of the total history of that subject. The tendency is to not want to investigate new occurrences, new developments of the product or to look at different applications. We may not feel we have the time, the money or the inclination to do it. It is especially difficult when living in a technical explosion. New products, new materials, new combinations, new chemical compounds, all add to the choice of combinations that are used to put together projects.

THE ATTITUDE SCREEN

Figure 2-2 is an attitude screen. During our progression through life, an attitude screen is developed. At birth our attitude screens are clear like a clean French window, but, it doesn't take long before clouds begin to develop within that attitude screen in the early years of our lives. As an example, we may have an aversion to ice-cream sodas. Our father, whom we love very much, comes home from a long week's work and is delighted to see his children. He takes us for a ride in the country, and we begin to feel nauseous. Dad then suggests that we stop for an ice-cream soda. We love ice cream, however, on this particular occasion, ice-cream sodas just don't sound appealing to us. Because Dad was being so kind, we decide to accept it anyway. We eat the ice-cream soda, and as a result become very sick from it. A cloud is developed in our attitude screen. For the next several years, we cannot

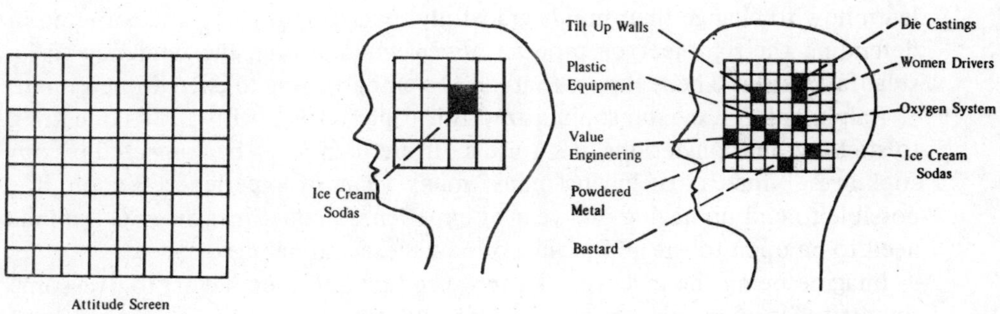

Figure 2-2. Attitude Screen. Unclouded at birth and gradually tempered by experiences.

stand the thought of ice-cream sodas. In reality, it was the motion sickness brought on from riding in the car that caused the illness; however, a cloud is formed against ice-cream sodas.

Now let's jump ahead in our life to the stage of a young engineer. The aspiring engineer has been gaining more and more experience, having gone through several projects and having designed and specified numerous types of materials, new combinations of processes and machinery. In one of these projects, PVC piping was used with poor results.

The poor experience came as a result of failure of the glues and compounds that were used to make the joints. The failure caused great embarrassment at the failure of the joints and the expense of repairing them. For the next dozen designs, plastic piping is not used in designs even though the total costs for plastic are far less than comparable materials. A cloud is formed in the engineer's attitude screen; it tells him, "Don't trust the plastic piping." In the five years since the initial poor experience with this type of piping, new materials and glues have come out that now make the joints more reliable. But, because of the bad experience, metallic pipe is still used in certain applications with a resulting cost far above what is really necessary. Why? Because of the failure to erase the cloud about plastic pipes long after *new information* should have erased the attitude cloud.

Is it true that by the age of 40 years our attitude screens are so filled with clouds that we can no longer view a problem with a clear and unbiased attitude? Is it true than an engineer cannot be objective after 40? No, this is not the case. Some people are obsolete at 30, while others are still pioneering new subjects and new creations at 70. What determines whether we are obsolete at 30, or pioneers at 70? The answer lies in the ability and willingness to erase clouds, to change one's mind when new information and new facts enter into the picture. Most progress requires some change. There needs to be a willingness to adapt to change, where appropriate, and make it an effective and useful part of our design.

There is a great deal of reality in the statement that *when we are through changing, we are through*. A technical explosion exists. The world changes as we walk to work. Many people would rather be steadfast than right; others would rather be right than steadfast. People who are steadfast often never learn how to change their minds gracefully, because they become cornered in defending their project or product. Even when wrong, the tendency to be steadfast exists. The feeling is that it is too embarrassing to change one's mind.

Ralph Waldo Emerson summarized this topic very capably: "It's one thing to stick by our convictions, it's quite a different thing to be convicted by our stickiness." Instead of having many, many years of experience at a job, it is possible to end up having one year of experience many times over. Our minds need to be open to the acceptance of new ideas and new processes.

Imagine being the inventor of a new product and then having to overcome the attitudes of people when they viciously attack your new idea. Let's look at some inventors and see how their inventions were first accepted.

IT CAN'T BE DONE

- One U. S. citizen predicted that the introduction of a railroad would require the building of many insane asylums, and people would go mad with the terror at the sight of locomotives running across the country.
- Commander Vanderbilt dismissed Westinghouse and his new air-brake system with the remark that he had no time to waste on fools.
- Those individuals who loaned Robert Fulton money for his steamboat project stipulated that their names be withheld for fear of ridicule should it be known that they had supported anything so foolish.
- Joshua Coppersmith was arrested in Boston for trying to sell stock in the telephone. "All well-informed people knew that it was impossible to transmit the human voice by wire."
- The editor of the Springfield Republican newspaper refused to ride in an early automobile, claiming that it was incompatible with the dignity of his position in society.
- Chancey M. Depew confessed that he warned his nephew not to invest $5000 in Ford stock because "nothing had come along to best the horse."
- When in 1907, DeForest put the radio tube in workable form, he was not able to sell his patent and let it lapse rather than pay $25 for its renewal.
- Scientist Simon Newcomb said in 1906 just as success of the airplane was in the offing, "The demonstration that no combination of known substances, known forms of machinery, and known forms of force can be united in any practical way by which men might fly seems to the writer as complete as possible for a demonstration of any physical fact to be."
- Henry Morton, the president of Stevens Institute of Technology, protested against the trumpeting of the results of Edison's experiment in electric lighting as a wonderful success, when everyone acquainted with the subject recognized it as a conspicuous failure.
- When rayon was first put on the market, a committee appointed by *silk manufacturers* to study its possibilities declared it to be a transient fad.
- When tractors were first invented small-town bankers refused for many years to lend money to purchase the tractors on the ground that they were a menace to farmers.

Imagine yourself being in the position of these famous inventors and having to overcome the resistance set up by acknowledged and prominent people in the field. The mental strain and anguish must have been significant. But yet these people persevered. They worked through their obstacles, and came up with progress that has aided in the development of our nation.

THE POWER OF A POSITIVE ATTITUDE

Our conscience is subjective in nature. In other words, it makes no decision on its own; it simply is subject to the decisions and the attitudes that are made in the conscious mind. It tries to synthesize the decisions and attitudes of the conscious mind. Suddenly it dawns on us that if our minds do contain hidden and unknown power, and it is directed by the decisions and attitudes of the conscious mind, then maybe we should be quite careful about the attitudes we assume at the beginning of a project.

In a value engineering study, we strive for an open-minded approach that will allow, (1) the designer to accept new ideas based on information furnished; and (2) the value engineering team to explore new ideas that will be of benefit to the owner.

The power of positive thinking is discussed by many authors. They indicate that the mind responds better to positive direction, rather than negative direction, because positive direction uses words that form the images we want rather than the images that we are unlikely to accept. People in professional communications learned a long time ago that if you put out a message that said, "use a file with a handle," you would get better results than if you worded it negatively by saying, "don't use a file without a handle." The reason is that in negative suggestions, your mind has to conceive of a different image than the word written to focus. Imagine the dentist using the words, "this won't hurt." Immediately, the patient begins to ready himself for the onslaught and the pain that will come. Another approach might be to say, "you won't feel this." Then you stay away from the visual image of "hurt." The analogy to a value engineering study is that when you run into a situation where the designer may say, "this won't work; that won't work; I've tried this; your solution can't be done," and shows you with an onslaught of ways that something will not work, you will know that he is not looking at the subject matter objectively. It is also very important that when the value engineering team comes forward with a solution and results that they be expressed in a positive manner. The positive aspect of the recommendations must be clearly outlined to the designer. When presenting your results, the VE team must be firm but not pushy.

When you get negative directions, there are always those who refuse to convert the message into a positive action. Hence, the desired results are difficult to obtain. Phrasing the subject matter in positive words gets better all-over results.

Psychologist William James, expressed the significance of these observations in the following statement: "Possibly the greatest contribution of my generation is that a man may change his life by changing his attitude." Psychologists tell us that if we believe and have faith that something will work out, the results are influenced positively; or, conversely, if we believe and have faith that something will not work out, we tend not only to believe but also to *act* in such a way as to not make it happen. The belief adopted in the beginning influences the end result.

A value engineering study depends a great deal upon the attitudes of the participants. Hence the object of this discussion is to alert people to the importance of their attitudes on the end results of a project.

REALIZING OUR TRUE POTENTIAL

As can be seen through illustrations of the trials and tribulations of past inventors, the road to implementing a new idea is a long and difficult one. The foremost achievements and advancements in technology were at first, and for a long time, a mere dream. The potential for a saving and improvement to project cost has been proven time and time again in numerous value engineering studies. The program works. It saves money, it improves the operation of a facility, it improves our ability to manage the project, and, it oftentimes saves our precious energy resources. Our prime purpose in discussing habits, roadblocks and attitudes has been to sensitize the reader to his full potential as an individual and as a member of the value engineering team. It is also our intention to sensitize the participant on the other end of the value engineering study, i.e., the designer whose project is being reviewed and analyzed. There is an innate tendency for people to throw up roadblocks to the analysis of their design. They view a value engineering study as a critique on their ability. The end result of VE is a better product and an improved design for the design engineer and the owner. People forget that every great inventor has had his design improved by lesser souls. The potential for value engineering can be summarized in the illustration of the acorn and the oak tree.

Figure 2-3. Within the Acorn Sleeps the Mighty Oak.

3
The Value Engineering Job Plan

INTRODUCTION

The organized and systematic approach of the Value Engineering Job Plan is the key to success in a value engineering study. It is through the job plan that the study identifies the key areas of unnecessary cost and seeks new and creative ways of performing the same function as the original part, process, or material. It works, and has been proven effective in manufacturing processes and procedures, and in the construction field. The job plan allows the study team to go farther than the usual design process.

THE INVENTIVE PROCESS

The Value Engineering Job Plan closely follows the steps used by inventors when they develop new ideas and procedures. Thomas Edison, the Wright Brothers, Kettering, and other prominent inventors followed the same basic steps that are used in the job plan. Architects, engineers, and contractors are inventors–their designs and methods of construction are the result of original thinking. New buildings are a combination of materials and configurations constructed to achieve a desired function. Table 3-1 shows the process of how an inventor thinks.

REASONS FOR USING THE JOB PLAN

The job plan is a proven format for reducing cost in a project and it helps to maximize the effectiveness of a VE study. The job plan provides the value practitioner with the following:

1. *An organized approach.* Value studies on construction projects could go on for extended periods of time if the studies were not organized and scheduled procedures were not used. The length of the study is restricted in order to get the job done quickly and to allow the designer to complete the design. Following a job plan allows project studies to accomplish more in a short period of time.

2. *It forces a concise description of purpose.* The Value engineering job plan directs the study team to define the requirements of the project and to assess its true *function*. It utilizes function analysis to delineate the com-

Table 3-1. How An Inventor Thinks.

INVENTORS	VE JOB PLAN	DESCRIPTION
INSPIRATION DATA GATHERING ANALYSIS OF KNOWN FACTS	Information Phase:	Information and background on the subject matter are sought so that patterns and combinations of ideas can be formulated. The required functions of the inventor's quest are broken down and identified.
EXPERIMENTATION - NEW COMBINATIONS	Creative Phase:	Ideas, ideas, and more ideas are formulated to hopefully arrive at the right formula.
ANALYZE AND JUDGE DATA	Judgment Phase:	The inventor needs a place to start, so he begins judging and evaluating his ideas, trying to arrive at the best combination.
DEVELOP DESIGN	Development Phase:	The inventor's dream nears the point of success as he begins building. He fails and tries again, each time learning by his mistakes and other people's suggestions.
SELL TO PUBLIC	Recommendation:	His new invention is complete and ready to go, only to meet with the reluctant supervisor, who sets every road block imaginable. He overcomes these road blocks and feels the true meaning of success.

ponents of the project that are performing the required function and those that are support functions.

3. *It zeroes in on high cost areas.* It allows the VE team to identify the concentration of cost, and to associate cost required to achieve a purpose.

4. *It forces people to think deeper than their normal habit solutions.* People are accustomed to using the first idea that enters their minds. The job plan directs and motivates people to make several comparisons and to analyze in detail how the total system works, as well as the function of each part.

5. *Objective approach.* The job plan allows an objective look at the project, concentrating on the life-cycle costs of the facility.

Participants in a value engineering study should be cautioned about the tendency to disregard the step-by-step approach of the job plan. Where the job plan is disregarded, the study tends to degenerate into a design review. The review will find the obvious high-cost savings. In the value field, we say that they will find the apples that have fallen to the ground. The job plan helps us to work through the apples on the tree and to select the ripe, juicy fruit.

6. *Universal approach.* The job plan is universal in its approach. It has been applied to manufacturing, systems processes, construction projects and software. In the construction field, value engineering has shown excellent returns. Highways, bridges, wastewater plants, chemical plants, power plants, buildings, transportation systems and other areas have been value engineered successfully. As long as there is a function required and money spent, the job plan will work.

THE JOB PLAN

There are several versions of the job plan. The procedures are all similar in their approach. Table 3-2 shows a comparison of the job plans as outlined by the US/EPA, General Services Administration, and the basic job plan as it originally started.

In this book, we will use the Five-Phase Job Plan to describe the procedure.

Job Plan

1. Information Phase
2. Creative Phase
3. Judgment Phase
4. Development Phase
5. Recommendation Phase

The job plan is a systematic approach that follows the five basic phases. A multidisciplined team of experienced personnel is brought together in a workshop setting to analyze the project. Time is also spent prior to the study gathering information and reviewing background data for the study. Chapter 6, Managing a VE Study, explains the steps in coordination, staffing and conducting a study. This chapter deals with the job plan. Each phase of the job plan is explained and illustrated with examples.

Table 3-2. The Job Plan.

EPA–Six-phase Job Plan
1. Information Phase
2. Creative Phase
3. Analytical Phase
4. Investigation Phase
5. Recommendation Phase
6. Implementation Phase

Standard–Five Phase Job Plan
1. Information Phase
2. Creative Phase
3. Judgment Phase
4. Development Phase
5. Recommendation Phase

GSA Job Plan–Eight-Phase Job Plan
1. Information Phase
2. Functional Analysis
3. Creative Phase
4. Judgment Phase
5. Development Phase
6. Presentation Phase
7. Implementation Phase
8. Follow-up.

Information Phase

The information phase of the VE job plan involves defining the project, obtaining background information that leads to the project design, limitations on the project, and a sensitivity to the costs involved in owning and operating a facility. The purpose of this phase is for the VE team to gain as much information and knowledge as possible on the project design.

It is important to realize that the design engineer or architect for the project has spent considerable time in developing the plans and specifications to this point. The value engineering team needs to know the information that went into the development of that design. What was the rationale used by the designer for the development of the project? What were the assumptions that he made in establishing the design criteria and in selecting materials and equipment to perform the required functions? The intention is not to dispute the work that the design engineer has accomplished. It is to come up with new and different alternatives and comparisons of designs that will reduce the cost of the project. In most cases, the design engineer can provide valuable information that will give a better feel to the circumstances that led to the project, and indicate areas that he feels have high costs.

Project Constraints

The project constraints are those areas of the design that are not subject to the value engineering study. Often these are specific requirements that have been made by the owner that are unalterable. This will save the designer and the value engineering team embarrassment at the end of the study by having many of their recommendations refuted by the designer with the expression, "these are constraints given to me by the owner."

Examples of project constraints used on wastewater treatment plants might be as follows:

1. Effluent criteria established by the health department.
2. Plant design capacity.
3. No bypass to the river.
4. Provisions to be provided for interim solids handling.
5. Architecture to blend in with surroundings.

The purpose of establishing project constraints is to identify areas in the design that must not change. This is not to say that the designer should indiscriminately list many of the elements of the project, so that the value engineering team does not have a chance to evaluate them. It does outline key areas that the owner feels he must have as a part of his project.

It is best to give the value engineering team as much latitude as possible in developing alternatives to be considered by the owner. Keep in mind that the value engineering team only makes recommendations, and it is up to the owner and designer to evaluate these recommendations and select the ones that they feel are worthy of incorporation into the design. By applying undue constraints to the value engineering team they are in essence eliminating ideas that may be of future benefit to them.

Information Needed from the Designer and Owner

The quality and completeness of information provided by the owner and the designer on the background of their project directly affects the quality of the value engineering team study. Much searching for facts and much prior thought have gone into the development of the design, and the value engineering team must rapidly analyze the available information in order to become knowledgeable about the project within a concentrated period of time. The team depends heavily on the designer and the owner to provide necessary information. There are several areas of information that are needed to conduct the value engineering study. Some of the most relevant areas are:

1. Design criteria (system requirements)
2. Site conditions (topography, soil condition, soil borings, surrounding area, aerial photographs)
3. Regulatory requirements
4. Elements of the design (process parts, construction components)
5. History of the project
6. Constraints imposed on the project
7. Available utilities

8. Requirements resulting from public participation
9. Design computations

A good background on these key areas will allow the value engineering team to empathize with the designer, and to better understand the rationale that has gone into the project development.

At the beginning of any value engineering study, whether it be on a water treatment plant, a power plant, a highway, etc., the value engineering team should outline the information that they would like to have to become familiar with the project. Table 3-3 is a sample of information requested from the designer and owner that was used by the value engineering team in a study of a wastewater treatment plant. Information provided on plans, specifications, design memoranda, local codes, etc., are all important background information.

The best sources of information on the project are the project manager and the other participants that have prepared the design. At the beginning of a value engineering workshop, the design team is asked to make an oral presentation on their project. The designer discusses the key parts of the project, and explains the reasons for the selection of the process, the layout, materials of construction, space orientation and other areas of the design.

Table 3-3. Information Needed from Designer and Owner.

Study 1–Conceptual Design

Facilities Plan
Design Criteria: Process Loadings; storage volumes; structural, heating, planning loads, etc.
Design Calculations
Soil and Foundation Reports
Alternate Designs Considered
Pertinent Correspondence with Government Agencies
Permit Requirements
Regulations covering Construction for Docks or Structures in Navigable Waterways
Design Drawings
Specifications
Operations Schedule and Estimated Costs
Maintenance Schedule and Estimated Costs
Power Rate Schedule
Estimate of Construction Cost (Quantity Take-Off)
Appropriate Building Codes
Architectural Concepts
Pilot Plant Results

Study 2–Working Plans and Specifications

Design Plans
Specifications
Calculations
Cost Estimate
Equipment Specifications and Drawings
Operations Schedule
Maintenance Schedule
Information Provided in Study 1

It is also helpful to know the comparisons that the design engineer has made in developing his design.

Site Visit

A site visit is often helpful to the value engineering team so its members may become familiar with the actual elements of the project. This is especially true when the project involves renovation work, or additions to an existing facility. The site visit not only gives the value engineering team a feel for the construction of the existing facilities, but it also gives them some indication of the quality and amount of the current operation and maintenance at the facility. This often influences their recommendations as to sophistication of equipment and complexity of design. In addition, it will indicate the types of maintenance embellishments that must be included in order to assist in the upkeep of the project. The old expression, "a picture is worth a thousand words," is especially true when trying to evaluate a design. Site visits have been especially helpful in past value engineering projects, and are usually well worth the expense incurred.

One way to summarize the need for gathering information on the project is as follows: *Get the facts so that you can do a competent job.*

Analyzing Cost Information

The *cost model* is used as a method of organizing costs into identifiable areas in order to determine the high cost areas of the design. All value engineering studies are done on the basis of life-cycle costs. Therefore, the cost needed from the designer of the project is not only the initial construction cost estimate, but his best estimate of the cost of owning and operating the facility. Much of this information has been prepared while analyzing concepts for the design. Because cost is the medium that is used for comparison of ideas, its importance and accuracy cannot be overstated. One of the first assignments of the value engineering team is to review the cost information of the project and to validate it. If there are apparent discrepancies in the cost information regarding unit quantities, unit costs, deletions from the cost estimate or errors, these should be brought to the attention of the designer so they can be adjusted. The cost estimate serves as a basis for comparison of future value engineering recommendations; its accuracy is mandatory. If the value engineering study starts off with poor cost information, the basis for evaluation is hampered.

Having established and verified the cost information, the next step in the process is to construct the *cost model.* There are two types of cost models that are commonly used for a value engineering study. One cost model uses the concept of the cost matrix to divide the project by system and construction trade. The other cost model divides the project into systems and subsystems, using cost per gallon, square feet, etc., depending on the type of project.

The *cost matrix* separates the construction trade components of the projects, and also distributes these components into the various elements and systems of the project. Figure 3-1 is the form for value engineering cost matrix. The description column is used to identify the construction components of the project. Normally these components follow the Construction Specification's Institute (CSI) format. This format is also used to break down construction project specifications. Cost estimates prepared by the engineer and architect organize the costs of a project in a format similar to the cost matrix. The horizontal breakdown of cost is done by system. The systems vary for different types of facilities. For a wastewater plant, they may be first broken down by site work, liquid stream and solids processing, and again by unit processes, such as pumping stations, primary treatment, secondary treatment, clarification tanks, disinfection, administration buildings, gravity thickeners, digesters, site work and miscellaneous. The cost specialists from the value engineering team must break down the cost for the project into these elements, as identified in the cost matrix. A complete cost matrix is shown in Figure 3-2.

The cost model is to serve as a comparison to use for further judgment of ideas. It helps to identify where the money in the project is being spent and what the owner is buying for each dollar spent. It also helps to decipher the value being obtained by the design. Similar models for energy and life-cycle costs are also prepared to determine high energy and operation cost factors.

Chapter 7 discusses the cost model in more detail and gives in-depth information about other types of cost models used for construction projects. Examples of cost models used on various other projects are also given.

Function Analysis

The *function analysis* for a project is used to identify *what it is we are trying to do* and also to identify *the associated cost.* The purpose of the function analysis is to clearly define the work involved and the requirements for the project. It also helps to separate those nonessential areas of the project that are being provided for support more than to perform the specified requirements. Function analysis also forces conciseness by identifying the work or function to be performed.

Function analysis is the cornerstone of value engineering. The best definition that we have heard today is: *Function analysis helps to identify what we really want to do and how much we really should have to pay for doing it.* Figure 3-3 is a worksheet used to perform the function analysis.

The first step in a function analysis is to identify the basic function of the system, project, building or area being analyzed. The basic function is the purpose of the item being studied. Only those parts of the project that perform the primary function are called basic functions. All other parts of the project are support or secondary functions.

Referring to the function analysis worksheet, the description column would be used to fill in the subsystems used in the analysis. As an example, if a power plant were the project, the function of the power plant would be to *generate power*. Under the description column we would list the subsystems of a power plant. They might be intake, fuel feed, combustion units, pollu-

PROJECT ________________
LOCATION ________________
CLIENT ________________
DATE ________________
PAGE ________ OF ________

INFORMATION PHASE

COST MODEL

ITEM NO.	DESCRIPTION	SYSTEM BREAKDOWN								PERCENT OF TOTAL	ITEM COST
	COST (SHEET ______)										
	WORTH										
	PERCENT OF TOTAL										

WORKSHEET No 1

Figure 3-1. Sample Worksheet-Cost Matrix.

COST MATRIX FOR WASTEWATER TREATMENT PLANT

		Liquid System					Sollos System		Support System				
Item No.	Description	Influent Facilities	Primary Clarifier & Pump Sta.	R.B.C.'s	Final Clarifier & Pump Sta.	Effluent Pump Sta. & Chem. Storage	Sludge Processing Bldg	Thickener	Tunnel	Control Bldg	Site Work	Percent	Totals
1	Major Equipment	150,000	194,400	1,142,000	176,500	617,900	841,400	198,000	-0-	37,500	-0-	30.7	3,367,700
2	Concrete	92,500	349,500	337,500	378,750	184,000	179,000	125,000	117,050	90,200	-0-	16.9	1,853,500
3	Site Work	2,000	259,500	119,500	311,500	65,000	43,000	39,500	-0-	4,000	826,000	15.2	1,670,000
4	Piling; 60 Ton	36,000	146,700	234,000	144,000	139,300	117,900	95,400	32,400	84,600	15,300	9.5	1,045,600
5	Architectural	12,000	-0-	-0-	-0-	278,500	185,000	-0-	-0-	328,800	-0-	7.3	804,300
6	Electrical	3,000	45,000	90,000	45,000	270,000	35,000	35,000	10,000	60,000	20,000	5.6	613,000
7	Inside Piping	35,000	75,600	-0-	50,300	180,000	30,200	41,300	41,200	-0-	-0-	4.1	453,600
8	Outside Piping	-0-	34,600	-0-	55,000	-0-	-0-	-0-	-0-	-0-	287,500	3.4	377,100
9	Instrumentation	10,000	15,000	10,000	15,000	60,000	40,000	10,000	-0-	140,000	-0-	2.7	300,000
10	Misc. Equipment	60,000	10,500	75,000	37,000	-0-	15,000	-0-	-0-	20,000	-0-	2.0	217,500
11	HVAC	5,000	2,600	2,600	2,600	15,000	60,000	2,600	2,600	112,000	-0-	1.9	205,000
12	Plumbing	1,000	2,000	2,000	2,000	2,000	12,000	2,000	1,000	36,000	-0-	0.7	60,000
	COST	406,500	1,135,400	2,012,600	1,217,650	1,841,700	1,558,500	548,800	204,500	913,100	1,148,800	100.0	10,987,300
	PERCENT	3.6	10.3	18.3	11.1	16.8	14.2	5.0	1.9	8.3	10.5		
				60.1			19.2			20.7			
										Contingencies 20%			2,197,700
										Total			13,185,000

Taken from a study conducted by Arthur Beard Engineers, Inc and Greeley and Hansen.

Figure 3-2. Completed Cost Matrix for a Wastewater Treatment Plant. (Courtesy of Arthur Beard Engineers and Greeley and Hansen)

PROJECT ____________

LOCATION ____________

CLIENT ____________

DATE ____________

PAGE ______ OF ______

INFORMATION PHASE

FUNCTION ANALYSIS

ITEM (SCOPE OF STUDY AREA)

FUNCTION : (FUNCTION REQUIRED)

FUNCTION ANALYSIS

ITEM #	(1) DESCRIPTION	FUNCTION (2) VERB	(3) NOUN	(4) KIND	COST (5)	WORTH (6)	COMMENTS (7)

Functional Analysis Steps

1. List Subsystem Description
2. Define action verb
3. Define measurable noun
4. Is the function basic or secondary?
5. What does it cost? (From Estimate)
6. What is it worth? (Speculation of least cost to perform the function)
7. Any additional information to be added
8. Total cost divided by the worth of the basic functions

ACTION VERB
MEASURABLE NOUN

KIND: B = Basic; S = Secondary

(Basic Function Only)
Cost/Worth Ratio = ________ (8)

WORKSHEET No 2

Figure 3-3. Sample Worksheet-Function Analysis.

tion control systems and administrative areas. Verb-noun descriptions would then be used to describe each of these elements.

Functions are defined by using two words: an *action verb* and a *measurable noun*. The two-word description should be general, so that it does not imply a solution but only the required function. As an example, pumping equipment has the function of *conveying fluid*. Had the function been identified as pump water, it would assume that pumping was required. The two-word description used in the function analysis forces a clear and concise description of the purpose. The function of a pipeline might be to convey flow. The function of a structural column might be to transmit load. The function of an automobile might be to transport people.

Each function is then classified as a *basic function* or as a *secondary function*. Basic functions must perform the function identified in the original scope of the analysis. For a power plant, the basic function would be to generate power. Only those elements for the project that actually generate power would be identified as basic functions. Other functions would be identifed as secondary functions. Secondary functions may be a necessary part of the overall project, but they are not identified as basic unless they actually perform the required function. The function of a project is separated into basic and secondary to distinguish between the components of the project that are actually doing the required job and those that support the main function. It gives a feel for the percentage of the cost that is being spent for performing the basic function as compared to those areas that are support requirements.

The next step is to identify the cost and worth related to each function. The cost of these components is listed under the cost column. Most of these costs should be available from the cost model previously prepared.

Worth is defined as *the least cost required to perform the function*. Assigning a worth is difficult, as it requires making comparisons and devising new ideas as alternates to the present design. There are two theories that are used to assign worth in the function analysis. One theory is that the worth should only be assigned to basic functions because the basic functions are actually performing the work. The other theory is to assign a worth to all of the described elements. By assigning a worth to all the elements of the project, the value analyst is generating alternative designs. Ideas for future development are often generated in this way.

The next step is to compare the overall system costs to the sum of the worth of the basic functions. The resultant is defined as the cost-to-worth ratio. Based on past experience in comparing cost, a cost-worth ratio greater than 2 will usually indicate possibilities for removing cost within the project.

More than one function analysis may be proposed in a study. The first step is to analyze the total system and then divide the project into its component parts. When analyzing a bridge, the approach would be to first analyze the entire bridge system, listing the major parts, such as foundation, pier, truss, deck, electrical, mechanical, etc. Next, we would do an analysis of each part, splitting the foundation into its pieces. We look at the *system first* to assure that major savings are not overlooked by system design. Having identified the basic function of the scope under study, the analysis continues by identifying the basic and support functions of each component part.

Specific examples of a function analysis for different types of construction projects are included in Chapter 4.

Having completed the function analysis and the cost model for the project, the value engineering team is now ready to venture into the creative phase. The cost, energy and life-cycle models and the function analysis have served to familiarize the value engineering team with the elements of the project and to determine the cost associated with each element. The value engineering team has also been given the opportunity to discuss the designer's viewpoint and his rationale for design. At this point, the value engineering team has the information that they need to start making comparisons of design and to generate ideas for future recommendations. If, after analyzing the project information and preparing the cost model, the value engineering team is still not sure of the process and elements involved in the project, it may be helpful to prepare a functional analysis systems diagram. The Functional Analysis Systems' Technique (FAST) is actually a road map of a function which helps to delineate the steps that are taken in a project in order to achieve its purpose and objective. The function analysis systems' technique is described in detail in Chapter 4.

Creative Phase

The creative phase of the value engineering job plan is intended to force the value engineering participants to think deeper than they are usually accustomed. Engineers and architects are creatures of habit, just like other individuals. Their instinct is to take the first solution that comes to mind, develop it, put it into the design, and cast it in concrete. In the course of their experience on projects, they may have several different alternatives that have worked well for them in the past, and which they traditionally use as solutions to designs.

Ideas come as a result of work done in the information phase and from group and individual creative sessions. Creative techniques are used to foster an open atmosphere of a free flow of information. The floor is opened, and all speculative ideas are aired and listed. For instance, one member of the team might notice that oil is used to run an incinerator to burn sewage sludge. He speculates on changing from vacuum filtration to a filter-press unit, resulting in a thicker sludge with less water. The more concentrated sludge requires less oil for incineration, at a vastly lower price. His idea is listed, to be decided upon later in a judgment phase. The VE team is looking for quantity and association of ideas.

Figure 3-4 is a creative and judgment phase worksheet used in a VE study. The creative ideas are listed in order in columns 1 and 2. The creative idea listing is completed before analyzing and judging any of the creative ideas.

All people have creative talents. Some of those talents are latent in certain individuals, while other individuals are willing to augment their present level

PROJECT ______________________
LOCATION ______________________
CLIENT ______________________
DATE ______________________
PAGE ________ OF ________

CREATIVE PHASE	JUDGEMENT PHASE
CREATIVE IDEA LISTING	IDEA EVALUATION

NO (1)	CREATIVE IDEA (2)	ADVANTAGES (3)	DISADVANTAGES (4)	IDEA (5) RATING

LIST ALL CREATIVE IDEAS BEFORE PROCEEDING TO JUDGEMENT PHASE. 10 MOST DESIRABLE 1 LEAST DESIRABLE

WORKSHEET № 3

Figure 3-4. Sample Worksheet-Creative and Judgement Phase (Creative Idea Listing and Idea Evaluation).

of knowledge with new and different possibilities for consideration. Members of the value engineering team are encouraged to not hold back on creative ideas. There are no roadblocks in a creative session; there are no judges to criticize and ridicule the ideas that people put out. There is a chance for each individual to express his thoughts openly. This often does not happen in a traditional design review setup. As ideas are brought forth, they are immediately recorded so that they will not be forgotten. Many ideas when first mentioned may seem ridiculous, but after careful consideration and study, these ideas may be worth countless dollars to the owner of the building or facility.

New ideas may also be added during other phases of the value engineering job plan. During the value engineering study, the value engineering team is continuously analyzing and synthesizing ideas to come up with the best balance between the cost, performance, and reliability of the project. Few pictures better describe the concept of analyzing or synthesizing a field of possibilities than W. C. Fields in his classic poker-face picture (Fig. 3-5).

Figure 3-5. What better description of analyzing and synthesizing possible alternatives than W. C. Fields in his classic poker face picture. (Source unknown)

Another point to be made about the creative session is that usually people are prompted by the interaction of other individuals. A multidiscipline team approach allows a diversity of ideas and opinions to be expressed. As an example, an architect may have an excellent idea dealing with project layout. Often the most creative ideas come from individuals with expertise outside of the study area. The reason for this is that these individuals are not burdened by their habit solutions, and by past precendents for designing a certain way.

Chapter 5 of this book contains a discussion of creative thinking with examples designed to be remembered.

Judgment Phase

The judgment phase of the value engineering study is used to screen the ideas previously listed in the creative phase. As the reader will recall, judgment was suspended during the development of creative ideas. It is in this judgment phase that we now evaluate those ideas to see if they can be developed further for recommendations resulting in increased value to the owner. The advantages and the disadvantages of each of the creative ideas are listed in columns 3 and 4 of Figure 3-4.

The evaluation of ideas should be as objective as possible. The team is looking for ways to implement the idea in such a way that a return can be given to the owner. Although the idea itself may not be worthy of development, there may be other areas resulting in residual benefit. It is important to try to find ways to make the idea work rather than to discard ideas at a first glance. There are also advantages when evaluating creative ideas in trying to look at the total list of ideas to see if one or more may be combined for one recommendation. The potential for cost savings for each of the ideas should also be evaluated. Cases with potentially high-cost savings and resultant savings in operation and maintenance costs of the facilities should be given high priority. At this stage, also, savings in energy costs might also weigh heavily.

Some of the criteria that are often used to screen creative ideas might be the following:

- Other obvious cost benefits to the recommendation.
- Does the proposed idea meet the required functional requirements?
- Is the new idea reliable?
- Are the original design requirements excessive?
- What is the impact on the design and construction schedule of the project?
- Is there excessive redesign required to implement the idea?
- Is there improvement over the original design?
- Has the proposed design been used in the past?
- Is there a past record of performance on the new design proposal?
- Does the idea materially affect the esthetics of the building or project?

After listing the advantages and disadvantages of each of the creative ideas, the ideas are rated on the basis of 1 to 10; 10 being the most desirable, and

1 being the least desirable. Ideas that are found to be irrelevant or not worthy of additional study are disregarded; and those ideas that represent the greatest potential for cost savings and improvement to the project are then further developed. If all the ideas on the creative list were rated with a 10, it would become obvious that the creative session was inhibited.

At this stage, we don't know whether some ideas will work or not, but the best possibilities are selected, and are researched first. They are developed to find out if they will work and if they will result in savings. If the idea does not work out later on in the development phase, then it is discarded. Perhaps we feel the idea does not save money; however, it would be something that the designer would ordinarily recommend as part of his own design. The VE team may eventually want to research it to see if the idea can be altered to save cost and retain the design benefits.

Development Phase

The development phase of the value engineering study takes the ideas remaining after judgment and further develops them into workable solutions. In this phase of the value engineering study, the ideas are thoroughly researched, preliminary designs are prepared, sketches of the proposed solution are prepared, and life-cycle cost estimates are made of the original design and of the new proposed recommendation. Background information and supporting calculations are necessary to augment and support the new recommendations. It is important that the value engineering team be able to convey the concept for their recommendation to the design engineer. If the proposal is not understood well, it is not likely to be accepted. It may well be discarded due to lack of information. Each recommendation is presented with a brief narrative to compare the original design method to the proposed change.

During the development phase, the value engineering team should try to empathize with the designer. The designer, when reviewing the value engineering recommendation, must make many decisions to properly judge and implement the value engineering team recommendations. First, he must be assured that the recommendation can be implemented and that it is a workable and reliable solution. Secondly, he must have adequate information to prepare the necessary drawing and specification changes that must be made to accommodate the revised design. Cost implication to the project and the effects that the change may have upon the schedule of the project must also be considered. The value engineering team should attempt to evaluate these areas of concern in the preparation of their recommendations.

This phase of the job plan is where the technical expertise of the team participants comes into play. Having the multidiscipline team together in one location helps in the development of value engineering ideas. All related areas of expertise can be utilized in the development of design alternatives. Documentation from each of the trades can be formulated in support of data required for the recommendation. In addition, outside sources of information may be called in to augment information available to the value engineering team.

The question often asked is, "how do you divide up the ideas for development among the team members?" The best policy is to take the areas with the most potential for savings, or those with the greatest potential for acceptance. Usually the individuals that were responsible for the creative idea will have the most interest in developing that idea for a positive recommendation.

It is important that key reference material relative to the changed design be available to assist the value engineering team in the preparation of their recommendations. Reference books, design manuals, specifications, catalog information, and design standards should be used as background material. When information is not available, use the telephone and other sources in order to find and document the facts. Find the best available source for information and back up all your assumptions with reference to the telephone number and the name of the individual whose information you are quoting. Worksheet No. 4 (Figure 3-6), for the development and recommendation phase, is used as an outline for presentation of value engineering recommendations. The development phase should include the following steps:

1. Make comparison design.
2. Sketch the original and proposed design.
3. Describe the recommendation and what it involves.
4. Compare life-cycle cost analysis.
5. Discuss the advantages and disadvantages that each recommendation entails.
6. Discuss briefly the implications and requirements to implement the value engineering recommendation.

It is also important to highlight the ramifications that this change will have on other areas of the design. As an example, if a value engineering recommendation is made to change the exterior enclosure of a building, there may be impact on the structural loading, on the heating and ventilating loadings and on the total construction time for the project. Cost estimates and preliminary calculations of these impacts should be included in the development of the recommendation. A discussion as to how these changes would impact other areas in the design, such as esthetics, safety, and operation and maintenance of the facility, should also be included.

The primary rule to remember in presentation of ideas is that each idea must be evaluated on its own merit. The designer may be able to understand your recommendation easily; however, you must be aware that other governmental regulatory agencies may also be reviewing your recommendations. Therefore, they must be complete to the extent that all the necessary information is included in the recommendation. Remember that the review agencies may not have plans, specifications and all the background information that were available during the value engineering study. So be complete,

PROJECT ____________

LOCATION ____________

CLIENT ____________

DATE ____________

PAGE ______ OF ______

DEVELOPMENT AND RECOMMENDATION PHASE

WORKSHEET № 4

ITEM: | NO:

ORIGINAL CONCEPT: (Attach sketch where applicable)

PROPOSED CHANGE: (Attach sketch where applicable)

DISCUSSION:

LIFECYCLE COST SUMMARY	CAPITAL	O & M COSTS	TOTAL
INITIAL COST— ORIGINAL			
— PROPOSED			
— SAVINGS			
ANNUAL COST— ORIGINAL			
— PROPOSED			
— SAVINGS			
PRESENT WORTH—ANNUAL SAVINGS			

Figure 3-6. Sample Worksheet-Development and Recommendation Phase.

be thorough and present your recommendations in a clear and concise presentation. Always work on specifics of the design rather than generalities. Generalities add an area of gray to a subject.

One way of checking the thoroughness of a value engineering recommendation is to have a team member not involved in the original preparation review it.

As an example, if the architect of the value engineering team prepared the recommendation to change the material in the wall section of the job, it may be advantageous to have the electrical engineer review the recommendation to see that it is understandable. This is a very valuable method in ensuring that our recommendations are clearly understood. The acceptance rate on value engineering recommendations that are thoroughly prepared is much greater than those ideas that are not well founded or well supported.

Using Outside Consultants

When using outside consultants as a source of information for a value engineering study, it is important to get the facts straight. It is often advantageous to ask the source of your information to come into the value engineering study so that you may have a face-to-face meeting with the specialist. This will improve your communication with that individual. Oftentimes, the suppliers will need to go back to their factories for price-quotations in order to assist you. This sometimes takes more time than is available during a value study. If there are prices that need to be researched, these areas should be approached first. It is also necessary that you document the source of cost information. If you have received a contribution of information from a supplier, or from some outside source, it is appropriate that you give credit to this individual or to the supply company for their assistance. Today's market is constantly expanding–new materials, new products, new processes are continually entering the marketplace. It is the job of the design engineer and the value engineer to recognize these new advancements and to use them where possible. Outside sources are a good fund of data for these new advancements.

Life-Cycle Costs

Life-cycle costs have been mentioned as one of the important parts of a value engineering study. It would be naive to recommend changes that would reduce the construction cost of a project and have major implications on the owner's ability to operate and maintain the facility. Design criteria have been changed by the recent impact of increased cost of fuel and other energy sources required to heat, cool and operate buildings and plant facilities. Life-cycle costs then become a necessary tool for the value engineering team. Worksheet No. 5 (Figure 3-7) is used for calculating the life-cycle cost of a project. This worksheet and the principles of life-cycle cost are explained in more detail in Chapter 8.

PROJECT ______ LOCATION ______ CLIENT ______ DATE ______ PAGE ______ OF ______	DEVELOPMENT PHASE LIFE CYCLE COST ITEM :	WORKSHEET Nº 5

	PRESENT VALUES	ORIGINAL	ALT. 1	ALT. 2
INITIAL COSTS	1. CONSTRUCTION COSTS			
	2. REDESIGN COSTS			
	3. TOTAL INITIAL COST			
REPLACEMENT COSTS	LIFE CYCLE EXPENDITURES			
	4. Year ______ a ______% Amount ______			
	Present Worth of Future Replacement Cost			
	5. Year ______ a ______% Amount ______			
	Present Worth of Future Replacement Cost			
	6. Year ______ a ______% Amount ______			
	Present Worth of Future Replacement Cost			
SALVAGE VALUE	SALVAGE VALUE (Pwf = ______)			
	7. Year ______ a ______% Amount ______			
	Present Worth of Salvage Value			
	8. Year ______ a ______% Amount ______			
	Present Worth of Salvage Value			
	ANNUAL OWNING OPERATING COSTS			
TOTAL COST OF OWNERSHIP (LIFE CYCLE COST)	(Crf = ______)			
	9. Amortized Initial Cost			
	a ______ % ______ Year ______			
	10. Replacement Cost			
	(Crf = ______)			
	(a) Year ______			
	(b) Year ______			
	(c) Year ______			
	11. ANNUAL COSTS (ACTUAL)			
	(a) Maintenance ______			
	(b) Operations ______			
	(c) Powers ______			
	12. TOTAL ANNUAL OWNING & OPERATING			
	13. Annual Salvage Value Credit (Crf = ______)			
	(a)			
	(b)			
	14. Net Annual Owning & Operating Cost			
	PW of LINE 14 (cwf (Unif. Pwf) = ______)			
	SAVINGS			

Figure 3-7. Sample Worksheet-Life Cycle Cost.

The life-cycle worksheet is used to make comparisons of the total cost of owning and operating a project or a building. The top half of the worksheet, under the categories, initial costs, replacement cost and salvage value, is used to calculate the present worth costs that are involved in a project.

Initial costs might include the construction costs, the cost of engineering, the costs of redesign resulting from the value engineering change, costs for planning, costs for the owner's coordination of the project, and costs for fees and licenses associated with the planning and design of the constructed facility.

The second category is replacement costs. Replacement costs are those costs incurred when equipment is replaced or major repairs must be done on a building. This might include replacement of mechanical equipment, resurfacing of roadways, repainting over the life of the project and other costs that would incur sometime in the future. To evaluate costs on an equal basis, replacement costs that occur sometime in the future are brought to the present worth. As an example, should the life of a project span over 25 years, it may be necessary to replace certain types of equipment during the lifetime of the project. Air-handling units, for instance, have a life of from 10 to 12 years. If a replacement were required at 12 years, and again at 24 years, it would be necessary to indicate the cost of those replacements 12 years from now and 24 years from now, and to bring those costs back to today's dollars. Figure 3-7, Worksheet No. 5, shows the calculations necessary to indicate replacement costs.

The third category under present values is the salvage value of the project. Salvage value is the amount that can be received in exchange should the project be sold in the life expectancy for the job. As an example, if a chemical plant with a life expectancy of 20 years, were constructed on a 200-acre site, at the end of the 20 years the plant facility may have no apparent resale value. However, the land on which the facility is situated may have some resale value. That resale value would be the salvage value. We bring the salvage value back to present worth so that all our costs are evaluated on an equal basis.

From the second half of the life-cycle cost worksheet, the annual owning and operating costs of the facility are calculated. These calculations take the present values that were previously calculated, and annualize them over the life of the project and add the annual operation and maintenance costs. All initial costs are annualized. Actual annual expenditures for maintenance, operation and power requirements for the facility are added as annual costs. Salvage values are also annualized, and are subtracted from the annual costs of the project. The result is the net annual owning and operating costs of the facility.

When evaluating life-cycle costs, we compare the annual owning and operating costs of the original design with the net annual owning and operating costs of the proposed design. The difference, then, becomes the annual savings.

To determine what the savings are in today's dollars, the present worth of the net annual owning and operating costs is calculated. The difference for the present worth of the original and the alternate under consideration then becomes the present-worth savings for the value engineering recommendation.

Because of the importance of life-cycle costs and the importance of energy in today's construction industry, a chapter is devoted to each of these subjects. Calculation of life-cycle costs are developed in Chapter 8, and the impact of energy on today's buildings and facilities is discussed in Chapter 9.

Matrix Evaluation

Up to this point, the evaluation of recommendations to be presented to the owner have been based primarily on cost. Cost is but one consideration in the total analysis of a project design. Other parameters must be considered in evaluating value engineering recommendations. Redesign costs, implementation time, performance, safety, esthetics and owner-preference are but a few of the criteria in the final judgment of ideas. For this reason, a matrix evaluation is used to augment our capability in evaluating value engineering recommendations.

Worksheet No. 6 (Figure 3-8) is a matrix evaluation form used by the value engineering team.

The several alternatives under consideration are listed in the left-hand column. The factors that are used to evaluate the recommendations are listed across the top of the worksheet. The first step is to weigh the importance of each of the factors under consideration. For instance, if the capital cost is the most important factor, it might be rated with a 10. Implementation time is not as important, and that might be rated as an 8. If esthetics have no consideration at all in evaluation, they would be rated a 1 or a 2. Weighted factors are evaluated on a basis of 10 to 1, 10 being a more important factor, and 1 being of least consideration.

The next step in the matrix evaluation is to take each of the factors, and to rate each item on a scale from 4 to 1. In the example, the capital costs for item 1, the Toyota, have an excellent rating. Item No. 2 has a fair rating, so it would be rated with a 1. Each of the alternatives is rated, based on the factor under consideration.

Having done this, the next step is to multiply the factor-weight by the rating to determine the weighted factor. All the weighted factors in the evaluation are added. The highest total number then becomes the recommendation.

Figure 3-9 is a completed matrix analysis for the evaluation of the purchase of a new car. The factors used in the evaluation included capital costs, operation and maintenance costs, esthetics, fuel consumption, performance, safety, repair costs, and Buy American. The vehicles evaluated were: (1) Toyota, (2) Mercedes, (3) Chevrolet Compact, (4) Ford Mustang. In this matrix evaluation, the most important factors were fuel consumption, which was rated with a 10; and other factors of importance to the evaluator were capital costs, and operation and maintenance costs, which were rated as a 9. Safety was then rated with an 8. Performance and repair costs were rated with a 7, and esthetics, lower on the priority list, were rated 6. Buy American was rated as 5 in importance. First, the capital cost was evaluated. It was felt that the Toyota had excellent capital costs; that the Mercedes, being high in cost was

PROJECT ______	RECOMMENDATION PHASE
LOCATION ______	MATRIX EVALUATION
CLIENT ______	ITEM :
DATE ______	
PAGE ______ OF ______	

WORKSHEET Nº 6

	FACTORS								TOTAL	RANK
	CAPITAL COST	O & M COST	REDESIGN	IMPLEMENTATION TIME	PERFORMANCE	SAFETY				
FACTOR WEIGHT 10 = MAXIMUM										

EXCELLENT = 4, GOOD = 3, FAIR = 2, POOR = 1

Figure 3-8. Sample Worksheet-Matrix Evaluation.

PROJECT ____________
LOCATION ____________
CLIENT ____________
DATE ____________
PAGE ________ OF ________

RECOMMENDATION PHASE

MATRIX EVALUATION

ITEM : Personal Car

WORKSHEET № 6

	FACTORS									
	CAPITAL COST	O & M COST	AESTHETICS	FUEL CONSUMPTION	PERFORMANCE	SAFETY	REPAIRS	BUY AMERICAN	TOTAL	RANK
FACTOR WEIGHT 10 = MAXIMUM	9	9	6	10	7	8	7	5		
1. Toyota	4	3	3	4	3	3	3	1		
	36	27	18	40	21	24	21	5	177	2
2. Mercedes	1	3	4	2	4	2	3	1		
	9	27	24	20	28	16	21	5	150	4
3. Chevy Compact	3	3	2	3	3	3	2	4		
	27	27	12	30	21	24	14	20	175	3
4. Ford Mustang	4	3	3	3	3	2	2	4		
	36	27	18	30	21	16	14	20	180	1

EXCELLENT = 4, GOOD = 3, FAIR = 2, POOR = 1

Figure 3-9. Completed Matrix Evaluation for an Automobile.

out of the price range and was rated with a 1; that the Chevrolet was a moderately priced car; and that the Ford Mustang also had good capital cost characteristics. Each of the factors were then evaluated on the basis of 1 to 4. The total weighted factor for each of the vehicles was recorded under the totals column. As you can see, the Ford Mustang was rated No. 1; the second rating was the Toyota; the third, the Chevrolet Compact; and the fourth was the Mercedes. The weighted factors being evaluated will be different for each individual. In a value engineering study, the average of each person's vote should be the factor weight.

When the owner evaluates the engineering recommendation, his factors may be different than yours. The matrix evaluation is a worthwhile tool in obtaining an objective evaluation of many different alternatives. It should be used when there is a necessity to evaluate factors other than just cost.

Recommendation Phase

All the work and effort that is put in by the value engineering team is wasted unless its recommendations are accepted and implemented by the owner. Not all recommendations will be accepted. Certain recommendations will fall outside the scope and requirements desired by the owner, or will not fall in compliance with the design engineer's objectives.

The recommendation phase is important, as it is the step in the process that brings our value engineering ideas into fruition. It is also perhaps one of the hardest steps in the value engineering job plan. Recommendations are essentially a challenge to the original design. It is a change to the design. Now that the value engineering team has developed a series of recommendations, it is up to the design team and the owner to review these recommendations and to adopt those that they see fit. Obviously, the savings by a value engineering study is the yardstick for measuring the study's success. The effort in bringing the recommendation to final acceptance is long and hard. However, unless the idea is accepted, the net result is zero.

Many new concepts will face a long uphill struggle for acceptance. Remember that the habit solutions that have been used by firms have taken a long time to develop and are usually entrenched within their organization. Your ideas must have special merit in order to persuade the designer and owner to accept the change. This was the reason that a great deal of emphasis was placed on the development phase. Each of the ideas was moved from its conceptual stage into its development, and now will, it is hoped, be accepted by the designer and the owner. Please refer to Chapter 2 on Habits, Roadblocks and Attitudes. This chapter deals with the roadblocks that are often run into when presenting value engineering recommendations.

There are several rules that will be helpful in making your presentation. First, your information must be summarized in a clear, concise manner, and each idea must be well documented, as previously discussed in the development phase. Secondly, it is helpful to touch base with the design engineer as the value study progresses. This will eliminate any surprises to the designer that may occur when you make your presentation. Picture yourself in the designer's shoes. You have been selected among many consultants to design a major building. You have developed this building along the basic guidelines given to you by the owner, and have come up with a design that you feel best meets the owner's needs. Now you are faced with the value engineering study. You have made your initial presentation on your rationale for the design at the beginning of the study. Throughout the study you have sat by and provided information to the value team, but you are totally unaware of the final results of the study. Now, at the end of the study, the value engineering team starts to make its recommendations, and you nervously sit there as the value team discusses ways that your design can be changed. Obviously, you will be very nervous.

Good human relations come into play here in recognizing the concerns of the designer. You will usually find that your acceptance level will be higher when you pay close attention to the basic rules of courtesy when conducting your value engineering study. There are also benefits in informing the designer of impending recommendations, as he will oftentimes interject information and objections to your proposals. This will allow you to redesign and to make modifications to overcome these objections. It will also help to improve the proposals with the contributions of the designer.

Value engineering recommendations are usually presented orally to the design team, to the owner, to regulatory agencies, to funding organizations and other individuals with an intimate involvement in the process. The key decision-makers that will be evaluating the recommendation should be present. It is also important to have top management involved in the presentations. Information discussed in the presentation often help to sell an idea.

Many times, when developing a new idea for recommendation, there may be questions that arise about the requirements of the owner and the requirements for the project. The value engineering team should feel comfortable in talking with the designer about the actual requirements for the project. This helps the designer to feel more a part of the engineering study. By increasing his input into the project, he will feel more comfortable with the end results.

One of the major areas of concern to the design engineer will be the impact of value engineering recommendations on the schedule for completion of the project. It has been the experience of the authors that design schedules have become increasingly stringent during the last several years. This has put an undue burden on the design team to produce a cost-effective design within the limitations not only of cost, but also of the time available to study alternatives for consideration and development into the contract drawings. If certain recommendations will have a substantial impact upon completion of the plans, that is, if the recommendation requires extensive redesign time, it may be necessary to develop a plan of implementation. Generally speaking, recommendations requiring major redesign will have to be worth the loss in time. Should the analysis of costs show that the delay in the project is warranted, then the cost impact of the schedule delay should become a part of your evaluation. Designers will be reluctant to make wholesale changes in the design. This stems from several reasons: first, the designer has been working on the project for six months to a year and is disappointed at having to make changes in his pride and joy; secondly, most designers don't like to make changes because they are more difficult to coordinate than the original design process. All these factors must be weighed in making your final recommendations to the owner.

We like to summarize the recommendation phase by the word "salesmanship." Table 3-4 represents some of the key factors to use when presenting and analyzing VE recommendations.

Table 3-4. Salesmanship.

VE Team

A. Good recommendations
B. Open-minded review
C. General, but persuasive, push for acceptance
D. Management support

Evaluators (Owner, Designer, VE Coordinator)

A. All projects have unnecessary costs.
B. The value engineering job is easier than the designers.
C. The value engineering goal is a better job for the owner.
D. The value engineering team is aiding in the design.

4
Function Analysis

FUNCTION AND ITS ROLE IN ACHIEVING VALUE

The goal of a value engineering study is to achieve true values for the owner. The value may come in the form of removing unnecessary costs to the project, or it may come in the form of providing a more workable product that would decrease the costs of owning and operating the facility. Value is that elusive commodity that we all attempt to achieve in our design. Value, in this context, is considered to be the amount of money that we receive in return for a product or service. The dictionary definition of "value" is the "worth of a product or thing." There are many ways to determine value other than by financial cost. As an example, today a high value is placed on a clean environment. Value is also evaluated in terms of the prestige or the esteem that a product returns to its owner. Let's look at value a little closer and examine four different types of value. (Table 4-1)

Use Value is a value received from the delivered function. It usually represents the properties and qualities which perform a function.

Esteem Value encompasses our emotional regard for the item which we are purchasing.

Exchange Value is the amount that we are willing to accept in trade for an item. Sometimes this amount is expressed in monetary terms, or it is a defined product or a certain quality that is acceptable in trade for other items.

Cost Value is the amount of money that we are willing to incur to produce an item. The cost value of a construction project would be its actual construction cost.

Other types of values are also used to assess the social qualities of our society. These values are often in abstract form and are difficult to quantify. The values that we use to analyze construction projects also follow the categories of quantifiable and abstract. The quantifiable values are those values that we can price. Abstract values relating to a construction project would be the esthetic values of natural undisturbed areas versus those where con-

Table 4-1. Four Kinds of Value.

1. Use Value
2. Esteem Value
3. Exchange Value
4. Cost value

struction has occurred. The importance placed on safety and protection of the employees working in facilities, and the degree of reliance that we are placing on the design of the project while not abstract are difficult to quantify.

At times it is difficult to quantify and qualify the importance of values other than those relating only to cost. In a value engineering study, we do our primary investigations centered around the cost and the price of the facility. The importance of abstract values and the final determination of the best alternative to recommend to the owner must, however, recognize factors other than cost. One tool used to analyze alternatives is the weighted matrix analysis which is defined and explained later in this chapter. The four kinds of value that have been defined, are for the most part quantifiable values. They can be related to a measurable means of worth.

Use Value

An example of use value can be seen in a highway project. The grooved surfaces on the curved bend of a highway deliver the function of reducing skidding. In his bid the contractor puts in a certain cash value for providing this grooved surface. The grooved surface then delivers the function for an identifiable price.

Cost Value

Cost value is simply an expression of worth in terms of the common measurement of money. It is the direct relationship of the amount paid for a part of a system in relationship to the sum required to produce the total item. As an example, if we were to get involved in a major concrete placement of a floor slab, the normal cost value of the floor drains, conduit, etc., would be the market value for which we purchased the product. However, if during the placement of that slab we suddenly find that one of the wall inserts is missing, the cost value of that item suddenly skyrockets because of the cost of labor and other factors that are being expended while searching for the missing item. If we were wiring the electrical system of a new house and had totally completed the project, with the exception of the circuit breaker and the panelboard, and were expected to complete construction of the house that day in order to avoid charges for liquidated damages, the price of the circuit breakers suddenly becomes a very high priority item.

Exchange Value

At one time bartering was a recognized way of doing business. People assessed commodities in terms of their value, and were willing to exchange other products at supposedly equal value. A good example of exchange value might bring back memories of our childhood. For instance, to obtain a baseball card that was very scarce, we may have been willing to give up four or five other cards in exchange. Politicians and economists in the United States are advocating the exchange of our grain supplies for much needed oil and petroleum products from the Mid East. Each of these commodities has an identifiable exchange value. Usually this value is based on the supply available and the demand for a particular product.

Esteem Value

Esthetics, appeal and emotions are the chief factors which influence esteem value. Consider the tie clasp used to hold a tie next to a person's chest. What is the function of the tie clasp? It has a valid function—to keep your tie out of your soup. If you had to send that tie to the cleaner several times, you would realize the value of the tie clasp. Now let us suppose that you are working around machinery. For several months, your tie clasp has no value. Then one day, you forget to wear the tie clasp, and your tie suddenly gets caught in the machinery. You suddenly realize the value of that tie clasp.

Now, let's look at its value more closely. Let's say that the cost of a tie clasp is $7.50. That doesn't appear to be an excessive amount to pay for a tie clasp. The *function* of the tie clasp is to *retain* the *tie*. However, the same function can be delivered with a paper clip. The paper clip costs one cent. How much is the esteem value in the tie clasp? It appears that $7.49 is for the esteem value and one cent is for the use value of the tie clasp. Not many people would go around wearing a paper clip on their ties. In value engineering, the objective is to become aware of just how much we are paying for the required function, and how much we are willing to pay for the esteem value of a product.

Another example of the comparison of several types of value is the paint on the outside of an airplane. What is the function of the paint? Is it to preserve the metal surface from rusting? Many people believe that is its purpose. But then, let's ask the question: "If the body of the plane is painted, then why not the wings?" The function of the paint on the body of an airplane is to advertise; so that the airline is identified and also to beautify the plane. The paint on the airplane has use value and esteem value. Its use value is that of identification; and its esteem value may be evaluated in the image it portrays and the resultant increased sales from people riding on the airplane.

CRITERIA USED TO EVALUATE VALUE

Table 4-2 shows some of the criteria which we use to determine value. The criteria used to determine the value of a product must be judged by the purchaser, by each individual, by the owner and partially by the design firm involved in the project. These factors will vary in importance depending upon the owner and his terms of ownership. As an example, a developer may place more emphasis on the initial cost of a product and be willing to sacrifice some of the operating and maintenance cost that will be incurred by the tenants of his property. Municipal governments, especially those receiving fed-

Table 4-2. Criteria for Evaluating Value.

1. Initial cost
2. Energy cost
3. Return in profit
4. Functional performance
5. Reliability
6. Operability
7. Maintenance ability
8. Quality
9. Salability
10. Regard for esthetics and environment
11. Owner requirements
12. Safety

eral funds for construction, will likely place greater emphasis on reducing the operating and maintenance cost, and the cost of power consumption of their plant or building while it is in operation.

FUNCTION: AN APPROACH TO OBTAINING VALUE

Function is the cornerstone of value engineering. The functional approach to value engineering is what separates it from other cost reduction techniques. The concept of function is used in a value engineering study to obtain a concise description of purpose. Of course, the determination of the function to be achieved is a prerequisite for any value engineering study. Utilizing the cost of a project and determining alternatives that can reduce cost cannot be intelligently analyzed without first determining the function that the project is to perform. The owner of a construction project has several purposes to perform. These purposes are the basis for designs.

Definition of Function

Function is the basic purpose of an item or an expenditure. It may also be a characteristic that makes the item work or makes it sell.

Miles defines function as: "The basic purpose of each expenditure, whether it be for hardware, the work of a group of men [people], a procedure, or whatever is to accomplish a function."*

Hart entends this definition to say that "function is anything that makes a product work or sell."

When an owner hires an architect or an engineer to design a project for him, he has a purpose in mind. He may want to produce a chemical product; he may want to manufacture some other product or commodity; he may want to provide office space to house employees in a workable atmosphere; he may want to clean wastewater or produce drinkable (potable) water for consumption. Breaking these requirements down to more definable and

*Miles, Lawrence D., *Techniques of Value Analysis and Engineering,* New York: McGraw-Hill, 1972, Second Edition, p. 29.

quantifiable categories is the first step in functional analysis. The customer wants something sheltered, moved, cooled, warmed, purified or some action that the product must perform.

First investigate the function of the total system of the project, and then break that system down into quantifiable parts. We find that thinking about what a system or assembly does and placing a worth on that action forces us to think in greater depth and to make more comparisons than we would have without the function approach.

The application of function in a value engineering study is *function analysis*. The project or product is evaluated by identifying the function in two words. A *verb* and a *noun* are used to identify what the item does. *The verb is an action verb, and the noun, a measurable noun*. As an example, an electrical cable has the function of *conducting current*. "Conduct" is the action verb, and "current" is a measurable noun. The following list of questions is used to help us arrive at the functions:

1. What is the purpose of the project?
2. What does it do?
3. What does it cost?
4. What is it worth?
5. What alternative would do the same job?
6. What would that alternative cost?

These questions are simple, yet the answers are sometimes difficult to arrive at. Usually people define functions in several sentences. In a value engineering study, you are asked to reduce the definition of "Function" to a two-word description, that is, the action verb and the measurable noun.

Let's look in more detail at the identification of action verbs and measurable nouns as they apply to function. The function of a water service line to a building could be described as being to "provide service." We run into a problem at this point because this is not a measurable function, thus making it harder to seek alternative solutions. To say "transports water" is a superior solution because the noun in the definition is measurable. Another danger in selecting functions is to choose definitions that imply a suggested solution. By choosing words such as "provide pump," to describe a function, we are guilty of a narrow definition that excludes alternatives. The function to *provide pump* assumes that a pump must be used to move the liquid. Hence, it is far better to choose the description "transport fluid," or "convey liquid." Try to avoid the word "provide" in determining functions because the noun reciprocal of "provide" usually is the implied solution. Choose a broad noun to avoid narrowing options.

Another way that the functional approach helps the participant to think deeper about the project is by classifying the functions between basic and secondary functions. *Basic Functions* are the specific work or purpose the product or project must complete. The basic function of a screwdriver is to apply torque. It may also be used to pry off hubcaps, or as a scraping mechanism. In these cases, the function is shifted to prying rather than rotating. In a water-treatment plant, the *basic function* is to *purify water*. Those elements of a treatment process that actually purify water are the basic functions within a water-treatment plant. The basic function of a power plant would be to generate power, and, similarly, the elements within the power plant that generate the power are the basic functions.

Secondary functions are *support functions* that may be a necessary part of the project, but do not perform the actual work. Table 4-3 defines the two types of functions, i.e., basic and secondary. Classification of the two types of functions give the analyzer some very valuable information. First of all, it identifies the costs of the projects that are really doing the work necessary to accomplish the primary function. As we will see later in the chapter, it will help to identify the costs that are associated with performing the basic function. By separating these functions into basic and secondary categories, the ratio of the amount of money spent to perform the functions and the amount of money that is being provided to support those functions is determined.

An ordinary pole-mounted luminaire offers an opportunity to further our understanding of the relationship between basic and second-degree functions. The basic function of the pole-mounted luminaire is to *produce light*. Figure 4-1 shows the pole-mounted luminaire and describes some of the parts. Table 4-4 is a function analysis of a typical pole-mounted luminaire. The first question we ask is, "What is the basic function of the pole-mounted luminaire?" Its function is to illuminate areas. When looking at the system as a whole, the only part that provides the basic function is the light bulb itself. We also might ask the question, "Could this light bulb be mounted on the side of a building, which would eliminate the necessity for the entire pole and foundation?" Now, let's shift ground a second and narrow our scope of decision-making to the part or the subsystem of the pole lamp (see Table 4-5). Each identifiable area scope now has its own basic function. Whether its function is basic or secondary relates directly to the scope of your decision or the area of your study.

In a value engineering study, it is prudent to perform a functional analysis on the total project first and provide separate functional analysis on each of the subsystem parts. Let's consider the functional analysis of a bridge. The basic function is to allow passage. The component parts of the bridge may be the bridge deck, precast T-beams, pile bents, pile cap, excavation and guard rails. The bridge deck itself is the only part that really allows access to traffic. Other elements of the bridge are support functions. In analyzing part of the bridge it is found that the structural fill used for embankment from the

Table 4-3. Types of Function.

Basic:	The specific work or purpose the product or project must complete.
Secondary:	Support functions that may be needed but do not perform the actual work

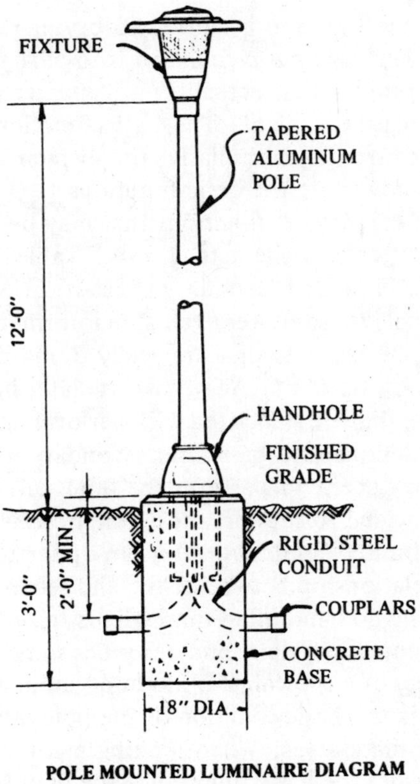

Figure 4-1. Pole Mounted Luminaire. Example for Function Analysis.

approach roads might be extended to eliminate several of the pile-supported deck sections. Thus, a part of the bridge deck is now replaced with the road surface, which provides the same function of allowing passage.

Another example is equipment buildings that are used to house electronic gear. The function of these buildings is to provide an environment with a specific temperature range which will allow the normal functioning of the equipment. In this case, the team analyzed the total project first. They broke the basic project down into concrete, exterior closure, roofing, interior finishes, heating, ventilating and air conditioning, electrical, plumbing and miscellaneous. Next they started functionally analyzing each of the parts of the project. During their analysis of the heating, ventilating and air conditioning, they noticed that the standard design for these equipment buildings provided air-conditioner units. The team decided that two exhaust fans would deliver the same required function of controlling the environment, within the operating limits of the electronic gear. The dual exhaust-fan system would operate effectively in 40 percent of the locations throughout the United States. Once the overall decision was narrowed down to the HVAC system, comparisons were made within that system of alternative ways to provide the required functions. Had the team decided that the air-conditioning system was needed,

Table 4-4. Functional Analysis Pole Mounted Luminaire.

Parts	Function	Basic	Secondary
Foundation	Support Load		
	Resist Loads		
	Transfer Loads		S
Anchor Bolts	Transfer Load		
	Hold Pole		S
Base	Holds Pole		S
	Supports Pole		
	Covers Bolts		
Pole	Raises Fixture		
	Supports Arm		S
	Protects Wire		
Extension Arm	Holds fixture		
	Spreads Light		S
	Protects Wire		
Housing (Fixture)	Holds Bulb		
	Transfers Electricity		
	Diffuses Light		S
	Reflects Light		
Lightbulb	Produces Light	B	
	Dissipates Heat		

When the scope of the decision is the pole lamp as a whole, the light bulb is the only element delivering the basic function.

they might have then narrowed their scope of study to the HVAC system, and broken that system down into component parts, i.e., the air-conditioner unit, the ductwork, insulation and the other component parts.

The question is often asked as to how many different levels and areas of function one should investigate. The answer is that it is a matter of judgment. It would be difficult to list every component and every part of a major project. However, by listing broad areas of study, i.e., systems first, and moving into smaller areas, the reviewer will become sensitive to those areas of the project that are representing the major costs.

QUANTIFYING FUNCTION IN TERMS OF ITS COST AND WORTH

Our primary means of measuring function is through its cost. Cost is what we are paying for an item. *The worth of a function is the least cost for performing the function* (see Table 4-6). The cost used in a function analysis is usually based on the engineer's estimate of the project. Chapter 7 deals with development of costs for a value engineering study. In performing a function analysis, the cost of the project is organized according to its func-

Table 4-5. Functional Analysis Pole Mounted Luminaire.

Parts	Function	Basic	Secondary
Foundation	Support Load		S
	Resist Load		S
	Transfer Load	B	
Anchor Bolt	Transfer Load	B	
	Hold Pole		S
Base	Hold Pole		S
	Supports Pole	B	
	Covers Bolts		S
Pole	Raises Fixture	B	
	Supports Arm		S
	Protects Wire		S
Extension Arm	Holds Fixture		S
	Spreads Light	B	
	Protects Wire		S
Housing (Fixture)	Holds Bulb	B	
	Transfers Elect.		S
	Diffuses Light	B	
	Reflects Light		S
Light Bulb	Produces Light	B	
	Dissipates Heat		S

When the scope is reduced to each part or subsystem than each area of scope will have a basic function.

tional components. Figure 4-2 is an example of the completed function analysis of a highway bridge.

The next step is to assign a worth to the parts of the function analysis. In assigning a worth, the team members must speculate on the least cost for performing the function. Many of the ideas may seem crude at first. However, the purpose of assigning worth is to develop a list of alternative solutions to the original design. It is often beneficial to apply a worth to each of the parts of the project. A comparison of the total cost of the project, divided by the worth of only the basic functions is then made. This ratio is called the cost-to-worth ratio. Experience has shown that cost-to-worth ratios greater than two will usually indicate that there is unnecessary cost in the project.

Table 4-6. Cost/Worth.

COST:	What we are paying for the item. (Engineers estimate)
WORTH:	Least cost for performing the function. (What ideas do we have that will perform the function at a lower cost?)

GRAPHICAL FUNCTION ANALYSIS

As a means of communicating the results of the function analysis, a graphical function analysis is prepared. A graphical functional analysis is a bar chart representing in descending order the highest cost to the lowest cost items of the project. The function of each of the parts is identified. Figure 4-3 is a graphic functional analysis. Other parameters may also be used. As an example, the energy and resource model described in Chapter 9 could be shown graphically. The measurable parameter would then be in terms of kilowatt hours, or it could also be expressed in Btus.

EVALUATE BY COMPARISON

Alternatives and comparisons are means to arrive at solutions to reduce the cost and increase the value of a project. Comparisons are obtained from his-

HIGHWAY BRIDGE
V.E. STUDY
GRAPHICAL COST MODEL

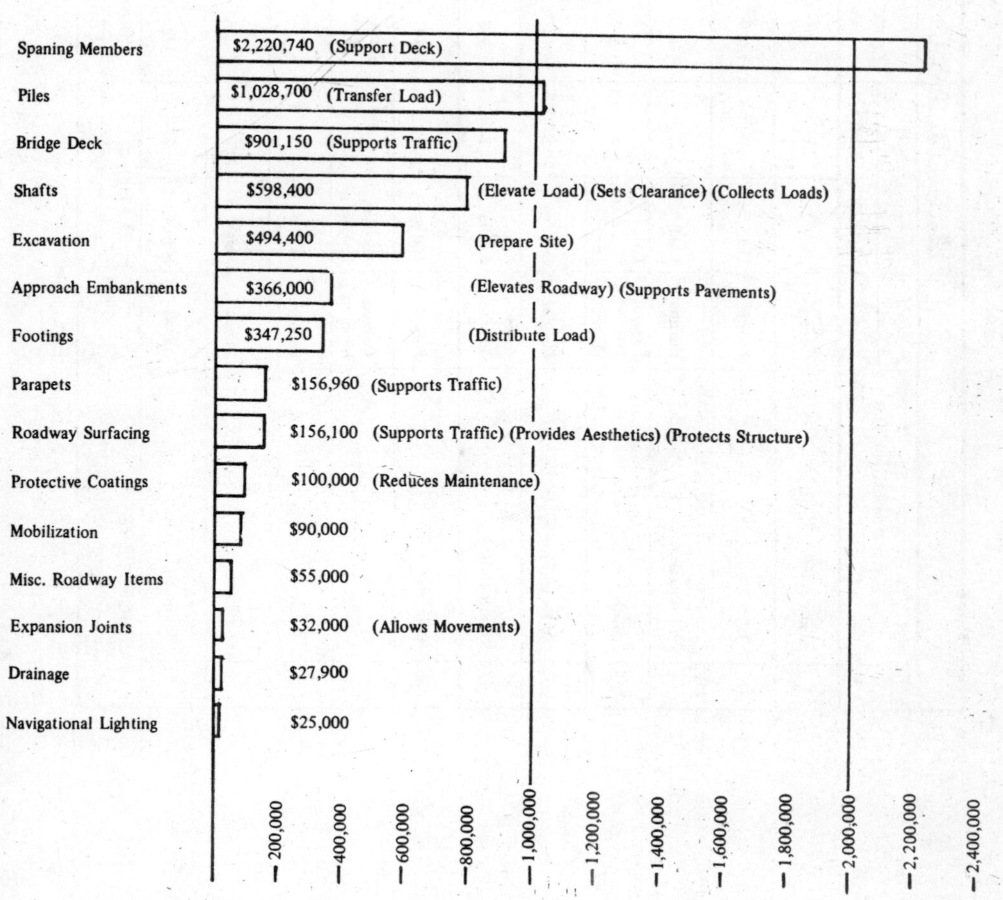

Figure 4-3. Graphical Cost Model-Function Analysis of a Bridge.

PROJECT ______
LOCATION ______
CLIENT ______
DATE ______
PAGE ______ OF ______

INFORMATION PHASE

FUNCTION ANALYSIS

ITEM : Bridge
FUNCTION : Support Traffic

FUNCTION ANALYSIS

ITEM #	DESCRIPTION	FUNCTION			COST	WORTH	COMMENTS
		VERB	NOUN	KIND			
	Excavation	Prepare	Site	S	491	0	
	Piles	Transfer	Load	S	1,029	0	
	Footings	Distribute	Load	S	422	0	
	Shafts	Elevates Sets Collect	Load Clearance Load	S	598	0	
	Spanning Members	Support	Deck	S	2,121	0	
	Bridge Deck	Supports	Traffic	B	968	968	
	Parapets	Protect	Traffic	S	157	0	
	Approach Embankments	Elevates Supports	Roadway Pavement	S	366	0	
	Roadway-Surfacing	Supports	Traffic	S	156	0	
	Drainage	Directs	Flow	S	28	0	
	Expansion Joints	Allows	Movement	S	32	0	

ACTION VERB
MEASURABLE NOUN

KIND: B = Basic; S = Secondary

(Basic Function Only)
Cost/Worth Ratio = ______ Cost in thousands

WORKSHEET No 2

PROJECT ______
LOCATION ______
CLIENT ______
DATE ______
PAGE ____ OF ____

INFORMATION PHASE
FUNCTION ANALYSIS

ITEM : Bridge
FUNCTION : Support Traffic

FUNCTION ANALYSIS

ITEM #	DESCRIPTION	FUNCTION			COST	WORTH	COMMENTS
		VERB	NOUN	KIND			
	Protective Coatings	Reduce Provide Protects	Maintenance Aesthetics Structure	S	100	0	
	Bridge Bearings	Support Anchor	Structure Structure	S	15	0	
	Misc. Road Items	–	–	S	55	0	
	Lighting	Provides	Safety	S	25	0	
	Mobilization	Prepares	Construction	S	90	0	
					6653	968	

ACTION VERB
MEASURABLE NOUN

KIND: B = Basic; S = Secondary

(Basic Function Only) Cost/Worth Ratio = $\frac{6653}{968} = 6.9$

WORKSHEET № 2

Figure 4-2. Example Function Analysis of a Bridge.

torical information on past projects, and from the development of new combinations that are assembled to produce the required function. The question of how else the function can be performed, and what its approximate cost might be, is a guiding question that helps us to arrive at comparisons for future evaluation. A checklist of questions for highway projects, buildings, power plants, water plants, and wastewater facilities has been accumulated. These questions are just the beginning to help you in your efforts to search out comparison solutions. These comparisons also will help to develop criteria for establishing a worth for the functions. A checklist of questions for function analysis is found below.

Larry Miles, in his book entitled *Techniques of Value Analysis and Engineering*, states that "the larger and more complicated the object undergoing analysis, the greater the number of comparisons necessary to make the analysis sufficiently comprehensive to establish the best value for each included function. This means analyzing a series of basic functions, each discovered by breaking the assembly down into its subsystems, components, and parts. In a way, the problem becomes perhaps one of comparing the use of one material with that of another; the style of one part with that of an equivalent; the application of one process of manufacture with that of another, etc."*

Typical Function Questions.

1. What does it do?
2. What is its projected use?
3. What is the design speed?
4. Who will use it?
5. How will it be used?
6. What is the location?
7. Are major cut and fill volumes required?
8. Is cut to be made in rock strata?
9. Do soils have good compaction characteristics?
10. Are right-of-way costs reasonable?
11. What type of bridge structures are needed?
12. Are standard specifications outdated?
13. Is steel or concrete more economical for bridge construction?
14. Are energy efficient (gas consumption) grades used?
15. Can planting save maintenance costs?
16. Are standard specifications for planting applicable to the entire state? Example: Florida may have several different growing zones. What will grow in one location, will not function in another.
17. What grade of steel is used?
18. Do flood levels and impact loads from river traffic affect bridge design?
19. Are pavement sections economical?
20. Are piles needed?
21. Is alignment optimized?
22. What is spent on signage structures? Can they be mounted on overpasses?
23. Can temporary barriers be used in the completed project?
24. Can natural noise barriers be utilized?
25. Will high mast lighting save money?
26. Is it cost effective to make provisions for future expansions (bridge widths, drainage structures, etc.)?

*Miles, Lawrence D., *Techniques of Value Analysis and Engineering*, New York: McGraw-Hill, 1972, Second Edition.

In a construction project, a comparison of the total system would be made, and then a comparison of each of the component parts.

Comparisons of the cost of the function that are being performed and their related cost must be made. Suppose, for instance, you are evaluating three bolts for an engine mount. One bolt costs $50, one bolt costs $5.00, and one bolt costs $1.00. Assume that all three bolts provided the required strength as outlined in the specifications and proven by testing. Which bolt would you buy? The $1.00 bolt provides the required performance functions at the least cost. Yet very often people try to persuade us to pay exorbitant prices on the ground that the failure of variance are great. Value is determined by comparison of viable alternatives, not by consequencies of failure.

In a wastewater treatment plant in western Colorado, the building exterior walls were constructed of cast-in-place, concrete-bearing walls with precast concrete double T's for roofing planks. A comparison was made on the cost of job-cast roof beams for the structure and the use of tilt-up nonbearing walls with a structural support system for the building. Insulation properties for both wall systems were similar. The designer-engineer further evaluated the roofing system, and its final design utilized a steel joist and metal-pan deck system for the roof. Cast-in-place exterior walls were modified slightly to complete the final design.

Comparisons are a normal step in the architect/engineer's procedure for doing a design. After completion of a function analysis, the value engineering team has a clearer picture of the purpose of the project and the related cost for performing that purpose. Clear insight into the high cost areas of the project help the reviewer to concentrate his efforts where the largest expenditures are being made.

ADVANTAGES OF FUNCTION ANALYSIS APPROACH

The function analysis approach has several advantages which have made it the focal point of value engineering. Table 4-7 is a listing of a few of those advantages which we have recognized. A two-word definition is not always easy; however, after we have bounced our ideas around and have communicated what each team member feels that function should be, we will have a better grasp of what the project is about. The advantage of the two-word definition is that it helps us communicate the ideas better to ourselves, and as a result we can communicate them to someone else with little ambiguity. It is a very powerful tool to make you think in greater depth about what you are doing. The exercise of the function analysis helps us to evaluate functions with a greater depth of thinking.

Don't be surprised if when performing a function analysis of a project you find something that is not performing a function and that can be totally eliminated. Why is it there? The answer might be: "Well, we always put it in these types of designs; it's been in our designs for the past 20 years." In the days when horse-drawn artillery was used in wartime, one man made sure that the horses didn't get away while the artillery was being fired. In addition, there were the individuals that loaded and fired the cannon. After this

Table 4-7. Advantages of Function Analysis Approach.

1. It forces conciseness and eliminates fog.
2. It identifies what the buyer wants in terms of function, not things.
3. It distinguishes between the parts and the functional approach.
4. It forces us to think in greater depth.
5. It helps us to communicate what we are actually doing into a more enthusiastic give or take discussion of cost versus worth.

process became mechanized, and men no longer used horses, it was discovered that there were still three men on an artillery crew. Further analysis showed that the third man really didn't have a function. When they traced back the origin of the make-up of the artillery squad, they found that this tradition of staffing an artillery crew had followed through into the era of mechanized artillery. Things like this often happen.

FUNCTIONAL ANALYSIS SYSTEMS TECHNIQUE (FAST) DIAGRAMMING

FAST is a systematic roadmapping of functions. It provides an organized method of exploring complicated processes or assemblies and determines in a step by step method the function required and a means to arrive at that function. FAST diagrams are applied to any series of functions that relate to each other. A complex timing mechanism can be diagrammed using FAST by diagramming each action or step required for the mechanism to function. In the construction industry, FAST is used to determine project functions as well as the function of each part of the project. FAST is best applied to clarify and to simplify an object or procedure into identifiable parts. The graphic presentation of functions is the FAST diagram. FAST stands for *Functional Analysis Systems Technique.*

The originator of FAST was Charles W. Bytheway, Value Engineering and Cost Reduction Administrator for UNIVAC of Salt Lake City, Utah. Bytheway first introduced his technique in a paper delivered to the Society of American Value Engineers at the 1965 National Meeting in Boston. This was the first major expansion of the functional approach originated by Lawrence D. Miles.

FAST has developed into an effective tool for evaluating existing procedures, structures, components, machines or other objects. It also serves as a problem solving technique by identifying the required functions to be performed and the other supporting functions. The final result is a proposed solution to the problem consisting of the steps required to achieve the function.

The application of FAST may be as a problem solving tool for existing objects, problems or procedures, or as a means to develop solutions knowing only the desired function. The purpose of FAST is to simplify the design, operation, plan, procedure or problem into identifiable functional parts thereby simplifying the problem. Each subsequent function is evaluated as to its effectiveness or usefullness with the hope of eliminating, modifying, or reducing functions. All functions are identifiable as two work verb-noun descriptions. Examples of FAST may be found in several application areas. In the design of a water treatment plant, FAST can be applied to develop alternative unit processes required to satisfy the basic function of purify water. In industrial plants FAST is applied to the manufacturing process by identifying each step in the assembly procedure. It can be used to evaluate existing processes or to arrive at new process approaches. Companies facing dwindling profits may apply FAST assuming the basic function is to increase profits and finding the required functions needed to make a profit. Insurance companies with complex procedures for filing and paying for claims will find FAST effective in simplifying the claims procedure to identifiable functional steps. Mapping the functions will quickly reduce the complex procedure into a manageable, identifiable set of lower level functions that will be much easier to evaluate and subsequently modify.

To understand the FAST technique it is first necessary to know definitions of the terms applied to the process. The diversity in definition of different types of functions substantiates the fact that FAST is a refinement and advancement in the normal functional approach.

A *Function* is the characteristic of an item that fulfills the needs or desires of the uses; it is that which makes an item work or sell; it is the purpose of an item or procedure. It is described by a verb and a noun without identifying the actual part or assembly performing the function.

A *Basic Function* is the required function, purpose or procedure that the item under study is required to perform. The purpose or performance feature which must be attained. It represents the primary objective of the items, whether it be hardware, software, procedures, methods or physical objects.

A *Supporting Function* is the characteristic of an item which is not essential to the user. Although often desired it does not contribute directly to the accomplishment of a basic function. It may make the item "sell" better or work better because of improved appearance or convenience of use.

An *Unnecessary Function* is an element or a characteristic which is not necessary for the item to work or sell. Unnecessary functions are usually the result of honest wrong beliefs and assumptions, or the perpetuation of obsolete requirements that can be removed or modified.

A *higher level function* is a function that appears to the left of another function in a FAST diagram. The higher level function can be found by asking the question *Why must the function be performed?*

A *lower level function* is a function that appears to the right of another function in a FAST diagram. The lower level function can be found by asking the question *How must the function be performed?*

Critical Path Functions describe sequentially how or why an adjoining function is performed.

Scope Line is an imaginary line drawn to the left of the basic function and to the right of the diagram to define those pieces under study. Functions to the left of the higher order scope line are higher order functions which may not be a part of the item being studied and those items to the right of the lower order scope line will likely be the solution to the project.

Applying the FAST Diagram

FAST uses three basic questions to begin breaking down seemingly tough problems. What is the problem? Why is a solution necessary? How can the solution be accomplished? A better understanding of the problem will result by asking these questions. Applying these questions to a function will result in a sequential higher or lower order function. The mapping of these functions is the FAST diagram. Higher order functions are usually the requirements defined by the user, while lower order functions are generally the solutions to the problems. (Figure 4-4)

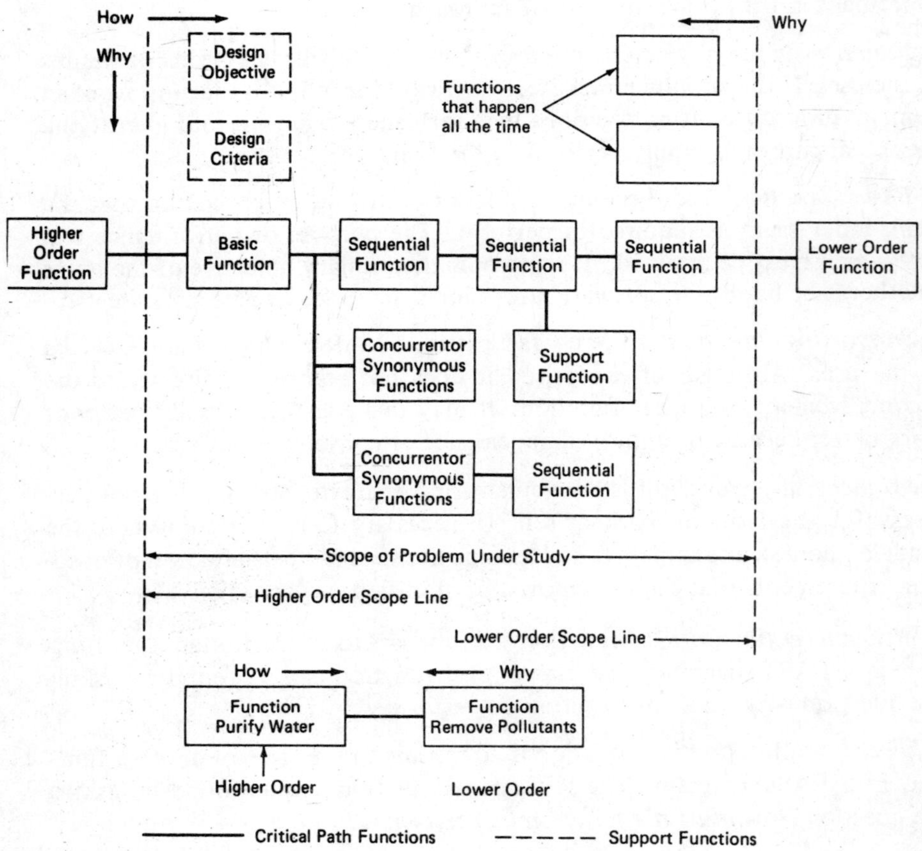

Figure 4-4. Ground Rules-Functional Analysis Systems Technique (FAST) Diagram.

Constructing a FAST Diagram

Start by drawing a scope line to the left side of the paper and placing the basic function immediately to the right of the scope line. This is the higher order scope line. By asking *Why* and *How* questions about the functions will result in other sequential or support functions. The answer to the *Why* question should be placed to the block to the left of the function and to the *How* question to the right of the function. For existing items index cards are often used to write down all the known functions and then arrange them in sequential order of occurrence.

Functions Which are Shown Horizontally Across the Diagram

Horizontally arranged functions, positioned as described above for the answers to the *Why* and *How* questions, must also meet a sequential order of events requirement-i.e., the earlier time functions appear in relative time sequence, starting at the right side of the FAST diagram. As a function occurs later in the sequence, it will be found progressively further to the left in the *Why* direction. Any function which does not meet this time sequence relationship is either located incorrectly in the horizontal chain of functions, or perhaps should be considered as a concurrent function and placed vertically below the function about which the *Why* or *How* question has been asked. As an example, the question *How* to remove pollutants may be answered by several concurrent functions, depending on the different types of pollutants. Functions which do have sequential relationships are arranged horizontally in accordance with the answers to *Why/How* logic questions, as follows:

The How Question. The answer should lie to the immediate right of the function about which the question was asked. If the function to the immediate right does not provide a logical answer to the *How* question, then the *How* answer function has either been described improperly or is in the wrong place. The *How* question should be phrased-"How do I (verb) (noun)?"

The Why Question. The answer lies to the immediate left of the function about which the *Why* question was asked. If the function to the immediate left does not provide a logical answer to the *Why* question, then the *Why* answer function has either been described improperly or is in the wrong place. The *Why* question should be phrased- "Why do I (verb) (noun)?"

Functions Which are Shown Vertically in the Diagram

Functions which do not have a time sequence relationship, should be shown below, or in some cases above, a particular function in a horizontal line of functions. These are functions which occur either at the same time or all the time and are called concurrent supporting functions. These functions can be required secondary functions, esthetic functions, or unwanted functions. If

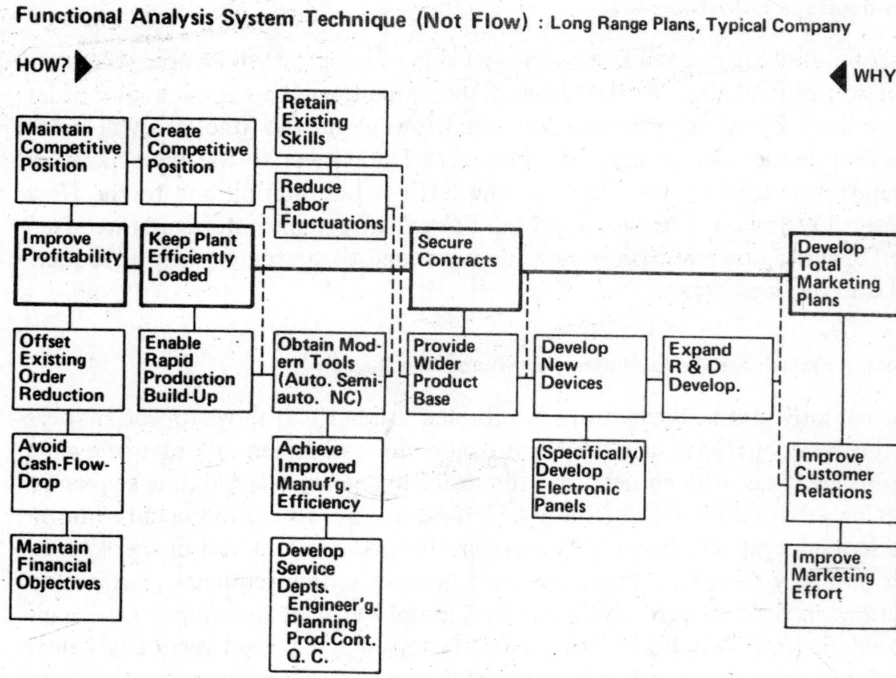

Figure 4-5. Functional Analysis Systems Technique: Long Range Plans, Typical Company. (Courtesy of Smith Hinchman & Grylls Associates, Inc.)

the function happens at the same time and explains or elaborates on some function in the horizontal chain of functions, it should be placed below the horizontal path function. If the function happens all the time, such as an esthetic function, it should be placed above the horizontal path function at the extreme right of the diagram. If there are specific design objectives to be kept in mind as the FAST diagram is constructed, they should be placed above the basic function and shown as dotted boxes.

Examples of the application of FAST diagramming are illustrated by the analysis of long range planning for a typical company. (Figure 4-5) The analysis of design requirements for a prison reception and processing center is shown in Figure 4-6. Portions of the text for FAST diagramming were taken from the value engineering workbook prepared by Smith Hinchman & Grylls Associates, Inc.

WATER AND/OR WASTEWATER TREATMENT PLANT

Total System

1. What does it do?
2. How large does it need to be?
3. What degree of treatment is needed?
4. How does it work?
5. What does it cost?

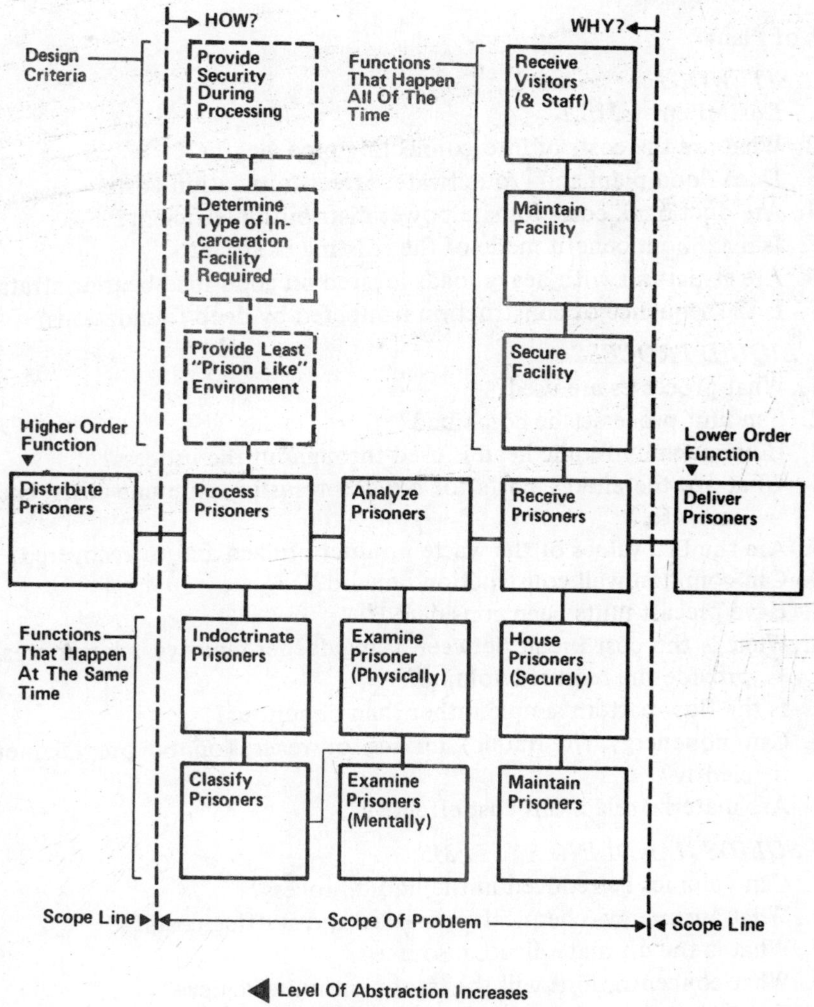

Figure 4-6. FAST Diagram – Prison Reception and Processing Center. (Courtesy Smith Hinchman & Grylls Associates, Inc.)

6. Are there any pollutants that materially increase the cost of treatment?
7. What is the cost per gallon of liquid treatment?
   For solids handling?
8. What are the percentage of costs for sitework, liquid treatment, solids handling and administrative services?
9. What is the cost associated with the type of pollutant treated?
10. Does the site require extensive conveyances and transportation to deliver the flow to the plant?
11. Are major pumping costs incurred?
12. Are elaborate foundations involved?
13. Is the groundwater level high?
14. Are major cut and fill necessary?

Parts of Plant

A. *SITEWORK*

1. Cost of cut vs. fill?
2. What are the costs of interconnecting pipe lengths?
3. Does flood plain and groundwater affect foundation costs?
4. Are duct bank costs for site power distribution efficient?
5. Is maximum benefit made of the existing contour?
6. Are structures with heavy loads located on good load-bearing stratas?
7. Is the sequence of construction hampered by deep foundations?

B. *LIQUID PROCESS*

1. What processes are used?
2. Can unit processes be combined?
3. How much hydraulic head is used throughout the process?
4. What are the energy costs for oxygen transfer, pumping costs, chemicals, etc.?
5. Are the Btu values of the waste product utilized and/or recovered?
6. Can common wall construction be used?
7. Have precast units been considered?
8. What is the cost break between using deeper tanks vs. a larger area to provide the required volume?
9. Is the flow pattern simple rather than circuitous?
10. Can nonenergy (hydraulic) mixing or reaeration be provided efficiently?
11. Are material selections cost effective?

C. *SOLIDS HANDLING SYSTEMS*

1. Can volumes be reduced in the liquid process?
2. What are energy, chemical, operation and staffing costs?
3. What is the ultimate disposal source?
4. What concentrations will the treatment units achieve?
5. Can energy be utilized from the Btu value of the sludge?
6. Is digestion feasible?
7. Can methane gas be used?
8. What is the break-point between adding chemicals and achieving a dryer sludge?
9. Can chemicals be recovered?
10. Will volume reduction of sludge save money in ultimate disposal?
11. Can storage be provided in the treatment process units?
12. Can chemical feed units be controlled to obtain efficient dosages?
13. Is heat efficiency retained by well-insulated units?
14. Can piping and pumping systems be optimized?

D. *ADMINISTRATION BUILDINGS*

1. What is the function of the buildings?
2. Is administration to be separated from the operating and maintenance staff?

3. What would be required if federal grants were not involved?
4. What is the cost per square foot?
5. Can functions within the building be combined?
6. Are the offices designed larger than the executive suite of a major corporation, or for the functional area required to do the job?
7. Is task lighting provided? Will skylights reduce lighting loads?
8. See Building Checklist for Other Questions.

E. *ELECTRICAL SYSTEMS*

1. Are dual power sources available or is on-site power generation needed?
2. What is the effect of demand change on power rate structures?
3. Can load shedding be applied at peak demand?
4. Can lighting levels be applied on a task basis?
   Are fixture units energy intensive?
5. Is the power distribution system for cable sizing and fault protection economical?
6. Can power factor corrections be made?
7. Can heat from motors be recovered and reused in the building HVAC system?
8. Are higher efficiency motors applicable for the systems?
9. Can two-speed motors be used at lower horsepowers to reduce demand?
10. Will variable speed units save energy by providing only the required amounts of oxygen, air, etc., instead of a constant amount at the peak demand?

F. *MISCELLANEOUS*

1. Are materials of construction available locally?
2. Do contracts allow competition?
3. Evaluate space allocation and equipment orientation within structures.
4. What percentage of building space is functional?
5. Are pipe runs routed efficiently?
6. Can acoustical treatment be localized?
7. Are standard specifications obsolete?

BUILDINGS

Total System

1. What is in the building?
2. What are the requirements?
3. What is the square footage area of the building?
4. What percentage of floor space is functional area?
5. What is the ratio of building exterior surface area compared to floo area?
6. What is the energy budget?
7. What percentage of exterior surface area is fenestration?
8. Are building materials suited to the locale?

A. *SITEWORK*

1. Are extensive utility relocations required?
2. Are cut and fill balances excessive?
3. Can sediment control structures be used in the ultimate drainage design?
4. How many parking spaces are provided per acre? Is it below average?
5. Is building oriented to achieve optimum sun angle?

B. *ENERGY CONSIDERATIONS*

1. Is make-up air and exhaust air minimized?
2. Can comfort levels be reduced to 68°F and 55°F where unoccupied?
3. Localize extreme loading areas such as laboratories, computer rooms, etc.
4. Use individual zone control where feasible.
5. Is heat from exhaust air recovered?
6. Is insulation sufficient? Are reflective coatings used on southeast and west exposures?
7. Are hot-water tanks and piping insulated?
8. Is task lighting utilized? Can heat be recovered from lights?
9. Can two-speed motors be used to achieve efficiency?
10. Is building orientation optimum for heat?
11. Is solar application feasible?
12. Are high-efficiency motors cost effective (i.e., do energy savings offset premium cost)?

5
Creative Thinking

INTRODUCTION

Industry and government are recognizing the benefits of promoting working atmospheres where creativity can thrive and be rewarded. Development of new ideas and techniques is resulting in better products, increased sales, energy savings and a more functional end-product. Inventors and innovative businesses have long recognized creative thinking as a problem-solving technique to promote progressive idea development. In contrast, it is not unusual for a company to select a solution to a problem, or to assume that there is no solution, without first checking the alternatives that may be commercially available or attempting to find a new and unique solution to the problem.

Traditionally, industry and government have done much to promote and recognize the education of an individual as a basis of the person's professional ability. While knowledge is an important factor, increasing emphasis is being placed on promoting an individual's imagination as well.

In VE, creativity plays an important if not a vital part in a project. The value engineering analyst is asked to develop new ideas that go beyond the original concept of the designer. The architect and project engineer exercise creativity by formulating a combination of materials, systems, processes and techniques to accomplish a required function. The VE team, on the other hand, begins with the designer's proposed plan and develops new ideas, combinations and techniques that go beyond the architect's and engineer's normal design techniques. Creative thinking is used to go beyond our normal pattern of problem-solving, and it makes us more productive. It saves cost in construction projects and adds to the total value of the project.

If an engineer has spent considerable time and effort on a design, then how can a value engineering team find ways to reduce its cost and/or increase its value? A specific period of time on each project is alloted to VE to encourage and create new problem-solving techniques. The creative phase of value engineering establishes an environment where a person can be creative and bring people together in a group where they can cross-fertilize each other's imaginations.

This chapter deals with the concepts of creative thinking and thought processes that impact on creativity. Much of the background for this chapter is excerpted from a creative-thinking lecture prepared by Glen D. Hart. The purpose is to sensitize the reader to the need to stretch our imagination beyond its normal limits when applying problem-solving techniques. The key points about creative thinking are illustrated by examples.

Realizing the potential benefits and the factors that influence the effectiveness of creativity will help improve our overall understanding of the subject. The goal is to outline ways to employ the concept in a useful and effective manner.

DEFINITION OF CREATIVE THINKING

Creative thinking is often associated with the development of a new thought or idea or concept that has not been thought of before.* Einstein's theory of relativity was a new concept. Likewise, discovery of uses for electricity can also be termed a new concept. Another definition of creative thinking is that it is a product of the imagination where a new combination of thoughts and things are brought together.** We have found the latter to be the best definition. The key word is "combination."

Frank Lloyd Wright, America's renowned architect, was unquestionably a creative individual. His designs were unique at the time of their development. And yet the materials used in his designs were readily available on the commercial marketplace. Concrete, timber, steel and masonry designs were proven techniques at the time. It was the *combination* of these materials and techniques that made Frank Lloyd Wright a renowned architect.

An excellent example of a new combination was the development of gunpowder. In 1242, Friar Roger Bacon of Oxford University published a book on how to make gunpowder. The ingredients of potassium nitrate (saltpeter), carbon and sulphur were known elements. What was not known was that if one combined these elements and ignited them, an explosion resulted. By changing the proportions, the force of the explosion could be controlled.

Creative techniques are used to bring about improvements and progress. Creative thinking may be seen as a means of overcoming problems that confront us. The solutions, our creative ideas, are often new and different from the original designer's concept. There is always a new proposition that improves the required function. Even if the basic premise is sound, there are always methods to improve that concept. When a project is value engineered, a good design is made more cost effective. The options are unlimited. Finding the best solution is where the challenge occurs.

CREATIVE PEOPLE

The capacity to be creative is likely a congenital trait. The actual creativity of an individual develops throughout his life with trial and error. Creative ability is nurtured from birth, and is in constant development throughout

*Koontz, Harold & O'Donnell, Cyrl, *Principles of Management: An Analysis of Managerial Functions*, New York: McGraw-Hill, 1972, Fifth Edition, p. 534.
**Miles, Lawrence, *Techniques of Value Analysis and Engineering*, New York: McGraw-Hill, p. 114.

adolescence and into maturity. This is contrary to the old belief that only geniuses, or persons with a very high I.Q., possess the ability to be creative. Albert Einstein, Thomas Edison and others were considered creative individuals because they were geniuses of their time. However, we now recognize that each individual has a certain amount of creativity within his own psychological makeup. We all know that architects, engineers and managers, to name a few, express their creativity by way of their designs and their ingenuity in managing a company. Creativity and high intelligence do not necessarily correlate. Individuals of high intelligence may be restricted to the point where their creativity and judgment are curbed.

Psychologists have studied the relationship between I.Q. and creativity. There is a diversity of opinion regarding the connection of high I.Q. and the amount of creative ability possessed by an individual. One thing is definite, however, and that is that everyone has some creative ability. Unfortunately, roadblocks traditionally get in the way of the development of a person's inborn creative talent. The influences of home and school often thwart the child's creative drive by not allowing him to experiment. The rules are often too rigid and inflexible.

Parents must learn to strike the proper balance between necessary discipline and an open educational environment. Finding that proper balance is certainly not an easy task.

Establishing an open environment to allow an individual creative capacity to develop is also a *goal* of the value engineering study. Let's look at some examples of creativity in our everyday life. A housewife must provide a plan for stretching her budget for feeding and clothing her family. As living costs continue to soar, she must devise new ways of stretching those dollars. Another example is the person who buys an old rundown house and uses his creativity to renovate, redecorate and reconstruct the house into a beautiful picture of architecture. Another example would be a minister who must divide his time between preparing and preaching a sermon and looking out for the welfare of his congregation; and, at the same time must also develop plans to increase attendance. It is becoming apparent that creativity is used everyday in our lives, and that creative individuals are not a part of one group.

In value engineering, we are interested in the creative capability of individuals, as this is one characteristic that is necessary to a value engineering team. Bringing out this creative ability is the key task of the value engineering specialist.

Let's explore the subject of who is a creative individual. Several different types of people have been identified as creative individuals:

1. *Small children*. The ingenuity and imagination of a child are almost unlimited. Parents, especially, wonder how their children can have so much imagination at the age of two, and how they can get into so much trouble. Children also must use their imagination because they do not have all the raw materials and resources available to grownups. They must improvise.

2. *Scientists*. Scientists are creative individuals because their jobs provide a forum for new combinations of chemicals, new properties of materials and new discoveries with which to perfect and to improve our existing products.

3. *Pioneers*. The early pioneers in our country and in other countries had to be creative in order to survive. They faced adverse weather conditions and a fear of the unknown. It was often their creative imagination and ingenuity that helped them to survive their ordeals.

4. *Seabees*. The Seabees were organized in World War II as the construction division of the U.S. Navy. While building in the jungles of Guam, the Seabees invented the chain saw that we now use in our homes today. They also invented the steel mesh that was used to build runways and roads for supporting vehicles in marshy, wet areas. Many of their discoveries were based on necessity.

5. *Writers*. Writers must be creative individuals. The writer must be able to express himself in new combinations of words and thoughts in order to express ideas and concepts to the reader.

6. *Housewives*. Several years ago, in a parking lot in Schenectady, New York, one of the authors observed a woman who was returning to her car after shopping. There were several inches of snow on the ground and very severe icy conditions. After the woman got into her car, she started the motor and began to back out of the parking space. The ice was very slick and the wheels began to spin. She reached into her grocery bag and picked out a box of graham crackers, pulled out the crackers, crunched them up, and threw them under the back wheels of the car. She then got back into the car, put the car into reverse, pulled out of the parking space and went on her way. She had developed a new combination to solve her problem.

7. *Architects*. Each new building or interior design is a new combination of materials, colors, space allocations and physical conditions. The verity and integrity of our buildings and structures are excellent representations of the creative capacity of our architects.

8. *Engineers*. Engineers, like architects, need a variety of materials, principles and properties to arrive at their designs. Prestressed concrete, for example, was virtually unknown 20 years ago. The concrete and reinforcing steel used in prestressed concrete were all materials that were previously available. However, the new process of prestressing the reinforcing steel involved a new combination of processes which has resulted in substantial savings to building owners throughout the country.

Judgment is a factor that affects the acceptance or rejection of creative ideas. Often, people of high intelligence will attempt to block an idea with little consideration of the facts. Slightly over 100 years ago, in 1878, Alexander Graham Bell offered the new invention, the telephone, to the president of Western Telegraph for $25,000. The president responded that he had no time to waste on toys, that they already had a communication system in the telegraph, and the telephone had no practical value. The president was a man of high intelligence, but his judgment in this instance was certainly poor.

In other words, if you have a great idea, just because a highly intelligent or high-positioned man tells you it's no good does not mean necessarily that he is right. In a televised interview, Howard Jarvis of California Proposition 13 fame, related the following story. He was advised by a banker he had consulted several years ago not to buy land that was for sale at 17½ cents a square foot in a California coastal town, as it would never be worth much more because of its poor location. Jarvis said he felt the bank official should know about land values, hence he decided not to buy the property on the banker's advice. As he walked out of a store and down the street, he saw a sign on a hardware store identifying carpeting for sale at 19½ cents a square foot. Jarvis thought, if that carpeting is worth 19½ cents, the land certainly should be worth more than the carpeting and that the banker must be wrong. He purchased the land, and made $100,000 profit when he sold it. The moral is: gather all the information you can, but in the final analysis use your own best judgment and not someone elses.

CHARACTERISTICS OF CREATIVE PEOPLE

When staffing a value engineering study, we look for creative individuals. It becomes important to know the characteristics of creative people in order to select the best team members for a value engineering team. We know that everyone possesses some degree of creativity; however, we are now looking for individuals who are ready to put their creativity to work.

We believe that the prime thesis behind creativity is that the individual must *believe that it can be done.* This thesis is taken from a book written by David J. Schwartz, entitled *The Magic of Thinking Big.** Believing that it can be done is often half the battle in finding the solution. If a person believes that something can be done, it will also activate his mind to seek ways that a solution can be found. On the contrary, if a person believes that the task is impossible, his mind will shut out potential solutions that may be valuable. Some people call this task "mind-tuning," or developing an appropriate attitude before entering into the problem-solving techniques.

Because value engineering is a proven technique, we know that better value will, in fact, come as a result of our value engineering studies. As value engineers, we believe that there is potential for removing unnecessary costs in any design or any process or project.

In this context, creativity in an individual may be manifested as active input into the design process. Another person may have latent creativity that is waiting for an opportunity and a situation in which to express itself. The following characteristics have been found to be representative of creative people. However, they are certainly not the only characteristics with which to judge a creative individual.

1. *Motivation.* First, they must have a desire to find a better solution for a project. Motivation is often expressed in enthusiasm for the challenge of

*Schwartz, David J., *The Magic of Thinking Big.*, p. 69.

attacking a new and complex project. People who are highly motivated will push themselves and the members of their team to go beyond their normal habit solutions.

2. *Flexibility in thinking.* It is difficult for a civil engineer to make comments and suggestions on a mechanical design. The civil engineer often believes that his background does not give him the experience to make suggestions on other areas of the project. In value engineering, engineers should not be reluctant to consider alternate approaches that may be new and creative. Many of the best recommendations come from people outside of their particular field of study. As an example, the pneumatic tire was invented by a veterinarian. A person must also be flexible in his approach to a project. He must be willing to reorient his thought processes with new and more effective information.

3. *Sensitivity to the problem.* A person must have an awareness and a feel for the problem areas. For value engineering on construction projects he must have a perception of where the high-cost areas are in the project, and be able to spot the areas where improvements can be made. Our experience in value engineering on construction projects has shown that certain people can zero-in on the high-cost areas of a project in a short time. They have a perception and a feel for the cost being paid for the required functions.

4. *Originality.* A creative person is able to come up with new and original ideas. He has a wide span of interests from which he can draw. He is able to combine ideas suggested by other team members with his own experience in an effort to improve the final product. The original thinker is an inquisitive individual who is unwilling to accept the statement, "we have always done it this way," as being a logical solution.

5. *Persistence or drive.* Emotional drive is the motivating force that helps us overcome adversity and roadblocks that we face when coming up with new and creative ideas. We have talked about the subject of roadblocks in the chapter entitled, "Habits, Roadblocks and Attitudes."

6. *Open to change.* The creator or innovator brings about change to our society. Resistance to change is often a steadfast thing in many people's minds. They are unwilling to take the risk that could result in failure. On the other hand, if there were no risk, there could be no change, hence no progress.

7. *Ability to abstract.* The field of engineering is based upon absolute principles and properties. There is very little abstract thinking that goes into our designs. They are primarily based on material properties, proven strength and scientific knowledge. Developing new ideas that are as yet unproven is not something that an engineer is used to doing.

8. *Tolerence of ambiguity.* In a value engineering study, we are often unsure whether our creative ideas will, in fact, be developed and eventually recommended. There is a reluctance, at times, to suggest ideas without having a clearcut, positive notion that the particular idea is, in fact, a better recommendation. There is always some ambiguity in coming up with a creative idea.

CREATIVE PROCESSES (TOOLKIT OF CREATIVITY)

The creative thought process is composed of three main categories: imagination, inspiration and illumination. These three creative processes were obtained by analysis of how creative thought comes about. If you were an inventor, such as Thomas Edison, the Wright Brothers, Henry Ford, Charles Kettering, or others, you would likely use this toolkit of creativity. If you were a song writer, a painter, a housewife, teacher, statesman, writer, etc., you would likely use the same toolkit. In other words, there is no difference in the toolkit; the difference lies in the application.

Imagination

Einstein once said that "imagination is more important than knowledge." It is interesting to note that he did not say that imagination was as important as knowledge; he stated that it is more important than knowledge. A good example of Einstein's thesis occurred at the turn of the century. Dr. Simon Newcomb, a leading scientist at that time, published this statement: "The demonstration that there is no combination of force or machinery that can be put together by which men shall fly is as conclusive as anything could possibly be " About the same time that this statement was made, two very intelligent bicycle mechanics, were enthusiastically working on their mechanical bird with manmade wings. They did not know all the theoretical principles of aerodynamics but they constructed a wind tunnel and collected information about shifts in the center of gravity and resultant lift on the airplane wings. They conceived the idea of varying the inclination of sections of the wing to aid in controlling the plane. The part is the aileron. They enthusiastically worked on their mechanical bird; and we all know what happened from these two bicycle mechanics in December of 1903. Their imagination and their persistence brought about the first successful powered flight. Perhaps that is what Emerson was talking about when he said "imagination is even more important than knowledge."

Enthusiasm and imagination go hand in hand. It is our enthusiasm which drives our imagination to endless limits. Ralph Waldo Emerson once observed that "nothing great was ever achieved without enthusiasm. It is the key to our imagination." Imagination is at its peak when our enthusiasm is in full swing. Imagination is a deliberate process that works in direct proportion to one's enthusiasm and does not seem to work if enthusiasm is not present.

Inspiration

Inspiration is a factor that is brought on by accidental stimuli. Knowledge and experience are often available but need some new elements that will trigger a new combination. We all, at times, receive inspiration from the people that we come in contact with, by our exposure to new ideas that are parallel to our own, and by contact with ideas that are a contrast to our proposed solution of a problem, or by some adjoining thought.

An excellent example of an inspirational discovery occurred in 1942, during World War II, in England. The Royal Air Force was charged with the destruction of three hydroelectric dams that supplied hydroelectric power to the Ruhr Valley, which produced much of the Nazi war machinery. Prior attacks had been made on the dam without noticeable results. Dr. Barnes Wallis came up with the idea that a 500-pound bomb could be dropped, not on top of the dam, but behind the dam, so that it would skip along the water. When it hit the dam wall, it could be stopped without bursting and sink straight down the side of the wall and be detonated by the water pressure. The explosion would combine the force of the power of the bomb, the pressure of the water and the containment of the explosion by the more dense water compared to the air above. These three forces would be sufficient to rupture the dam wall. Prior attempts at bombing the top of the wall had failed. The problem was, how to drop the bomb so that it would skip across the water at the correct velocity. It was determined by experimentation that the bomb must be dropped 600 yards in back at the wall at an altitude of 60 feet above water level. The distance from the dam wall was easily determined by a sight-gage mounted on the airplane's window. The sight-gage would be lined up with the dam spillway. There was, however, no solution for determining a precise altitude of 60 feet above water level. One solution was a plumb bob suspended by a piano wire. Others were tried, but were unworkable. There must be a way without redesigning the altimeter itself. Guy Gibson was attending a night club show in downtown London one evening. The show was at the famous Windmill Theater, whose motto was "we never close." They operated through the London blitz. As Guy Gibson was watching the show, he observed that the spotlights focusing on the female performer sometimes combined into one spot, and sometimes two. He turned to view the two corners of the theater, and noticed there were two spotlights, each focused on one location. An idea materialized! Why not place one spotlight in the left wing-tip and another in the right wing-tip, and position them so that at exactly 60 feet above water, only one spot would show. Guy Gibson was inspired by an accidental stimuli of spotlights crossing on the stage.

One light was placed in the nose, and the other in the tail. Nineteen airplanes were sent on that raid. Eight were shot down. Fifty-six men were killed, but the RAF destroyed the Eder and the Moehne dams. Forty-two factories were wiped out from the tidal wave alone.

Illumination

Illumination is what happens when the idea about a project you have been working on simply arises from your subconscious to your conscious mind. Illumination is brought about by the addition of new information that enlightens us in alternate ways of performing the same function. James Watt's development of the steam engine condenser came as a result of illumination. He had viewed the model of a cylinder with a piston. Heat was introduced into the cylinder, pressure in the cylinder would build, and the piston would be pushed out. Cold water was then injected in the cylinder, and the pressure inside would drop, causing the cylinder to be returned. The potential for work was obvious to James Watt. If only they could make it move faster. The in and out action of the cylinder was too slow. Watt worked for several months trying to resolve his problem. According to Watt, he was enjoying a relaxing day walking home from church, when suddenly it popped into his mind that steam was an elastic body. Why not save the elastic steam in a condenser and have two units working in tandem. Details for the design began falling into place. He could hardly wait to get home to his design board to record and sketch his thoughts. His conscious mind had not been thinking of the problem; however, subconsciously he had been working on the solution. We bring up these three examples of the creative thought process to make the reader aware of his potential for creating and developing new and exciting ideas. Each individual is stimulated in different ways to bring about new concepts.

PSYCHOLOGICAL BASIS OF CREATIVITY

Aristotle gave us these three basic elements of the association of ideas under three laws of creative thinking:

1. Similarity–or like ideas
2. Contiguity–or adjoining ideas
3. Contrast–or opposite ideas

These three laws need to be explored in order to show their true potential in a creative-thinking process.

Similarity

What do we mean by similarity of ideas? Again, the example of similarity of ideas can be found in the development of the typewriter. The typewriter is designed similar to the piano. If a man or woman could sit down to a piano keyboard and select the notes desired to play a certain melody, then certainly they could sit down with a similar keyboard of the alphabet and select the letters to develop words and paragraphs.

Another example of similarity of ideas may be found in the wastewater field. Composting is a relatively new process which is used to stabilize wastewater sludges so that they may be placed back on the land and used for soil conditioners. The process used in composting is very similar to the process that nature uses in the bacteriological breakdown of decaying organic matter. The composting process modifies and speeds up nature's process.

Contiguity

Contiguity is the process of the association of adjoining ideas. When you look up and see a cloudy sky, the adjoining thought that you have is that it might rain. Louis Pasteur, in his development of the inoculation process, is a good example of contiguity. Louis Pasteur had been experimenting on the development of a cure to combat chicken cholera. In the middle of the experimentation, Pasteur became ill and was forced to go to bed. Pasteur had been using chickens in his experiment. He asked his landlady to care for his chickens and cholera bacteria. She agreed to feed the chickens but refused to touch the cholera culture. Thus the germs became weak. At the time of his illness he had divided them into groups: one with severe chicken cholera, the second with mild cholera, and the third, a group that had never been exposed to the disease. He had also been successful in isolating various cultures of chicken cholera. Pasteur observed that some of his chickens survived cholera that previously had been severely ill with the disease, while others that had been exposed to mild cases, survived. Once they had had either a mild or a severe case of cholera, they never contacted the disease again. He suddenly thought of his weak chicken cholera cultures and wondered if, by introducing the weak germs into the chickens which had never been exposed to cholera, it would build an immunity within them. Thus, inoculation was born. What was the main process or association of thoughts? It was contiguity.

Contrast

The third law, contrast, obviously means the opposite idea. We use contrasting thoughts and processes everyday in our designs. A good example is the design of highways. To provide a smooth ride and save on fuel consumption, highway designs strive for straight roadways with minimal slopes. On dangerous curves, the chances of losing control because of skidding is a potential hazard. The skidding occurs because there is not enough friction between the road surface and the vehicle wheels. On dangerous curves, highways are now being constructed with special aggregate material that is sometimes grooved to increase the friction of the paved surface and aid in stopping the vehicles. The opposite idea of increasing the friction of the smooth paved surface has helped to save the lives of many of the nation's motorists.

Another example is in the design of building structures to counteract buoyancy. We counteract buoyancy by adding extra weight to hold the structure down. It is an opposite reaction to the buoyant force.

Pennsylvania was one of the earliest states to have a railroad. They experienced a plague of grasshoppers while ascending a steep grade. The wheels on the mighty steam engine began to slip on the rails which were made slippery with crushed grasshoppers. They asked themselves what was the contrast to the slippery grasshoppers. Someone mentioned sand. A sandbox was installed high on the engine with pipes running to a point in front of the wheels. A slight amount of sand was put on the rails. It stopped the skidding. To this day, somewhere on the modern diesel railroad engine you will still find the useful sandbox. The contrasting idea helped solve the problem.

WHAT STIMULATES CREATIVITY?

What prompts us to go beyond the normal solutions to problems? For people who are creative thinkers, traditional thinking can be one of our worst enemies. It freezes our mind, it blocks our creative thoughts, and prevents us from developing further.

Charles Kettering was one of the more progressive inventors of our century. Many of his ideas and inventions met great opposition when first proposed. Kettering made this observation about the development of new ideas:

"Man is so constituted as to see what is wrong with a new thing, not what is right." To verify this, submit a new idea to a committee. They will obliterate 90 percent of the rightness for the sake of 10 percent wrongness. The possibilities a new idea opens up are not visualized because not one man in a thousand uses his imagination. Yet, faced with this adversity, progress still occurs. Let's look at several reasons and factors that motivate our creativity. We should add that many of these factors came from participants in our 40-hour value engineering workshops.

1. *Search for beauty.* This factor was added to our list at the request of an architect. Architects are continuously looking for beauty in their structures as an enhancement to our environment.

2. *Discontent with status quo.* Creativity is spurred on by an unwillingness to accept the statement that design is optimized to the fullest extent. Constructive discontent is a good example of this principle. American industry would soon fail if they thought that further improvements were impossible. Successful businesses live with the question of how they can improve the quality and performance of their products. Because we are human, all of our designs can be improved. Optimum balance between cost, performance and reliability can always be improved.

3. *Wars.* Wars are placed on the list for subjects that motivate creativity because many new inventions have come out of desperation of war. Such inventions are bred out of necessity.

4. *Ignorance of the past.* So often, if you don't know that something can't be done, you go ahead and try to do it anyhow. Often, knowing too much about the problem willl discourage you from further investigation. Charles Kettering had a system that he used in these situations. If he had a problem that dealt with chemical composition, he would assign it to two people. He would assign one man with a strong chemical engineering education, and another individual who was not educated in the field of chemistry. He would keep them separated while they were working on the problem. Many times, the chemical engineer would come up with the better solution. At other times, the fellow who had no education in chemical engineering would come up with a better solution because he was viewing it from a different direction.

Our past experience will sometimes lead us away from a viable solution. Not all the answers are found in the mathematical or scientific solutions that have been previously developed. It is often necessary to look beyond our own area of expertise to find the solutions to a problem.

5. *Necessity*. It is said that necessity is the mother of invention. With the change in the availability and the price of energy, we are now faced with critical problems that affect not only our ability to heat our homes and provide gasoline and oil for transportation purposes, but also the inflationary spiral of our business economy. The point where we must devise alternate energy resources has been reached. A good example of necessity is the development of our space age resources to put a man on the moon. Shortly after the Russians launched their first sputnik into outer space, the U. S. felt the need to put a man on the moon within the following decade. American industry responded accordingly.

6. *Greed*. Criminals and businessmen often devise creative, and often devious ways to make money. White-collar crime has come to the forefront as a new way of beating the system. In this case, it gets in the way of proper judgment.

7. *Curiosity*. The old saying that curiosity killed a cat may be true, although curiosity and experimentation have also made men rich. A creative individual has an overwhelming desire to invent, to create and to refine. A curious person is also an individual who is not satisfied with the obvious solutions. Curiosity also leads the way for the quest for further knowledge and a further understanding of our fields of study.

8. *Knowledge*. It has been the experience of the authors that the more a person learns about a subject, the more he desires to further broaden the depth of knowledge in that subject. Take, for example, the bridge designer who has a basic knowledge and understanding of loads on highway bridges, materials of construction and design procedures. That individual would be most interested in new developments in the field, new designs, new materials and new insight into construction methods.

9. *Competition*. Competition is what makes our society function. To be successful a company must keep up with the latest advances in technology; it must also attempt to be at the head of development of new ideas and products. An excellent example of competition is in the manufacture of hand calculators. The transistor, printed circuit boards and electronic chips now perform the same functions that tubes and other electronic gear used to perform. Competition and the development of the transistor has brought the price down substantially.

WHAT STIFLES CREATIVITY?

Development of an ingenious and innovative idea is a trying task. It often requires going out on a limb with an idea that is a change from our norm. It requires a proposer to risk the possibility of being wrong in his idea. In contrast, it is easy to stifle a creative idea. Ideas are usually stifled by individuals with a quick response. Experienced individuals, knowledgeable in the field of construction, said that the first steel framed building structure would not last because the contraction and expansion of the steel would crack all the plaster material and all that would be left would be the steel frame. This was a quick response and a roadblock to the development and progress of our society.

Charles Kettering, who received the award of merit of the American Alumni Council in 1948 for his work as a scientist, a humanitarian, inventor, philosopher, college graduate and an American, had two significant points that he would often make. The first point was that guidelines that were established were often rigid and unbending. The other point was that we don't teach people the proper attitude to adopt when they meet with failure.

On the first point of making guidelines too rigid, he noted that all too often people feel that because something is written down in the guidelines, there is only one way to do it. Kettering relates the story of his invention of the automatic self-starter for an automobile, and notes that the important guidelines requiring wire of a certain minimum thickness to carry a minimum current. This had been a good standard because it prevented people from improperly wiring houses, machinery and other electrical devices. Wires that were too thin or poorly insulated to carry the required current continuously heated up and often caught fire. Kettering, however, felt that they did not have his potential self-starter in mind when they set these standards. Had he chosen to use the wire size specified in the standard, the self-starter would have been almost as big as the engine. Kettering's design used wire that carried five times the allowable current set by the standard for continuous use. His defense for violating the rule was that he only carried the current for a short period of time sufficient to start the automobile.

Kettering's self-starter was first used on a 1912 Cadillac. Shortly after, he was invited to speak at a meeting of the American Institute of Electrical Engineers. Kettering's talk centered on his development of the self-starter. After his presentation, one of the individuals in the audience stood up and made the following statement:

> No wonder the man can make a self-starter. He transgresses every fundamental law of electrical engineering. If you want to make a self-starter that way, you are welcome to it. I'm an honorable electrical engineer, and I refuse to do that.

But, as Kettering remarked:

> All human development, no matter what form it takes, must be outside the rules; otherwise, we would never have anything new.*

Kettering's invention went past the normal rules that were used at the time. New applications, revised guidelines and an ingenious idea made Charles Kettering's self-starter an instant success.

The second point that Kettering made is that inventors and innovators are scarce because people are not taught how to fail with the proper attitude.

---

*Boyd, T. A., *Professional Amateur–the Biography of Charles Franklin Kettering*, (New York: E. P. Dutton & Co., 1957), p. 76.

Often, when people fail, they meet with derision and scorn from their associates. Kettering's main thesis was that once you fail, get up and try again, and again, and again. Look for new combinations, new ways of doing things, and stretch your imagination beyond the limits of normal solutions. Chapter 2, "Habits, Roadblocks and Attitudes," talks about the resistance and the failure that individuals experience before coming up with their final quest, or their final solution.

The following are excerpts from remarks by Charles F. Kettering on receiving the Award of Merit of the American Alumni Council at Ann Arbor, Michigan, on July 13, 1948. The remarks are transcribed from a radio broadcast by Station WJR, Detroit:

> Now what you want to do is learn how to fail intelligently. After you've failed, analyze it and find out why you've failed because every failure is one of the steps that leads up into the cathedral of success and you can't make that final step unless you come all the way up.
>
> Why do we always fail in these things? Well, the thing is very elementary again because the first time you do anything you're doing it as a very rank amateur 'cause that's all an amateur is—a person doing a thing for the first time. And his ability to succeed on the first time would be purely accidental on anything outside of the most mediocre attempts. So this question then of practicing how to make each step. Sometimes you have to practice, practice, practice, practice. That's the reason why we can never tell you how long it's going to be after we start a project before you get the answer because we don't know how much practice we have to do on the road. You can call it experimentation—anything you want to—research is only a word for giving failure a respectable nomenclature. That's all.
>
> . . . . it's much more difficult to reverse the thinking of people than it is to give them a new idea. We have that problem stepping up here a little bit on a new type of engine which we developed. The new type of engine is exactly like the old type, but we rearrange certain parts of this engine differently from what it's been. We went out and got the consensus of studied opinion on that, just for fun, and even in our own organization, where people are paid to be open minded (laughter), the consensus of studied opinion was no good.
>
> . . . Let the job be the boss and you follow it around and run errands for it and that's the way you get things done. In this thing of studied opinion, there is no possible way in which you can overcome the negative attitude or the wrong attitude to a thing by any argument, philosophy, logic, or anything of the kind. Any time you are arguing on a thing like that, you're just wasting time. The only thing that will solve that problem is a sample—a working sample.

Contentment with the *status quo* greatly diminishes creativity and is a threat to progress. All progress requires some change. It is our ability to manage that change that will determine its success. You can't steal second base unless you leave first.

Anything that is new or is a change is full of unknowns. A creative individual who is enthusiastic about his new concept runs into possible danger from the negative thinker who is fast to squelch any new ideas. The emphasis on the negative will quickly diminish the benefits of a new idea. Many of us have been to staff meetings with the managers of our firms. A new idea, a creative solution to a lasting problem, is brought up by a staff member. Oftentimes that new idea is met with a barrage of reasons as to why it won't work. People will not take the time to think of a reason why it will work, but will be free with their advice as to why it will not work. In today's society, we are facing more and more the problems of a bureaucratic government. A key example of stifling creativity comes in the form of contractor-incentive clauses. Contractors are given the opportunity to use their creativity to come up with innovative ways to reduce the cost of construction, which will result in savings not only to the contractor, but also to the owner. Most contractors are reluctant to submit such changes, due to the red tape and bureaucracies that they must wade through in order to get their ideas and their concepts accepted and implemented. On construction jobs, they cannot afford the time required to implement such changes.

CONDUCTING A CREATIVE SESSION

Alfred North Whitehead, the philosopher and mathematician, pointed out that in order to encourage our creative thinking certain guidelines are useful. The following summarizes Whitehead's philosophy:

1. Dare not to be apparently illogical.
2. Overcome inertia toward change, toward the unconventional.
3. Realize that insight does not necessarily flow from a plan or a logical sequence.
4. Remove all mental blocks and personal inhibitions. Let the imagination grow.
5. It helps to have crazy ideas; they should be encouraged and not ridiculed.
6. Remember—all truly great ideas seem absurd when first proposed.

This list of suggestions gives us effective guidelines to follow when conducting a creative session. Whitehead's suggestions apply, whether you are indulging in a solo creative session or a group creative session. Most of our thinking is done in solo sessions, though when circumstances are arranged, we can have group creative sessions that pay off handsomely.

The creative session is a valuable tool in a value engineering study. A creative session allows the participants to express themselves freely without fear of being judged harshly or improperly. In a value engineering study, we ask each of the team members to participate during the creative session. The group-creative session may last anywhere from two to four hours. Each of the team members is asked to think beyond his normal habit solutions to come up with as many ideas as possible of new combinations, new systems and new approaches to the problem.

The first rule in a creative session is to define the problem. Having defined the problem, the team develops as many ways as possible of solving that problem. They may come up with an entirely different approach, or they may take the basic approach that is proposed and modify and change certain parts of it. None of the ideas that are generated during a value session are discarded; they are all written down, regardless of their merit. The following basic suggestions are helpful to keep in mind when conducting a value engineering study:

1. The team members must believe that there can be improvements made to the project.
2. There is always room for improvement in the design.
3. Be receptive to new ideas.
4. Eliminate the word "impossible" from your thinking.
5. *Suspend judgment.*
6. Develop as many ideas as possible.
7. Look for association of ideas.
8. Don't be afraid to experiment.
9. Encourage all team members to participate.
10. Test your own views in the form of questions.
11. Help your team members work through their ideas.
12. Record all your value engineering ideas.

The leader in a creative session should encourage the free flow of information from participants. It is important that he gently but firmly ensure that judgment is suspended during this session. The leader should also prompt and encourage each team member to freely participate.

CRUX OF CREATIVE THINKING

The crux of creative thinking, as applied in a value engineering study, requires that you separate the creative portion of your mind from the judgment portion of the mind, for two reasons: (1) To allow more associations of ideas; and (2) to accumulate a greater quantity of ideas.

You cannot dictate to your mind how it chooses to associate and build on other ideas. Our train of thought usually follows any path of association that it chooses. An example of the association of ideas may be found in the following example:

During World War II, a destroyer was halted because it had encountered a 500-pound mine that had appeared near the bow of the ship. Normal procedure would have been to destroy the mine with a machine gun. However, the ship was too close and needed to back up to avoid the mine. The captain noticed that there was another mine that had drifted across the stern. Clearly, it was impossible to blow up either of the mines without damaging the ship. One of the chief petty officers remarked: "With all the windy guys that we have on this ship, we should get them up here and blow the mine away." This remark caused someone to think: "Maybe we could use a high-pressure air hose." That thought promptly brought up another idea, and that was to use a water hose. The water hose was turned on the mine and it moved away from the ship. The first mine was destroyed, and the ship moved out in turn to detonate the second mine. The association of ideas went from the silly idea of the windy guys to the better idea of the air hose, and then to a still better idea of the water hose. Had the initial idea been forbidden or stifled, the entire train of thought association might never been brought to the final solution.

The second principle of gathering a quantity of ideas is especially difficult for engineers to accept. Time and again, we take the one best and most reliable solution that we have used in the past, place it in our designs and build the project. Let's compare the principle of a quantity of ideas with the experience of the professional pearl diver. If you were a pearl diver, would you walk to the edge of the beach, climb in your boat, row to the oyster bed, put on your diving gear, swim to the bottom, find one oyster, then swim up to the top of the water, climb into the boat, then take off your diving gear and open that oyster, to find that there is no pearl? Would you then repeat the process, going down to the bottom of the ocean again to find one oyster and bring that up to the boat, to find that it, too, had no pearl? We can see that the physical action taken is a very clumsy process. However, people will follow the same clumsy mental processes without realizing it. If you were a professional pearl diver, you would put on your swim gear, dive to the bottom of the ocean, fill up the entire basket with oysters, then swim back up to the surface of the water, get in your boat and open all of the oysters until you found a pearl. When you are holding your creative session, you are looking for ideas, just like the pearl diver looks for oysters, in quantity, and you will delay opening them looking for pearls until you have a quantity of them. People often follow mental procedures that are clumsy because mental processes are abstract and thus more difficult to detect clumsiness.

The objective is to accumulate a large number of ideas. Do not start looking at those ideas, or judging them, in selecting the potentially best ideas for development until you have collected a large number of ideas. This is a far more efficient approach toward unearthing and selecting creative ideas for development.

Why do we push hard on this subject of separating the creative portion of the mind from the judgment portion of the mind? Because it is very difficult for cautious professional engineers and architects to do so. Their training tends to make them very conservative and to squelch far-out speculation in favor of conservative habit solutions. Creativity is not a result of training. It has to be released from within people by creating the circumstances and climate that release it!

THE CREATIVE PROCESS

Many inventors have been interviewed about the thought processes that result in their inventions. Some of the points in their responses are often the same. The first step in tackling any problem is to first define that problem. The second step is to gather information and background on the problem, and to educate ourselves as best we can as to how the problem might be approached. One needs to become familiar with the project, without worrying about what the final solution might be. It helps also to define the requirements and what is actually needed in the design. The next step in the process is to speculate, or to develop creative ideas about ways of providing the function of the project. The ideas are then sifted through to find the ones that have the best potential for development and eventual implementation. There may be 20 or 30 ideas brought up for the solution to a problem. The final stage is the development and creation of the solution to the problem.

When you are working on a problem, work hard during the working day. When the workday is concluded, forget the work and turn to something that relaxes you. The reason: You can go only so far with your conscious mind. Then, by stopping conscious work, *you free your subconscious from conscious limitations.* Relieving the mind of anxiety permits the subconscious to incubate the problem until a new combination may be formed.

Recreation is derived from the word meaning "re-create." Let's not overlook the benefit of leisure and relaxation in the creative process. Many great discoveries have been made when the inventor's attention was directed to other unrelated areas.

When the idea materializes, be sure to write it down. Chances are great that your idea may be forgotten if it is not written down and captured on paper when it occurs.

CREATIVE PROBLEM-SOLVING TECHNIQUES

There are several creative problem-solving techniques that can be used when leading a value engineering session:

Brainstorming

In brainstorming, a group of individuals representing different disciplines in a construction project are brought together in a group. Usually, the group is led by one individual, and a recorder picks up all the ideas that are generated by the group session. The team participating in the study must have reviewed the background information for the project and have become familiar with the requirements of the owner. Prior to the session, the individuals in the study are briefed on the design project and on the requirements and limitations that are imposed.

The rules for brainstorming that were previously stated are reviewed with the team participants. A creative brainstorming session may start with an example of a project or a problem that requires creative thought. The practice brainstorming session is started by having each individual first list his creative ideas for the problem. After that is done, the team is asked to come together as a whole and work as a group in determining creative solutions to the problem. By using an example, the team quickly catches onto the concept of the free flow of thinking.

The creative session provides an environment for open thought. It is an ideal situation for being yourself and being able to express yourself clearly without fear of retribution. Psychological safety and freedom must be a part of the creative session. External evaluation by team members must be completely absent.

Gordon Technique

This technique is also a group-creative technique. In many ways it is the direct opposite of the brainstorming technique. The group meets without any prior knowledge of the problem or project being studied. The leader of the session guides the team into broad areas in which the problem might be identified. As an example, the problem is to design a wastewater treatment plant to treat sewage. The discussion might center on purification. The leader leads the discussion through the consideration of the purification process and into ways that the process takes place. He might first, for instance, discuss the natural means of purification that are available in nature. Evaluation of the solutions is encouraged. The exact solution of the problem is not identified until the leader feels that all possible solutions have been explored.

Checklists

Past history and precedents on prior studies may have resulted in an accumulation of ideas that resulted in savings to the owner. This list of ideas serves as a basis for comparison on new studies. We have found it helpful to check back on past projects to see if there are any ideas that continuously occur.

Morphological Analysis

Morphological analysis is a systematic ranking of alternatives. The first step is to define the problem in terms of its parameters. Next, a model is developed that lists all the potential combinations that might be used in deriving a solution to the project. This often employs a system analysis to come up with the best solution. One axis of the analysis shows unit processes. The vertical axis represents the parameter used for design, and the third axis represents the type of equipment that could be used for the solution. There are many possibilities and combinations of solutions that are available in this analysis.

Attribute Listing

Attribute listing uses the parts approach. It lists the various elements of the project, and changes are modified in each of the characteristics. This technique allows new combinations of characteristics or attributes to solve the problem.

A coordinator for a value engineering study must evaluate the project itself, as well as the composition of the team members, to determine the best technique to use in his creative session. With any of these techniques, however, these basic guidelines may be followed.

1. Express ideas free of criticism by suspending judgment until you reach the judgment phase of the job plan.
2. Assume that each idea will work.
3. Research ideas without restriction.
4. Capitalize from cross-fertilization of ideas.
5. Participate in a competitive spirit.

These simple rules will enhance the results of your creative session.

6
Managing the Value Engineering Study

Perhaps no one element contributes more to the success of a Value Engineering (VE) Study than its management. For this is the area that influences the success of the study by determining whether the recommendations of a VE study are accepted or rejected by the owner. The end result is the benefit to the owner in cost savings or improved operation. Proper precautions in establishing the necessary communications and environment necessary to foster a free flow of information is required for an effective study. A value engineering study involves participation between three main entities: the owner, the designer and the value engineering consultant. Unless the project is properly managed, its success will be hindered. Each participant has a role in the value engineering study. It is the job of the value consultant to ensure that all participants know their responsibilities ahead of time; are properly organized to carry out their responsibilities; that the staffing and team expertise necessary to carry out the study are provided; that the work is directed in an effective manner; and that the end product produces results that are well founded and will result in cost savings or ease of owning and operating the owner's facility.

How this task is performed and the elements that are involved is the subject of this chapter. The basis for much of the information included is from the experience gained by the authors in previous value engineering studies and workshops. Participants in 40-hour value engineering training workshops have raised many questions about the methodology used to ensure the proper results from a value engineering study. At the same time, owners and design engineers whose projects are being value engineered have also raised certain questions and have outlined certain criteria which they feel are important to the overall success of a project.

WHY THE PROGRAM WORKS

Value engineering is a proven management tool to ensure the cost effectiveness of design or construction projects. The program has shown excellent results in all fields of construction and manufacturing. Participants in our value engineering project studies and training seminars have been questioned about what they feel is the most effective part of a value engineering effort. They have also been asked why they feel value engineering is so effective.

The responses cover a wide range of answers; however, there are certain elements that seem to be prevalent among the responses.

1. Value engineering is a straightforward and effective approach. It uses a *job plan*. The job plan is a key to value engineering. Its organized approach is very similar to that of the inventive process which seeks out information, stimulates the thought process in a group or single session and evaluates these thoughts and ideas and produces recommendations for implementation. Value engineering ensures that the free flow of information is not hampered. The pitfalls of premature criticism are detoured by separating the creative aspects of the study from the judging aspects. A value engineering study uses certain worksheets as a tool to guide the value engineering team through the steps of the job plan. It should be said that the value engineering worksheets used in the study are somewhat different from those used by other firms or organizations.

2. Another reason why the program works is the fact that all designs have some unnecessary cost. Because each design is a creative process itself, there are an infinite number of combinations of designs, materials and methods that can be used to achieve the ultimate goal of the project. Whether or not they include the best balance between the cost, the performance and the reliability of the project is the real question. Each designer working on a project meticulously develops a number of comparisons that can be used to perform a function. Often, due to the time restraints of the schedule and the necessity to meet a budget for the design itself, that number of comparisons is limited. At the same time, new information and data on the background of the project and an objective second look by someone not involved directly in the design may change the outcome of previous comparisons. All designers would like to study and develop more comparisons to verify their design. However, there are a million-and-one details to pull together in that final design. Hence, the designer may be obliged to bypass many comparisons and to use past experience in the interest of meeting due dates and design budgets.

The number of evaluations and comparisons made in arriving at a final design greatly influences the cost of a project. It has been interesting to the authors, in the course of the value engineering studies which they have conducted, to see the benefits and results of effective comparisons. Having worked with over 25 design consultants, a wide variety of approaches and methodologies have been observed which compare design alternatives. It is heartening, as a fellow designer, to see the engineering excellence exhibited in the projects studied. From past histories of design projects, the depth and thoroughness of the design are shown to be directly proportional to the time and fees allocated. Given the time and the resources, the proper comparisons may be performed to help optimize the design.

There has been more and more concern recently over the cost and the methods for selecting design consultants. Efforts have been made to curtail the fees that architects and engineers receive. On the other hand, construction projects are left with little attention given to the amount of money being spent. In other words, the low bidder gets the job. As a general rule, the design for a project represents anywhere from 5 to 10 percent of the overall cost, although there are cases where the fees are less than 5 percent. As a rule, the lower the fee the fewer number of alternatives. The result is that the owner usually gets what he pays for in terms of design. A worthy investment is to provide resources in the front of the project that represent 5 to 10 percent of the cost of the project rather than risk having a design that is not the most cost effective, especially in light of ever-rising life-cycle costs. While construction aspects represent over 90 percent of the initial costs of the project, operation and maintenance costs must be absorbed throughout the total life of the project.

Skimping on the design often results in a project that may not include the most cost-effective, economical operation and maintenance costs. While this statement may not be true in all cases, it is the rule rather than the exception.

3. Motivation is a force that drives us beyond habit patterns and procedures that we are accustomed to using. Value engineering team members are uniform in their response to motivation as a key force in a value engineering effort. A multidiscipline team provides motivation to its members by the very fact that they are participating in a group-thinking process. A successful design project involves cooperation between the various elements involved in the design, i.e., sanitary, electrical, civil, mechanical, architectural, structural, etc. Hence, a design is dependent upon the cooperation that exists between these various groups. Often the basic physical limitation of an office set-up prohibits the free flow of information between these groups. What better way to cross-fertilize a design effort than through a value engineering study with a multidiscipline group? It is an excellent step toward mobilizing and uniting the individual talents of each member to obtain the design goals involved in the project.

It also provides an atmosphere such that when questions arise, design expertise in all areas is available to properly answer those questions. In this way, false assumptions are not made as to the proper solution.

Many design firms do not provide the atmosphere for a multidiscipline participation within the design effort. Unfortunately, the norm is that the main process is designed by one group, it is then given to another group for their input, and follows a successive chain of events which ultimately culminate in the end product. While the process design, which is the first element involved, is often designed efficiently, the support elements, such as structural, architectural, HVAC and electrical must *fit the design.* The VE effort seeks to blend these disciplines at the beginning of design.

In the design process, most thinking is done in solitude. It is unusual for a group to sit down and decide to think. A value engineering team operates for the most part as a group-thinking technique. The VE team is stimulated by the group input, and is motivated through the influence of the value engineering team and coordinators. The coordinators' responsibility is to motivate the participants and to capitalize on their talents and experiences. Presentations on creativity are offered to free the team from roadblocks and to clear the way for open thinking. Pointed questions which serve to analyze the design and stimulate the thoughts of the individuals are analyzed. It provides the catalyst for pulling out the creative capabilities of each team member. All minds are fluid and are influenced by external stimuli provided by presentations that seek to motivate people.

There is a story that highlights the fact that motivation is a force. A gentleman walking home one evening was a bit inebriated. He took an old familiar shortcut across the graveyard that wound under trees where no light penetrated. Suddenly this gentleman fell into an open grave that had been dug across his familiar path. Picking himself up, he tried to climb out. After many attempts at jumping up the side of the grave and falling back because the sides were too slippery and because it was too deep, he concluded it was impossible to get out of the hole without help. So he scooted down in a dark corner and began to doze. It was not very long before a second character came along that same shortcut, and he, too, fell into the same open grave. He started jumping and scrambling to get out, completely unaware of the other character in the corner. He was also about to give up when his efforts and the noise he was making awakened the snoozer in the corner. The snoozer raised his head from its resting place on his knees and said in a deep voice, "You can't get out of here." *But the second man did!* With a mighty leap and scramble, he cleared the edge and got out of the deep hole. HE WAS MOTIVATED. So motivation is a force in our everyday life.

4. Still another reason why the program works is that the circumstances can be taken into account as a result of the design development process. When designing a project, you are creating. Often this creation is by its nature made in step-by-step fashion. As the design develops, the pieces are pulled together into a whole. You are using the deductive reasoning process of which the major mental process is the recall of past knowledge.

Oftentimes, the piece-by-piece process that evolves comes from new requirements added by the owner. Changes in requirements of regulatory agencies, changes to the design as a result of site conditions and a myriad of other influences. Designers would often like to revise their designs midway through the project to update the design. New technology is one element that affects designs. Value engineering provides for a means of making changes well into the design phase.

The design process for major construction projects may now be as long as three to four years from the time a project is planned until the time the project is bid. In that time, technology often changes to the point where a new design would be more cost effective than that proposed in the original plans.

When performing a value engineering analysis, the pieces have already been pulled together and the inductive reasoning process is used to analyze the project. In this case, the major mental process is the comparison of alternatives. We all know that it is much easier to evaluate a given idea than it is to come up with the original concept, just as it is easier to quarterback the Sunday afternoon game on Monday morning or to improve an invention such as the airplane rather than create it originally.

5. Value engineering is a system that helps to promote *progressive change*. Change is very hard for many people to handle. Value engineering promotes change. It tries to establish an atmosphere whereby change can be made gracefully without anyone losing face. As human beings, our brain sometimes finds it is not searching for truth but for advantage. It is a mechanism used to provide for our selfish needs. Many times self-interest allows our thoughts to be dominated by our desires. This is a very thought-provoking concept. It is a regular occurence in engineering circles. As an example, an excellent idea may be proposed by a value engineering team. However, an engineer or architect, realizing that he must face the fact that a change is being made to his design, will sometimes try to slant the information to his own advantage. They may forego the information and facts and choose the design alternative, which apparently puts them in an advantageous position. This is a very important point.

6. It is important to remember that in value engineering, *the goal of the value engineering team is identical to that of the designer. That is, to provide a design for the project that meets the owner's requirements at the best balance between cost, performance and reliability*. Keeping this in mind, it is easier for the designer to realize that the value engineering team is a supplement to his design effort. A second look is taken at the design in an attempt to improve the cost impact of the project. It is not intended as a criticism of his work.

7. Value engineering saves money. Experience in both the manufacturing and the construction field have shown the benefits of value engineering to owners. In the first 35 studies on value engineering of construction projects conducted, Zimmerman has managed projects where an average of over $50 could be saved for each dollar spent on value engineering. This is not to say that all projects save that much money. Some project studies result in very little savings. But nonetheless, these figures indicate that value engineering is an excellent investment. What other method can be used to obtain returns of over $50 for each dollar spent?

THE RELATIONSHIP BETWEEN OWNER-DESIGNER AND VALUE ENGINEERING CONSULTANT

The best designs of buildings, plants, highways, industrial complexes or other construction projects are the combined efforts of the owner, a construction manager, a design engineer, a contractor and in cases where value engineering studies are performed, the value engineer himself. During the design phase, the owner, designer and value engineer function as a team to achieve a project that is low in cost while still performing the required functions of the project. Owners are also striving to ensure that the facilities are easily maintained, have low operating costs, and operate efficiently in terms of fuel and power consumptions. Traditionally, responsibility for the major part of the project was centered with the owner, who presented the user with the building. The owner may be a public utility, the federal, state, or a municipal government, the owner of an office building or some other complex, the owner of an industrial company or the ultimate user of the building. The designer for the project may be an architect, an engineer or a design-construct firm. The designer, basing his work on the requirements outlined by the owner, designs the building or plant facility to meet these requirements. The contractor is responsible for constructing the facilities.

With the boom in construction and rising costs, the traditional designer-contractor organization of project management has been diversified. Some of these additions are welcome, while some are not. Construction managers and value engineers are often included in this overall project scheme. In today's larger projects, designers may be charged not only with the design of buildings, but of major complexes involving transportation systems, buildings, utilities, office space and recreational facilities. The projects are indeed complex and challenging.

Regardless of how small or how large the project may be, someone must be responsible for the development of plans and specifications to achieve that need, and someone must interpret the plans into an actual project.* The value engineer has an important part in the overall project management process. His responsibility is to provide a second look at the design to assist the owner and the designer in achieving maximum results. The effort must be a concentrated one based on the cost aspects of the project. The value engineer is not liable for the design. That liability lies with the designer. Many design firms are also incorporating value engineers into their design process.

Figure 6-1 is a management organization chart for a value engineering study. It indicates the line of responsibility of each party to the project. On environmental projects, often the state funding agency and the Environmental Protection Agency provide construction grants for the project. Their input is required to approve the grant funding for the design and value engineering. They also have the ultimate approval on the value engineering study results. The owner of the project holds the prime responsibility for the job; including the selection of the value engineering consultant, negotiation of fees for the services, and for ensuring that the value engineering study is done in accordance with specified requirements. The designer for the project is charged with designing for the owner the facility required to meet the owner's functional requirements. The designer may also be charged with obtaining the necessary permits for construction and to assist the owner in bidding the project. Often the designer also participates during the construction phase by providing construction inspection and coordination services.

The owner and the designer are responsible for reviewing the recommendations made by the value engineering consultant. This fact is very important and should be identified at the onset of any value engineering study. The

** The Building Estimator's Reference Book,* Chicago: Frank F. Walker Co., 1973, 18th edition, p. 2.

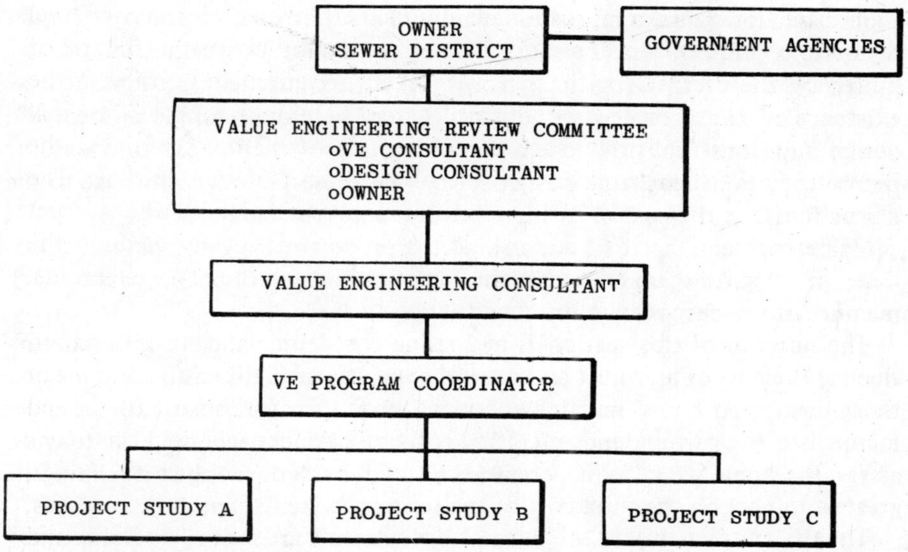

Figure 6-1. Management Chart for a Typical Value Engineering Study.

value engineering team is not performing a review of the design. It is performing a cost study of the project. Recommendations made by the value engineering team must be evaluated and accepted by the owner and the designer before being implemented into the designer's plans.

To ensure that an objective analysis of value engineering recommendations is carried out, a review committee is often formed consisting of the owner, the designer and a representative of the value engineering team. The results of the value engineering study are analyzed and a decision is made to accept the recommendations that are of the best benefit to the owner.

The value engineering coordinator is responsible for the overall value engineering effort. The coordinator must identify to the designer and the owner their responsibilities during the value engineering effort. The coordinator is also charged with developing a rapport with the designer and reassuring the designer that the intention is not to criticize the design for the sake of criticism itself. By explaining the value engineering effort and the work involved, the designer will have a clearer picture of how the process evolves and will have the assurance that the value engineer is benefiting the project. The coordinator is also responsible for directing the value engineering team through the workshop process.

Each team should have a value engineering team coordinator (VETC), whose responsibilities are further outlined later in this chapter. Last but not least, are the value engineering team members, whose job it is to analyze the design for high cost.

WHO INFLUENCES THE COST OF A PROJECT?

Development of public utilities, buildings, industrial complexes, commercial office space and other construction projects has become a drawn out, complex procedure. There are a myriad of requirements that stipulate the government regulations and codes to be met. These are in addition to the function required by the user. Oftentimes a government requirement accounts for the existence of the project itself. Projects that were once simple and easy to design and construct now face a complex maze of roadblocks to overcome before they even reach the design stage. All these factors contribute to the dramatic rise in the cost of owning and operating the facility.

Value engineers need to understand the procedures in the development of a design. It gives them an understanding of the influence and impact of each member of the design team on the project.

The purpose of this section is to outline the people and the areas that influence the cost of a project and to find a way to further identify and manage those costs. To know and to understand how the decisions of the designer factor into the owning and operating costs of a facility will help the team to assess the time when value engineering can best be applied to have the greatest impact on the total cost of the project.

Time is another important factor in determining impacts of cost on a project. Planning and design costs represent a small part of the overall facility cost. Initial construction costs represent a significant amount of money, but are expended in one time frame. In the case where the project is financed, the initial construction cost may be spread over the time frame of the loan payment. Operation and maintenance costs, while usually at a lower annual rate than the initial construction cost, are absorbed throughout the life of the project. It is also important to note that as time progresses and equipment wears down, the efficiency of that equipment also decreases. The end result is a gradual rise in the cost of maintaining the equipment and an increase in the fuel consumption used to power it. These costs gradually increase throughout the life-span of the project and are subject to inflation.

Owner/User

The owner or the user of a facility has the greatest impact on the cost. It is the owner and/or the user that established the size, magnitude and the required function of the facility. Selection of the quality of construction, the size and capacity of the facility, the life expectency required in the design, and the comfort levels to be associated with the operation of the facility are primarily the responsibility of the owner/user. Their decisions are also felt during the design phase when the design consultant is selected. They work with the designer during the preparation of plans and specifications. They also influence the operation and maintenance stages of the project by the amount budgeted for providing materials and personnel to maintain the facility properly. Owners and users also come under the influence of federal, state, and local regulations governing the construction of buildings and the stipulations of various regulatory agencies. In the environmental field, as an example, state health agencies are responsible for setting stream effluent standards which establish the degree of treatment necessary for wastewater treatment plants. The degree of treatment as well as the capacity of the plant are the two foremost factors in establishing the costs of owning and operating the facility.

Design Consultants-Architects/Engineers

The design of the facility encompassing both the planning stage and the preparation of plans and specifications also has an impact on the cost of a project. The time frame for the design portion of the project is limited, usually ranging from one to four years. During that time, the architect or engineer works under the direction of the owner/user and prepares a set of plans and specifications to meet the functional requirement of the owner's/user's needs. The designer's selection of materials, structural systems, architectural concepts, electrical distribution, system control, automation, building orientation and reliance on energy and other resources significantly impact initial construction costs, as well as the cost of operating and maintaining the facility. The design professional has an option of investing significantly in the initial cost while saving costs of owning and operating the facility. He may also design the same facility with a low initial cost which will result in higher owning and maintenance costs for the facility. The selection of these alternatives made in conjunction with the owner's requirements have a significant impact on the total life-cycle costs of the project. It is for this reason that coordination between the owner and the design professional is such an important part of the overall project management for a facility. Design professionals are also becoming more and more aware of the impacts of O & M costs on their plant designs. The smart designer will consult with the operation and maintenance personnel of similar existing facilities to determine which systems have been the most cost effective for their region and for their level of personnel employed to maintain and operate the facility.

Contractors

Contractors have a one-time tangible impact on cost related primarily to the costs of construction. The intangible aspect, however, is in the reliability and quality of workmanship applied to the finished product. A well-constructed facility with good workmanship and quality of construction lasts longer and operates more efficiently than a poorly constructed facility. Again, the contractor's work effort is within the restricted time of construction. The results are experienced throughout the life of the project. The contractor's efforts may last from one to five years, depending upon the size, magnitude and complexity of the facility. In terms of total costs of owning and operating a facility the contractor's costs are major, but they are only a part of the cost of operating and maintaining the facility.

Operation and Maintenance

Operation and maintenance costs are for staffing the facility, purchasing materials to continue the operation of the facility, fuels required to power equipment, power to run equipment, salaries for staffing of operators and maintenance personnel.

As a result of dramatic increases in fuel cost, operation and maintenance costs have become a more important factor in the determination of the design of a facility. More emphasis is being placed on investing dollars today to decrease the operation and maintenance costs over the future life of the facility. The primary focus of these added dollars is to relieve the energy dependence of the mechanical aspects of the project. These characteristics can logically be accounted for in the design phase of the facility. After a project is constructed and ready to be operated, the operator must make do with the constructed facility. If the project has been designed with operational flexibility, with minimal stress on the equipment and with a high reliability factor, the facility will likely operate more efficiently and effectively. The design engineer and the value engineer must be aware of the importance of the operational and maintenance aspects of the project.

While operation and maintenance costs on an annual basis may not appear to be monumental, these costs add up to a significant factor in the total cost of owning and operating the facility. Because operation and maintenance costs are subject to inflation and supply and demand, they are subject to dramatic change. Energy costs are presently escalating at approximately 20 percent per year, while labor costs, the major cost of maintenance, are rising from 7 to 15 percent.

The operation and maintenance of a facility are affected by many factors. The workmanship of the contractor affects the quality of construction and the facility's ability to operate effectively over a long life-span. The quality of equipment plays a big part in the operation of plant facilities, as well as buildings and commercial establishments. We have mentioned the physical aspects of the equipment and workmanship; however, the skill and experience of the maintenance personnel of a facility also are important. Their ability to detect and prevent equipment failures may mean the difference in plant shut-downs with loss of revenues. Labor relations also affect operational efficiency and cost. Operation and maintenance personnel who take a great deal of pride in their plant will likely save money and lengthen the total life of the plant facility.

Facilities designed with operational designs of 25 to 50 years or more must be capable of withstanding stresses, corrosive effects, erosion and general wear and tear. A well-planned and thought-out maintenance schedule must be implemented to protect and enhance the operational efficiency of the equipment and of the overall facility.

FACILITY LIFE-CYCLE PROCESS

The development of a new facility goes through many stages from the time of its inception until it is usefully occupied and operated. To see where value engineering can be applied effectively, the design process must be understood. The facility life-cycle process involves six major steps.

1. Project Conception Phase
2. Project Planning Phase
3. Project Design Phase
4. Bidding and Construction Phase
5. Facility Operation Phase

Project Conception Phase

The project concept phase is the initial investigation to determine the project feasibility and the potential return on investment. As an example, a developer may want to construct housing units on a given piece of land. An economic comparison is performed to determine the total project costs of design, construction and operation. The developer is interested in the amount of money that must be invested, the time frame for the investment, the cost of money, and the costs to keep the facility operational. Many government agencies, when evaluating the need for a new capital improvement, will determine the benefit of the project.

Cost-benefit ratio is a means of evaluating the total life-cycle cost in comparison to the total benefit that might be received from the facility.

As an example, a local government may be interested in constructing storm drainage improvements to a flood-prone area. During the course of determining the need for such a study, it was found that facilities to combat erosion and flooding might run as high as \$3.5 million. At the same time, it was expected that the agency would have to spend an additional \$60,000 per year for the next 25 years to operate and maintain the facility. The need for the facility had been brought about by past floods, accounting for approximately \$150,000 damage from erosion and flooding each year. Every fifth year, major storms had accounted for \$2.2 million in damage. In determining the cost-to-benefit ratio, it is necessary to equate both the cost and the benefit on one given monetary basis—that is, to compare apples to apples. Figure 6-2 shows calculations for the life-cycle comparison. The initial cost of \$3.5 million is for construction of storm water impoundment basins and various channel improvements. The annual operation and maintenance cost of \$60,000 represents cost for labor and materials to clean out the storm-water impoundment basin and to periodically monitor and maintain the equipment within the facility. The \$150,000 annual benefit represents the estimated savings realized from damages that should not occur because of the decreased storm-water flows downstream. This is because the storm-water is now impounded in a retention basin. Major floods in the watershed had in the past accounted for approximately \$2.2 million in destruction of personal property and in damage to roadways, sanitary facilities, and public property within the watershed. In computing the cost-to-benefit ratio, all costs are first projected to a present-worth status. The costs of \$4,045,620 represent the present-worth cost of owning and operating the facility. The benefit received from the facility would amount to approximately \$4,633,222, which represents the present worth of the total benefit as a result of constructing the facility. It can

A. *Cost*

1. Initial Cost $3,500,000
2. Annualized Initial Cost (25 yrs. @ 10%)
   (3,5000,000 x 0.1102) = $385,700
3. Annual Operation and Maintenance Cost $ 60,000
4. Total Annual Owning and Operating Cost $ 445,700

   Present Worth $4,045,620
   (445,700 x 9.077)

B. *Benefit*

1. Annual Benefit $150,000
2. Recurring Benefit

		Present Cost
5 yrs.	$2.2 million x 0.6209	$ 1,365,980
10 yrs.	$2.2 million x 0.3855	848,100
15 yrs.	2.2 million x 0.2394	526,680
20 yrs.	2.2 million x 0.1486	326,920
25 yrs.	2.2 million x 0.0923	303,060
3.	Present Value	$ 3,270,740

4. Annualized Recurring Benefit
   (0.1102 x $3,270,740) = $ 360,435
5. Total Annual Benefit $ 510,435
6. Present Worth Total Annual Benefit $ 4,633,220

   Cost to Benefit Ratio 4,045,620 ÷ 4,633,220 = 0.87

Figure 6-2. Example of the Application of Cost to Benefit Ratio in the Project Conception Stage.

be seen that the cost-to-benefit ratio of 0.87 makes the project a worthwhile venture. The cost-to-benefit analysis is one method that is used in the Project Conception Phase to analyze whether a project is worth further consideration and planning. Other factors besides cost may also influence this decision.

Project Planning Phase

Planning of a project or a facility is a stage where the conceptual idea is developed further into a workable solution. *Planning is the setting of objectives and goals required to meet a given requirement.** Planning takes the conceptual idea and develops it further to ensure that a project is, in fact, realistic, and to also obtain direction as to what approach should be applied. Planning is deciding in advance what to do, how to do it, when to do it, and who is to do it. Planning bridges the gap of where we are and where we want to be. In the engineering field, and more particularly the facilities construction field, planning is also a stage of setting objectives. It encompasses the setting of parameters, the financial aspects of various site locations, the size of alternative solutions, and a myriad of other areas that are required to meet the objectives of the project. It helps to establish the size of the facility, it analyzes the physical characteristics and limitations of the particular site under question, it services the needs of the employees that will be working in the facility, it evaluates the environmental impacts of the facility and surrounding area, it establishes

*Koontz and O'Donnell, p. 113.

the basis for physical embellishments of the building facilities, it budgets for the cost of construction and the eventual impacts of operation and maintenance of the facility. In essence, it is the mechanism that will determine the total scope of the eventual facility being constructed. The plans and specifications for construction will usually be prepared on the basis of the planning report. It also helps to assure the owner that his project is, in fact, feasible.

The importance of planning cannot be overlooked in the overall scheme of a project. *Value engineering has a real impact in the planning stage.* Major impacts on the life-cycle cost of a facility are usually determined at this stage of the project. As an example, the sizing of a major water facility would likely be done during the planning stage. The need for such a step would become evident during the conceptual stage of the project. The planners would identify the basic area of need and would locate several potential sites for a facility. The next step would be to determine the facility size. This determination often has the greatest impact on the total cost. If it is overdesigned, excess funds are being expended unnecessarily. However, if it in turn is underdesigned, another expansion may be necessary farther down the road. At the same time that the size of the facility is being determined, its process flow scheme and method of operation is set down. These two factors, that is, sizing and the process of the facility, usually have the greatest impact on cost of construction and on cost of owning and operating the facility.

Value engineering is a likely candidate for the planning stages of a project. It is increasingly being applied earlier in the project because this is where major decisions on the overall scope and magnitude are made. Once the project moves further into design development, it is more difficult to make major recommendations that are centered around planning.

In the planning stage of a project, the scope and objectives that are established must be compatible with the overall needs of the company or the owning organization. A good example of the planning stage for a project may be seen in the illustration of a master plan for an industrial plant. During the planning stage, the owner outlined the requirements for the project. These needs were categorized and formed the basis for the design. The next step was to determine and locate a site for the physical facilities. One such site was the 1300 acre plot southwest of Waterloo, Iowa. The project was the 2.1 million square foot, John Deere Tractor Works. A consultant was retained to prepare a site analysis and master plan for the specific site. Figure 6-3 shows the overall site analysis plan. The owner's specific objectives and the physical site limitations were analyzed to determine the most compatible makeup of facilities with the available site constraints. The site analysis is an excellent graphic example. It illustrates the areas within the site most suitable for development. It shows the impacts of surrounding areas, the available utilities to the site, access and egress for traffic control, the location of the site in relationship to other strategic facilities, and the areas within the site that can be used to meet the owner's objectives. The natural drainage patterns and the desire to restore agricultural uses around the development zones influence the selection and development concepts. The valley edges set the limits of development while the topography of the ridges establishes the orientation

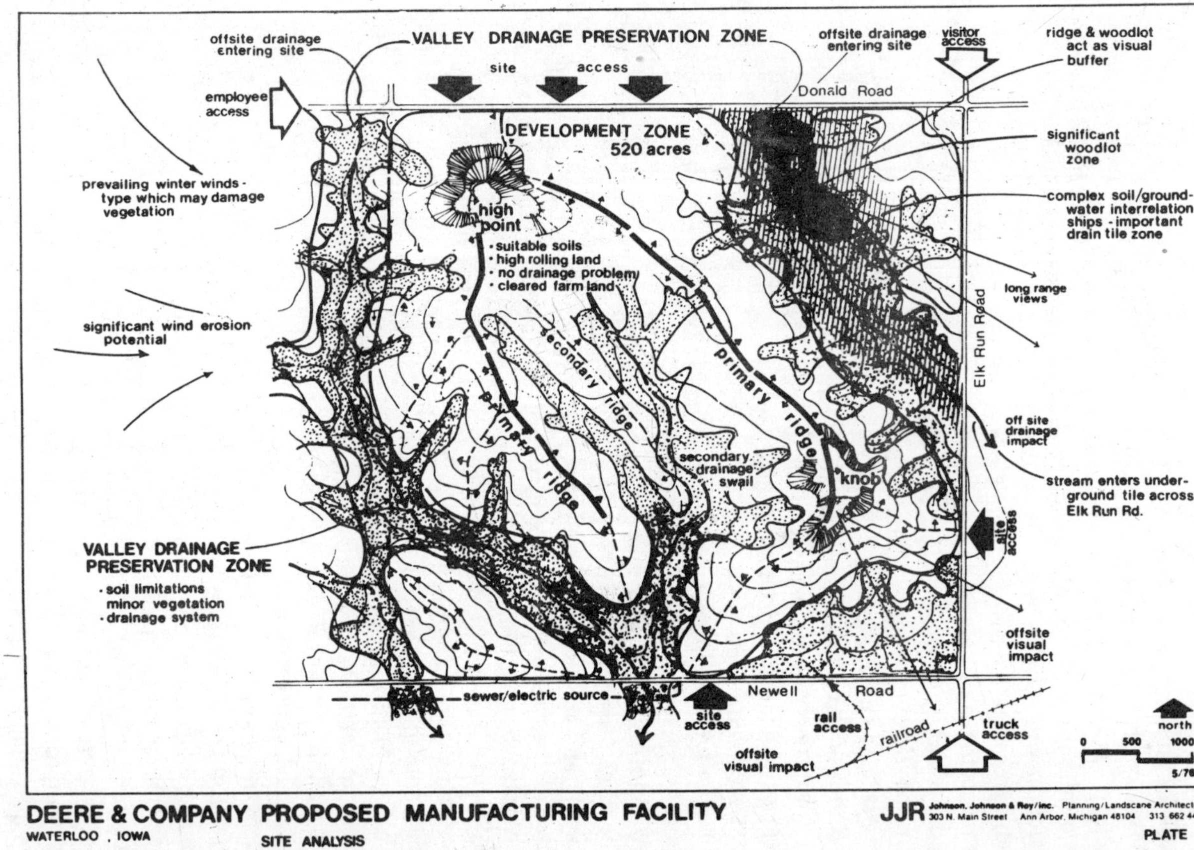

Figure 6-3. Site Analysis Plan. (Courtesy of Johnson, Johnson and Roy, Landscape Architects, Ann Ar Michaigan and John Deere Company)

of the complex allowing the perimeter to be restored to a cropland buffer. Dominant land forms are retained to buffer parking and storage areas. Figure 6-4 is the final accepted plant layout and site rendering for the facility.

At this point in the project, a value engineering study may be performed. A physical plan and preliminary building plans with costs allows the value analyst to equate function and cost for an effective effort.

Project Design Phase

The actual project design takes information from the planning stage and develops it into a set of plans and specifications to allow the project to be built. The design stage determines the actual materials of construction, the configuration, comfort levels, space utilization, process design, mechanical facilities and processes, the control and operation of the facility, the site layout, drainage and all the other physical aspects of the project. And we should not ignore the psycholcgical impact of the facility design on workers and the surrounding public. It interprets the objectives and outlines procedures made during the planning and conceptual stages, and shows how they can be made into workable solutions. It further gives instructions to the constructor to allow him to first determine a price to bid and to later construct the facility.

A project design uses engineering and architectural principles and decisions to achieve the required function at the desired cost. It further sets the standards for operation and maintenance of the facility. It also helps to determine the later impact on safety, ease of maintenance, comfort and efficiency of the final product.

Value engineering has traditionally been applied in the design stage of the project. Here the actual construction elements of the project can be viewed and analyzed with specific costs placed on each item. Recommended value engineering changes are easily evaluated at this stage by the difference in quantities and costs of materials as well as the labor and materials required to construct the facility. Thus far, value engineering has had its greatest impact during the design phase. Value engineering studies have successfully reduced the initial costs and energy dependence of major projects. Project design is probably one of the most difficult stages in the total facility life. At this point, speculation is turned into reality. Here, actual facilities are being designed. Yards of concrete, tons of steel, brick and mortar and other physical materials are combined for the final end product. Literally millions of details must be considered in combination with site limitations in order to arrive at an end product. Indeed, the task of the designer is challenging, whether he be an architect or an engineer. As discussed in previous chapters, the design engineer is a true inventor and a true creator. The task of the designer is probably the most difficult task in the total facility.

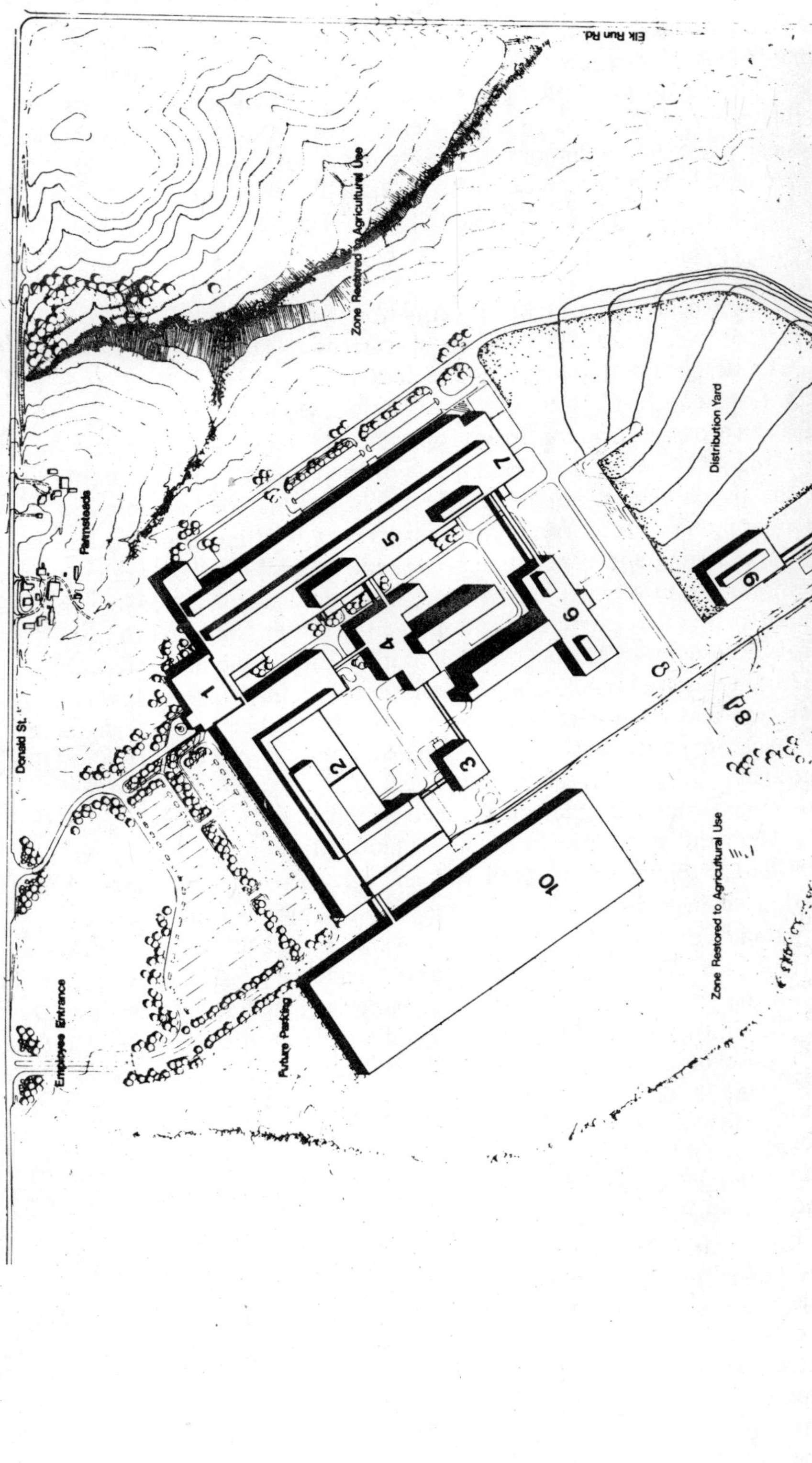

Figure 6-4. Master Plan. (Courtesy of Johnson and Roy, Landscape Architects, Ann Arbor, Michigan and John Deere Company)

Figure 6-4. Master Plan. (Courtesy of Johnson, Johnson and Roy, Landscape Architects, Ann Arbor, Michigan)

Bidding and Construction Phase

The bidding stage is when the plans and specifications are advertised to allow contractors to prepare an estimated cost for constructing the facility. Plans and specifications are interpreted by the contractor and a price determined for the cost to build the facility. It is obvious that the completeness and thoroughness of the plans and specifications help to avoid any gray areas that might be open to speculation once the contractor begins the job. Contractors usually base their bid price on quantity take-offs and actual quotations for furnishing and installing materials of construction. A contractor in determining a cost for construction has analyzed the material costs, the labor cost and methods of construction that will give him the best competitive edge in the bidding process.

Value engineering can play an important part in the construction phase of the project. Many municipal and government agencies allow value engineering sharing clauses as a part of their contracts for construction. These clauses allow the contractor to share in the savings of money as a result of recommendations to reduce the cost of the facility. As an example, the contractor may propose a different type of material for the roof of a building. The material provides the same insulating properties; however, it can be obtained and installed at a savings of $100,000. The contractor can participate in instant savings based on a percentage of the initial savings and a collateral savings. Collateral savings are based on a percentage of the owning and operating costs. As an example, if a contractor makes a recommendation that he will save money in future years of operating the facility, he may be entitled to a percentage of the savings for the first year of operating the facility. These means of sharing in savings from ideas are called contractor-incentive-sharing clauses. The amount of savings and the regulations for submittal vary. Contractors should be aware of the potential in these areas when they bid a project.

The biggest drawbacks experienced thus far in using contractor-incentive-sharing clauses have been in the long delays experienced by contractors in receiving approval of their recommendations. The delay is often the result of incomplete submittals on the part of the contractor. In order to evaluate a contractor-incentive-sharing proposal, a complete idea of what the contractor is proposing, how it impacts the project, the specific differences in the original and the proposed design, a detailed description of the comparison costs, and the impact on the total schedule of the construction of the project should be explained. In most cases, however, the time delay attributed to contractor-incentive-sharing clauses is involved in the red tape of the various review agencies.

Facility Operation Phase

Operation and maintenance costs began to soar within the last decade. The increase in cost of energy, and inflationary increases in labor and material have brought about an awakening to public and private plant owners. More and more emphasis is being placed on reducing the maintenance burden and easing the operating costs of a plant or building facility. Operation and maintenance costs are continually increasing throughout the life of the project. They will fluctuate from year to year with inflation and with the escalating costs of fuels, chemicals, lubricants and other supply materials. While operation and maintenance costs escalate, the construction cost is fixed. In many cases, the advantages of investing money during initial construction will result in operation and maintenance savings throughout the project life. In terms of value engineering, it is best to evaluate the operation and maintenance aspects of a facility during the design stage so that the characteristics of the facility can be changed or altered accordingly.

Can value engineering be applied to plants that are already operating? The answer is a resounding "yes." The approach in this case focuses on the Value Engineered Energy and Resources. The same tools of the value engineering job plan are applied: energy model (power, fuels, etc.); resource modeling (accounting of staffing, chemical, maintenance and benefit costs); functional analysis and the multidisciplined team approach. The chemical and process industries have been successful in reducing costs of production and increasing their profits. In these cases, the total costs of the plant operation are evaluated.

It is the opinion of the authors that the best place for value engineering is in the planning and design stages. The major reason is, of course, that if changes can be found at this stage, the major cost savings can be realized by the owner and not shared with the contractor. The other element involved is the time frame. Contractors make their highest profits when they can start a job, follow the schedule rigidly, finish the job, and move off the site. In many cases, the savings that could result from a value engineering incentive clause may be eaten up by having to reschedule construction events and alter the scheduling of the project. Unless the savings is substantial, contractors are usually not willing to take the risk.

WHO INFLUENCES THE COST OF A PROJECT?

Planning, developing and constructing a project in today's marketplace is involved and often a lengthy task. Rigorous and complex regulations and standards add to the difficulty and the cost. Input into the design from the owner, engineer, contractor and the operation and maintenance personnel comprise a large matrix of people that influence the design and eventual cost of a facility.

The main impact comes from the owner of the facility who sets the requirements and objectives of the project. The owner has a certain function to perform and an idea of the size of the facility. The design engineer interprets these requirements and develops them into a workable solution. The designer impacts the construction cost and the operation and maintenance costs. The contractor impacts the project by the cost required to build the facility and the resultant quality of construction. The quality of construction and life-span of the facility are due to the contractor's skills. Operation and maintenance personnel must keep the facility running. They are required to operate the plant given to them, or to change it. Their maintenance skills and perseverance are key factors that influence operation, longevity of equipment, and cost. The value engineer also influences the cost of a project. His input into the design saves money in both the areas of construction costs and the total life-cycle costs of the facility.

In many federally funded projects, the regulatory agencies are involved. As an example, the regulatory agencies of the U. S. Environmental Protection Agency and the state health departments, which set strict standards, greatly influence the costs of wastewater facilities required to meet stringent effluent guidelines. Figure 6-5 shows the impact of the major decision-makers on facility cost. As can be seen, the using agency has the greatest impact, as they set the overall criteria for the project. The architect-engineer also influences the project to a great extent because their design impacts the construction cost and the operation and maintenance cost throughout the life of the project. The initial contractor influences the costs by the bid price. However, that bid price is a one-time cost in the life of the project. Operation and maintenance personnel are forced to operate the facility. Therefore, their actual impact is small; however, it is stretched over a long period of time.

WHEN IS THE OWNER READY FOR VALUE ENGINEERING?

An owner's decision to employ value engineering on a project is difficult. An engineer or an architect is selected to design the facility, and it is hoped

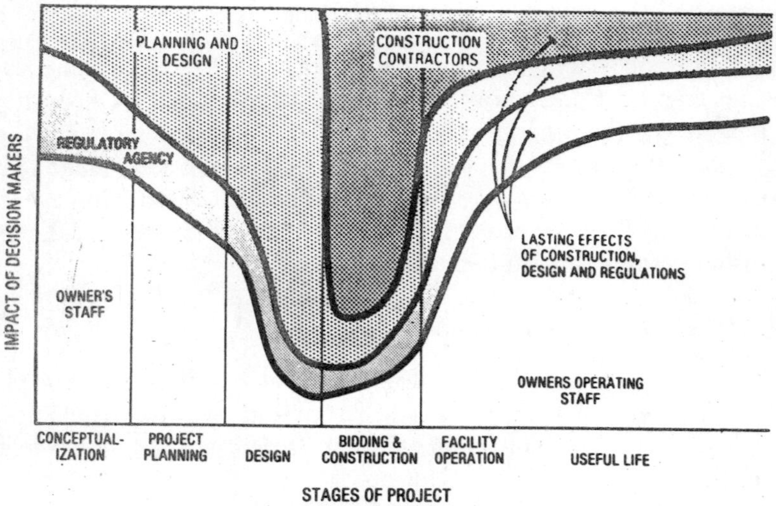

Figure 6-5. Impact of Decision Makers on a Facility.

to design it at the optimum cost. The owner has spent much time and effort in arriving at a proposed plan and has certain criteria to be met. The designer is vigorously employed working on the project trying to get all the details pulled together during the planning stage so that he can progress rapidly into design. At this stage, there are many details to be brought together. It is often difficult to sit back and take an overview of the project to make sure that the designer is, in fact, on the right road.

We have found that value engineering is best employed as an overview of the total planning process and during the actual design stage of the facility. The planning stage offers an opportunity to analyze the conceptual ideas and the conceptual thinking for the project. At this stage, the value engineering team has the advantage of not being tied closely with the project. They have an objective viewpoint. They can and should review the project without being overburdened by the critical schedules and outside influences of the design concept. Value engineering applied during the planning stage also allows an opportunity to make changes without affecting the cost or the schedule of the project. Value engineering, in this case, is a second look, and has shown itself to be effective in yielding savings to the owner.

As the design progresses, value engineering should also be applied in the design stage of the project. It has been our experience that value engineering is best applied in a two-step approach at the design stage. One study should be employed at the point where the basis for design has been developed. At this stage, the value engineer is looking at the design criteria for the process; the layout of the facility on the site; foundation conditions; the physical layout of the facilities, space allocations; functional areas required for operating the facility; the theory and concept for operating and controlling the facility; the electrical one-line diagram and system design; the architectural concept to be employed for the project; climate and comfort control levels and corresponding heating, ventilating and air-conditioning conceptual design; building layout; and other factors that help to show the overall concept of the project. Value engineering at this stage of design is usually employed when the project is approximately 20–40 percent complete. The value engineer should state in specific terms what areas he wishes to evaluate to ensure that the designer and VE consultant agree on the level of completion of the project.

A second value engineering study is conducted at approximately the 60–80 percent design-completion stage. At this time, the value engineering team is interested more in the construction elements of the project. It is very difficult to evaluate process, layout and concepts for the design during the second study because, at this stage, working drawings are nearing completion. Major changes to the design at the 60–80 percent stage would cause delays in the scheduling of the project. High cost for redesigning and redrafting would also occur. The team's focus is on construction procedures, configurations, materials of construction, construction operations, instrumentation and control, mechanical equipment, electrical control and instrumentation and on analyzing very closely the impacts on the operation and maintenance of the overall project. The owner's staffing requirements should also be analyzed as an input to the overall operation costs of the project. Staffing requirements should be made jointly by the owner and the value engineering team. The specifications for the project are the most important part of the second value engineering study. Often overlooked is the high cost in the specifications that instruct the contractor in the material and equipment to be used and the construction procedure. Specifications should be closely evaluated as a part of the second value engineering study.

Having determined that the owner is interested in employing value engineering, the next step is to determine how value engineering should be conducted and to select the appropriate value engineering staff.

SELECTING A VE CONSULTANT

Value engineering is a systematic approach at identifying and removing unnecessary cost in a project. The key elements to the success of a value engineering study are knowledge and experience in the field of value engineering, coupled with the technical expertise in the area of study. Each of these rudimentary elements is an important aspect in the success of a project study. As a rule, the participants in a value engineering study should not be associated with the original design. Team members specifically should not have participated in the original design. The reason for this is that the original designer is often biased in his viewpoint when analyzing a value engineering alternative. Obviously, the designer's input and experience in the factors leading to the design are important and he should be asked to provide input on background of the project. The designer should also have input on the evaluation of VE recommendations as they develop.

There are several criteria that should be used in evaluation and selection of a value engineering consultant. The criteria, of course, follow the guidelines that would be used to select most consultant services.

1. Experience in the field of value engineering. Proper application of VE methodology.
2. Technical experience (design, construction, operation, etc.).
3. Past record of performance on similar projects.
4. The approach to the value engineering work.
5. Avoidance of conflicts, especially competition with the designer.
6. Results of past value engineering studies, including implemented savings.
7. References on past projects.
8. Ability to work with the designer and the owner as a team on the project.
9. Ability to perform value engineering study on short notice and to provide a quick turnaround time so that the project design may remain on schedule.

STAFFING AND STRUCTURING TEAMS FOR A VE STUDY

One question often asked is, how does one properly organize and staff a value engineering study? The subject needs to be addressed because of its importance and eventual impact on the success of a value engineering study. Far too many studies are conducted with individuals lacking an understanding of the application of value engineering. While these studies save money, they may omit areas that would have been found using sound value techniques. for staffing a study. However, we would like to share some of the logic that has been used in the development of project-study teams.

A successful VE study of a facility requires a knowledge and expertise in the technical field of study and a solid background in the principles of value engineering. It has been our experience that selecting individuals without prior VE experience sets the team back. Most people when they think of saving money envision reducing the cost by removing a part or cheapening the material. Therefore, when an engineer or an architect without VE training is selected, their initial response is to do a design review and find the apparent cost-cutting areas. In contrast, it is apparent that a study with a high level of VE talent and technical background will produce effective results.

Level of Training

Team participants in a project study should have a 40-hour value engineering training course as a minimum requirement. This places everyone at an equal footing when starting a study and allows for each participant to be actively employed on the study. Special consultants are sometimes used in a VE study because they are experts in a certain field. These people are often doctoral level and are hard to get to a 40-hour training seminar. One has to make the decision of the importance of the added expertise versus their experience in value engineering.

Value engineering training workshops are conducted by a number of sources. A VE training seminar should be one that is conducted by a certified value specialist and recognized by the Society of American Value Engineers (SAVE). Value seminars are also taught in the manufacturing field, and it is important that one recognizes the area the workshop emphasizes.

Many government agencies will require a varying level of value engineering training, depending on the size (cost) of the project and its complexity. Recommendations on the varying level of VE experience are usually specified by the government agency or owner. As an example, the US/Environmental Protection Agency may require that the team coordinator have completed at least two VE studies, and the team members each have completed a 40-hour training workshop.

Selecting VE Team Members

Value engineering teams operate under the premise that two minds are better than one, and, in many cases, one mind is motivated or prompted by the free flow of ideas and the stimuli of discussion. Not all individuals are alike in their personality, their ability to communicate, their perception of ideas and their ability to put their ideas into salable products. Research has told us that individuals might be categorized in three types:

1. Idea people
2. Communicators
3. Developers and organizers

Obviously, all these talents are needed to mold the team into a productive group.

Idea men contribute heavily to the success of a VE study, as their concepts form the basis for recommendations for cost savings. Will Rogers once said that we could get rid of all the German submarines in World War I by boiling the oceans. Will was obviously an idea man. A VE team needs idea men who can perceive new combinations of materials, new layouts, new processes, optimized utilization of energy and other areas of potential savings to the owner.

Communicators are the individuals in a study who relate available information on the background of a building, mechanical system or piece of equipment that allows comparative ideas that force us to go beyond our normal thought process. Newman and Summer define communication as the exchange of facts, ideas, opinions or emotions by two or more people.* Communication is one element that makes group studies effective.

Developers and organizers are the people that put words and concepts into reality. In the construction field they are the engineers, architects, estimators, operators, and contractors who develop ideas into real designs for the owner. Development of ideas is important and often overlooked. Many good ideas are killed because they are not presented completely. *Do not leave questions for the designer to assume judgment.* Developers ensure that recommendations are well conceived and well presented. Remember that unless the idea is well presented and sold, it has no basic value to the owner.

A diversity of talents and expertise are needed for a study. Providing the information and exchange of thought, speculating on a solution and developing the concept into a workable solution are essential requirements of the VE study.

Larry Miles identifies eight essential qualifications for value work as:

1. Knowledge
2. Imagination
3. High degree of initiative
4. Self-organization
5. Personality
6. Cooperative attitude
7. Experience
8. Belief in the importance of value
9. Diplomacy (added by authors)
10. Salesmanship (added by authors)

We would add diplomacy and salesmanship to that list because the importance of these essential traits can be seen as the VE team identifies recommendations to the designer that modify the design.

Most individuals approach a VE study enthusiastically because of the challenge, the opportunity to work and share ideas with their peers and the sense of satisfaction which is derived from improving on a project cost or operation. The studies are rewarding to the participants and to the designer as well. One of the side benefits gained by the team participants is the exchange of technical data from other fields (multidisciplined team members) and from other firms.

Value Engineering Team Coordinators (VETC)

Value engineering team coordinators (VETC) are given the responsibility of organizing and leading the value engineering studies. The VETC is the cornerstone of the project. The VETC's duties include: (1) Deciding on

*Newman, W. H. and Summer, C. E., Jr. *The Process of Management*, Englewood Cliffs, NJ: Prentice-Hall, Inc., 1961, p. 59.

the number of VE teams and the disciplines necessary for each study; (2) assigning team members; (3) coordinating the study schedule with the owner and designer; (4) managing the designer/VE consultant/owner relationship; (5) leading the study team through the job plan; (6) organizing the oral presentation of results; (7) preparing the VE report; and (8) assisting the owner and designer in the implementation of VE recommendations. Value coordinators should have a great deal of experience in the techniques of value engineering and should have strong leadership and communication capabilities. To ensure that VE principles are followed it is beneficial to utilize the services of a Certified Value Specialist (CVS).

A CVS is registered by the Society of American Value Engineers (SAVE) to perform value work. The registration ensures a high level of expertise in the application of value techniques. The requirements for certification may be obtained by writing to SAVE, 220 N. Story Road, Dallas, Texas, 75061.

Multidisciplined Teams

A multidisciplined team has proven to be the most successful structure for a value engineering study. The exchange of ideas and knowledge from other disciplines provide an objective analysis of the project design.

Anomalies frequently arise in a value engineering study. It is often the architect or structural engineer that will generate ideas that are part of the project, but not in their field of study. Why? Because many of the solutions that we use are based on our habit solutions and not on objective thinking. Value consultants have found that many firms operate through design divisions. The structural work is performed by the structural division, the electrical work by the electrical division. Often these divisions *do not communicate.* Experience has shown that just having all the project disciplines together will enhance the design because each discipline will have its respective impact on the total plant design. The importance of objectivity is evident in the example previously cited.

Project staffing for a value study can best be illustrated by an example of a past project.

The City of Oklahoma City required value engineering on their North Canadian Wastewater Treatment Plant. The facility was planned for an ultimate expansion to 80 million gallons per day (MGD). Forty MGD was under construction at the time of the study. The scope of the value engineering study included the next 20 MGD incremental expansion to bring the design flow up to 60 MGD. Solids handling facilities were also a part of the study.

It was decided that two value engineering studies would be conducted; one at the 20–30 percent design completion stage and one at the 60–70 percent stage. The first study analyzed the conceptual design, including such things as layout, process, equipment selection, hydraulic profile and conceptual designs for architectural, electrical and mechanical systems.

The objective of doing one study early in the design is to recommend changes early so that the impact on schedule and redesign effort is not as critical. The second study analyzes the working drawings, paying special attention to equipment design, architectural features, piping and mechanical design layouts, lighting, primary and secondary power distribution, energy and fuel utilization, structural design development and economic comparisons for construction.

VE Study Teams – North Canadian Wastewater Treatment Plant

The study teams for the North Canadian Wastewater Treatment Plant were as follows:

Study A – 20–30% Completion (Conceptual Design)

Team 1 – Certified Value Specialist
Sanitary Engineer
Landscape Architect
Sanitary Engineer
Structural Engineer
Owner's Representative

Team 2 – Team Coordinator/Certified Value Specialist
Sanitary Engineer
Cost Estimator
Electrical Engineer
Civil Engineer
Chemical Engineer

Study B – 60–70% (Design Completion)

Team 1 – Team Coordinator
Mechanical Engineer
Sanitary Engineer
Cost/Construction Estimator
Owner's Representative

Team 2 – Team Coordinator
Structural Engineer
Electrical Engineer
Civil Engineer
Architect
Mechanical Engineer

Selection of team members must fit the specific requirements that are pertinent to the project being studied. If unusual foundation problems are evident, a soils engineer should be included on the study. Other specific expertise should be provided accordingly.

An example of a value engineering team for a bridge might comprise the following:

VE Study Team – For a Bridge Design

1. Value Engineering Team Coordinator
2. Structural Engineer/Bridges

3. Foundation Engineer
4. Civil Engineer/Transportation
5. Construction Engineer

An important aspect of the total life-cycle cost over the life of a project is the operation and maintenance of the facility. Operation and maintenance considerations are a necessary part of most project studies. On a water or wastewater treatment plant, the input of the plant superintendent or chief operator is necessary, as the operation and maintenance may cost more over the project life than the original cost of the plant. Studies on power plants may require the maintenance engineer and operations supervisor. Studies on buildings may benefit from having a stationary engineer on the study team.

In addition to the operations and maintenance personnel, the owner is encouraged to participate, as he has an overview of the total project needs and cost constraints.

CONDUCTING A VE PROJECT STUDY

Success of a value engineering study depends heavily on its organization and management. In many cases, owners and design engineers are not familiar with value engineering and how it is performed. Their first impression is that someone is looking over their shoulder and oftentimes picking at their design. Another concern that runs through a designer's head is that the value engineering consultant might purposely be critical of a design in an effort to sway the owner on future projects. The integrity of the project schedule that may result as part of the value engineering effort is another monumental concern. One can see how both of these concerns are delicate and that they must be handled properly.

In any value engineering project study, whether it be during the planning, design, construction or operation stage, it is important to remember that the value engineering team is a part of the overall project and their goal is very similar to that of the design engineer: *to ensure that the owner receives a well-designed facility with the required balance between cost, performance and reliability*. In reality, the value engineering consultant is a great asset to the design engineer for a project. His efforts to identify alternate solutions to a problem will benefit the overall project. Remember that the design engineer and the owner have the final word on adopting value engineering recommendations. The design engineer and the owner still have the responsibility for the final design of the project.

The value engineering consultant must not lose sight of the fact that the design engineer has been involved in the project for a long time. Many comparisons and evaluations of alternate processes and design concepts have been prepared. The designer will undoubtedly feel that the project is his pride and joy.

Figure 6-6 is a task flow diagram which outlines the primary steps of a value engineering study. The study can be viewed in three separate phases: (1) the Prestudy Phase, (2) the Project Study Workshop, and (3) the Post VE Study

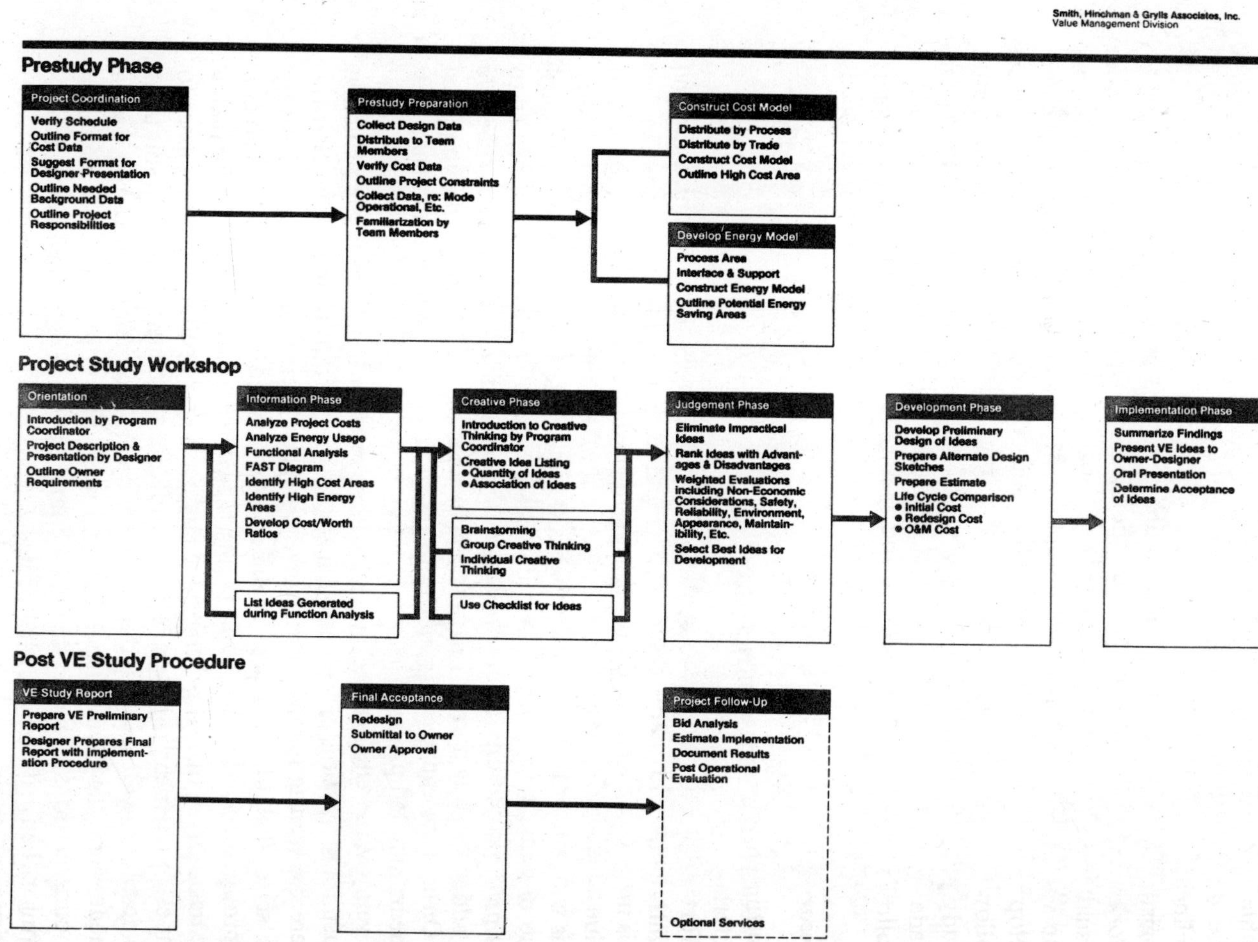

Figure 6-6. Value Engineering Studies Task Flow Diagram. A summary of the tasks necessary to conduct a VE study.

Procedure. The *Prestudy Phase* is the period of time used to familiarize the value engineering consultant with the project to be studied; to familiarize the design engineer with the value engineering process and procedure; to delineate the information needed for the study, and to arrange for the logistics and the set-up for the actual workshop session. The *Project Study Workshop Phase* is where the actual value engineering effort takes place. Usually a value engineering workshop lasts for a set period of time in which the value engineering team meets together and applies the job plan to develop alternatives for consideration. The *Post-VE Study Procedure Phase* follows the value engineering workshop. During this phase of the project study, the necessary reports and evaluation of the recommendations are made, and efforts to implement these recommendations are brought forward. Follow-up and accounting of implementation results are also beneficial.

Prestudy Phase

Getting off on the right foot on a VE study is akin to starting a new job. Laying out the responsibilities of each participant will lead to a well-coordinated effort. We have found that this can best be handled in an orientation meeting jointly with the owner, the design engineer, and the value consultant. At this meeting, the value engineering team coordinator should outline the entire value engineering process. It is important to remember that in many cases, this will be the designer's and the owner's first exposure to value engineering. The designer is perplexed, realizing that the value consultant is evaluating his project. There will be many underlying fears and questions that should be addressed in this session.

One of the most important concerns to the design engineer will be the schedule for the value engineering work. The value engineering schedule must fit very closely with the designer's schedule. The value consultant realistically must accommodate himself to any changes to the designer's schedule. Should there be delays in the project, the value engineering consultant must adjust his schedule accordingly. While discussing the subject of schedules, it is appropriate to mention the longevity of the value engineering effort. Once the designer has scheduled a date for the project study workshop, the consultant should establish the schedule for the balance of the VE effort. Submittal of design data, preparation of cost and energy models, review time and schedule for completion of VE reports must be set. This time frame should be compressed as much as possible. Keep in mind the primary objective during the design phase is to get the design completed. Therefore, the value engineering effort should be handled in a most expeditious manner.

At the beginning of the VE workshop, the designer is asked to make a presentation outlining the steps taken during the design development stages. To assist the designer, the VE coordinator should outline a format for the designer to follow. The format will outline the key steps which should be covered in the designer's presentation. It is not to say that this is a rigid outline, but it helps the designer to understand more clearly what the value engineering team is looking for.

The value engineering study is an abbreviated effort in terms of the total scheduled time for the design of the project. The value engineering team must, therefore, quickly become familiar with as much information on the project background as possible. The team coordinator for the value engineering study is responsible for collecting design information as well as plans and specifications for the project. An outline of information required for a value engineering study is shown in Chapter 3. This information should be sent to the value engineering team two to three weeks prior to the VE workshop. It is distributed to each team member so that he can become familiar with the material before the workshop session. The VE team members will then be prepared to ask pertinent questions during the designer's presentation.

In arriving at a project design, the design engineer may be given certain directives by the owner which serve as project constraints. Project constraints are often the major objectives of the project, and they are required functions that must be performed. *It is necessary to outline project constraints prior to the value engineering workshop.* In this way, the value engineering team does not make recommendations that are contrary to the desires of the owner. Project constraints should be formalized in writing by the owner, the design engineer and the value engineering consultant.

Because cost is the primary criterion for comparison of ideas, it is important that the value engineering team have complete and accurate costing information. The value engineering consultant, during the initial coordination meeting, should identify the format required for cost data. In this way, the design engineer can respond accordingly with information that is appropriate for a value engineering study.

Upon receipt of cost and energy information from the designer, the value engineering team will prepare a cost model for the project. The first step in preparation of the cost model is to validate the cost information provided by the design engineer. The reason for verifying cost information is to ensure that both groups agree on the unit prices and quantity of materials that went into preparation of the cost estimate. If there are discrepancies in the cost, these should be identified early to avoid confusion or misunderstanding during the implementation phase of the project. To construct the cost model, the value engineering team coordinator and/or the estimator on the value engineering team distributes cost by process, by trade, by system and other identifiable areas. This helps the value engineering team at the beginning of the study to know where the major costs are to be found. Pareto's law of economics indicates that 80 percent of the cost will normally occur in 20 percent of the items being studied. (See Figure 6-7.) This is usually true of a construction project. The cost model helps to identify this 80 percent of the project cost. During the prestudy phase, also, a graphical cost model is also prepared. An outline of the high-cost areas of the project is identified at this point so that when the engineering team meets jointly for their study session, the costs are well organized and the team can use its time effectively.

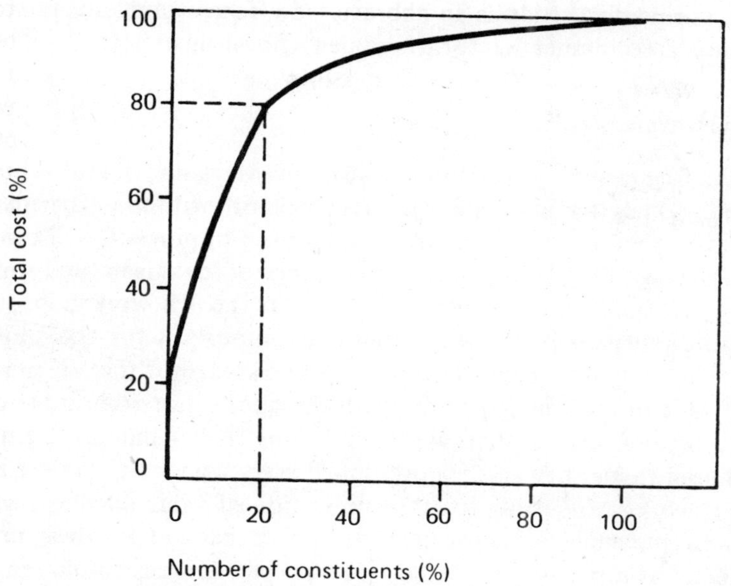

Figure 6-7. Pareto's Law of Distribution.

Energy and life cycle models are frequently constructed during the pre-study effort.

Each member of the value engineering team is to spend a specified period of time in going through the background information of the project. Usually, 8 to 16 hours per man is allowed for this task, depending on the size and magnitude of the project. Familiarization can be done independently.

The logistics of a value engineering study are a consideration to the overall project. Keep in mind that the value engineering effort is an intense effort employing a group of people. Therefore, it is helpful to have the study in a place where interruptions are infrequent and the arrangements are comfortable. Oftentimes, the studies are conducted in hotel conference rooms or other conference areas that are isolated from the main working stream. Outside calls coming into the value engineering team should be restricted. Other disturbances should also be kept to a minimum. It is also helpful to have facilities with windows that open to the outside. This helps to provide a good working environment. For a value engineering team of five to six people, approximately 800–1000 square feet of meeting area should be provided. The team should also have available reproduction machines and other supplies required for the study. The location of the value engineering study may be in the city where the owner or the designer is located or in the offices of the value engineering consultant. Where an existing plant is involved where unusual site conditions warrant, the study should take place near the site. This gives the value engineering team a chance to visually observe the location and surrounding area of the project. In any event, a site visit by the value engineering coordinator and one or more of the other value engineering team participants is recommended for the value engineering effort.

Project Study Workshop Phase

The Value Engineering Workshop is a participative session of multidisciplinary skilled individuals that integrate their technical skills with the VE methodology in an effort to reduce cost or improve the project or product. An atmosphere that pulsates with free discussion and exchange of ideas is needed to arrive at alternate solutions to the original design. In the VE workshop, the value engineering job plan provides a structured framework for the VE team to follow. The practical technical skills and knowledge of the VE team members are used in conjunction with VE techniques. The skills are required to make recommendations that work, and the VE techniques are a proven method used to identify and remove unnecessary costs.

Why a workshop setting for the application of value engineering? Can't this same value engineering job plan be applied back at the design office by the designer as a part of the design? Certain techniques employed in value engineering can be applied by the designer on his own project. However, the value of bringing together the various disciplines involved in a major project into an uninterrupted session for a period of 40 hours or more is unique to the design field. Traditionally, engineering firms used design review committees to evaluate project designs. These projects fall under the scrutiny of the principals of the firm and their most experienced designers. The thrust of their reviews, however, is to ensure that the project functions properly. It's primary function is to ensure a workable product. The value engineering workshop, however, has as its primary goal the reduction of the life-cycle costs of the project. The VE team is directing its attention at specific and precise methods of reducing the cost of the project.

Bringing together a group of highly skilled design professionals for an extended period of time is an obvious challenge. First, pulling skilled technical people from their normal assignments for an extended period of time is not profitable. Second, most designers are interested in doing what they know best, that is, designing the project. Their specific interest may not be to corroborate the cost and value, but to ensure successful performance. The VE coordinator conducting the workshop has to manage and coordinate the session to ensure an open and free exchange of ideas and to assimilate the ideas into specific recommendations to the owner and the designer.

Another task of the VE team coordinator is to bring together the designer's knowledge and background of the project, the owner's history of the existing plant, and the specific purpose for the project. During the workshop session, the designer is asked to submit his design for review before both the owner and the VE team. Maintaining flexibility and performance are the primary concerns of the designer. The owner wants a final product to meet his requirements and to yield the best potential benefit to the taxpayer, user agency or company. The VE team is interested in providing a better project, and, at the same time, in saving money. The common denominator is that the final project meets the functions required by the owner at the lowest life-cycle cost commensurate with the owner's needs.

The value engineering job plan previously outlined in Chapter 4 forms the framework for the VE workshop. The team coordinator must be familiar with the techniques of VE required by the job plan. The VE team coordinator must disseminate data on the project design to team members prior to the study and *lead* the workshop session keeping it on course and on schedule.

At the beginning of a VE workshop session, there is a joint meeting of members of the design team, owner representatives and the VE team. It is helpful for the VE team coordinator to outline the steps to be taken in the workshop session. High-cost and high-energy-use areas should also be described as a result of preparation of the cost model and the energy model. It is also wise to reassure the designer that the VE team is interested only in improving the project. It helps to relate to the designer while in the owner's presence that all projects have unnecessary costs no matter which design firm has been preparing the project. The thrust of the VE workshop is very similar to a second look at the project.

Another major concern of the owner and the designer will be the impact of the value engineering workshop effort on the schedule for design completion. At the beginning of the workshop session, the VE team coordinator should be prepared to outline the scheduled dates for the completion of the workshop sessions, the submittal of design recommendations to the owner and the designer, the schedule for oral presentation of results, and the time frame for submittal of the VE report by the value consultant. The designer's responsibility for addressing each of the VE recommendations should also be coordinated.

The mood of the value engineering workshop is usually set during the first half-hour of the workshop. It is, therefore, very important that the coordinator take the proper steps in order to ensure an efficient and compatible start. Starting on a firm foundation will ensure a stable ground upon which to build. A project description and presentation by the designer can often provide the missing link that the VE team members need to understand and to appreciate the background effort of the designer. In every project, unusual circumstances will be responsible for influencing project designs. As an example, during the public hearings for environmental impact statements on a wastewater treatment plant, the community may have set unalterable stipulations on the design. Pertinent correspondence between review and regulatory agencies help to illuminate and justify design decisions. The designer's presentation should include as a minimum, a description of the project's physical components, rationale for the design, a review of how the design evolved, description of design criteria, alternative solutions investigated, owner and regulatory agency requirements and important factors that have influenced design-decision making. An outline of information that might be used for a designer's presentation is included as Figure 6-8. The designer should be available throughout the study for questions that may rise about the project.

Upon completion of the designer's presentation, the VE team should be encouraged to question the designer and the owner about any questionable aspects of the project design. All members of the VE team, the design team and the owner's representative are encouraged to participate freely in discussion of the project design. Upon hearing the designer's presentation, the VE team may want to revisit the site to analyze any questionable areas and to become more familiar with the particulars of the plant design. This initial phase of the VE study, along with the time spent during the prestudy phase in evaluating background information is of great benefit to the VE team in becoming familiar with the project in a short amount of time. Further investigations into the project cost and energy model as a result of the designer's presentation may reflect new information. At this point it is appropriate to revise and to

OUTLINE FOR VE PRESENTATION

The designer of a project has been actively employed in the planning and design of the project to be value engineered. He has spent a great deal of time and effort in comparing alternatives.

The design has also been influenced by outside input during public participation meetings, in preparing environmental impacts, and from requests made by the owner and regulatory agencies and other sources. The value engineering team needs to know this data to get an idea and a flavor for factors that influence the design. The object is to avoid duplication of effort and to aid the team in becoming familiar with the project.

To achieve this objective, the designer is asked to give a presentation at the beginning of the VE workshop session. To assist the designer, we have outlined information that, as a minimum, should be addressed.

1. Scope of the Designers Effort
2. Participating Firms
3. Projected Flows
4. Effluent Criteria
5. Influent Characteristics
6. Existing Site Conditions
7. Regulatory Requirements
8. Basis of Design
9. Rationale and Steps in Development of Design
10. Design Concepts for Architectural, Structural, Mechanical, Electrical, Controls, Etc.
11. Methodology of Operation
12. Pertinent Information from Public Participation
13. Constraints Imposed by the Owner
14. Appropriate Codes
15. Explanation of Information Provided by Designer
16. Summary of Cost Estimate

The outline is provided to aid the designer. The presentation is the Designer's responsibility and he may conduct the initial presentation the way he feels is most comfortable. Remember that there will be other people involved in the presentation so that graphics, slides, viewgraphs, etc., should be planned accordingly.

Figure 6-8. Outline for Designers Presentation. An outline to assist designers to prepare for a VE study.

refine both the cost model and the energy model where appropriate.

The next step in the VE study is the functional analysis. During the function analysis remember to start with the total system first before analyzing the functional components. The function analysis is set up to stimulate the creative process. By analyzing the project in terms of function, the team is forced to think beyond its normal thought processes. Caution should be exercised at this point in the VE study about skipping over the function analysis step. Our experiences showed that the function analysis sets the stage for the creative session which follows. By analyzing the function of the total plant and each of its component parts, the VE team will become intimately familiar with what the plant is supposed to do and alternative ways of performing that function. Apportioning costs associated with the function gives the team a framework for comparison. Speculation of the worth of each of the functional areas forces the VE team to think of new and different ways of providing that function. Each new method then becomes a potential creative idea. Remember that Kettering started outside the bounds of the normal solution when he designed the self-starter for the automobile. This may be true for your project. Don't be inhibited by what you see on the plans. Look beyond that solution for new and exciting concepts.

During the information and creative phases of the value engineering workshop, the VE team may feel pressure to complete the study. They feel as though they should jump ahead to development of ideas. The information and creative phases of the job plan are important. Time invested in the earlier stage of the project will result in even more significant time savings later on during the development and implementation phases.

If the VE team is involved in a very complex project, it may be appropriate to use the functional analysis systems technique (FAST) to simplify and to clear up any difficulties and questions that the VE team may have about the design. The functional analysis systems technique is a technique used to organize the functional elements of a project. It is a roadmap of functions used to delineate a clear understanding of how the project functions. (See Chapter 4.)

To ensure some semblance of order in the value engineering workshop session, the VETC may designate one of the team members, preferably one with good handwriting, to record the steps followed in the value engineering procedure. In this way, background data will be retained for eventual use in the VE report. The project scribe should also be charged with the responsibility of recording each VE idea that is suggested by the team members. Although the team should refrain from jumping immediately into the creative idea listing, there will be certain ideas that will crop up during the early information-gathering part of the project. Make sure these ideas are captured in writing so they aren't lost. Remember that in each idea the potential exists for major savings.

Next, the VE team moves into the creative phase. The creative phase is one of the more interesting parts of the VE study. All team members are asked to participate in the VE creative phase. The team is looking for a *quantity of ideas and an association of ideas.* In this stage of the VE study, judgment is suspended, and the VE coordinator should make sure that team members are not criticized for openly expressing their thoughts. Keep in mind that often individuals are unfamiliar with such an open forum. This is especially true of team members without prior VE training. The VETC should be able to assess any reluctance on the part of team members to express their thoughts. Often the situation occurs where one individual will dominate the thought process. Even though his ideas may be good, he may be thwarting the thought process and the contributions of other team members. One way to bridge this gap is to have several types of creative sessions. One creative session might be a group session where all the team members are encouraged to participate. The second creative session might be broken down into groups of two to three individuals that have established a rapport and a working relationship during the earlier stages of the project. The third part of the creative session would be the listing of individual ideas gathered during an individual creative session. All the ideas are then pooled into one common list for further judgment. Checklists of ideas that were generated on other projects also may be a valuable asset to the VE team.

A technique used by Smith, Hinchman & Grylls in their workshop is to replace the traditional "*no,* it won't work" response with a "*yes,* it will work *if* we do this." A more positive approach that generates positive results. The owner's participation in this part of the study is encouraged so he will be aware of the type of ideas generated.

After the VE team has completed the creative phase, each of the VE ideas is evaluated in terms of the advantages and the disadvantages. Impractical ideas are eliminated from the list. Other ideas are evaluated on a scale from one to ten, depending on the potential for cost savings, the potential for implementation and the credibility of the idea itself. The VE team will usually start developing other ideas from the creative idea list.

Keep in mind that during the development of value engineering ideas, the VE team should refrain from recommendations and changes that they would not make on their own designs. Each of the VE ideas that passes through the judgment phase and goes into development should have the support of the VE team and should have a strong practical application to the project. The VETC's judgment should be used in cases where there is vast disagreement on the rating scale by the team members. If the judgment phase and the rating of ideas is starting to take an inordinate amount of time, the democratic process might be employed. In this case, each of the VE team members is allowed to cast his vote in the idea rating. The votes are then averaged to give a weighted score. Remember that the main objective of the judgment phase is to thin out those ideas that are impractical and to concentrate on the best ideas for further development. If one team member feels strongly about the merits of an idea that others reject, let that person develop it. He may be viewing the idea from a different and possibly useful angle.

The team coordinator should take special care in assuring that each VE idea that proceeds to the development phase is thoroughly analyzed to give a clear picture of the scope and purpose of the recommendation. All VE recommendations should include a description of the original design concept and the proposed design; the reason for the recommendation; advantages and disadvantages as a result of the revised design; sketches of the original design and the proposed alterations; and a life-cycle comparison of the original and proposed design. Before he will accept the idea and implement it into the design, the designer must be assured that the recommendation will benefit the project. He must be able to understand your rationale for the VE recommendation. A clear avenue for implementation of the recommendation will reduce the burden of acceptance.

As in the development of any design, the VE recommendation should be checked to ensure that all calculations and cost data are accurate and correct. VE recommendations should also be specific and not written in terms of generalities. The importance of specifics is illustrated in the story of the Bengal tiger. A man on safari in India was told a tiger would never attack a man carrying a flashlight at night. They left out one little detail and that was provided he carried it fast enough. A similar analogy applied to the VE recommendation. Specifics will help give a vivid picture of the VE team concept.

The implementation of value engineering recommendations require skillful diplomacy at best. Keep in mind that your recommendation may be an idea that the original designer had not thought of, and remember he has an ego, too. On the one hand, he has a professional responsibility to provide the best possible project for the owner within the limits of fee and time. On the other hand, pride of authorship makes for a natural reluctance to accept ideas that are not our own.

An intelligent negotiating team, which is really what the VE team is doing when presenting its ideas, will ensure that all parties to a negotiation are treated fairly. During your presentation of VE results, if the designer has excelled in certain areas of the design, then he should be rewarded. At the same time, if there are major areas of improvement to the design, it is important that the recommendations be presented gracefully. A gentle but firm push for acceptance often achieves the best results.

The presentation of VE results is done in the form of an oral presentation. The VETC may handle the entire presentation, or rely on each of the team members to present the recommendations they worked on. There is no set format for an oral presentation. We have found the best results have occurred in an informal setting where the designer, the owner and the VE team can freely discuss the merits of each recommendation. The oral presentation may take place the last day of the workshop, or the VE team may want to organize the material further and present the recommendations sometime during the following week. In any case, the VE worksheets should be reproduced and presented to the owner and the designer to facilitate their review and analysis of the VE results. The worksheets represent the recommendations and the background leading up to them.

Post-VE Study Procedure Phase

The post-VE study procedure is the time spent after the workshop in the preparation of the value consultant's preliminary report, and in the further implementation of value engineering recommendations by the designer and the owner. After presenting the oral report to the designer and the owner, the VE consultant then finalizes the results of the value engineering workshop into a report. The VE consultant's report will include a summary of results of the VE workshop session.

The Final VE Report is prepared by the designer in concert with the owner. Each recommendation is evaluated and accepted or rejected. Often an idea will be rejected because a small portion is not acceptable. The reviewer is encouraged to seek out the usable parts of each idea. When ideas are rejected the reason for rejection should be stated. The final report should have a summary of accepted ideas and the resultant savings. The designer's response report addressing acceptance of each recommendation is referred to as the *final report.*

To maintain the integrity of the design schedule, the VE consultant is encouraged to complete the VE report as soon as possible after the workshop session.

It is up to the designer and the owner to select those ideas which they feel benefit their project. All value engineering results are *recommendations.* Owners should also be aware that the designer should be entitled to redesign costs where appropriate to implement value engineering ideas into the design. The redesign costs should be accounted for in the designer's evaluation of value recommendations.

After analyzing the preliminary value engineering report, the design engineer may have questions regarding certain VE recommendations. The VE coordinator should be available to answer these questions and to go over the designer's final VE report to ensure that no misunderstandings have evolved in the designer's or the owner's interpretation of the recommendations.

The last step in the VE process is the follow-up on the final results of the VE study. The follow-up may be equated to the post-audit. It also provides the VETC with valuable information on ways that he might improve future value engineering studies. We have also found great value looking at the project two or three years later to verify the life-cycle costs and energy consumption.

7
Cost Modeling

Cost is a major frame of reference used to assess the value of the things that we purchase. In construction projects, cost represents the amount of money expended for the construction of the facility. Cost is the primary means used to compare value. This value might be in terms of the quantity, quality, esthetics, image or other criteria. In the comparison of alternatives cost adds the element of objectivity needed to analyze alternatives.

In achieving the required function of the owner a certain cost must be expended. In most cases, the owner outlines the requirements for the architect or engineer to follow to achieve that function. A cost budget is also established. Reducing the cost of the building or facility and achieving the function at the same time is the goal of the value engineering study. Combining functions and eliminating unnecessary functions are two means of reducing cost. Keep in mind that function, reliability, operability or maintainability are not jeopardized in the effort to reduce cost.

Costs are used in the construction field from the very conceptual planning stages, through design and construction, and during the operation (useful life) of the facility. During the preliminary planning stages of the project, the degree of accuracy of costing is usually limited. The estimates made at this stage are usually conceptual in nature and are based on past trends and historical knowledge of similar projects. As the project develops, more and more detail is generated to enhance cost integrity. Costs can be applied to a given set of parameters established as a part of the design. As an example, during the preparation of schematic drawings, the various building system alternatives can be compared in arriving at a final solution. The systems can be costed in terms of square footage, cubic footage, footprint area, and other quantified amounts. The final estimate and the contractor's construction estimate are then based on definitive quantities and amounts, often described as unit price estimates.

The purpose of this chapter is not to outline procedures and processes for cost estimating. It is, however, intended to show the degree of accuracy required at various stages of design, and to show how the cost estimates are transformed into cost models used to relate and compare alternatives.

A cost estimate and a cost model are communication tools. It is a tool used by the owner, the architect, engineer, contractor, operating personnel, bankers and consumers to arrive at a common language to assess value. A standard frame of reference that will give all parties a means to understand the exchange value received in return for investment dollars. A good complete cost estimating system therefore provides the following:

1. It ensures consistency in estimating over time and from project to project.
2. It allows costs related to different stages of development to be forecast, and design to be made based on preset budget parameters.
3. It provides a checklist to reduce error and improve accuracy.
4. It reduces ambiguity and facilitates communication between all members of the project team.
5. It provides a continuing frame of reference to develop and maintain project cost control.
6. It provides for a comparison of alternatives and evaluates ideas to select the most cost-effective design.
7. It aids in financial planning and product cost budgeting.

COST VALIDATION

In value engineering, we assure the accuracy of costs by validating costs before the workshop session is conducted. Verifying costs early in the study wards off disagreements on recommended ideas. The aim is to evaluate ideas based on their design integrity and to have all members of the project team agree on costs. We detour the pitfalls of criticizing cost by arriving at an agreed upon basis for costs.

Cost-estimates are usually prepared by the design consultant for the project. In some cases a complete estimate is prepared by the value consultant. In any case, the VE consultant must be assured that costs are accurate. If the original estimate is suspect, the consultant should validate it. Because cost is the basis for evaluation, its accuracy is necessary if meaningful responses are to accrue.

COST ESTIMATING

Cost estimates can be used for a variety of purposes. The type of estimates will also vary to correspond to the purpose, complexity, accuracy and time that the estimate is made. In a project's infancy stages when the need for a facility is being assessed, gross estimates are used. The opposite extreme is when a detailed set of plans and specifications have been prepared and quantity takeoffs and unit prices assigned.

Cost estimates are prepared using different levels of complexity (Figure 7-1). User units expressing a cost per unit quantity of function performed are the basis for first and second order costs. Examples of user units are cost per bed in a hospital design, cost per gallon of chemical produced, cost per capita per day for treatment of sewage. User costs are applied to obtain a gross estimate of the total project cost. Often user costs are applied before a site is selected. Spatial cost parameters are based on linear feet, square feet

Parameter \ Project Phase	Planning/Budget	Schematic/Conceptual	Preliminary Design	Working Drawing	Construction
User Units/Functional Units	X	X			
Square Foot/Cubic Feet or Million Gallons per day		X			
Subsystem Evaluation		X	X		
Quantity Takeoff			X	X	X

Figure 7-1. Estimating Methods Used at Various Stages of Design. (Chart derived from Value Analysis in Design and Construction, O'Brien, James J. Copyright 1976. Used with permission of McGraw-Hill Book Company, New York, 1976)

or cubic feet. The costs are also grouped by functional systems and subsystems. Building types are grouped in functional areas by building subsystems. Costs are derived by using square footage costs extended by multiplying by spatial area to arrive at the total cost. To account for height, cubic footage costs are also used. Another category of costs is parameter cost. In the wastewater field cost per pound of BOD removed is a parameter cost. Parameter costs are frequently used in the process industry to describe costs for systems and unit operations. And finally unit costs are applied to quantity takeoffs. Unit costs are the cost of each piece of material and labor hour used in the project.

Cost estimates form the basis for cost models used in a VE study. Depending on the completion stage of a project, the organization of the cost estimate and the subsequent cost model will change. To show the likely variation we have organized costs into five orders of complexity. A wastewater project is used as an example of the complexity of costs.

1. *First order costs* represent the total cost of the facility. User units are the basis for first order cost estimates as they are gross estimates based on a quantified functional use. Costs per million gallons per day describe a total cost estimate.

2. *Second order costs* use a combination of system costs combined to compute the total cost. System costs of a wastewater project would be the liquid system, solids handling system and support systems.

3. *Third order costs* represent a further distribution of cost by subsystem. Costs for each unit process fall into this category. The liquid system of a wastewater facility might include preliminary treatment, primary clarification, activated sludge, final clarification and disinfection.

4. *Fourth order costs* are distributed by subsystems or components and by construction trade. Costs for a wastewater project would include sitework, concrete, structural steel, architectural, major equipment, miscellaneous metals, interior piping and valves, exterior piping and valves, HVAC, plumbing, electrical, and instrumentation and controls.

5. *Fifth order costs* are detailed estimates based on actual costs of material, labor, overhead, profit and any other cost needed to construct the project.

A VE team is likely to see several types of estimates depending on when the study is conducted. User units, spatial and parameter estimates will likely be used when studies are performed during the conceptual stage of the project. Emphasis on studying the total function of a project first corresponds readily to the use of these gross estimates. Studies conducted later in the design schedule depend more on unit prices as the study is likely to focus on component parts rather than the total system. Several cost models are included in this chapter to show system, subsystem and trade breakdown of costs.

COST MODELS

Categorizing costs into identifiable functional areas will aid the VE effort and start the search for high-cost areas. The cost model is the tool used to organize and distribute estimated costs into functional areas that can be easily defined and quantified. The purpose is to use past historical costs and the experience of team members to compare with the present design to ascertain those areas with abnormally high costs. As an example, costs for a building could be functionally distributed into sitework, structural, exterior closure, finishes, plumbing, HVAC, and electrical. Structural costs for the structural steel building are expressed in dollars per gross square foot. The cost is $12.00. Comparing other system costs showed that a concrete cast-in-place structure should cost about $10.00 per square foot. The cost differential represents an area of potential cost savings. Elements of the cost model should relate to a cost estimating system that can be organized easily into functional areas and trade breakdowns. Two types of cost models are used. One is a cost matrix that reflects costs by functional areas and by construction trades. Total costs or cost per unit may be used. The second cost model identifies functional areas within the project.

MATRIX COST MODEL

Figure 7-2 is a cost matrix for a wastewater treatment facility. Costs are organized by functional system and subsystem along the horizontal axis, and by construction trade or other component breakdown on the vertical axis. A matrix cost model is especially useful for process plant designs where there are more than one unit process and where a large complex of component parts is repeated throughout each unit process. Percentages are also calculated to find the high-cost areas of the design by unit processes and also by component parts. Over the course of some 50 VE studies on wastewater treatment plants, we have accumulated valuable information on the approximate percentages associated with each unit process and component part. Using this historical data, abnormal costs for a given type and size of plant can be determined and high-cost areas identified. The cost matrix can be readily understood and utilized by the designer to analyze cost per process function and cost per trade element (concrete, sitework, etc.). The worth of the project elements is estimated to account for what the project could be built for. Depending on the project, cost can be reflected with functional quantities. A wastewater project would reflect cost per million gallons of flow, a chemical plant might be expressed in cost per square foot or cost per cubic foot. In any case the costs should be organized so that one can equate the cost with an identifiable functional quantity.

FUNCTIONAL COST MODELS

The functional cost model breaks down the project costs by functional area. Costs used in the model include two types. The estimated construction cost or in the case of an existing building the actual cost and the target costs or worth. The worth or target cost is the VE team's estimate of the least cost to perform the function. Cost engineers are often assigned to the project to ensure that realistic costs are applied. Constructing the cost model and identifying the estimated costs is usually done prior to the VE workshop session. Identifying the project target costs is done jointly by team members. Past cost experience by team members, experience on previous similar jobs and cost references serve as the basis for projecting the worth of each area. The worth is the least cost to perform the required function. Projecting a worth on the various cost categories stimulates team members to devise alternative solutions to the original design. Eventually these alternatives become the ideas that form the basis of final recommendations.

Figure 7-3 and 7-4 are cost models for a building and a wastewater project. Differences between estimated costs and target costs are fertile ground for cost savings. Analysis of the building cost model indicates high-cost areas for the mechanical and architectural areas. The largest difference between estimated cost and the target cost (worth) are in the plumbing, HVAC and exterior closure. Team investigations are directed to these areas.

The cost model of the wastewater treatment plant (Figure 7-4) is for a covered facility constructed on an existing concrete platform. Costs are divided by unit process where possible. In the cases where several functions are included in one building, the cost of the total structure is used. The cost model indicates that the major costs of the plant by process are in secondary clarification, and by construction trade are concrete, electrical and heating,

COST MATRIX OF WWTP

No.	Description	Head Works	P. Clarifier	Aeration System	Secondary Clarifier	Disinfection	Effluent P.S.	Gravity Thick
1	Major Equipment	491,000	270,000	380,000	500,000	16,000	521,000	164,300
2	Concrete	378,600	819,000	1,958,000	1,481,000	526,000	209,000	92,400
3	Piles	44,000	213,000	-0-	-0-	-0-	-0-	-0-
4	Excav. & Backfill	12,200	73,200	132,000	211,000	53,000	21,000	7,700
5	Dewatering	50,000	140,000	175,000	180,000	55,000	40,000	30,000
6	Sitework	-0-	-0-	-0-	-0-	-0-	-0-	-0-
7	Inside Piping	31,900	7,800	205,000	12,000	1,000	410,000	54,200
8	Inner Unit Piping	-0-	-0-	-0-	-0-	-0-	-0-	-0-
9	Architectural	68,500	-0-	228,000	-0-	-0-	61,000	3,600
10	Gates, Weirs	22,800	80,000	194,000	55,000	21,000	-0-	9,800
11	Electrical	-0-	-0-	-0-	-0-	-0-	-0-	-0-
12	HVAC	-0-	-0-	-0-	-0-	-0-	-0-	-0-
13	Plumbing	-0-	-0-	-0-	-0-	-0-	-0-	-0-
14	Misc Equip.	-0-	-0-	-0-	-0-	-0-	-0-	-0-
	COST	1,099,000	1,603,000	3,272,000	2,439,000	672,000	1,762,000	362,000
	WORTH	1,019,000	1,603,000	3,000,000	2,240,000	600,000	856,000	360,000

Figure 7-2. Cost Model of a Wastewater Treatment Plant.

ventilating and air conditioning. The cost model also identified the high cost for covering the plant.

There are three models currently used in a value engineering study. The cost model just described organizes initial costs of construction, design and administration. Energy costs for operating the facility are identified in the energy model. The energy model and the cost model do not predict the total costs for owning and operating the facility. A project life-cycle model serves to account for all costs of ownership. Project cost models and energy models are prepared before the life-cycle costing model. An example of a life-cycle costing model is found in Chapter 8 and an example of an energy model in Chapter 9.

Models involving cost play an important part in the value engineering process. For this reason team members with a keen sensitivity to cost should be chosen. Up-to-date experience in local conditions including the availability of labor and materials help to augment the VE teams.

Flotation Thick	Digesters	Oper. Solids	Site Work	Site Piping	Misc. Items	Percent of Total	Totals
248,000	648,000	1,192,000	-0-	-0-	-0-	23.5	4,430,300
133,000	991,600	206,800	-0-	-0-	-0-	36.1	6,795,400
-0-	-0-	121,600	-0-	-0-	-0-	2.0	378,600
15,000	84,000	8,800	-0-	85,000	-0-	3.7	702,900
40,000	65,000	18,000	-0-	-0-	-0-	4.1	793,000
-0-	-0-	-0-	413,000	-0-	-0-	2.1	413,000
36,000	118,600	48,000	-0-	-0-	-0-	4.8	924,500
-0-	-0-	-0-	-0-	900,000	80,000	5.1	980,000
126,000	49,800	245,800	-0-	-0-	-0-	4.1	782,700
-0-	-0-	-0-	-0-	-0-	-0-	2.0	382,600
-0-	-0-	-0-	-0-	-0-	1,010,000	6.8	1,010,000
-0-	-0-	-0-	-0-	-0-	835,000	4.3	835,000
-0-	-0-	-0-	-0-	-0-	167,000	0.9	167,000
-0-	-0-	100,000	-0-	-0-	-0-	0.5	100,000
598,000	1,957,000	1,941,000	413,000	985,000	2,092,000	100.0	18,695,000
532,000	-0-	700,000	-0-	-0-	-0-		10,810,000
					Contingencies Bond, Ins.		200.00
					Total		$18,895,000

Figure 7-2. Cost Model of a Wastewater Treatment Plant.

USES OF PROJECT MODELS

Use of the cost, energy and life-cycle costing models is by no means restricted to value engineering. As value engineers, we encourage the use of these tools during the design process to control and manage costs. Rather than designing the project to completion before coming to grips with cost over-runs, why not budget realistic figures for functional areas within the project and design the project to the budget?

As value engineers, we are finding that owners are looking to consultants to come up with better ways to manage their money. The tools of cost, energy and life-cycle costing models are tools that can be used during the design process to manage cost.

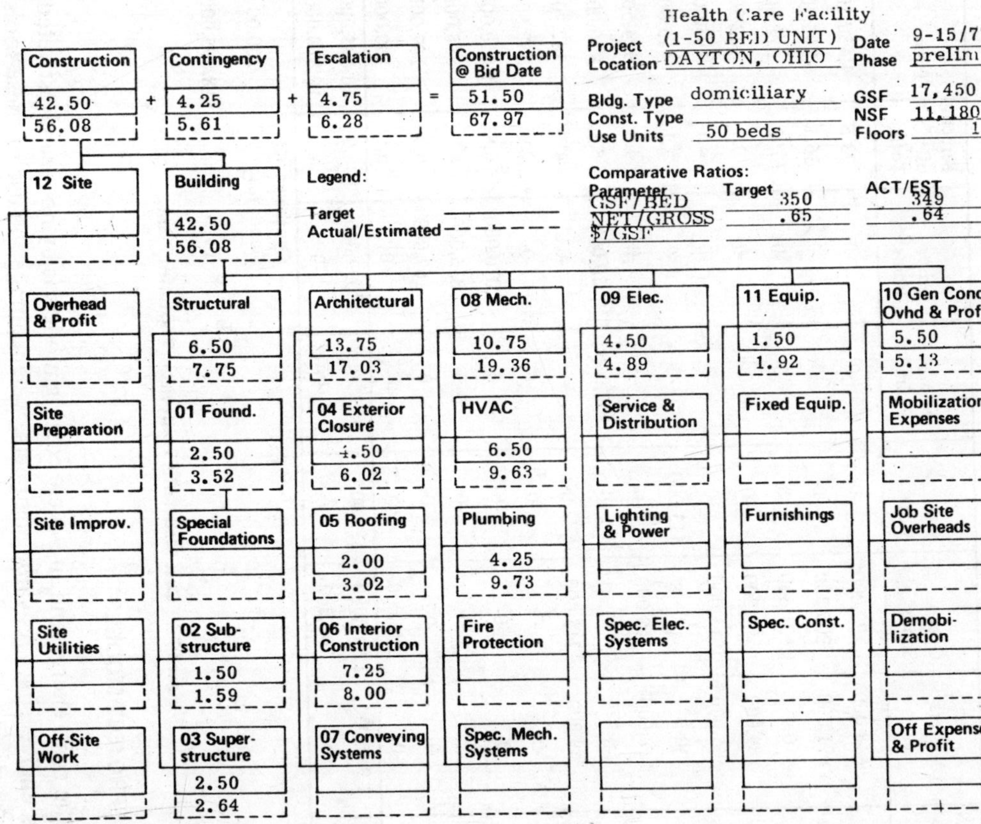

+ without connecting passageways
* program net area

Figure 7-3. Cost Model of a Health Care Facility. (Courtesy of Smith Hinchman and Grylls Associates, Inc.)

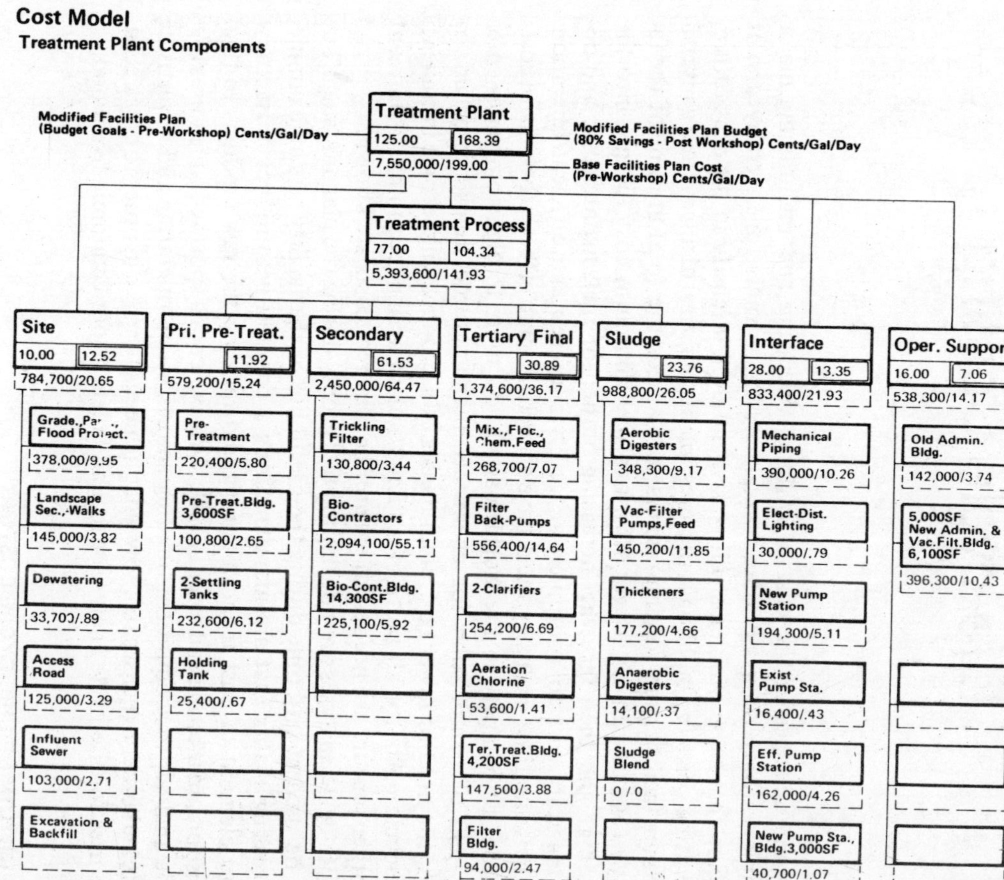

Figure 7-4. Cost Model of a Wastewater Treatment Plant. (Courtesy of Smith, Hinchman and Grylls Associates, Inc.)

8
Life-cycle Costing

Dynamic changes in the cost of owning, operating and maintaining major complexes have been a burden to planners and owners for several years. It appears that these problems will persist and even intensify in the near future. Operating costs for building structures, plant facilities, highways and a myriad of other facilities are forcing owners to plan for the total lifetime of the facility. Owners can no longer afford to pay minimum cost to "get into the building" and then face the increasing burden of fuel, maintenance and operating staff cost to continue the facility's upkeep and efficient operation. At the same time, industry must have a mechanism to effectively control costs in order to compete in the world market. As more foreign companies enter the field of competition for chemicals, manufactured items and other services, the need to lower cost of all phases of a product will become imminent. Life-cycle costs for all parts of a facility, plant design, economic investment or other venture are needed to ensure that the real costs are known.

Life-cycle analyses are not limited to use only during the planning stage, but can be used at any time during the useful life of the facility. As an example, processing plants that are manufacturing a competitive product must know every element of cost from obtaining and refining the raw products to final transport, marketing and eventual sale. An owner of a sports complex uses life-cycle analysis to account for building amortization, operating and advertising costs and other expenses to know what he needs to make in order to break even. The uses for life-cycle analysis affect all facets of our economic livelihood.

DEFINITION OF LIFE-CYCLE COSTING

There are many definitions of life-cycle costing that are in vogue. *The American Institute of Architects—Life Cycle Cost Analysis Workbook No. 2* defines life-cycle costing as follows:

> Any technique which allows assessment of a given solution, or choice among solutions, on the basis of considering all relevant economic consequences over a given period of time (or life cycle).*

---

*David S. Haviland, *Life Cycle Cost Analysis—Using It in Practice*, Washington, D. C., American Institute of Architects, 1978.

Smith, Hinchman and Grylls Associates in their *Life Cycle Costing Workbook* defines life-cycle costing in a similar manner.

> Life Cycle Costing–An economic assessment of competing design alternatives expressed in equivalent dollars.

The definition could be expanded slightly to broaden the use of life-cycle costing into all facets of our every day economic life. It can be used as a tool to make economic assessments and comparisons at any point in time.

> Life cycle costing is the total economic cost of owning and operating a facility, manufactured process or product. The life cycle costing analysis reflects present and future costs of the project over its useful life. It allows an assessment of a given solution and it is a tool for making comparisons.

The underriding theme is that life-cycle costing is a unversal tool to express the multifaceted elements of cost and time in a uniform criteria of equivalent dollars.

PURPOSE AND IMPLICATIONS OF LIFE-CYCLE COSTING

Use of the life-cycle costing technique has a broad range of applications. In the analysis of facilities, it can be applied during the conceptual, planning, design, construction and operating stages for a facility or product. Its application as an aid for analyzing economic alternatives for purchases at home and in the marketplace has been used by all of us. With the drastic rises in the interest rates and rising inflation, the use of life-cycle costing has been expanded. The impacts are astounding as will be seen later in this chapter. Before explaining the applications of life-cycle costing, facts about its application need to be addressed.

While LCC provides an excellent tool for decision making, its application should be understood to avoid possible pitfalls in its use. Fiscal managers especially should know the facts as LCC dollars may not be the same as budget dollars. One of the problems is that cost estimates may not be applicable as budget estimates because they are expressed in constant dollars (excluding inflation) and all cash-flow dollars are converted to equivalent monies at a common point in time. LCC estimates are not necessarily equivalent to the obligated amounts for each funding year.*

While LCC provides an excellent tool to assist in decision making, the analysis of results is based solely on economic factors. The estimates are only as good as the background data forming the basis for costs. Final analysis should account for noneconomic criteria that have intrinsic benefits that do not lend themselves to finite cost evaluations. Factors such as safety, reliability, operability, environmental factors, to name a few, may be more important

---

**Life Cycle Costing* National Bureau of Standards–Building Science Series 113, p. 3.

than monetary savings. The final decision on abstract factors relies heavily on judgment. Each set of circumstances is different and the criteria for analysis varies with project complexity. The most useful advice is to obtain as much background information as possible and make your analysis thorough and objective.

Criteria for making life-cycle analyses include many areas that force decisions using *soft* numbers such as future energy costs, system efficiencies, annual operating and maintenance costs, long-term cost of money, salvage values and expected life of equipment. Forcing decisions on soft numbers creates a margin of error inherent in the LCC process. However, the order of magnitude of the cost comparison makes life-cycle costing a worthwhile tool. It is the best tool available for computing order of magnitude comparisons.

ECONOMIC PRINCIPLES USED IN LIFE-CYCLE COSTING

Costs reflected on a time basis help us to get a clearer picture of the differences between expenditures made at the present time and the equivalent value of that money at some future date. Economic formulas are the mechanism used to equate the factors of time, interest, present costs, future costs and annual costs. The effects of escalation may also be equated.

The term commonly used for applying mathematical formulas to economic principles is *discounting*. Application of these formulas helps to equate costs at different time frames and at differing discount (interest) rates. Discounting is the method used to express costs at any given time on an equivalent basis. A good example of discounting is in two alternatives for equipment selection. Alternative A is a $14,000 expenditure for equipment to last 20 years. Alternative B is for one piece of equipment today at $10,000 and an additional expenditure of $10,000 10 years from now. Using a 10 percent discount rate, we would need to place $3,855 into the bank to meet the $10,000 expenditure in 10 years. The present worth of Alternative B is ($10,000 + $3,855).

Formulas for discounting analysis are for single payment and uniform payments. Single payments are one-time expenditures and uniform payments are for equal payments over a given time frame. (Formulas and diagrams were based on information taken from the *Life Cycle Cost Analysis–A Guide for Architects** published by the American Institute of Architects.) Figure 8-1 graphically explains the formulas used for discounting.

ACCOUNTING FOR ESCALATION

With escalating costs of petroleum products, there is a need to establish a more accurate picture of the actual economic perspective of comparison decision making. When evaluating uniform annual payments, the assump-

---

**Life Cycle Cost Analysis–A Guide for Architects*, Washington, D. C., The American Institute of Architects, 1977.

DISCOUNTING FORMULAS

SINGLE COMPOUND AMOUNT (SCA)
Given P (present worth)
Find F (future worth)
$F = P(1 + i)^n = P(SCA)$

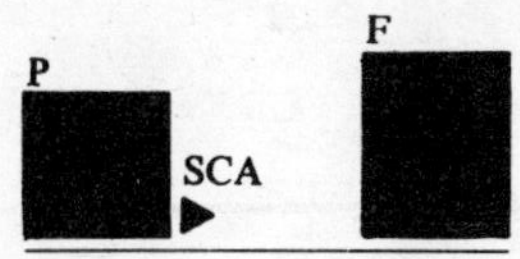

$1000 is placed in an account earning 10% annual interest compounded annually. How much is it worth in 5 years?
The SCA factor for 10% and 5 years is 1.611.
F = P X SCA, or $1,000 X 1.611, or $1,611.

SINGLE PRESENT WORTH (SPW)
Given F (future worth)
Find P (present worth)
$P = F(1 + i)^{-n} = F(SPW)$

$20,000 is needed for your daughter's education 15 years from now. You are willing to make a single deposit in an account which earns 10% annual interest compounded annually, and to let it grow. What do you deposit?
The SPW factor for 10% and 15 years is .2394.
P = F X SPW, or $20,000 X .2394, or $4,788.

UNIFORM PRESENT WORTH (UPW)
Given A (a uniform annual payment)
Find P (the present worth of all these payments)

$$P = A\left[\frac{(1 + i)^n - 1}{1(1 + i)^n}\right] = A(UPW)$$

Starting this year you will be obligated to pay your son's college $4,000 a year for 4 years. What single present sum of money should you deposit in an account paying 10% annual interest compounded annually in order to have enough money for the payments?
The UPW factor for 10% and 4 years is 3.170.
P = A X UPW, or $4,000 X 3.170, or $12,680.

Figure 8-1. Time Value for Money-Discounting Formulas. (Chart Derived from Life Cycle Cost Analysis—A Guide for Architects, Reprinted with permission of the American Institute of Architects) Further reproduction in part or in whole is not authorized.

UNIFORM CAPITAL RECOVERY (UCR)
Given P (the present worth of a series of annual payments)
Find A (value of those annual payments)

$$A = P\left[\frac{i(1+i)^n}{(1+i)^n - 1}\right] = P\,(UCR)$$

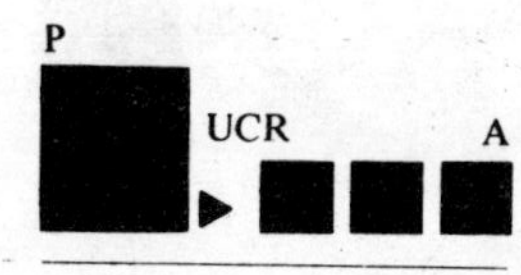

You take out a \$30,000 mortgage at 10% annual interest, compounded annually, for 25 years. What is the constant annual payment required to repay the loan?
The UCR factor for 10% and 25 years is .1102.
A = P X UCR, or \$30,000 X .1102, or \$3,306.

UNIFORM COMPOUND AMOUNT (UCA)
Given A (a uniform annual payment)
Find F (the future worth of all these payments)

$$F = A\left[\frac{(1+i)^n - 1}{i}\right] = A\,(UCA)$$

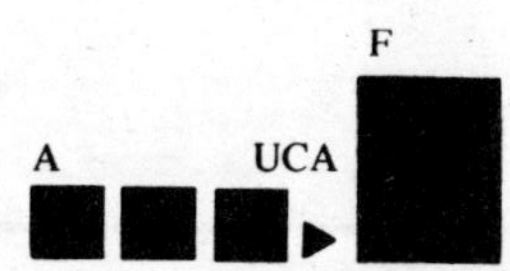

You set up a savings account and plan to add \$1,000 a year for the next 5 years. If the account pays 10% annual interest compounded annually, how much do you have after 5 years?
The UCA factor for 10% and 5 years is 6.105.
F = A X UCA, or \$1,000 X 6.105, or \$6,105.

UNIFORM SINKING FUND (USF)
Given F (the future worth of a series of annual payments)
Find A (value of those annual payments)

$$A = F\left[\frac{i}{(1+i)^n - 1}\right]$$

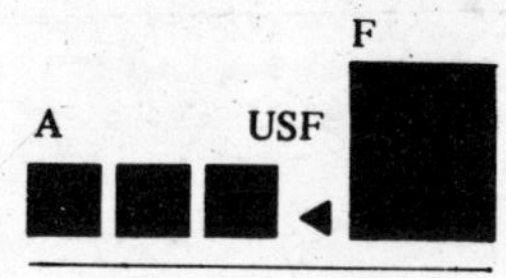

Back to your daughter and her school plans. If you want to have $20,000 for education costs 15 years from now, and cannot afford the single present payment calculated above, what uniform annual payment would you have to make for each of 15 years into an account paying 10% annual interest compounded annually to get $20,000?
The USF factor for 10% and 15 years is .0315.
A = F X USF, or $20,000 X .0315, or $630.

LEGEND

P = Present Worth
F = Future Worth
A = End of Year Uniform Annual Payment
i = discount rate
n = number of interest periods
e = excalation rate

* Many economics books use a different nomenclature for economic factors. The comparison nomenclature is shown for clarity.

	Other Terminology
SCA - Single Compound Amount	caf - compound amount factor
SPW - Single Present Worth	pwf - present worth factor
UPW - Uniform Present Worth	pwf^1 - present worth uniform payment
UCR - Uniform Capital Recovery	crf - capital recovery factor
UCA - Uniform Compound Amount	caf^1 - compound amount factor uniform payment
USF - Uniform Sinking Fund	sff^1 - sinking fund

Figure 8-1. Time Value for Money-Discounting Formulas. (Chart Derived from Life Cycle Cost Analysis—A Guide for Architects. Reprinted with permission of the American Institute of Architects) Further reproduction in part or in whole is not authorized. (*Continued*)

tion is that the annual expenditures will be uniform. It does not account for rising labor rates, fuel costs or unusual costs of other commodities. Figure 8-2 gives an indication of the impact of energy cost escalation depicting past history as well as trends for the future. Note the gap between inflation and escalation. To account for escalation, the following formula is applied:

$$P = A\,\frac{\left[\dfrac{1+e}{1+i}\right]\left[\left(\dfrac{1+e}{1+i}\right)^{n} - i\right]}{\left(\dfrac{1+e}{1+i}\right) - 1}$$

e = escalation rate
i = interest
n = years

TYPES OF LIFE-CYCLE COSTS

Cost categories to be used in a life-cycle cost analysis encompass a broad area. Monies for a project may be spent from the time frame of years leading up

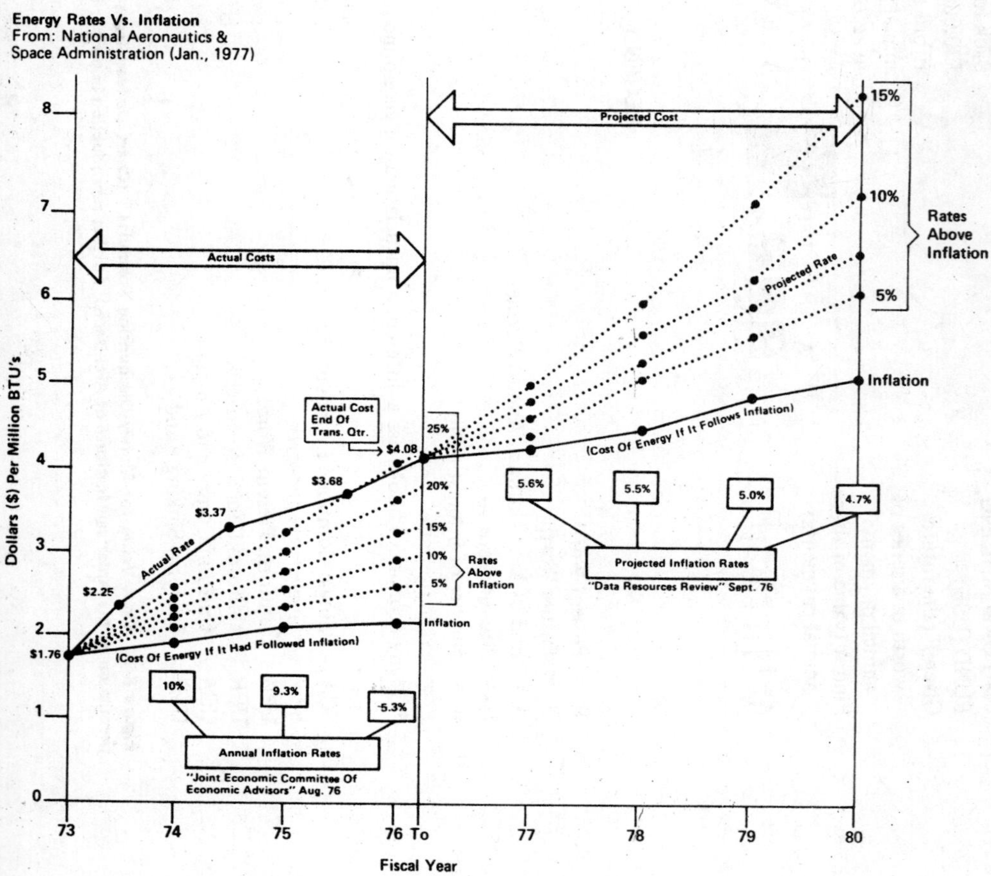

Figure 8-2. Energy Rates Vs. Inflation (From NASA, January 1977).

to the completion of an actual facility to the time when the facility has outlived its usefulness and must be disposed of. Table 8-1 includes a listing of costs that might factor into a total facility's life. This is not to say that these are all of the costs involved. However, it serves as a reminder of the major cost factors to look for when performing life-cycle comparisons.

1. **Investment Costs.** The amount of money expended for assessment of market potential, for time and expenses involved in analyzing site alternatives and expenses incurred for development of a financial plan. Investment costs may also include expenses for obtaining a line of credit and other financing alternatives. Preparation of stock and bond sales may be another type of investment cost.

2. **Land Acquisition Costs.** Costs for realty fees, title searches, legal fees, deed filing fees, insurances, cost of land and the interest on borrowed money for the purchase or leasing of land for use for a facility.

3. **Engineering Costs (Planning, Design and Construction Inspection).** Costs associated with the planning, design, bidding, construction, inspection and initial start-up of the facility. Any anticipated future costs for design modifications should also be included.

4. **Redesign Costs.** The cost of modifications to the original plans and specifications to accommodate value engineering changes. Often included in the redesign costs are any costs from delay in completion of the project directly attributed to making VE modifications.

5. **Construction Costs.** The cost of constructing the building or facility.

Table 8-1. Types of Life-cycle Costs.

1. Investment Cost
2. Land Acquisition Costs
3. Engineering Costs (Planning, Design and Construction Inspection)
4. Redesign Costs
5. Construction Costs
6. Administrative Costs
7. Replacement Costs
8. Salvage Costs
9. Operating Costs
    - Staffing
    - Fuel
    - Electricity/Demand Charge
    - Chemicals and Supplies
    - Operating Schedule
    - Outside Services
    - Resource Recovery
    - Transportation
10. Maintenance Costs
    - Lubricants/Parts
    - Staffing/Labor
    - Preventive Maintenance
    - Cleaning
    - Durability of Products
11. Time Cost of Money

6. **Administrative Fees (Legal and Administrative).** Generally the cost of managing and coordinating the project. Included are the owner and administrative staff that does the planning, contracting, personnel recruitment, staffing, marketing and the legal costs associated with the project.

7. **Replacement Costs.** Future costs to modify or replace a portion of the project. Usually the equipment is the major source of replacement costs. Based on the expected life of the equipment, several replacements may occur during the total project life. Painting and other maintenance requirements may also fall in this category.

8. **Salvage Value.** The value of the project or product at some future time. Usually salvage value is the amount received from the sale at the end of the life-cycle period.

9. **Operating Costs.** Costs required to operate the facility. These costs are the day-to-day costs of staffing; energy costs to create and maintain a working environment and to operate equipment; costs of outside services such as waste disposal, water and sewage costs; chemicals and other resources needed to manufacture or to process a product; and the costs of transportation from the source of raw materials to the final delivery point. These costs are often periodic costs falling at scheduled intervals.

A. **Staffing.** Costs of salary and fringe benefits of personnel required to operate the facility or system.

B. **Fuel.** Cost of gas, oil, wood or other fuel sources used as a part of the process for system operation or to create a comfortable environment. It also accounts for fuels required for operating equipment or unit processes. In life-cycle cost analysis, fuel and labor costs are often escalated to account for escalation and/or inflation.

C. **Electricity/Demand Charges.** The cost of electricity to operate equipment, lighting, and to provide heat. Note that costs for heating, cooling and ventilation (HVAC) are part of electricity for operating HVAC equipment. Demand charges are a multiplier that is applied to electrical bills. The multiplier is based on the peak electricity demand at a given time related to normal usage. If a user has a single high-use day, the entire electrical usage will be multiplied by the demand charge. In many cases, the demand charge can drastically increase electrical rates.

D. **Chemicals and Supplies.** The costs of materials required to keep the system or building functional. Chemicals, paper products and cleaning supplies are but a few of the examples.

E. **Operating Schedule.** The mode of operation of a system affects the cost of operation. As an example, a processing plant has five presses that operate 8 hours per day. An alternative might be to have three presses and operate the system 16 hours per day with one unit as a standby.

F. **Outside Services.** Cleaning services, refuse disposal, maintenance contracts, etc., are examples of outside services.

G. **Resource Recovery**. In many cases the raw product that is being processed has specific properties that may result in a cost savings. As an example, sewage sludge has a heat value (in methane gas) formed in the anaerobic system that can be recovered and used to operate equipment.

H. **Transportation.** When analyzing alternatives the differences in transportation modes and haul distances should be evaluated. Transportation costs, especially in the processing industry, are significant and often go unnoticed.

10. Maintenance Costs. Factors included in maintenance costs would include labor, cost of parts, materials, cleaning materials and equipment, and preventive maintenance. Also included are normal maintenance and repair of equipment, painting, etc.

11. **Time and the Cost of Money**. Time has a high price tag when evaluating alternatives. The longevity of a project and the life-span of individual components must be considered in the decision-making process. Cost of money is the interest that is charged on borrowed money for the project.

Elements of cost in a life-cycle cost analysis are for the total facility life. Some costs are one time expenditures that occur before the project is built. Others are single expenditures that are amortized for periods up to and beyond the useful life of the facility. The elements of cost and the span of time that they occur are illustrated in Figure 8-3.

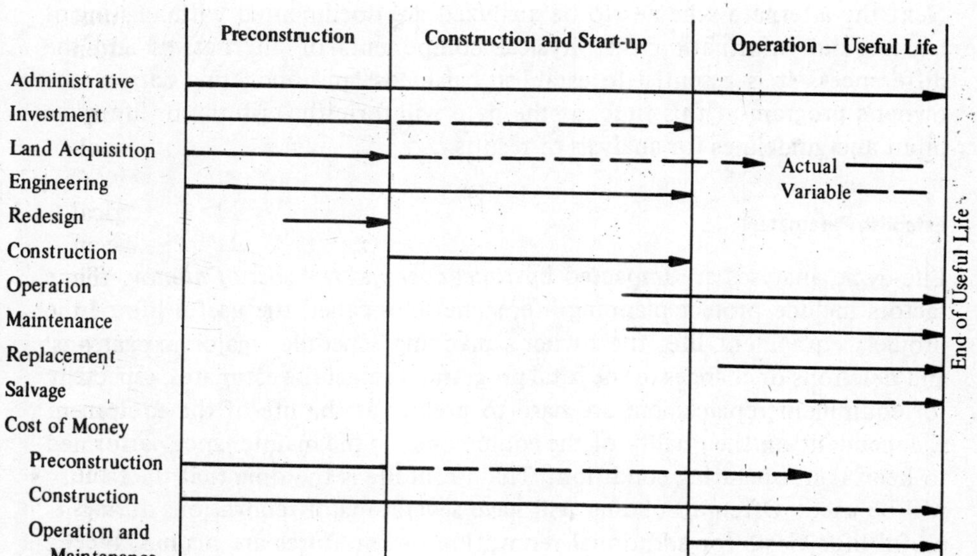

Figure 8-3. Time Frame of Life Cycle Cost Occurrences.

USING LIFE-CYCLE COSTING AS A TOOL

Using life-cycle costing will aid your decision-making process and increase the sensitivity to cost for operating facilities. Life-cycle costing is actually a series of computations applying economic factors to monetary expenditures. The validity of the comparison like all estimates is dependent on the quality of the cost estimates used in the analysis. There is no good substitute for sound cost figures. Therefore, before proceeding with a life-cycle analysis be certain of the quantity and the validity of cost parameters to be sure of the accuracy of the results.

Figure 8-4 outlines the life-cycle costing approach and the types of data needed to perform the analysis. It may be used as a format and checklist when applying life-cycle costing.

Problem Statement

As life-cycle costing can be used as a decision-making tool, its first step involves identification of the problem to be solved. A problem statement will help to focus on the basis of the comparison. A description of the physical facilities and the alternatives to be compared should be defined thoroughly. Before going further into the analysis, check to see if your objectives will be met by the comparisons and the cost parameters in the analysis.

Establish Alternates

Next the alternate schemes to be analyzed are documented with a listing of background information on physical components of alternatives and the differences. It is essential to establish basic cost and budgeting data of the owner's program at this time, as the data will form the criteria for life-cycle input and guidelines for analysis of results.

Establish Parameters

Life-cycle analyses are impacted by *time, cost and the cost of money.* Time factors include project planning life, sometimes called the useful life of the project; equipment life; the owner's planning schedule; major expansions; and deletions or changes to the total program. Project life estimates, especially for equipment replacement are hard to predict as the life of the equipment is dependent on the quality of the equipment and the maintenance performed to keep it in operating condition. The useful life is the time that the facility will be used. Often a building will have several major renovations during its useful life. Costs for additional renovation expenditures are planned by the owner and are usually included in life-cycle comparisons. Cost parameters have been outlined previously. Major impacts are being felt by owners from escalating energy, labor and maintenance costs above the normal inflation rates. These fluctuations in cost are accounted for by use of escalation rates.

Problem Statement	Establish Alternates	Establish Parameters	Economic Analysis	Analyze Results
Description of Total Project Identify Alternates Rationale For Alternative Selection Description Of Original And Proposed Alternates Objectives To Be Met	Physical Description Of Alternatives Cost Factors Used In The Analysis Useful Life Of Facility Source Of Background Information Cost Background Information	Time Basis • Planning Period • Economic Life Of Major Assets • Equipment Life Cost Parameters • Investment Cost • Land Acquisition • Engineering • Redesign • Construction • Administration • Replacement • Salvage • Operation • Maintenance Cost of Money • Interest Rate • Escalation Rates • Tax Benefits • Penalty for Early Payments • Inflation Rates	Point Of Time For Projecting Cost Estimate All Costs Project Future Costs Select Present Worth Or Annualized Cost Basis For Study Convert Cost Using Economic Formulas Construct LCC Model	Compare Cost Results Determine Sensitivity of Results Check Cost Validity Consider Non-Economic Criteria

Figure 8-4. Life Cycle Costing Approach. Steps in conducting a life cycle analysis.

The cost of money is taken into account by setting interest, inflation, and escalation rates. Monetary loans for financing and tax benefits are part of the analysis.

Economic Analysis

Figure 8-5 is a list of data to be used in a life-cycle cost analysis. It includes many of the parameters just described and other criteria used in a study of a building. Figures 8-6 through 8-12 are used as a checklist for life-cycle cost comparisons on building structures. They can be used when accounting for all the costs associated with a building structure. Worksheets for structural, exterior closure, interior construction, mechanical and electrical equipment, and sitework are used as they closely follow the method of estimating used by designers. A summary of life-cycle expenditures for the total project is summarized on the worksheet in Figure 8-13. The graphical solution for computed life-cycle data is compiled in the life-cycle cost model, in addition to showing costs of the existing system and allowing for targeting of cost-reduction potentials. (This data provided courtesy of Smith Hinchman & Grylls Associates.)

To illustrate the application of life-cycle costing an example for a wastewater treatment plant is shown in Figure 8-14. The model illustrates the magnitude of construction costs that must be absorbed throughout the life of the project.

Data Required For Life-Cycle Cost Estimating

Type	Variable Symbol	Nomenclature	Units Of Measure	Reference	Design Quantities Original	Alternative 1	Alternative 2	Alternative 3
Economic	AA	Building Economic Life	Years	R-2				
	AB	Project Discount Rate	% Of Cost	R-2				
	AC	Escalation Rate/Yr.–Labor & Materials	% Of Cost	R-2				
	AD	Escalation Rate/Yr.–Heating Fuel	% Of Cost	R-2				
	AE	Escalation Rate/Yr.–Cooling Fuel	% Of Cost	R-2				
	AF	Escalation Rate/Yr.–Lighting Fuel	% Of Cost	R-2				
	AG	Escalation Rate/Yr.–Domestic Hot Water Fuel	% Of Cost	R-2				
	AH	Escalation Rate/Yr.– Maintenance	% Of Cost	R-2				
	AI	Escalation Rate/Yr – Associated Costs	% Of Cost	R-2				
Facility	BA	Gross Area Of Building	Sq. Ft.	Sketch				
	BB	Normal Building Population	Each	Project				
	BC	Required Lighting/Year	Hours	Project				
	BD	Average Amount Of Lighting Power Required Over Floor Area	Watt/Sq. Ft.	R-5				
	BE	Domestic Hot Water Boiler Energy Required/Gallon Heated	BTU/Gal.	Manuf.				
	BF	Domestic Hot Water Usage/ Year	Days	Project				
	BG	Daily Hot Water Gallons/ Person	Gallon	R-6				
	BH	Estimated Hourly Heating Load	BTU/HR	ASHRAE				
	BI	Estimated Hourly Cooling Load	BTU/HR	ASHRAE				
	BJ	Air Conditioning Power Per Design Ton	KW	R-7				
Site & Climatic	CA	Area Design Cost Factor	N/A	R-8				
	CB	Fuel Costs – Heating	$/Million BTU	R-8				
	CC	Fuel Costs – Cooling	$/KWh	R-8				
	CD	Fuel Costs – Domestic Hot Water	$/Million BTU	R-8				
	CE	Fuel Costs – Lighting	$/KWh	R-8				
	CF	Equiv. Full Load Hrs. A.C. Equip. Per Year	Hr.	R-8				
	CG	Heating Degree Days	Day °F	R-8				
	CH	Summer Inside Design Temperature	°F	R-8				
	CI	Winter Inside Design Temperature	°F	R-8				
	CJ	Summer Outside Design Temperature	°F	R-8				
	CK	Winter Outside Design Temperature	°F	R-8				

Figure 8-5. Data Required for a Life Cycle Cost Estimate.

Structural Life-Cycle Cost Estimate
(Foundations, Substructure, Superstructure)

		Original		Alternative 1		Alternative 2		Alternative 3	
		Estimated Costs	Present Worth	Estimated Costs	Present Worth	Estimated Costs	Present Worth	Estimated Costs	Present Worth
Initial Costs	**Element** (See Reference R-1)		1						
	01 Foundations								
	011 Standard Foundations								
	012 Special Foundations								
	02 Substructure								
	021 Slab On Grade								
	022 Basement Excavation								
	023 Basement Walls								
	03 Superstructure								
	031 Floor Construction								
	032 Roof Construction								
	033 Stair Construction								
	Total Initial Cost								
Maintenance Costs	**Annual Costs @____% Discount Rate**		2						
	Escal. Rate____% PWA (With Escal.) Factor								
	01 Foundations								
	A. Inspection								
	B. Routine Repair, Moistureproofing, Resealing								
	C.								
	02 Substructure								
	A. Inspection								
	B. Routine Repair, Moistureproofing, Resealing								
	C. Painting, Touch-up, Routine Refinishing								
	D.								
	03 Superstructure								
	A. Inspection								
	B. Cleaning & Sweeping Of Flrs., Strs. (If No Arch. Fin.)								
	C. Painting, Touch-up, Routine Finishing								
	D.								
	Total Annual Maintenance Costs								
Replacement Costs	**Single Expenditures @____% Discount Rate**		3						
	Item Replaced: / Year: / PW Factor:								
	A.								
	B.								
	C.								
	D.								
	Total Replacement Costs								
Associated Costs	**Annual Costs @____% Discount Rate**		2						
	Escal. Rate____% PWA (With Escal.) Factor								
	A.								
	B.								
	C.								
	Total Annual Associated Costs								
Salvage Value	**Final Value @____Year PW Factor**		4						
	01 Foundations								
	02 Substructure								
	03 Superstructure								
	Total Salvage Value								
LCC	**Total Present Worth Costs**								

PW – Present Worth **PWA – Present Worth Of Annuity**

Figure 8-6. Structural Life Cycle Cost Estimate Worksheet.

Architectural Life-Cycle Cost Estimate
Part I (Exterior Closure, Roofing)

		Original		Alternative 1		Alternative 2		Alternative 3	
		Estimated Costs	Present Worth	Estimated Costs	Present Worth	Estimated Costs	Present Worth	Estimated Costs	Present Worth
Initial Costs	Element (See Reference R-1)		1						
	04 Exterior Closure								
	041 Exterior Walls								
	042 Exterior Doors And Windows								
	05 Roofing								
	0501 Roof Coverings								
	0502 Traffic Toppings & Paving Membranes								
	0503 Roof Insulation & Fill								
	0504 Flashings & Trim								
	0505 Roof Openings								
	Total Initial Cost								
Maintenance Costs	Annual Costs @____% Discount Rate		2						
	Escal. Rate____% PWA (With Escal.) Factor____								
	04 Exterior Closure								
	A. Cleaning Windows, Spandrels								
	B. Routine Erection Of Screens, Awnings								
	C. Touch-Up, Resealing, Routine Refinishing								
	D. Routine Replacement Of Glazing, Panels								
	E.								
	05 Roof								
	A. Inspection								
	B. Routine Maintenance Of Roof Surface								
	C. Cleaning Gutters, Drains								
	D. Resealing, Skylight Repairs								
	E. Parapet Repointing								
	F.								
	Total Annual Maintenance Costs								
Replacement Costs	Single Expenditures @____% Discount Rate		3						
	Item Replaced: / Year: / PW Factor:								
	A. Exterior Restoration								
	B. Exterior Painting								
	C. Roof Covering								
	D. Painting, Reflashing								
	E.								
	F.								
	Total Replacement Costs								
Associated Costs	Annual Costs @____% Discount Rate		2						
	Escal. Rate____% PWA (With Escal.) Factor____								
	A.								
	B.								
	C.								
	Total Annual Associated Costs								
Salvage Value	Final Value @____Year PW Factor____		4						
	04 Exterior Closure								
	05 Roof								
	Total Salvage Value								
LCC	Total Present Worth Costs								

W – Present Worth PWA – Present Worth Of Annuity

Figure 8-7. Architectural Life Cycle Cost Estimate Worksheet. (Exterior Closure, Roofing.)

Architectural Life-Cycle Cost Estimate
Part II (Interior Construction, Conveying Systems)

		Original		Alternative 1		Alternative 2		Alternative 3	
		Estimated Costs	Present Worth	Estimated Costs	Present Worth	Estimated Costs	Present Worth	Estimated Costs	Present Worth
Initial Costs	Element (See Reference R-1)		1						
	06 Interior Construction								
	061 Partitions								
	062 Interior Finishes								
	063 Specialties								
	07 Conveying Systems								
	0701 Elevators								
	0702 Moving Stair & Walks								
	0703 Dumbwaiters								
	0704 Pneumatic Tube Systems								
	Total Initial Cost								
Operation Costs	**Annual Costs @____% Discount Rate**		2						
	Escal. Rate____% PWA (With Escal.) Factor								
	A. Salaries (Operation, Etc.)								
	B. Elevator Energy Cost								
	C. Moving Stairs & Walks Energy Cost								
	D. Dumbwaiter Energy Cost								
	E. Pneumatic Tube System Energy Cost								
	F.								
	G.								
	Total Annual Operation Costs								
Maintenance Costs	**Annual Costs @____% Discount Rate**		2						
	Escal. Rate____% PWA (With Escal.) Factor								
	06 Interior Construction								
	A. Cleaning & Dusting Partitions, Chalkboards								
	B. Maintenance Of Operable Partitions								
	C. Carpet Cleaning, Sweeping								
	D. Tile. etc., Floor Cleaning & Sweeping								
	E. Stair Cleaning (If No Arch. Finish, Use Struc. Form Plan)								
	F.								
	07 Conveying Systems								
	A. Preventative Maintenance, Inspection								
	B. Routine Cleaning								
	C. Repair, Adjustment								
	D.								
	E.								
	Total Annual Maintenance Costs								
Replacement Costs	**Single Expenditures @____% Discount Rate**		3						
	Item Replaced: / Year: / PW Factor:								
	A. Motors, Lifts								
	B.								
	C.								
	D.								
	Total Replacement Costs								
Associated Costs	**Annual Costs @____% Discount Rate**		2						
	Escal. Rate____% PWA (With Escal.) Factor								
	A.								
	B.								
	C.								
	Total Annual Associated Costs								
Salvage Value	**Final Value @____Year PW Factor**		4						
	06 Interior Construction								
	07 Conveying Systems								
	Total Salvage Value								
LCC	**Total Present Worth Costs**								

PW – Present Worth PWA – Present Worth Of Annuity

Figure 8-8. Architectural Life Cycle Cost Estimate Worksheet. (Interior Construction, Conveying Systems)

Mechanical Life Cycle Costing Estimate

		Original		Alternative 1		Alternative 2		Alternative 3	
		Estimated Costs	Present Worth	Estimated Costs	Present Worth	Estimated Costs	Present Worth	Estimated Costs	Present Worth
Initial Costs	Element (See Reference R-1)		1						
	08 Mechanical Systems								
	081 Plumbing								
	082 Heating, Ventilation, & Air Conditioning								
	083 Fire Protection								
	084 Special Mechanical Systems								
	______								
	Total Initial Cost								
Operation Costs	Annual Costs @____% Discount Rate		2						
	Escal. Rate____% PWA (With Escal.) Factor								
	A. Salaries (Operation, Etc.)								
	B. Domestic Hot Water Energy Cost		5						
	C. Heating Energy Cost		6						
	D. Ventilation Energy Cost								
	E. Air Conditioning Energy Cost		7						
	F. Pumps, Motors, Etc. Energy Cost								
	G. Fire Protection Energy Cost								
	H. ______								
	I. ______								
	Total Annual Operation Costs								
Maintenance Costs	Annual Costs @____% Discount Rate		2						
	Escal. Rate____% PWA (With Escal.) Factor								
	08 Mechanical Systems								
	A. Plumbing & Sewage Cleanout/Repair								
	B. Domestic H.W. System Repair, Adjust.								
	C. HVAC Preventative Inspection, Testing								
	D. Routine Cleaning: Ducts, Plenums								
	E. Routine Cleaning: Boilers, Controls								
	F. Repair Heating System								
	G. Repair Ventilation System								
	H. Repair Air Conditioning System								
	I. Adjust Controls & Instrumentation								
	J. Routine Replace Filters, Insulation								
	K. HVAC System Balancing								
	L. Fire Protection System Cleaning								
	M. Fire Protection System Repair								
	N. ______								
	O. ______								
	Total Annual Maintenance Costs								
Replacement Costs	Single Expenditures @____% Discount Rate		3						
	Item Replaced: / Year: / PW Factor:								
	A. H.W. Boiler								
	B. Pumps, Motors								
	C. Control System								
	D. ______								
	E. ______								
	F. ______								
	Total Replacement Costs								
	Annual Costs @____% Discount Rate								
	Escal. Rate____% PWA (With Escal.) Factor								
	A. ______								
	B. ______								
	Total Annual Associated Costs								
Salvage Value	Final Value @____Year PW Factor		4						
	08 Mechanical System								
	Total Salvage Value								
LCC	Total Present Worth Costs								

PW – Present Worth PWA – Present Worth Of Annuity

Figure 8-9. Mechanical Life Cycle Costing Estimate Worksheet.

Electrical Life Cycle Costing Estimate

		Original		Alternative 1		Alternative 2		Alternative 3	
		Estimated Costs	Present Worth	Estimated Costs	Present Worth	Estimated Costs	Present Worth	Estimated Costs	Present Worth
Initial Costs	Element (See Reference R-1)		1						
	09 Electrical								
	091 Service & Distribution								
	092 Lighting & Power								
	093 Special Electrical System								
	Total Initial Cost								
Operation Costs	Annual Costs @____% Discount Rate		2						
	Escal. Rate____% PWA (With Escal.) Factor								
	A. Salaries (Operation, Etc.)								
	B. Lighting Energy Cost		8						
	C. Communications/Alarm Energy Cost								
	D. Emergency Light/Power Energy Cost								
	E. Electric Heating Energy Cost								
	F.								
	G.								
	Total Annual Operation Costs								
Maintenance Costs	Annual Costs @____% Discount Rate		2						
	Escal. Rate____% PWA (With Escal.) Factor								
	A. Inspection, Testing, & Maint. Of Safety								
	B. Relamping And Routine Replacement								
	C. Repair Communications/Alarm System								
	D. Repair Electric Heating System								
	E.								
	F.								
	Total Annual Maintenance Costs								
Replacement Costs	Single Expenditures @____% Discount Rate		3						
	Item Replaced: | Year: | PW Factor:								
	A. Distribution System								
	B. Lighting System								
	C. Commun./Alarm								
	D. Emergency Generator								
	E. Elec. Heat Equip.								
	F.								
	G.								
	H.								
	Total Replacement Costs								
Associated Costs	Annual Costs @____% Discount Rate		2						
	Escal. Rate____% PWA (With Escal.) Factor								
	A.								
	B.								
	C.								
	Total Annual Associated Costs								
Salvage Value	Final Value @____Year PW Factor		4						
	09 Electrical								
	Total Salvage Value								
LCC	Total Present Worth Costs								

PW – Present Worth PWA – Present Worth Of Annuity

Figure 8-10. Electrical Life Cycle Costing Estimate Worksheet.

Equipment Life-Cycle Cost Estimate		Original		Alternative 1		Alternative 2		Alternative 3	
		Estimated Costs	Present Worth	Estimated Costs	Present Worth	Estimated Costs	Present Worth	Estimated Costs	Present Worth
Initial Costs	Element (See Reference R-1)		1						
	11 Equipment								
	111 Fixed And Movable Equipment ______								
	112 Furnishings ______								
	113 Special Construction ______								
	Total Initial Cost								
Operation Costs	Annual Costs @____% Discount Rate		2						
	Escal. Rate____% PWA (With Escal.) Factor ______								
	A. Salaries (Operation, Etc.) ______								
	B. Food Service Equip. Energy Cost ______								
	C. Vending Equip. Energy Cost ______								
	D. Waste Handling Equip. Energy Cost ______								
	E. ______								
	F. ______								
	G. ______								
	Total Annual Operation Costs								
Maintenance Costs	Annual Costs @____% Discount Rate		2						
	Escal. Rate____% PWA (With Escal.) Factor ______								
	A. Inspection And Testing Of Equipment ______								
	B. General Cleaning, Dusting Of Equip. ______								
	C. Repair Food Service Equipment ______								
	D. Repair Vending Equipment ______								
	E. Repair Waste Handling Equipment ______								
	F. ______								
	G. ______								
	Total Annual Maintenance Costs								
Replacement Costs	Single Expenditures @____% Discount Rate		3						
	Item Replaced: | Year: | PW Factor:								
	A. ______								
	B. ______								
	C. ______								
	D. ______								
	Total Replacement Costs								
Associated Costs	Annual Costs @____% Discount Rate		2						
	Escal. Rate____% PWA (With Escal.) Factor ______								
	A. ______								
	B. ______								
	C. ______								
	Total Annual Associated Costs								
Salvage Value	Final Value @____Year PW Factor ______		4						
	11 Equipment ______								
	Total Salvage Value								
LCC	Total Present Worth Costs								

PW – Present Worth PWA – Present Worth Of Annuity

Figure 8-11. Equipment Life Cycle Costing Estimate Worksheet.

Sitework Life-Cycle Cost Estimate		Original		Alternative 1		Alternative 2		Alternative 3	
		Estimated Costs	Present Worth	Estimated Costs	Present Worth	Estimated Costs	Present Worth	Estimated Costs	Present Worth
Initial Costs	Element (See Reference R-1)		1						
	12 Sitework								
	121 Site Preparation								
	122 Site Improvements								
	123 Site Utilities								
	124 Off-Site Work								
	Real Estate								
	Total Initial Cost								
Operation Costs	Annual Costs @____% Discount Rate		2						
	Escal. Rate____% PWA (With Escal.) Factor								
	A. Salaries (Operation, Etc.)								
	B. Lighting Energy Cost								
	C. Snow Melting System Energy Cost								
	D.								
	E.								
	Total Annual Operation Costs								
Maintenance Costs	Annual Costs @____% Discount Rate		2						
	Escal. Rate____% PWA (With Escal.) Factor								
	A. General Site Cleaning								
	B. Landscaping Maintenance								
	C. Snow & Ice Removal (Parking, Walks)								
	D. Relamping And Routine Replacement								
	E.								
	F.								
	Total Annual Maintenance Costs								
Replacement Costs	Single Expenditures @____% Discount Rate		3						
	Item Replaced: / Year: / PW Factor:								
	A. Trees, Shrubs								
	B. Parking Pavement								
	C.								
	D.								
	E.								
	Total Replacement Costs								
Associated Costs	Annual Costs @____% Discount Rate		2						
	Escal. Rate____% PWA (With Escal.) Factor								
	A.								
	B.								
	C.								
	D.								
	Total Annual Associated Costs								
Salvage Value	Final Value @____Year PW Factor		4						
	12 Sitework								
	Total Salvage Value								
LCC	**Total Present Worth Costs**								

PW – Present Worth PWA – Present Worth Of Annuity

Figure 8-12. Sitework Life Cycle Costing Estimate Worksheet.

Life Cycle Cost Estimate Summary

		Original		Alternative 1		Alternative 2		Alternative 3	
		Estimated Costs	Present Worth	Estimated Costs	Present Worth	Estimated Costs	Present Worth	Estimated Costs	Present Worth
Initial Costs	**Initial Costs**		9						
	Planning, Design, Special Studies Fees								
	Structural								
	Architectural (Parts I & II)								
	Mechanical								
	Electrical								
	General Conditions & Profit ____% (If Approp.)		10						
	Equipment								
	Sitework								
	Other								
	Contingencies ____%								
	Escalation ____%								
	Total Initial Cost								
Owning Costs	**Operations**		9						
	Architectural (Part II)								
	Mechanical								
	Electrical								
	Equipment								
	Sitework								
	Other								
	Total Annual Operations Costs								
	Maintenance		9						
	Structural								
	Architectural (Parts I & II)								
	Mechanical								
	Electrical								
	Equipment								
	Sitework								
	Other								
	Total Annual Maintenance Costs								
	Alterations		3						
	Item(s) Altered / Year / PW Factor:								
	A.								
	B.								
	C.								
	D.								
	Total Alteration Costs								
	Replacement		9						
	Structural								
	Architectural (Parts I & II)								
	Mechanical								
	Electrical								
	Equipment								
	Sitework								
	Other								
	Total Replacement Costs								
	Financing Costs		2						
	Functional Use Costs		2						
	Denial Of Use Costs		2						
	Associated		9						
	A.								
	B.								
	C.								
	D.								
	E.								
	Total Annual Associated Costs								
	Total Owning Present Worth Costs								
Salvage Value	**Salvage**		9						
	Building (Struc., Arch., Mech., Elec., Equip.)								
	Other								
	Sitework								
	Total Salvage Value								
LCC	**Total Present Worth Life Cycle Costs**								
	Life-Cycle Present Worth Dollar Savings		11						

Figure 8-13. Life Cycle Cost Estimate Summary Worksheet.

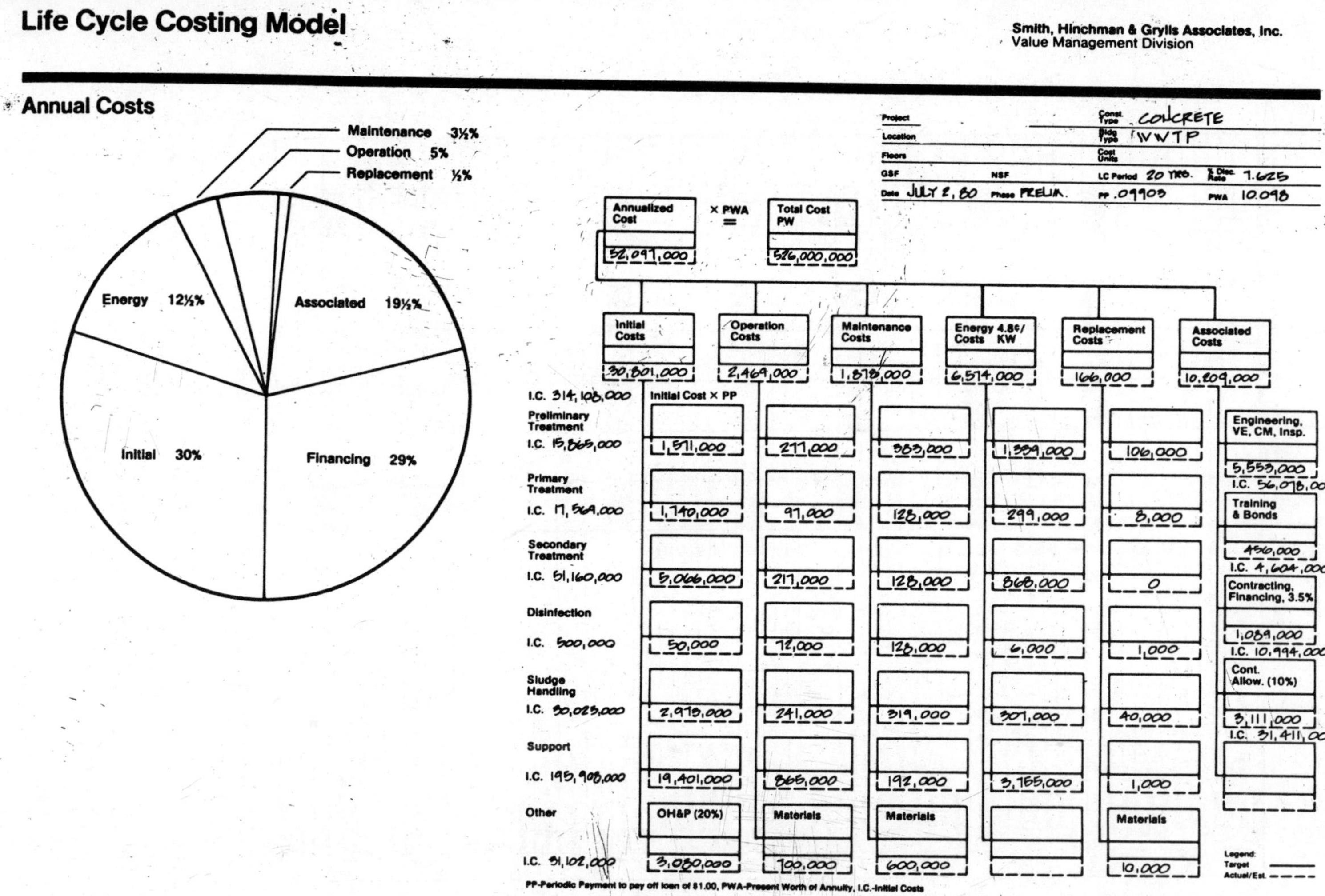

Figure 8-14. Life Cycle Costing Model-Wastewater Treatment Plant. (Courtesy of Smith, Hinchman and Grylls Associates, Inc.)

9
Energy

INTRODUCTION

The energy consumed by buildings can be reduced by 30 percent if buildings are redesigned. These savings have been obtained on many projects. With the cost of energy rising and availability decreasing, the need to provide energy-efficient designs becomes more important. Designing buildings, water and wastewater projects, highway facilities and power plants is one of our most demanding challenges.

The purpose of addressing the subject of energy in a value engineering text is to sensitize the owner, designer and value analyst to the impacts of energy and power on the cost of constructed facilities. Escalating energy costs are changing our design habits. It is no longer possible to design structures without specific reference to the projected energy consumption. The unclear picture of the path of our energy future presents many problems. The trend, however, is very predictable: The cost of energy will escalate at a rate far greater than the rate of inflation. Supplies of nonrenewable energy sources will drop, causing a shortage of fossil fuels and a move to natural and possibly nuclear energy sources.

As a proponent of increased value, our knowledge of energy must be expanded. Sources of energy and the availability of energy must be understood. This is especially true in relationship to the design life of projects, consumption rates, equipment efficiencies, system designs and other factors that contribute to waste of energy.

ENERGY RESOURCES AND CONSUMPTION

In the past energy resources have been assumed to be an inexhaustible commodity. Investigation of the design of building structures and plant facilities shows that designs in the past focused primarily on the initial cost of getting the plant in operation. It was assumed that the cost of fuel to heat, cool, ventilate, light and power the operating equipment in plant facilities would be paid on an annual basis once the facility was in operation. Owners of projects are now anxious to invest in energy-efficient structures. Part of the reason is the dwindling supply of fuels and increased dependence on other nations for energy to maintain our economy.

The sources of our energy problems require further analysis to understand how we suddenly arrive at an energy deficit. Let's examine the cause of the energy shortage by looking at our past history of energy use. Two centuries ago there was no energy problem. Fuels were used in meager quantities for cooking, heating of homes and public building facilities, and for the manufacture of metals and glass. Our primary source of work was a strong back and the use of natural sources of power, such as wind, water and animals. Industry centered around waterways to benefit from nature's free source of power. The invention of the steam engine brought about a new source of power and helped start our industrial revolution. Industry was no longer forced to locate near water bodies, but could move closer to the source of their raw material, or to locations of more favorable transportation sources. Soon the railroads opened up new frontiers to development. New continents were opened to travel and commerce. Standards of living rose as new conveniences were introduced. Industry expanded accordingly, and man's productivity multiplied. Our dependence on energy and our corresponding consumption of energy were in full swing. Introduction of the internal combustion engine brought about the automobile, which resulted in a major increase in energy use. Our energy consumption from the year 1850 to 1973 depicts the dramatic rise in our energy use. Note the sudden rise in per capita consumption at the turn of the century, primarily from the automobile (Figure 9-1).

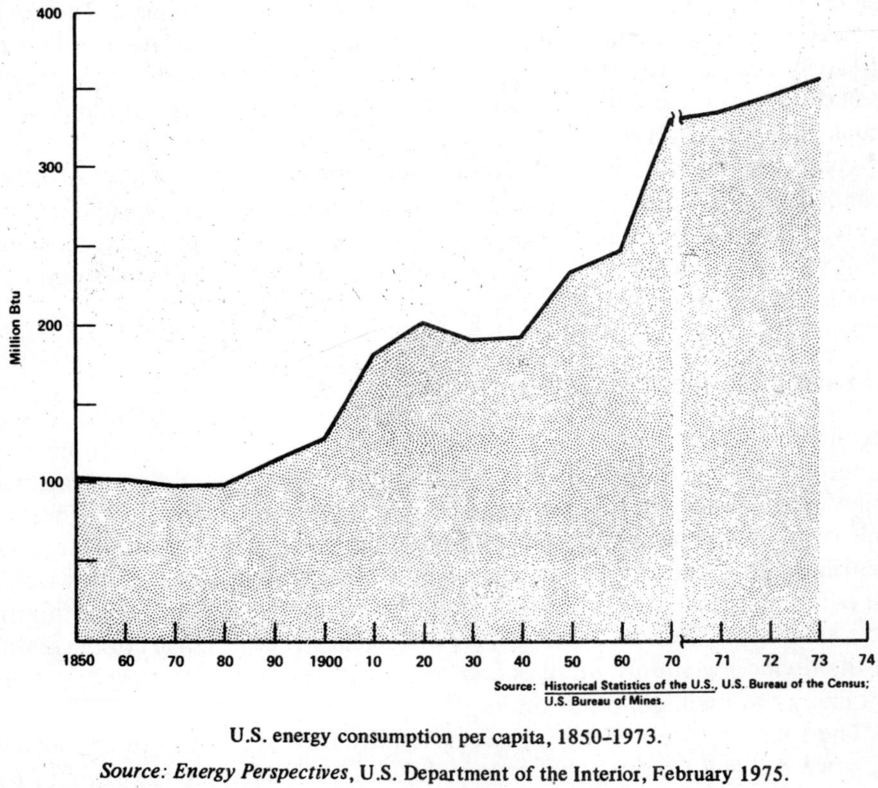

Figure 9-1. U.S. Energy Consumption Per Capita, 1850-1973. (Source: Energy Perspectives, US Department of the Interior, February 1975.)

Our total energy demand has risen steadily with the increase in population and with the improvements to our life-styles. Our historical and projected energy demand shows a growth rate of 3.6 percent from 1955 to 1970. Projected growth rates through the 1970s were approximately 4 percent (Figure 9-2). Further analysis of energy consumption trends shows a fairly uniform increase in consumption for industrial, transportation, and household and

NPC—U.S. ENERGY BALANCE

Historical and Projected U.S. Energy Demand

(Quad. BTU)

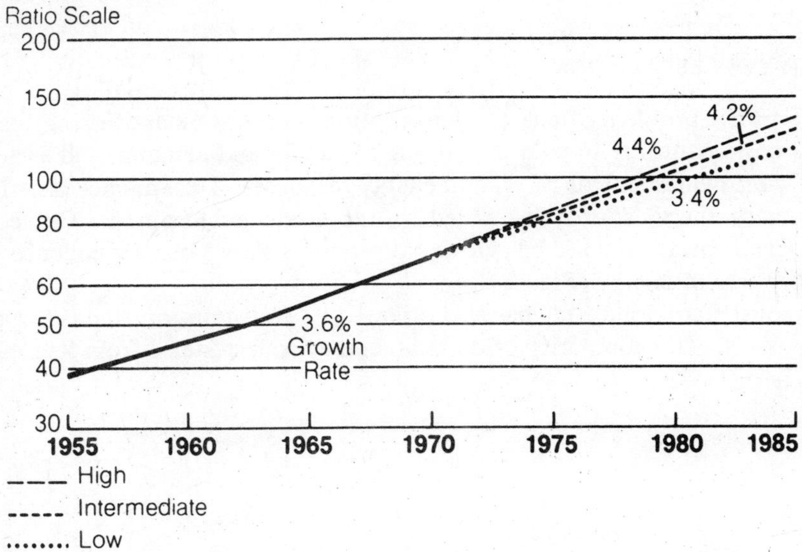

Energy Demand Trends to 2000

	Volume (Quadrillion BTU)		Growth Rate	
	1985	**2000**	**1971-85**	**1985-2000**
High Case	130.0	215	4.4%	3.4%
Intermediate Case	124.9	200	4.2%	3.2%
Low Case	112.5	170	3.4%	2.8%

Source: Guide to National Petroleum Council Report on United States Energy Outlook, National Petroleum Council, Washington, D.C., December, 1972.

Figure 9-2. Historical and Projected U.S. Energy Demand., (Source: Guide to National Petroleum Council Report on United States Energy Outlook, National Petroleum Council, Washington, D.C., December 1972.)

commercial demands (Figure 9-3). These energy demands will continue to rise with the increase in population and with the industrialization of other countries.

In the past, the United States has been virtually energy independent. The supply of oil, natural gas and coal appeared to be in abundant supply. Fuel costs closely followed the gradual rise in inflation. In the 1950s, the United States was energy self-sufficient, with ample supplies of coal, oil, gas and hydroelectric power generation capability. In the 1960s, a trend toward oil as a source of energy and the increase in consumption resulted in the import of 15 percent of the crude oil used in the U. S. In 1976, the U. S. relied on imports for over 40 percent of our energy needs. Today, we import 50 percent of our energy needs.

ENERGY COST ESCALATION

Adding to the problem of energy consumption is the problem of rising costs. Energy costs continue to soar as a result of supply and demand, and as a result of worldwide control of oil and energy resources. Dependence on oil as our primary energy source has added to our energy predicament. Our consumer trend toward the use of petroleum products shows our dependence on oil as a source of energy (Figure 9-4).

The construction industry has also oriented its consumption trends toward the use of oil. The popularity of oil as an energy source stems from its clean-

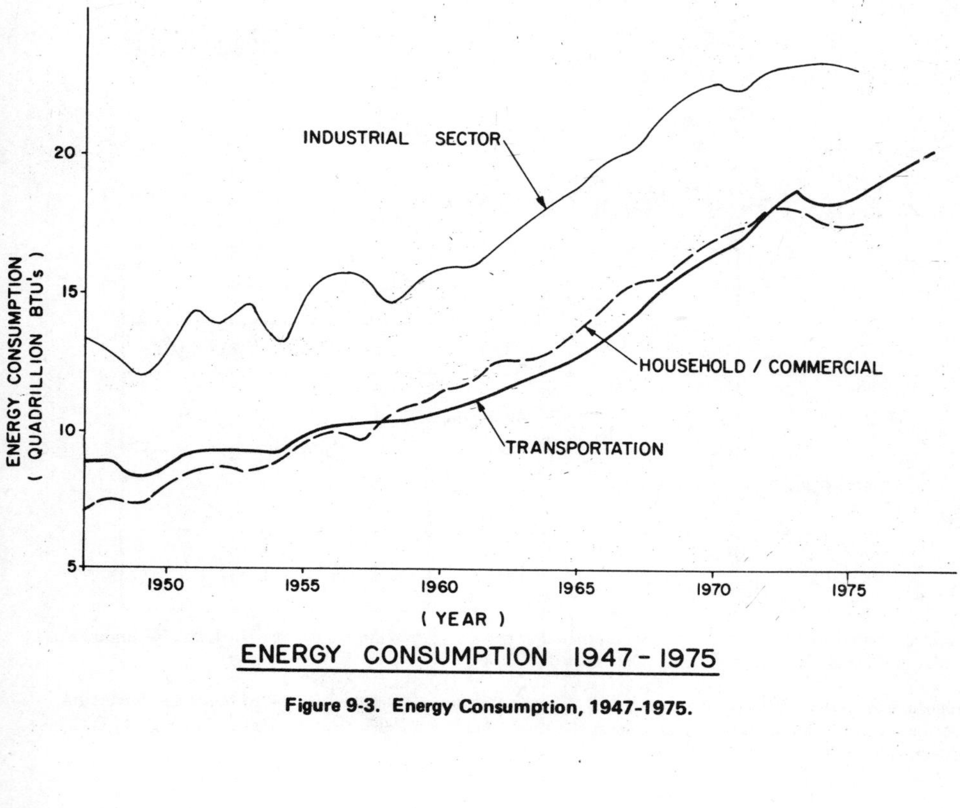

Figure 9-3. Energy Consumption, 1947-1975.

4-12 / U.S. ENERGY CONSUMPTION 1850–1975

U.S. Energy Consumption Trends, 1850-1974
(Quadrillion Btu)[1]

YEAR	COAL	PETROLEUM	NATURAL GAS	HYDROPOWER	NUCLEAR	FUEL WOOD	TOTAL
1850	.2	–	–	–	–	2.1	2.3
1860	.5	–	–	–	–	2.6	3.1
1870	1.0	–	–	–	–	2.9	4.0
1880	2.0	.1	–	–	–	2.9	5.0
1890	4.1	.2	.3	–	–	2.5	7.1
1900	6.8	.2	.3	.3	–	2.0	9.6
1910	12.7	1.0	.5	.5	–	1.9	16.6
1920	15.5	2.6	.8	.8	–	1.6	21.3
1930	13.6	5.4	2.0	.8	–	1.5	23.3
1940	12.5	7.5	2.7	.9	–	1.4	25.0
1950	12.9	13.5	6.2	1.4	–	1.2	35.2
1960	10.1	20.1	12.7	1.7	–	–	44.6
1970	12.7	29.5	22.0	2.7	.2	–	67.1
1971	12.0	30.6	22.8	2.9	.4	–	68.7
1972	12.4	33.0	23.0	2.9	.6	–	71.9
1973	13.4	34.7	22.8	2.9	.9	–	74.7
1974	13.0	33.8	22.3	2.9	1.2	–	73.2

[1] 1 Quadrillion Btu = 500,000 barrels petroleum per day for a year
= 40 million tons of bituminous coal
= 1 trillion cubic feet of natural gas
= 100 billion kWh (based on a 10,000-Btu/kWh heat rate)

Source: Energy Perspectives, U.S. Department of the Interior, February 1975.

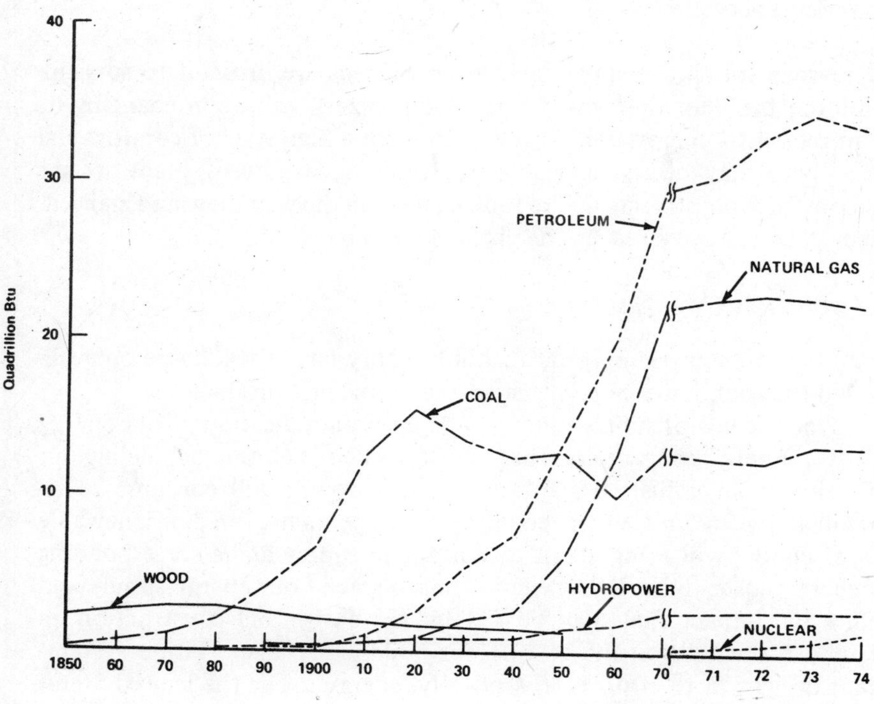

Source: Historical Statistics of the United States, Bureau of the Census; U.S. Bureau of Mines.

U.S. energy consumption trends, 1850–1974.

Figure 9-4. U.S. Energy Consumption Trends, 1850-1974. (Source: Energy Handbook, Van Nostrand Reinhold, New York, 1978.)

liness as opposed to coal. Major plant modifications were made to accommodate the use of oil instead of coal as our primary energy source. Most building systems for heating have been designed around oil-fired heating systems. In addition to its use as a heating source, oil has also been used in power generation and in the manufacture of petroleum products, such as plastics, asphaltic materials, containers and a wide variety of other commodities.

At the present rate of consumption, our supplies of petroleum-derived fuels are rapidly being depleted. The reasons for the high rates of consumption might be the following:

1. Population growth increasing the number of consumers.
2. Increased demands for a cleaner environment.
3. Design of structures and processes that waste energy. Many older buildings have heating systems that were designed when fuel costs were minimal.
4. The comfort level that we have been accustomed to is, in no way, conducive to energy conservation.
5. Leisure time from shorter working hours means more traffic miles.
6. Developing countries in Asia, South America and Africa are raising their industrial production levels and their energy consumption level is rising accordingly.

The reasons for our energy consumption trends are difficult to sum up. Much of the problem that will be faced by society will be in changing its habits in regard to energy use. Past demands for a high level of comfort and leisure activity may be facing a new era. Building structures, plant designs and all construction projects will require changes in the way they are financed, designed, built and operated.* The challenge is ours.

SOURCES OF ENERGY SUPPLY

Man's source of energy supply throughout history has varied, based on availability and the economics of conversion to a usable end product.

The economic law of supply and demand gives an indication of our energy perspective. Energy consumption has a historical basis closely paralleling our nation's rise as an industrial giant. Economic growth will continue to be accompanied by an increase in energy use. Dependence on nonrenewable sources of energy will bring about a shortage in supply and a corresponding rise in energy costs. Now let's explore the sources of our energy supply and determine the impact that may be felt by the design and construction industry, and ultimately on the cost of our buildings, transportation systems and plant designs in the future. Historically, energy use in the United States has been supplied from petroleum products, natural gas, coal, hydroelectric power, nuclear and from wood. The supply rate has easily met the needs of residential, commercial, transportation, and industry needs.

---

*Watson, Donald, *Energy Conservation Through Building Design*, New York: McGraw-Hill, 1979, p. 13.

Energy sources may be categorized as renewable and nonrenewable. Renewable sources are those fuels that can be replenished within an identifiable and useful time frame. Nonrenewable energy sources are those that once spent are not replaceable within a usable time frame. Oil, gas, and coal, the main sources of our energy, are, for all intent, nonrenewable sources. With diminishing supply of oil and natural gas, the future use of these fuels as power sources will likely change. Building and plant design will change accordingly.

Renewable energy sources such as peat, wood, food, animal power, wind and water have proved inadequate to meet energy needs for the future. Oil, coal, and natural gases are being depleted rapidly, giving rise to the use of nuclear fusion with uranium and thorium. But these sources, too, will be depleted within the next thousand years.* Nuclear fusion and solar energy remain at present as available sources as supplies of petroleum products diminish. The trend from nonrenewable to renewable sources will change design habits as well as actual building designs. Nuclear fusion may well be the ultimate energy source once it is technically perfected.

END USE OF ENERGY

Energy consumption trends have been used to depict the rise in energy usage. The total energy picture is not complete, however, without exploring the major energy users that are responsible for the demand for energy. Specific attention should be paid to the areas where energy conservation and improved design can be beneficial. Figure 9-5 illustrates the areas where our various sources of energy are used—transportation, heating systems, and electric power for process systems. More efficient automobiles and reduced speed limits will help reduce our energy dependence. More efficient designs for building systems and industrial processes will also sharply decrease the amount of energy consumed.

A further breakdown of energy use is illustrated by Figure 9-6. The specific uses of energy from industrial, commercial, residential and transportation also indicate where conservation techniques can be applied with the greatest hope of fuel savings. Energy use can also be divided into areas that use energy for operation and energy expended to construct the product (Embodied Energy). Energy required for operation is a continuous use and embodied energy is a one-time use.

ENERGY EMBODIMENT OF CONSTRUCTION MATERIALS

More emphasis is being placed on the energy-efficient designs of buildings and plant facilities to reduce consumption during the operation life of the structures. Energy consumption for buildings represents approximately 33 percent of the total national energy use. Aside from energy consumption during operation of buildings and plant facilities, the energy required to build a fa-

*Loftness, Robert, *Energy Handbook*, New York: Van Nostrand Reinhold, 1979, p. 29.

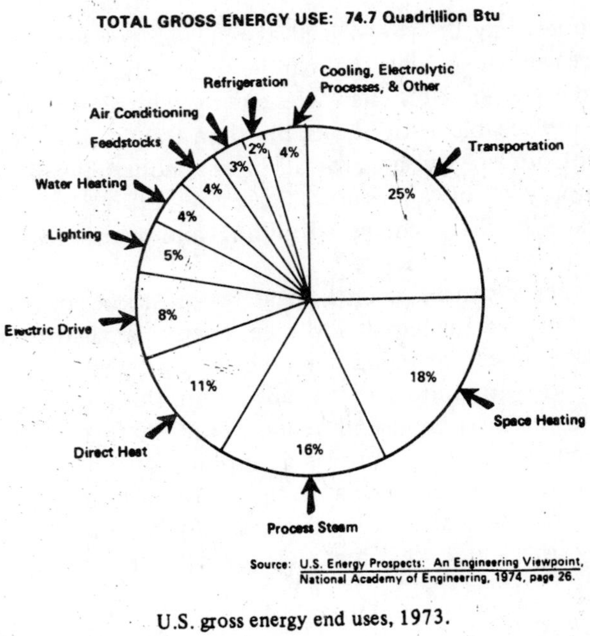

Figure 9-5. U.S. End Use of Energy. (Source: Energy Perspectives, U.S. Department of the Interior, February 1975.)

cility is significant. Stein and Serber in their article on "Energy Required for Building Construction" distinguish between the energy required for construction and the energy required to use the structure for its intended purpose—*operational energy.** The analogy of life-cycle cost and life-cycle energy use soon becomes apparent.

As energy availability and cost fluctuate, the need to analyze initial energy (energy required to construct the facility) will become more important. Initial energy will play a larger part in determining the value of a building. The subject of energy embodiment is intended to augment the designer's and value engineer's grasp of the total energy picture of a building, plant, highway or other construction project. Embodied energy is the energy required to manufacture materials, transport them to the site and to construct the facility.

Obviously, there is a difference in the Btus. required to produce various building materials. Let's look at the energy intensity of building materials found in the majority of construction projects. Table 9-1 lists common construction materials and their energy requirements.

Indications are that energy life cycles (total energy required to construct and operate a facility) will soon be a consideration in building and plant designs. Energy models will be used to determine the high energy of materials

*Watson, Donald (Editor), *Energy Conservation Through Building Design*, New York: McGraw-Hill, p. 183.

and building systems. Research is also needed to extend our knowledge in the historical norms for facility designs. In addition to costs, designers will soon need to know the energy consumption per unit quantity so that meaningful comparisons of alternatives can be made. It is expected that building systems may soon be evaluated in terms of energy as well as cost. Historical energy data will be most helpful to the value engineer in determining the initial energy expenditure and the consumption of energy in proportion to the benefit received as a result of energy uses.

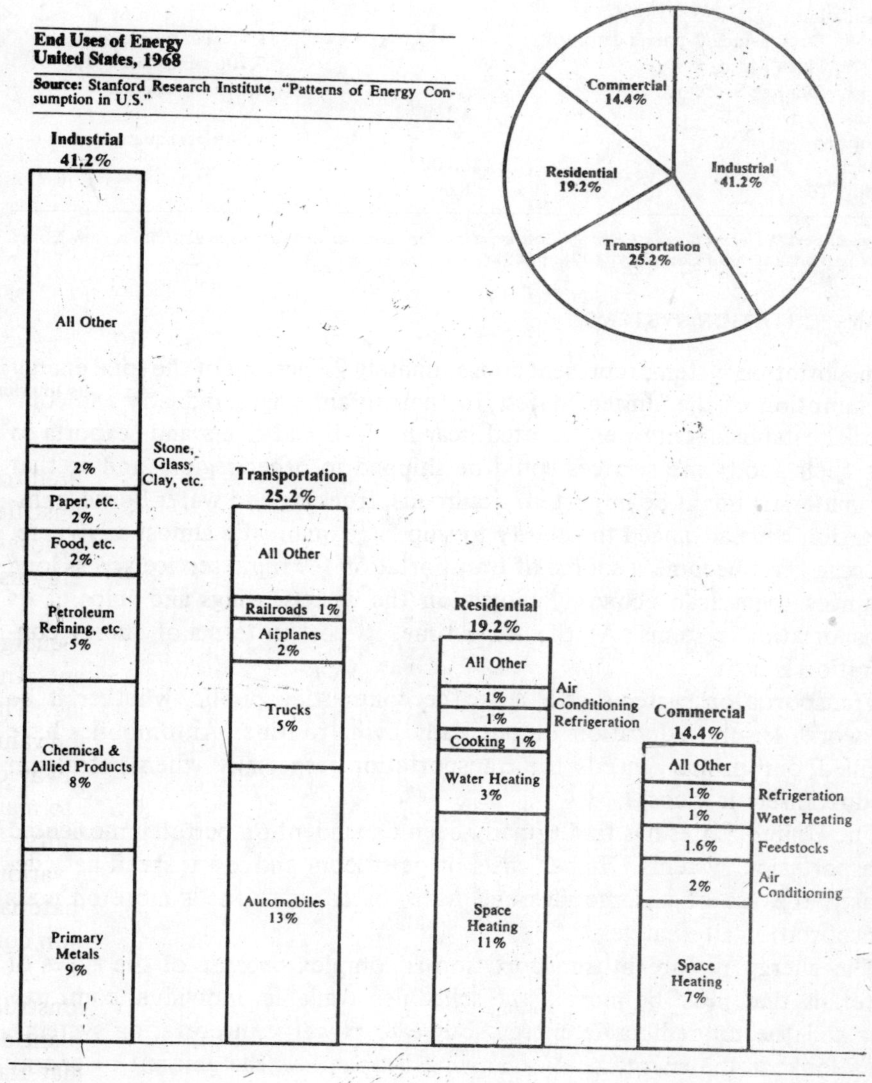

Figure. 9-6. Exploring Energy Choices, Energy Policy Project of the Ford Foundation, 1974, Copyright The Ford Foundation.

Table 9-1. Energy Intensiveness of Typical Building Materials.

Material	Btus/Pound	Btus/Unit
Aluminum	41,000	
Ceiling Materials	1,500	
Concrete	413	
Concrete Blocks (8 X 8 X 16 inches)		15,200 per block
Copper	40,000	
Dry Wall	2,160	
Glass	12,000	
Insulation		
• Duct (1-inch/3-pound density)		51,400 per square foot
• Pipe (2-inch)		7,700 per square foot
• Building Board		2,040 per square foot
Paint	4,134	
Roofing		6,949 per square foot
Steel	13,800	
Vinyl Tile	8,000	

Roose, Robert W., *Handbook of Energy Conservation for Mechanical Systems in Buildings,* New York: Van Nostrand Reinhold Company, 1978, p. 35.

TRANSPORTATION SYSTEMS

Transportation systems represent approximately 25 percent of the total energy consumption of the United States. In their infant stages, industry and commercial establishments were located near navigational rivers and seaports so that their goods and services could be shipped to other regions and so that raw materials might be imported. Railroads, trucking and water-borne transportation have advanced the ability to ship large quantities almost anywhere. Air cargo has become a source of transportation for rapid service across long distances. American economy moves on the wheels, wings and ships of its transportation systems. At the same time, its cost in terms of energy consumption is high.

Transportation systems also serve the commuting public, whether it be for work, leisure, education or our daily living routine. Automobiles have fulfilled our primary needs for transportation, especially when petroleum products were low cost.

The United States has traditionally been dependent on petroleum-oriented transportation systems. Higher costs of petroleum and lower speed have decreased the use of automobiles and have forced us to focus more on mass transportation alternatives.*

The energy picture in transportation is complex because of the types of materials that must be moved, the schedules available, individual comforts, cost and the unpredictable energy source to power transportation systems. Let's look at the energy cost of moving people, i.e., the amount of energy required on the average to move from one location to another. A comparison

*Smith, Craig B., *Efficient Electricity Use–A Practical Handbook for the Energy Strained World,* New York: Pergamon Press, Inc., 1976, p. 303.

of energy use for several modes of transportation is shown in (Table 9-2). In the analysis of future transportation systems, energy will play a significant part in the planning picture. Higher energy costs will require that energy consumption rates for various modes of transport be thoroughly evaluated. From knowledge of the cost and consumption rates of transportation systems, the following conclusions might be considered:

1. More people will be moving closer to their area of employment so that they can walk, bicycle or use public transportation for commuting.
2. There will be more dependence on mass transportation.
3. Shortages of fuel may cause rationing of fuel for vehicular transportation.
4. Car-pooling will have a significant effect on energy consumption rates.
5. Smaller, more efficient cars will be used.

Because transportation systems account for approximately 25 percent of our energy consumption, it is prudent to investigate the potential for energy conservation. Although mass transit systems, airports and railroads contribute to energy consumption, the main culprit is the automobile. Therefore, highways will be our framework of investigation. When value engineering the energy components of a highway or rail system, the first step is to analyze the source of power requirements.

Power Requirements for Highway Systems

1. Friction from rail or road surface. Power required to overcome frictional forces.
2. Power to overcome gravitational force. Grades on highways or rail systems.
3. Power required for acceleration. Weight of auto.
4. Power to overcome aerodynamic drag.
5. Efficiency of automobile. Gas consumption.
6. Speed or velocity of travel.
7. Idle time in traffic.

Table 9-2. Typical Energy Use for Passenger Transport.

	mJ/Passenger-km	Assumed Load Factor
Bicycle	0.13	1.0
Walking	0.20	1.0
Bus	0.80	0.5
Railroads	1.10	0.5
Automobiles	3.00	0.5
Airplanes	6.50	0.5

mJ = 10^6 Joules

Load Factor = Amount of total capacity

Smith, Craig, *Efficient Electricity Use: A Practical Handbook for the Energy Strained World.* New York: Pergamon Press, 1976, p. 304.

8. Lighting of roadway systems.
9. Traffic control by coordination of flow by various systems.

A cost model for a highway project would be difficult to prepare. It would include power consumptions found in the highway lighting systems, the fuel consumption rates of automobiles and trucks, energy for construction, maintenance energy, traffic patterns, and related energy use of support systems. Consumption rates for vehicles are influenced by highway designs as well as

Figure 9-7. Mass Transit Systems Provide Economical Use of Energy.

automobile efficiencies. Even before highway designs are analyzed, the obvious energy benefits of mass transit should be analyzed. The future designers of our highway systems might well consider designs for electric cars.

WATER AND WASTEWATER TREATMENT

Wastewater treatment facilities are constructed in an effort to preserve and protect the natural sources of our water supply. Oceans, rivers, lakes and streams have faced the onslaught of industrial, residential and commercial development. These facilities are also energy and resource dependent. Treatment of wastewater is unique for each facility. Chemical composition of wastewater characteristics, effluent requirements, caliber of operating personnel, quality of design and other conditions are varying factors for each facility. Each factor also influences the energy required to operate the facilities.

The rising cost of energy is having an impact on the design and operation of water and wastewater facilities. The rise in energy costs is forcing us to take a new look at processes that are energy intensive, and to also explore more closely the value of wastewater itself as a potential resource.

The importance of energy and other resources is recognized in a value engineering study through the use of an energy and resource model. The energy and resource model is a tool used to account for the elements of a facility that influence its energy and resource use now and in the future. We have distinguished between the cost model and the energy and resource model to get a clear picture of the chemical and energy use of the design. The impact of fluctuating costs of energy, chemicals, water, labor and supplies can be categorized by a model thus producing greater sensitivity to the future operation and maintenance costs of the facility.

The energy model was first introduced to the value engineering field by Bernard W. Stainton. Stainton summarized the need for an energy model in an article which appeared in *Plant Engineering*, March 22, 1979 entitled "VEE-Value Engineered Energy."

> Until the past few years, most (owners) have not been too concerned about getting maximum exchange for their dollars because of abundance or relatively low cost of fuel and power . . . . Value engineered energy provides an organized approach that assures total energy sensitivity during the design process.

Design of a water or wastewater treatment plant includes a wide range of design areas. A facility may include sanitary structures, office buildings, chemical processes, laboratory buildings, industrial buildings, storm drainage, power generation, transportation systems, computer designs and a number of other elements depending on size, complexity, and design of the system. Accounting for the energy and resources in the facilities is a major task. No two energy and resource models for an individual treatment plant will be the same. It is therefore difficult to develop a model that can be used universally. The model must be modified to fit the unit processes and the mechanical and electrical system designs in each facility. Figure 9-8 is an energy model used to categorize energy consumption in a facility. The primary areas of energy consumption in a water or wastewater facility are shown in Table 9-3.

As the cost of a plant design is influenced by energy and resource consumption, it is important to be able to recognize when a project is energy intensive. In this manner, alternative solutions can be developed to conserve energy. Referring to the outline for energy and resource utilization, an energy model may be prepared as shown in Figure 9-9.

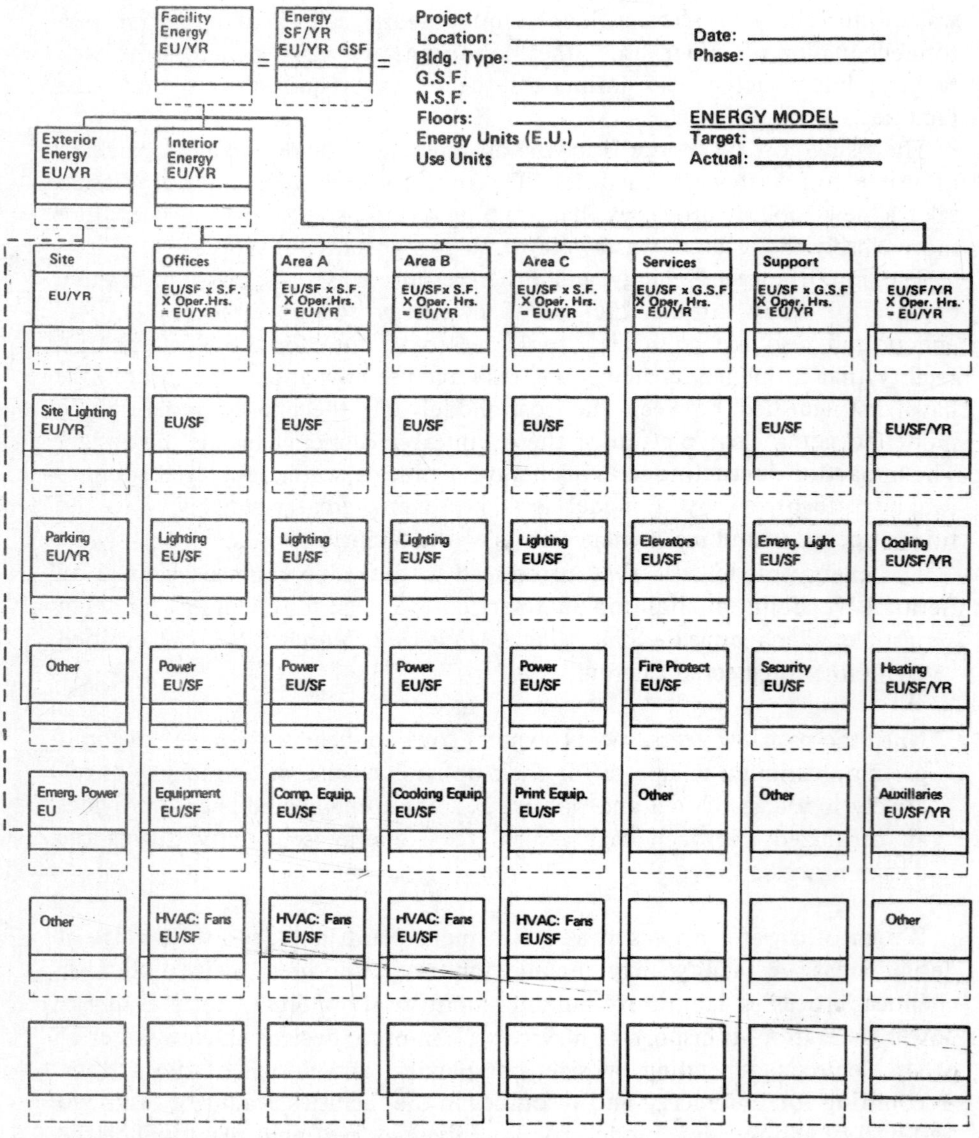

Figure 9-8. Typical Energy Model (Courtesy of Smith, Hinchman and Grylls Associates, Inc.)

Table 9-3. Energy Consumption in a Water or Wastewater Treatment Plant.

1. *Pumping Costs.* Electric costs of conveying sewage, sludges, plant water, potable water, chemical slurries, dry chemicals and other liquid or semiliquid materials.
2. *Hydraulic Head.* Headloss due to hydraulic design must be evaluated. The model differentiates between hydraulic head and pumping head to draw specific attention to the cost of hydraulic losses.
3. *Equipment Power.* Energy requirements of unit process systems are evaluated by consideration of electrical power, steam, fuel and other energy uses. Consideration of energy required to exhaust or cool equipment areas because of excess equipment heat must be considered.
4. *Waste Energy Utilization.* Waste products are also a source of energy. Heat values of sewage sludge gases converted for use in space heating or as electrical energy must be included in an energy balance.
5. *Transportation.* Energy utilized in the transportation of sludges, chemicals and other materials contribute to a plant's energy consumption. Alternative transportation systems, haul volumes, distances and cost of disposal sites influence energy use as well as life-cycle costs.
6. *Lighting.* As in buildings, the type of fixture, controls and operating voltage influence power and energy use.
7. *Space Heating.* Comfort control in the form of heating, ventilating and air conditioning are often areas of wasted energy in a plant facility. In plant designs, major emphasis is placed on the system operation at the expense of support systems. Plant designs are also complicated by the heat generated by unit processes and equipment. Much of this energy can be converted to a useful source of heat. System design and control of mechanical HVAC systems are recognized in this section of the energy model.

   It should be noted that the building envelope and environmental systems should be evaluated as a part of an energy model for a water or wastewater plant.
8. *Chemicals.* Water and wastewater treatment processes offer many alternative solutions to treatment. Chemicals applied to the treatment process represent major costs of operation. These costs continue for the operating life of the facility. Chemical dosage rates are based on characteristics of the water or wastewater, flow rate, temperature, mixing energy required to get the chemicals into solution, pH, and the allowable detention time. Millions of dollars each year are wasted because of poor management of chemicals. We pause here to study the effects of chemical usages and the conditions under which they are used.
9. *Staffing Costs.* Cost of personnel for operation and maintenance of a facility are also part of the resources involved in a project. Costs vary with the wage scale, quality of workmanship, productivity, process requirements and working conditions.

BUILDING AND ENERGY DESIGN

Energy consumption for constructing and operating buildings represents approximately 30 to 40 percent of our total national energy usage. This is the equivalent of 70 quadrillion Btu of energy use.* It is estimated that approximately 30 percent of the total energy consumption in buildings could be eliminated through the use of energy conservation and the redesign of existing buildings and structures. New buildings are being designed with more emphasis on the efficient use of energy. Figure 9-10 is an illustration of the projected energy reduction that can be obtained from building design. Of this amount, it is estimated that approximately 39 percent of that energy use is directly related to building energy requirement. It is further estimated that approximately 13.6 percent of that amount could be saved through conservation, solar heating and other design modifications. This is certainly a sizable amount of our overall energy needs. It would also help to decrease our reliance on nonrenewable energy sources. To express this in terms of

*Watson, p. 50.

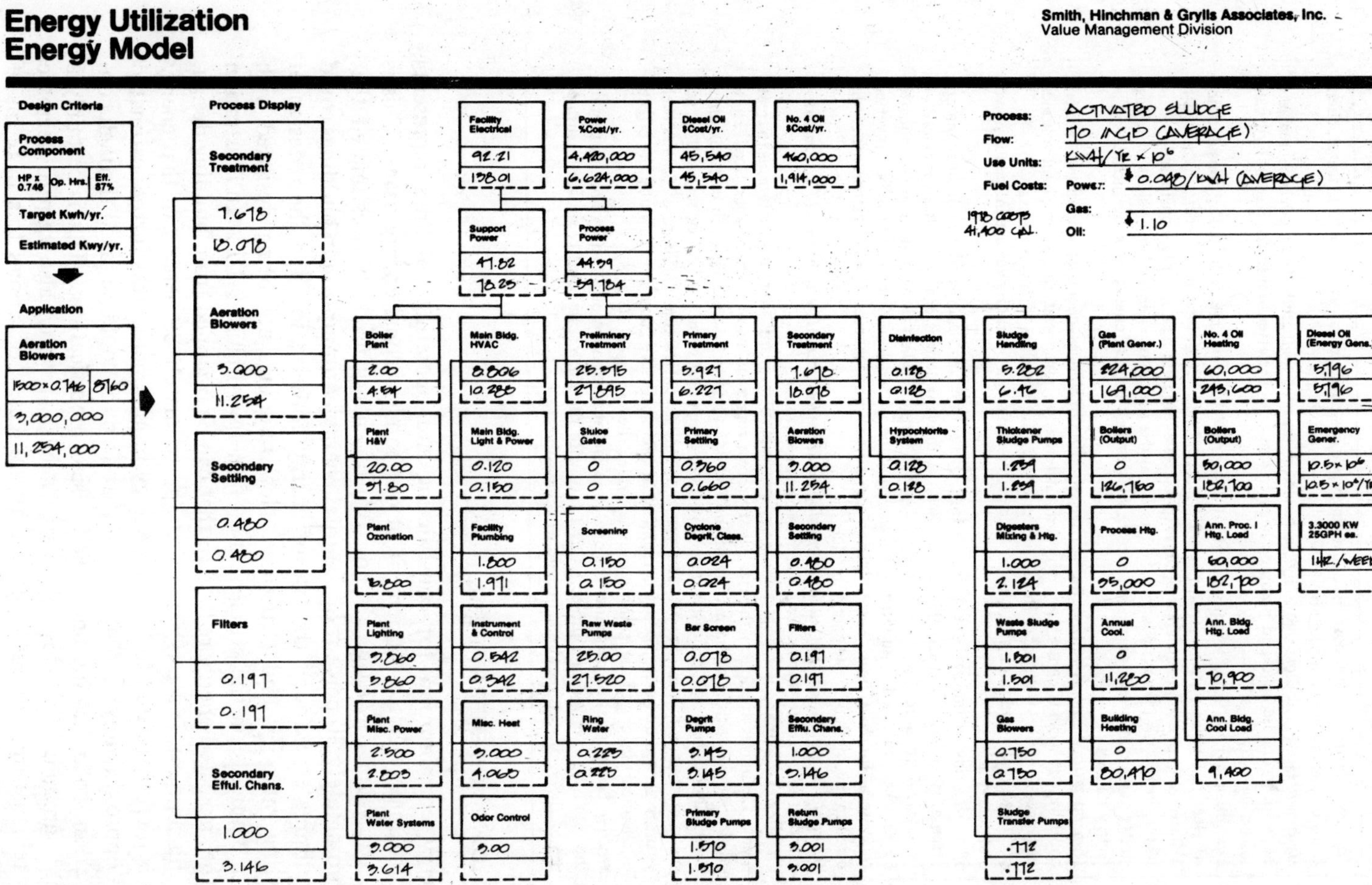

Figure 9-9. Energy Model of a Wastewater Treatment Plant.

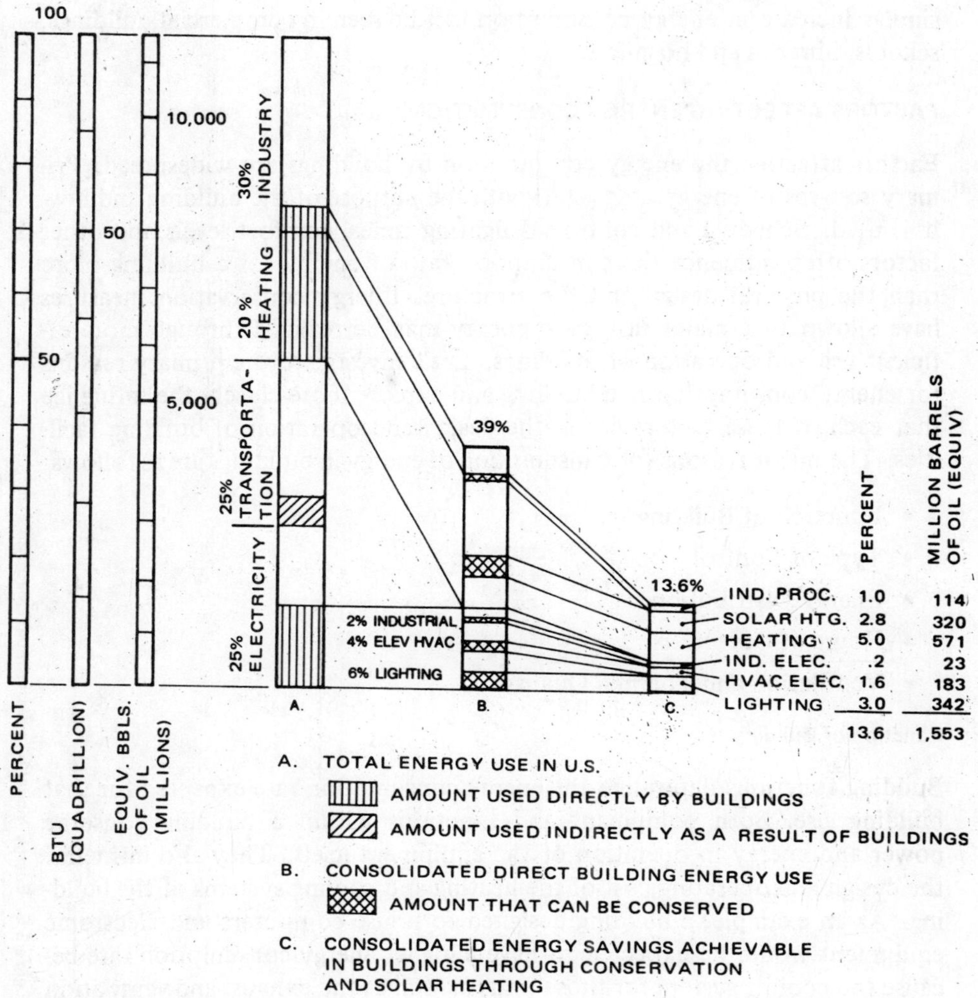

Figure 9-10. Available Energy Reduction of Buildings. (Source: Watson, Donald, Energy Conservation Through Building Design, McGraw-Hill Book Company, New York, 1979.)

individual energy consumption, let's look at the per capita energy consumption of individuals in the United States compared to those in the rest of the world. The average per capita energy use of Americans is about 330 million Btus per year, compared with an average per capita energy use for the rest of the world of about 39 million Btus, or nearly 10 times more than the average for the rest of the world. This represents a distinct difference in the way the rest of the world lives as compared to the United States.

While the American style of living has changed over the last fifty years, the average per capita consumption rate of energy has increased substantially. Residential energy usage has doubled and tripled over the last decade. A

---

*Watson, Donald, *Energy Conservation Through Building Design*, New York: McGraw-Hill, 1979, p. 49.

similar increase in energy consumption can be seen in commercial buildings, schools, libraries and hospitals.

FACTORS AFFECTING ENERGY CONSUMPTION

Factors affecting the energy consumption by buildings are widespread. Primary sources of energy usage start with the purpose of the building and how it is used. Schedule and control of lighting times, comfort levels and other factors often influence the consumption rate of energy for a building more than the physical design and the structure. Energy conservation measures have shown that major savings in energy may be realized through more efficient use and operation of buildings. Let's investigate the primary reasons for energy consumption in a building and explore more closely the influence that each of these factors has in the design and operation of building facilities. The major reasons for consumption of energy in buildings are as follows:

- Function of Building
- Type of Control
- Energy Distribution
- Hours of Operation
- Ventilation and Thermal Quality

Function of Building

Building functions determine the energy consumption rate expected for that building use. Both equipment and functions within a building consume power and energy in operation of the equipment itself. They also influence the design and operating cost of the heating and cooling systems of the building. As an example, a building designed to house computers and electronic equipment would be expected to have a higher energy consumption rate because the cooling system for those units as well as the exhaust and ventilation requirements would raise the total energy used. Industrial buildings are often designed for minimal occupancy and thus have lower comfort-level requirements and less energy use. On the other hand, schools might have a higher energy consumption because of the comfort levels required for the learning process. One of the first steps in analyzing a building is to determine the basic function of the building system. In terms of the heating load, it is also necessary to determine the allowable limits of comfort zones and to determine if those comfort levels are required throughout the building. It may be appropriate that various levels of comfort be provided, dependent on the function of the building space and the total area that it encompasses.

Type of Control

Control systems for buildings and equipment are becoming more and more sophisticated. The type of control in a building system used to regulate heating, ventilating and cooling operations can greatly influence the energy use of a building.

These controls can be either direct or indirect. Direct controls supply the need for energy at the rate required to fulfill the energy needs. Energy is supplied or consumed to meet the need at exactly the rate required.* Examples of direct control would be a simple thermostat control which senses the need for additional heat or cooling and turns on the furnace or air conditioner at the appropriate times. Although this is one form of direct control, a more direct reading would be from a room-by-room thermostat with heat or cooling supplied to each specific area. Another example of direct control would be sprinkler systems for fire protection. Sensing devices detect a rise in temperature indicative of fire and relay a message to open up the sprinkler heads and begin watering the fire down.

Indirect controls are building components that are energy users in which the amount delivered or consumed is not directly related to a need within the building structure. Examples of indirect controls would include cases where energy systems are designed for peak energy uses, usually during extreme weather conditions. However, the system operates at this peak design condition throughout the life of the structure. As a result, an inordinate amount of energy is consumed to satisfy the most extreme condition. Other examples would be heat and power loss due to improper design of ductwork, piping and heat exchangers. These are the hidden costs that often go unnoticed when evaluating electric bills at the end of each month.

Energy Distribution

This represents the energy required to convey heated air and cooled air to the point of use. Energy costs for the distribution of gases and liquids may result from power used in pumping system pressure for domestic water supply, power line losses and inefficiencies. Energy distribution also includes the conversion of the raw source of fuel into the ultimate heat or power source. Energy is consumed in the combustion and/or conversion of the raw source. Energy is used in pumping liquids and blowing heat into the required occupied space. Often it requires more energy to transport heat or coolant than to raise or lower the original air temperature. We might look also at the air-conditioning system as a means to draw hot air out of the building and to replace it with cooled air from the chilling systems of the air-conditioning system. All these processes take energy. Watson notes that, while the magnitude of horsepower required for these systems may not be great, the duration of operation is significant. Load factors for these types of equipment are usually at full load during the period that the building is occupied. Load factor is the percentage of time that the equipment is in operation. A pump operating 24 hours a day would have a 100 percent load factor.

Hours of Operation

Can you remember when you set the thermostat in your home at the beginning of the winter season and left it intact throughout the following cold months?

---

*Watson, p. 59.

In other words, we kept a constant temperature in our homes and our factories, and often in our office spaces, whether in the evening or during working hours. We all know the impact of running heating systems at such a load factor. Twenty-four-hour-a-day operation of heating and cooling systems has a substantial and adverse effect on the size of our heating and cooling bills. Setting back our thermostats in the winter and ahead a bit in the summer, while our buildings are unoccupied, will reduce the amount in our energy bill (See Figure 9-11).

Ventilation and Thermal Quality

This is the area that we're most familiar with in terms of energy related costs. Knowledge regarding insulation properties of buildings is an area in which

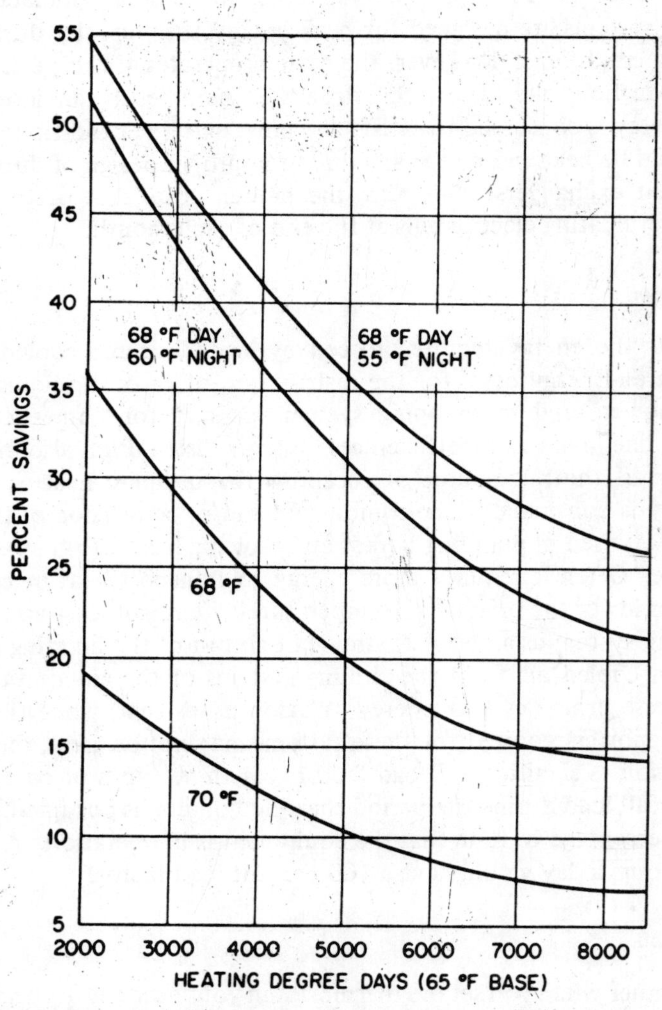

Figure 9-11. Energy Savings from Thermostat Setback. (Source: David Pilati, The Energy Conservation Potential of Winter Thermostat Reductions and Night Setbacks, Oakridge National Laboratories, National Science Foundation, 1975.)

we know how to conserve energy. ASHRAE regulations now provide minimum standards in which to design building and occupied spaces. These determine the minimum U coefficient of transmission to ensure a minimum building standard for building insulation. Added insulation will save energy. In addition, the design criteria used to determine the number of air changes, and comfort levels used to design buildings greatly influence energy use. Building orientation, described later in this chapter, also impacts energy use.

ENERGY MODELS

A means of accounting for the energy uses for the construction and operation of buildings and plant facilities is needed. More specifically, it is necessary to know the areas within a building which are energy consumers and to learn how much energy a building uses as a comparison to the amount of energy that a building should use. The categories in a building that utilize or consume energy are the heating systems, cooling systems, ventilation, water heating requirements and lighting requirements. Other energy consumers include miscellaneous equipment which is specifically related to the function of the building. Cooking equipment, computer equipment and other machinery used within a building are a part of the power consumption and ultimate energy use within that structure. In addition to the areas contributing to energy consumption in a building, it is also important to be able to recognize the time span into which energy consumption occurs. Energy consumption is tailored to the months or seasons of the year to account for the changing weather conditions and the building systems that service the structure. Figure 9-12 is an energy model for a typical building design. Energy consumption in Btus is plotted along the ordinate, and the time frames in months of the year are plotted along the abscissa. Consumption rate in Btu square feet is also shown. Each of the energy-consuming sources in the building are plotted, and a total annual energy picture is projected.

Another example of an energy model for a building can be seen in Figure 9-13. This energy model also depicts the energy requirements of the shopping center. It also depicts the categories of heat-consuming processes. This model is used to account for the energy consumption used in a building. The purpose is to give the designer a sensitivity as to where energy is being consumed, the time of the year it is being consumed, and the impact of the change in operating hours and weather conditions that will alter energy consumption rates.

ANALYZING BUILDING ENERGY USE

Having discussed the energy model and its use, now let's look into the methods used to analyze energy consumption in a building. In his article "Energy Management for Commercial Buildings: A Primer,"* Fred Dubin outlines seven key steps in analyzing consumption in existing commercial buildings. These seven steps are as follows:

---

*Dubin, Fred & Long, Chalmers, G., *Energy Conservation Standards for Building Design, Construction and Operation*, p. 207.

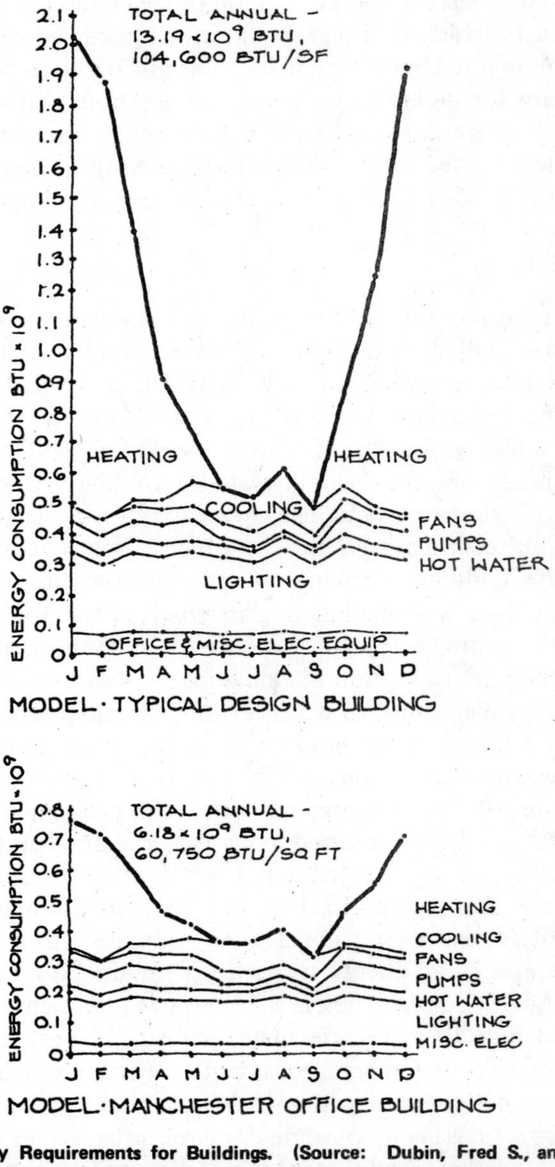

Figure 9-12. Energy Requirements for Buildings. (Source: Dubin, Fred S., and Long, Chalmers, Energy Conservation Standards, McGraw-Hill Book Company, New York 1978.)

1. Specific factors which cause energy to be used in a building.
2. The extent to which excess energy is being used to provide environmental control (heating, ventilating, cooling, elimination, hot water and essential services).
3. The opportunity to change the level of environmental control and/or functional use of the building and its operating and maintenance practices to reduce energy consumption.
4. The period of the mechanical and electrical system and the potential to reduce energy consumption by modifications to the hardware and

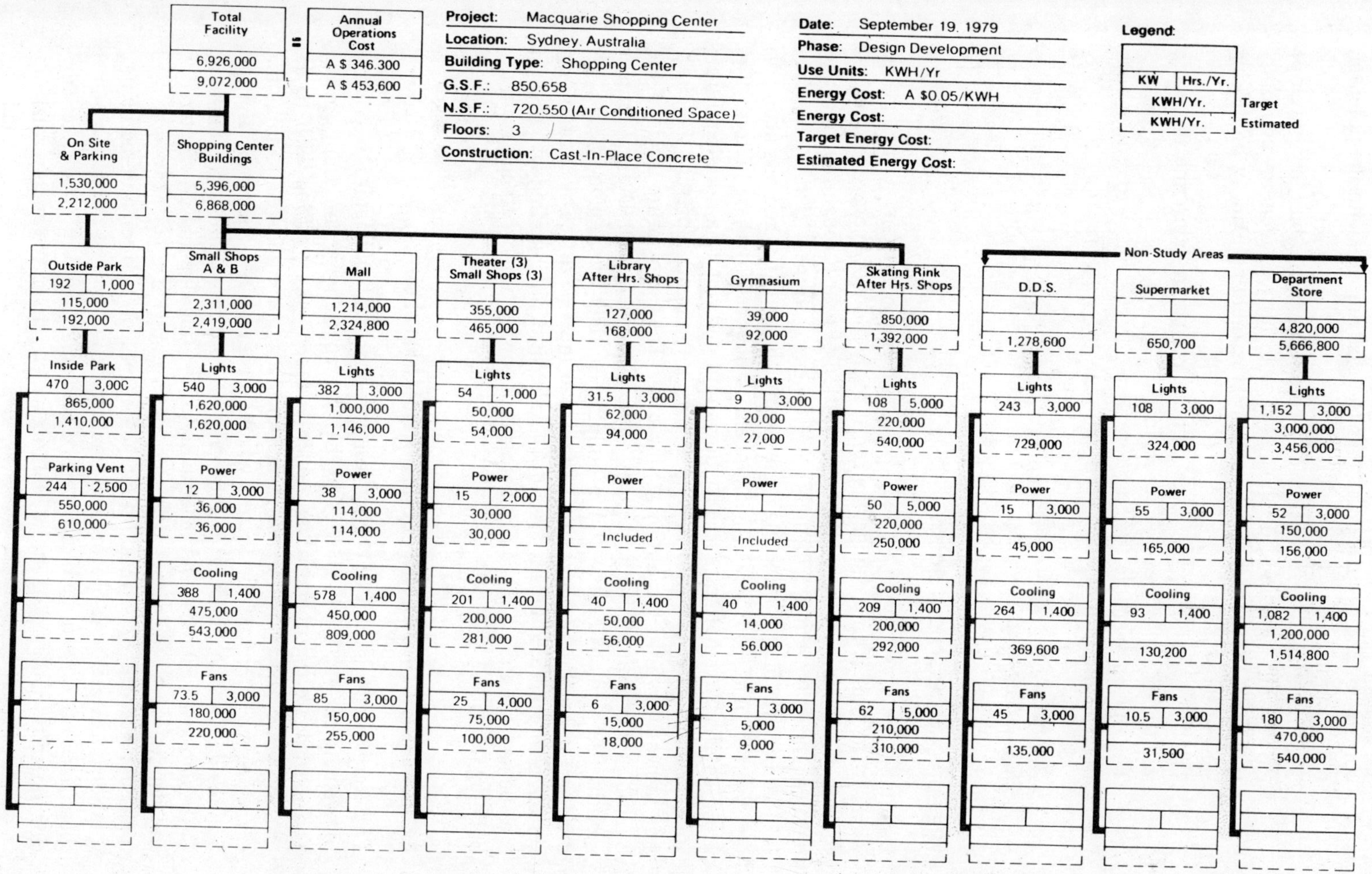

Figure 9-13. Energy Model of a Shopping Center. (Courtesy Smith, Hinchman and Grylls Associates.)

control, or their replacements, as the case may be, with the potential reduction in energy use by doing so.

5. The materials, configuration and condition of the building envelope (roof, walls, windows, doors) and their influence on energy consumption, and the potential for reducing the building load by modifying the envelope.
6. The load profile during each 24-hour period to determine the cause and the extent of peak electrical loads.
7. The option available to use alternative energy sources to reduce both the consumption of fossil fuels and their resulting cost.

As we can see by the outline, the energy model plays an important part in cataloging these factors.

THE BUILDING AS A HEAT BODY

Building structures may be viewed as a closed energy system. Temperatures within the building only change as a result of the flow of energy from several sources. Heat radiated by sunlight, infiltration of heat through building, and heat generated by equipment, lights and other functions within the building itself are several factors affecting temperature change. In a like manner, cooling systems, or the absence of heat are also influenced by these factors. Figure 9-14 is an example of the heat flows into and out of a building during summer and winter conditions. The arrows in the figure represent the direction of heat flow into and out of the building. The temperature inside of the building is, of course, influenced by these exterior forces. During summer months, the gain in heat within a building is offset by cooling systems. A drop in temperature during winter conditions must be offset by the building system heat generated by a heat source. Analysis of the building system must include an evaluation of each of the forms of energy transfer to and from the building itself.

FACTORS IMPACTING ENERGY CONSUMPTION IN BUILDINGS

To determine the impact of energy consumption in a building, it is important to evaluate the factors in the design that influence energy consumption, and also to evaluate the operation and maintenance of the building itself to determine what energy conservation methods may be employed to minimize energy usage. Many of the factors which impact energy consumption must be included in the building design—such as 1) orientation of the building; 2) insulation to establish thermal quality of the building and, 3) fenestration and window areas to increase the amount of passive energy that can be used to offset higher fuel bills. In addition, these three factors are all non-mechanical solutions, i.e., artificial heating and cooling are not part of the design. Once these parts are constructed, they cannot be changed without major construction retrofits. Other areas in the building which impact the energy consump-

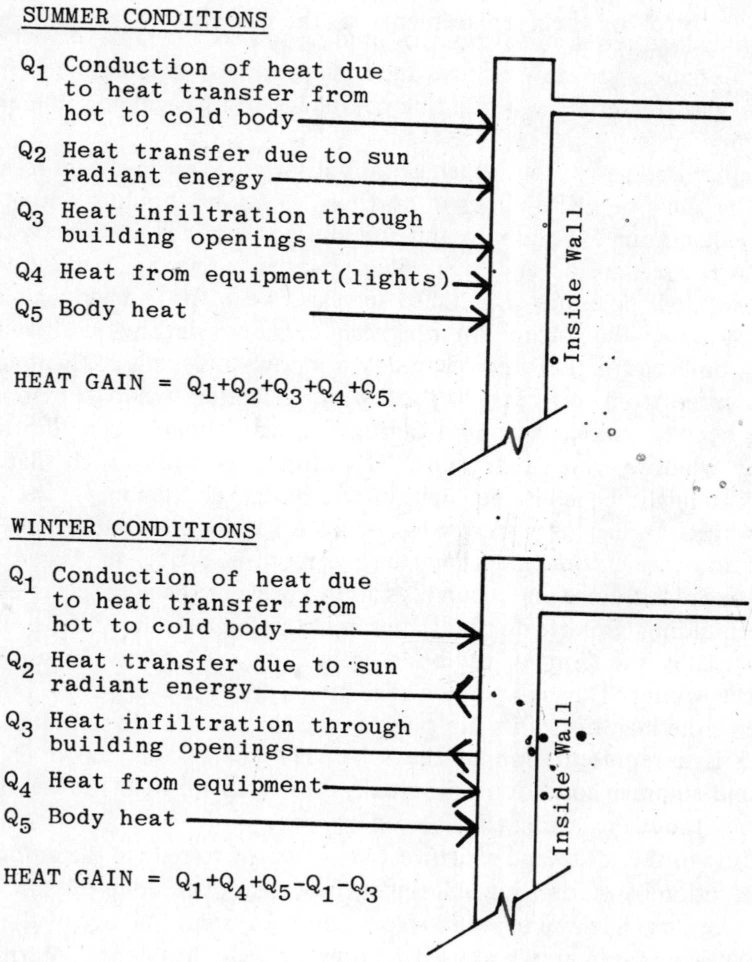

Figure 9-14. Heat Flow in a Building. (Source: Plant Engineers and Managers Guide to Energy Conservation, Van Nostrand Reinhold Company, 1977.)

tion are mechanical systems. These systems include heating, ventilating, cooling, hot water, domestic water, lighting and other power systems used to meet the functional requirements of the building. Let's look at each of these sources of energy consumption to determine how they influence the design and operation of the building.

Orientation of Building

Building orientation is the siting of a building to provide maximum benefit of sun exposure or shading to reduce energy needs.

Building orientation impacts the amount of heat energy absorbed within the building. Heat gain can be a benefit to buildings during winter months when heat loads are high, or a detriment to a building during summer months when excess heat radiated through the windows must be offset by the air-conditioning load required to cool the building to a comfortable temperature. Building designers are now using windows, openings, shading mechanisms, reflective glass materials and building overhangs to manage available energy for building design.

In northern climates, south-facing walls absorb heat from the direct radiation of the sun's rays. Buildings in northern locations should be situated so that the maximum exposure to the sun during winter conditions is to the east or to the south side of the building. Heat is radiated into the building through window openings which also serves to keep the outside wall of the building warmer than usual. In northern climates the obvious benefit of orienting buildings is that on a clear day windows and walls are heat gainers when oriented from southeast to southwest. Insulated windows help retain radiated heat to reduce heat loss during the sunlit hours. The addition of shades or window drapes reduces the U factors of windows such that additional heat might be contained within the building. Of course, the shade must be open during the period when there is sunshine available and closed when there is no sunshine. During summer months, reflective glass is often used to keep out more direct sun rays and to prevent the absorption of heat into the building. For residential structures, the longer side of the building, which is usually the front of the building, will be exposed to the sun's rays during the winter. During summer conditions, that same northern building will receive the majority of its sun rays toward the roof of the structure. Figure 9-15 is a representation of the solar views of a house taken in both winter and summer conditions. The daily heat gain through the east-facing windows without the shading device can be seen.

Buildings in the south and southwest are oriented to reduce the amount of heat absorption by minimizing building surface areas exposed to the sun. Maximum energy use in these regions is from cooling systems. Many of the same building design parameters are used to prevent heat flow from entering the building. The most obvious effect of building orientation can be seen in the use of solar heating. Solar collectors must be oriented and pitched such that they receive the direct rays of the sun. In this manner, their efficiency is greatly enhanced.

Building Configuration

The climate, the site and the geographic location influence the energy absorption of a building. The building configuration should be set up to use the available energy systems that are most useful for a given locale. As an example, natural light saves energy for lighting systems, and if available, may be advantageous to expose as much exterior surface of the building as possible. In extreme climates, however, more energy is conserved by using artificial light with fewer windows. It is also helpful in cold climates to reduce the amount of exposed exterior surface of the building subject to heat loss and heat gain. Designers in northern climates often use the ratio of total square footage of exterior surface divided by the interior square footage of useful office space

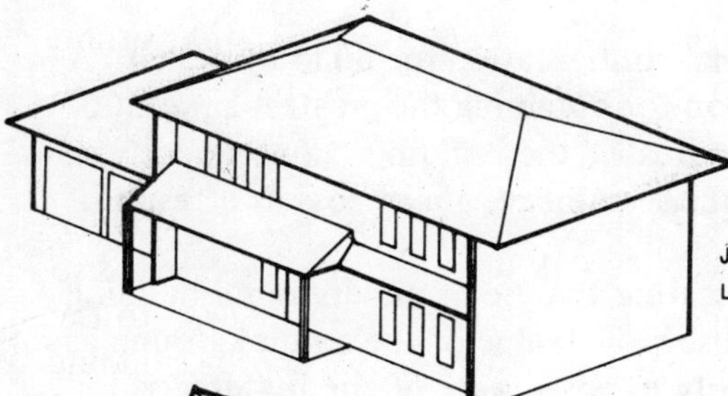

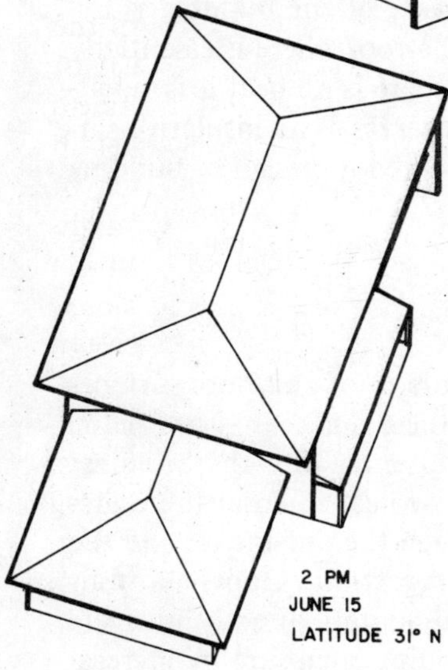

Winter and summer solar views of a house.

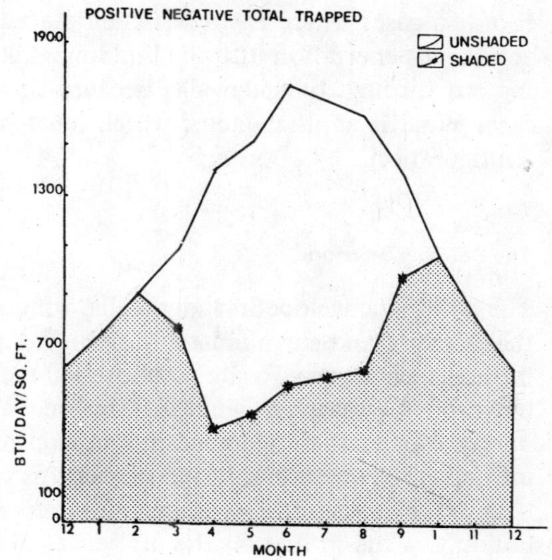

Daily heat gain through an east-facing window, with and without a fixed shading device.

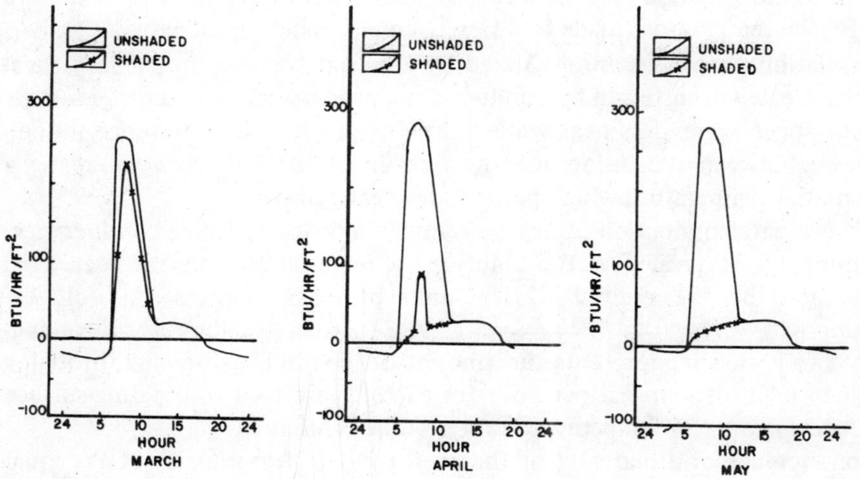

Instantaneous rates of heat gain or loss through an east-facing window comparing the values when the shading device is in place with values when the shading device is not in place.

Figure 9-15. Effect of Building Orientation. (Source: Watson, Donald, Energy Conservation Through Building Design, McGraw-Hill Book Company, New York, 1979.)

as a criterion for evaluating the optimal configuration for building design. A square building is the best configuration for obtaining the greatest amount of gross square footage area per surface area of the building. Consequently, a square building will also experience the least heat gain or loss as a result of its shape.

Many building designers are investigating the use of underground building structures to take advantage of the absorption value of the natural ground as an insulator. In this situation, the only exposed area of the building is the roof. In cases where earth has been placed over the roof, there is essentially zero heat penetration into the building. Likewise, there is no heat loss radiating out through the sidewalls, because the ground serves as an insulative surface. Wind is another factor which must be considered in design of building configuration.

The Building Envelope

The building envelope includes walls, windows, doors, roof and floor surfaces that enclose and surround the building. Each of these surfaces is subject to different elements. Windows allow light energy to enter into the building; however, they prevent wind infiltration. Walls allow heat to enter the building by way of the difference in temperature between the outside air and the interior air temperature. This property is called *convection*. Doors allow air to enter by *infiltration*. When doors are open, air enters directly into the building. Wind influences the properties of the building enclosure by increasing the amount of infiltration of air into the building structure. And the roof structure itself, which is often given little consideration concerning energy loss in building design, is influenced by heat from the direct rays of the sun and by the temperature loads resulting from accumulation of snow.

Insulation properties are evaluated by the heat transfer properties of materials. Heat is transferred by conduction, a property of heat transfer whereby one space surrenders heat while another gains it. The difference in temperature between the inside and the outside of the wall surfaces creates a differential temperature which perpetuates heat transfer.

We evaluate conduction of heat in terms of a property called *conductivity*. Conductivity is defined as the ability of a material to transmit heat. It is represented by the symbol K. The units of K are expressed as follows: Conductivity (K) = $\frac{(\text{Btu})\ (\text{in})}{(\text{hr})\ (\text{ft}^2)\ (^\circ\text{F})}$. Another way of looking at conductivity (K) is that it represents the amount of heat in Btus flowing through a one-inch layer of material per hour for each square foot of building surface per degree change in temperature expressed in Fahrenheit.

Conductance of a material, or the coefficient of transmission (U) is equal to the conductivity divided by the depth of material.

$$\text{Coefficient of Transmission } (U) = \frac{K}{d} - \frac{\text{Btu}}{(\text{hr})\ (\text{ft}^2)\ (^\circ\text{F})}$$

It is represented in Btus per hour-foot squared-degrees Fahrenheit. U factor is often applied to various types of materials, such as wallboard, brick, masonry, woodsiding and other materials of construction. The reciprocal of conductance is referred to as the resistance (R).*

$$\text{Resistance } (R) = \frac{1}{U} = \frac{d}{K} = \frac{(\text{hrs})\ (\text{ft}^2)\ (^\circ\text{F})}{\text{Btu}}$$

Thus the properties of a building wall can be evaluated to determine its thermal quality. Figure 9-16 shows the transfer of heat through common building materials. An example of the application of materials is shown in Figure 9-17. Two composite wall designs of a residential building are used for comparison. The first wall indicates a two-by-six stud wall with 5-1/2 inches of fiberglass insulation. The exterior wall surface is a face brick design with a 1/2-inch drywall used for the interior surface. The second wall is a 4-inch exterior brick surface with a two-by-four wall construction with 3-1/2 inches of fiberglass insulation. Again, the 1/2-inch drywall is used as an interior wall surface. The respective resistance (R) of wall A is 21.1 and for wall B, 14.8. The conductant, or the reciprocal of resistance, is 0.05 for the wall A and 0.067 for wall B. Assuming a 100-square-foot surface area and a change in temperature of 15°F, the heat transmission through the wall surface is 75 Btus per hour for the Wall A, and 100.5 Btus per hour for the Wall B. One can quickly understand the importance of insulation properties and materials and the amount of heat lost between two different thicknesses of insulation material and wall construction. We might also add that both of these wall

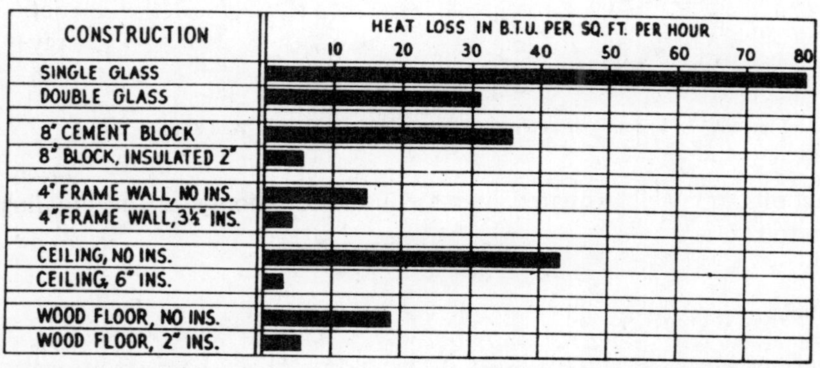

This bar graph shows transfer of heat through common types of material. Next to glass, the big losers are concrete and uninsulated frame construction. Adequate insulation and double glass lower heat loss from 17% to 70%, depending upon materials and location.

Source: Conservation and Efficient Use of Energy, Part 1, Joint Hearings before certain Subcommittees of the Committees on Government Operations and Science and Astronautics, House of Representatives, June 19, 1973.

Figure 9-16. Heat Transfer in Building Materials.

*Thumann, Albert, *Plant Engineers and Managers Guide to Energy Conservation*, New York: Van Nostrand Reinhold, 1977, p. 109.

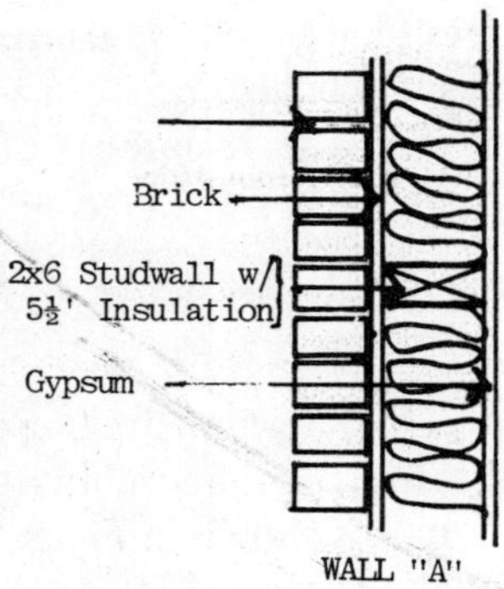

		Resistance
1.	Outside air film at 15 MPH	0.17
2.	4 inch Brick	0.44
3.	Sheathing	2.06
4.	5½ inch Aluminum Foil Fiberglass Insulation	7.03
5.	2x6 Studwall @ 24' o.c.	
6.	Gypsum	0.45
7.	Inside Film	0.66
		21.20

$$q = UA(t_o - t_1)$$
$$= 0.05(100\ ft^2)(15^oF)$$
$$= 75 \text{ Btuh (Btu's per hour)}$$

$U = 1/R = 0.05$

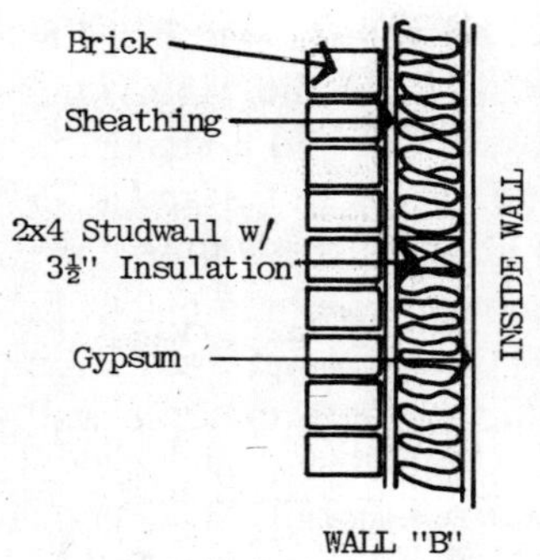

		Resistance
1.	Outside air film at 15 MPH	0.17
2.	4 inch Brick	0.44
3.	Sheathing	2.06
4.	3½ inch Aluminum Foil Fiberglass Insulation	11.00
5.	2x4 Studwall @ 16'' o.c.	
6.	Gypsum	0.45
7.	Inside Film	0.68
		14.80

$$q = 0.067(100\ ft^2)(15^oF)$$
$$= 100.5 \text{ Btuh}$$

$U = 1/R = 0.067$

Figure 9-17. Example of Thermal Properties of Comparative Wall Systems.

constructions are well insulated and are used commonly in the building industry today.

Fenestrations

Fenestrations are glass surface areas of a building. They have traditionally been used to allow outside light to enter the building as a means of providing a pleasant working atmosphere. In the past these esthetic qualities of the design have been costly when considering the insulating properties of the glass itself. New types and thicknesses of glass have now been developed which allow designers to use glass materials more effectively without fear of energy loss. Insulated glass is now being used because it is low in conductive value (U value). Reflective coatings, tinted glass, material thicknesses and double-pane construction now make glass and fenestrations an integral part of our building design. Tinted glass is normally used for its heat-absorbing properties. Reflective glass has also gained in popularity, as it greatly reduces the solar heat gains that increase building cooling loads.* In the composition of the total building structure, the percentage of the surface area attributed to fenestrations must be taken into consideration in developing the heating and cooling loads for the building. The properties of single and double glazing may be seen in Table 9-4.

Lighting

Lighting systems serve as illumination sources for the building occupants. Design of lighting systems has in the past been based on the footcandle method in which the footcandle requirement of the highest lighting intensity is provided over the total surface area of the building. This method of lighting is called broadcast lighting. In contrast to broadcast lighting is a point-by-point method in which specific lighting levels are applied to task areas requiring higher lighting levels, and broadcast lighting is provided at a lower footcandle rating. The point-by-point method has also been identified as task lighting. Task lighting greatly reduces the total wattage requirement for lighting design. Lighting systems can be evaluated by means of the following criteria:

1. Illumination output per watt of the lighting fixture.
2. The bulb and fixture efficiency.
3. The hours of operation of the fixture based on number of starts per hour.
4. The cost of the lighting fixture.
5. The intensity of the lighting.
6. Control and on-off switching of lighting.

In evaluating a lighting system, it is important to analyze the different light outputs or illumin outputs of the various available light fixtures. Maximum efficiency of lighting fixtures can be evaluated by determining the highest illumin output per watt. There are several categories of lighting fixtures. Incandescent lights are the lights that are commonly used in residential con-

Table 9-4. Fenestration Heat Gain Properties. Total solar transmittance, SC and U-value for clear single and double glazing using 1/8- and 1/4-inch thick glass with a 1/2-inch air-space width.

	Glazing Type			
	Single Glass		Double Glass	
Thickness (in.)	1/8-in.	1/4-in.	1/8-in.	1/4-in.
Solar Transmittance	0.86	0.78	0.71	0.61
Shading Coefficient	1.00	0.94	0.88	0.81
U-Value, Btu/(hr ft^2 °F)	1.10	1.10	0.49	0.49

*Thumann, Albert, *Plant Engineers and Managers Guide to Energy Conservation,* New York: Van Nostrand Reinhold Co., 1977, p. 163.

struction. Fluorescent lights are used throughout commercial establishments and apartments, and high-intensity discharge lights are used extensively in commercial and industrial applications.

Efficacy is the measure of the efficiency of a lighting system. It is measured in lumens per watt. The variations in lighting efficacy can be seen in Table 9-5.

The differences in efficacy of these lamping systems indicate possibilities for energy savings in building designs. Of course, a high-intensity discharge lighting system may not be applicable to task lighting because it is a very bright light source.

Many building designs are currently using the available outside sunlight as a source of illumination for buildings during daytime operations. Lighting levels at the outside of the building are provided through natural light sources. At nighttime, fluorescent fixtures are turned on. With this system, the design of lighting systems must be adaptable in order to operate in a dual mode. Control of lighting systems, therefore, becomes an important part of the total lighting design. We mentioned task lighting earlier in our discussion of lighting design. Suggested lighting levels for task lighting are shown in Table 9-6.

In addition to the lighting requirements that are needed, consideration must also be given to the heat given off from the lighting system. During the cooling mode, this heat must be removed by the ventilation system and replaced with cooled air. During winter months, the heat from the light system is beneficial to the building and serves as a dual function of providing light and heat. When lighting and air conditioning operate simultaneously, the systems operate against each other. Fred Dubin and Chalmers Long indicate that for each kilowatt of lighting, an additional 0.4 kw is expended for cooling of the additional heat provided by the lighting fixture.* Because heating systems are more efficient than lighting, the loss when air conditioning is used is not offset during the heating season.

A suggested guide for review of lighting systems is as follows:

1. Reduce lighting levels. Uniform lighting may be unnecessary in many areas of the building. The highest required lumination level is required over the specific task, but not over the total area. Lights should be

Table 9-5. Lighting Efficacy.

1. High Intensity Discharge:	
a. Sodium Vapor	83 to 140 lm per W
b. Metal Halide	80 to 115 lm per W
c. Mercury Vapor	20 to 63 lm per W
2. Fluorescent	31 to 83 lm per W
3. Incandescent	4 to 25 lm per W

*Dubin & Long, *Energy Conservation Standards*, p. 205.

Table 9-6. Suggested Lighting Levels.

Circulation areas between work stations	20 fc.
Background beyond tasks at circulation areas	10 fc.
Waiting rooms and lounge areas	10–15 fc.
Conference tables	30 ESI fc, with 10 fc for background lighting.
Secretarial desks	50 ESI fc with auxiliary localized (lamp) task lighting directed at paper holder (for typing) as needed. 60 ESI fc in secretarial pools.
Area over open drawers of filing cabinets	30 fc.
Courtrooms and auditoriums	30 fc.
Kitchens	Nonuniform lighting with an average of 50 fc.
Cafeterias	20 fc.
Snack bars	20 fc.
Testing laboratories	As required by the task, but background not to exceed 3:1 ratio footcandles.
Computer rooms	As required by the task. Consider two levels, one-half and full. In computer areas, reduce general overall lighting levels to 30 fc and increase task lighting for areas critical for input. Too-high a level of general lighting makes reading self-illuminated indicators difficult.
Drafting rooms	Full-time, 80 ESI fc at work stations. Part-time, 60 ESI fc at work stations.
Accounting offices	80 ESI fc at work stations.

Dubin and Long, p. 206

turned on only when needed. Use two-level switches or dimmers when changes in levels of light are needed.

2. Provide switching to turn off lighting systems when not in use. Switching systems should have enough flexibility such that all the lighting is not turned off with one switch.
3. Automatic turn-off switches with overrides for controlled illumination levels. Photocells are used for overhead lighting.
4. Account for natural light on the outside of the building. Adjust shades and drapes to allow daytime sunlight. Evaluate skylights using prismatic lenses to spread and diffuse light.
5. Use high-efficiency lamps where possible.
6. Install 277-V fluorescent fixtures where possible to preserve electric power.
7. Clean light bulbs on a regular basis to maintain a high efficiency illumination.

Heating, Ventilating and Air Conditioning (HVAC)

Energy is required in our building systems to remove air, as a means of ventilating; to provide a reservoir of heat to draw from to heat our buildings; and to provide chilled air to cool buildings. These three forms of climate control help to provide a pleasant environment and working condition for the building occupants. Requirements for heating, ventilating, and air-conditioning systems might also include a controlled environment for the operation of essential equipment. Building designs provide HVAC systems to control climatic conditions within the structure or area of influence. Variations in temperature, relative humidity and air characteristics are the major parameters that influence system design. As an example, our heating and cooling systems are used to maintain a temperature between 65 and 75 degrees during winter conditions. During summer conditions, the temperature range may go to 72 to 78 degrees. At the same time, the relative humidity is maintained between 20 and 60 percent in order to avoid dryness in air that produces static electricity and uncomfortable working conditions. Ventilation is provided in order to keep air fresh. It helps to avoid a build-up in body odors, and maintains a level of oxygen content within the air system. It also acts as a means of purging noxious gas and smoke, and can be used to control air temperatures within the building.

For the purposes of discussion of energy in buildings, the goal is to inform you of the parameters that impact building design and those areas that might be altered through a value engineering study. Heating, ventilating and air conditioning systems are primarily mechanical-type systems. Their major energy use comes in providing fuel as a source of heat energy and providing power to operate fans, pumps and other electrically powered equipment. The design criteria, the equipment systems selected, and the building systems design all influence the energy consumption levels for the heating, ventilating and air conditioning systems.

Examination into existing building systems has shown that as much as 30 to 40 percent of the energy required for providing comfort control in buildings can be saved as a result of more efficient design and effective control of operating equipment. Of course, the percentage of energy that can be conserved is different in each area of the country. As an example, in the northern climates, the primary energy source is for heating for winter conditions. Conversely, the major energy saving in southern parts of the country is from cooling systems required to offset the high temperatures experienced during most of the year.

Temperature Control

In the past, Americans have been accustomed to placing their thermostats between 72–75° for winter heating, and in summer conditions anywhere between 65–70°. During the oil crisis of 1978–1979, the temperature levels were dropped during the winter to somewhere between 66–68°F, and as high as 78–80°F, with a 60 percent relative humidity during the summer.

These changes have saved considerable amounts of energy, and if allowed to become part of our design of buildings, would permit the use of more energy-efficient systems (See Figure 9-18). American Society of Heating, Refrigeration and Air Conditioning Engineers (ASHRAE) Standard 90-75 permits the use of more energy efficient environment controls. It is a more realistic outlook on energy design and takes into account the savings that can be made with minor changes in the comfort levels that people have become accustomed to. America's per capita consumption of energy is ten times higher than the average of the rest of the world. The major part of that is due to the comfort level we have come to expect in our building and residential home designs. In the future, more and more thermostats will be turned down during the winter and up during the summer to save precious energy reserves.

The amount of energy required to heat and cool our building systems has often been based on extreme temperature conditions. This has resulted in excess waste and inefficiencies in equipment operation. Rather than designing for extreme conditions and running equipment inefficiently during the balance of the year, new buildings are being designed with more flexibility of controls. Variable equipment speeds, variable pumping rates for cooling waters and variable air volume systems are efforts to operate at optimum efficiency levels. Buildings are now being designed so that heating and cooling systems may be operated independently, based on the occupancy level and the actual requirements of the specific area. Although this accounts for

Increases in Thermostat "Comfort" Settings During Summer Season Possible Through Clothing Changes

Women	Raise Thermostat Setting (°F)	Men	Raise Thermostat Setting (°F)
Replace light slacks with light skirt	1.5	Replace heavy trousers with light trousers	.6
Replace long-sleeved dress with sleeveless dress	.2	Replace winter-weight jacket with summer jacket	2.5
Replace dress made of tightly woven cloth with one having an open weave	.5	Replace long-sleeved shirt with short-sleeved shirt	.8
Remove stockings	.1	Replace long light trousers with Bermuda shorts	1.0
Replace full slip with half slip	.6	Remove summer weight jacket	2.0
Remove full slip	1.0	Remove undershirt (T-shirt)	.5
Replace pumps with sandals	.2	Remove tie and open collar	.2
Remove hat	.2	Replace knee-length socks with ankle ankle socks	.6
Remove light long-sleeved sweater	1.7	Remove light long-sleeved sweater	2.0
Remove heavy long-sleeved sweater	3.7	Remove heavy long-sleeved sweater	3.7

Chart provided by Dr. Ralph Goldman, U.S. Army Ergonomics Laboratory and the John B. Pierce Foundation, New Haven, Connecticut.

The Federal Energy Administration has estimated that raising the thermostat setting during the summer season by 1°F would save the equivalent of 100,000 barrels of oil per day in the United States.

Source: Energy Reporter, Federal Energy Administration, Citizen Newsletter, August/September 1975.

Figure 9-18. Thermostat Comfort Settings.

larger investment, in terms of capital costs of the building, major savings in the operation of the building as a result of energy cost can be realized.

The control of our building system is another key factor in the evaluation of energy consumption in a building. Building designs should be able to operate efficiently and effectively during normal occupancy time frames and be set back during hours of nonoccupancy. Temperature setbacks have been responsible for a large part of the energy savings from building redesigns. The major source of the savings is based on heating or cooling only the areas that are occupied at any time. This may include designing systems to heat and cool occupied areas, or it may also result in setting back temperatures at nighttime when the buildings are vacated.

Another source of energy savings is using lower comfort levels in unoccupied areas, such as lobbies, corridors, storage areas and other areas that require little use. As an example, many federal buildings are now using temperature setbacks to 65° in unoccupied areas. Building system designs should account for automatic building temperature setbacks so that during daytime operation they can take advantage of the heat brought into the buildings by fenestrations.

KEY FACTORS AFFECTING ENERGY CONSUMPTION IN BUILDINGS

There are several key factors that are important to evaluate when determining the impact on the total overall building energy consumption. These factors are more specific applications of those previously discussed regarding lighting, insulation, and fenestration design.

1. *Volume of Outside Makeup Air.* Outside air introduced into a building may be categorized into three groups. The first category occurs when the air temperature of the outside air is much lower than the required building temperature. In this case, heat must be added to the air to raise it to a desirable comfort level. The second category occurs within a narrow band of temperature differentials when outside air can be used directly in the building systems as a form of climate control. The third category involves the situation when air of a higher temperature is introduced into the air intake and must be cooled to a temperature suitable for building operation. Bringing in outside air with a wide temperature differential from that desired means that energy must be applied to raise or lower the temperature. One method of lowering outside air quantities is by using a variable air-volume (VAV) system. Variable air-volume design is very similar to the process of pumping, in which variable speed controls are used. It is a method that is used in order to raise and lower heating and cooling and ventilation loads in building areas. Mechanical systems provide a means of changing the heating, cooling and ventilation loads that are distributed throughout the building. Designers are being more and more cognizant of the fact that fluctuations in the occupancy levels of building and the HVAC loads are in a dynamic state. Fluctuations of required HVAC loads allow wide ranges of air-volume requirements. Variable-air-volume systems are used because they can reduce by 40 percent the amount of recirculation air versus a constant volume system.

The use of variable air-volume systems cuts down on the total use of air. The result is a reduction of fan horsepower, fuel savings during the heating season and savings of energy during the cooling season. Variable-air-volume systems may be the best method that we have available for regulating the total amount of air distributed to a given area in response to required loads within that area. They prevent the unnecessary waste of energy by broadcast heating or maintaining the same air volume to various parts of the building, whether the heating load in that area has changed or not.

2. *Efficient Allocation of Building Function.* In severe cold weather, the inside of the exterior wall will be considerably lower than the room temperature. As the day progresses, heat from sunlight may raise that temperature appreciably. The result is a fluctuation in temperature being felt by the people situated in the building. Those close to the wall will often request that thermostats be turned up, which will result in a differential temperature in other areas of the building. Distribution of heating, as well as placement of people within a building, will greatly affect the comfort level required for heating and cooling loads.

3. *Relative Humidity.* Humidification in a building protects the health of the occupants by preventing severely dry air. It also is a means of protecting the furniture and equipment within a building structure. Humidification systems raise the moisture content of the air in the building. Dubin and Long, in their book entitled *Energy Conservation Standards for Building Design, Construction, and Operation* indicate that a heat input of approximately 1000 Btus is required to vaporize each pound of water used in the humidification process.* Very low levels of relative humidity will result in static electricity and the obviously uncomfortable effect of severely dry air. Relative humidity of approximately 20 percent should be provided for areas that are occupied more than the majority of the working day. Relative humidity as high as 30 percent may be required to prevent the static electricity discussed previously. An example of its impact is shown by the fact that it requires twice as much energy to maintain a 30 percent relative humidity in a building as opposed to a 20 percent level required under normal conditions. Many building proprietors are now starting out with the relative humidity of 20 percent and adjusting it upward to arrive at a desired moisture level that is comfortable to the people and at the least cost to the operation of the building.

4. *Control of Heating, Ventilating and Air-Conditioning Systems.* HVAC systems use energy in the form of fuel and power required to run and operate mechanical equipment. The power use is calculated based on electrical current used and its operational schedule. Shutting down system operations or using temperature setbacks would greatly reduce the energy required. In current design practices, controls are provided such that the systems may be turned down and adjusted during nonoccupied hours. The shut-back occurs near the end of the normal occupied hours of building operation, so that by the time the building is unoccupied, comfort levels have been reduced. Auto-

*Dubin & Long, p. 104.

matic timers are now being installed in buildings to shut off fans, to turn down thermostats on temperature controls, to shut off humidification cycles, to automatically close air dampers and to totally shut down building systems in certain areas of the building that are not in use. A great deal of flexibility in building-system operation and design are required. More time, effort and thought will be required in building design to provide controls and equipment to operate buildings more energy efficiently.

5. *Mechanical Distribution Systems.* Ductwork and pipelines are two means used to distribute and collect air and liquid materials. Energy losses occur in pipelines and ductwork in two forms: first, energy losses occur as a result of heat loss through the wall of the unit; and, secondly, losses result from friction, which increases the cost of power of operation of the fan blowers or pumps required to operate the system.

Heat losses due to poor insulation of pipeline and ductwork are significant factors. Let's analyze what happens when we turn on hot water in our homes. We may wait several minutes for the water to turn hot. What has happened? The temperature of the gas or liquid has approached ambient temperature because the pipeline was uninsulated. The result is that when we call for hot water, cooler water is first purged from the system, and new hot water is delivered almost directly from the hot water heater. The result is the loss of heated water and an increase in the amount of energy required to heat that water. The amount may seem insignificant for a residential home, but picture the impact on a multistory office building. Unit hot-water heaters are often installed in extreme locations, such as private bathrooms, isolated laboratories, and other areas in the building that are not close to the prime source of hot water.

Insulation on ductwork saves valuable energy. Insulation on ductwork serves a dual purpose: first of all, it conserves energy during the heating cycle, and it also serves to prevent condensation on the exterior ductwork when the cooling systems are in operation.

Losses of energy also result from excessive frictional losses in piping and ductwork systems. Many new buildings are now evaluating their past designs in determining distribution systems. Designs are becoming even more complex by the various zone controls that are required for heating, air-conditioning and ventilation loads. Utilization of plenum designs for office buildings has done much to reduce the frictional losses in fan and equipment operation. A new look must also be given to pipeline and duct computations in lieu of the escalated price that will have to be paid for electricity in powering pumps, blowers and fans that are used in the building system design.

6. *Reduce Ventilation Requirements.* In the past ventilation rates for buildings have been set based on comfort levels. These comfort levels are a result of the amount of air needed to exhaust body odors and to maintain the oxygen level within the building. However, the primary source of building ventilation has been to exhaust noxious odors of which the primary factor is that caused by smoking. Cutting back on the required ventilation rate will have a major impact on energy consumption on a building design. Prohibiting smoking may increase energy savings even more.

7. *Enthalpy Control.* Enthalpy is the amount of heat required to raise one pound of water from 32°F to a liquid state at another temperature. An enthalpy controller senses the total heat content of the return air and outdoor air sources and mixes both streams in an optimal manner to cut total energy loads. As an example, when the outdoor air is cooler than the supply air temperature required in a system, the enthalpy logic controller will maintain 100 percent outside air to cool the building. Enthalpy controllers have been used very successfully in new office buildings and in the retrofit of existing buildings in order to keep down the amount of outside air required in the building systems. A certain amount of fresh air is, of course, required in order to maintain client comfort conditions.

In many cases, designs are including the use of air filters to remove smoke and odor-laden air particles. This further reduces the volume of required outdoor air. Previously, toilet facilities, electric closets and other areas, such as conference rooms, were provided with separate exhaust systems which brought in fresh air immediately from outside. With the increase in energy costs, new designs have included filters which eliminate the need to bring in excessive amounts of outdoor air.

8. *Exhaust Hoods.* Kitchen, laboratory and industrial exhaust hoods require a large amount of exhaust air in order to function properly. Common problems in these areas are two-fold: first; these areas require smoke, heat and fume exhaust in order to function properly. The air required for these processes depends on the type of chemical or air being removed. In many cases, air is drawn through the building and up through the exhausts of the hood. It is more efficient to design a system such that direct air-intakes immediately adjacent to the fume hood can be turned on in order to supply the necessary exhaust air requirements and to avoid drawing unnecessary heat from other areas in the building. In many cases, it is not usually necessary for make-up air to be heated or cooled to the same degree required for occupancy comfort.* A separate system may be provided which directly introduces air at a location immediately adjacent to the exhaust hood.

9. *Solar Energy.* In many areas of the country, the application of solar heating is an effective tool in reducing energy costs. Its application serves both as a use in heating of buildings and hot-water supplies. Solar heating is also used to reduce the peak energy demands during extreme winter conditions. Solar energy sources can be both the passive and the active type of energy application. Passive solar uses are those designs which absorb heat during the day and store the heat for use at night. Added emphasis has been going into the use of passive energy systems as a heat sink.

The solar reflector is used to thermally collect and transfer solar energy. It is called a collection device in a solar set of systems. Factors that affect solar heating include the angle of incident of the sun's rays hitting the collection surface and the efficiency of each collection mechanism itself. The efficiency of the collection system is also dependent on the differential in temperature between the collector itself and the air temperature. Heated fluid flows

*Dubin and Long, p. 120.

through the collector mechanism, and after being heated through the collector, it is then fed to a storage tank to serve as either hot water or domestic hot-water systems, or as a heat reservoir to be used as a source of space heat. The efficiency of the solar systems is also dependent upon the location and the angle of incident of the rays. The best applications of solar systems are the systems which follow the sun's rays.

IMPACT OF MAINTENANCE ON ENERGY SAVINGS

Building maintenance is often neglected. Many building managers feel that they can get by for just a little bit longer without investing additional money into their equipment. As a result, there is a definite decrease in efficiency in system operation and a resultant loss of revenue and energy. Inefficient operations of building systems spells energy waste.* Leaks in pumps, pipelines, crusting of piping systems causing decreased flows and increased losses, improper maintenance of rotary equipment, improperly operating steam traps and uninsulated pipelines all serve to add increased cost to our building system designs. Combustion equipment also suffers from improper operating temperatures, incomplete combustion and poor controls. In lighting systems, one of the major maintenance problems is light loss due to improper cleaning of fixtures. As much as 50 percent of the lumin capacity of fluorescent lights can be preserved by proper cleaning of the fixtures. Relamping is also a method used to replace lighting fixtures before their efficiency drops off substantially.

DEMAND CHARGES FOR ELECTRICAL ENERGY

Power companies are the primary source of the electricity produced for industry, residential, government and private electricity uses. The public is dependent on these companies to provide power at an affordable rate. They provide service to a definite geographic area which prevents duplication of costly generation and transmission services. In addition, costs are optimized by reducing the peak demand by the customers.

High peak demands will result in higher average costs per kilowatt-hour for energy used. In commercial buildings, higher peak demands are more likely to occur during hot spells when the demand on HVAC systems are the greatest. A system for shutting off noncritical loads during these times will help keep peak demands lower and reduce costs.

Generation facilities for producing power must be sized to accommodate these peak demands, or must rely on supplemental energy sources. The time frame for operating at peak demand is usually 5 percent or less of total system operating time. By reducing total system peak demand, the size of the generating system may be reduced, which results in substantial cost savings.

---

*Thumann, Albert, *Plant Engineering: Manager's Guide to Energy Conservation*, 1977, p. 243.

To reduce peak demands of the consumer, the power companies adjust their rate structures to discourage abnormal usages. This helps to average out the customer usage.

Power costs for the year are based on the actual consumption multiplied by the peak demand charge. If, during the year, there was a period of abnormally high energy use, the power company applies a multiplier to the entire year's energy costs.

How does this affect the designer? It impacts his approach to design of mechanical systems of a project. As an example, a pumping station is designed to convey a combined sewage (sewage and stormwater) flow of 440 MGD during wet weather conditions. During dry weather, the sewage flow is 30 MGD. Electric drive motors are used to power the dry weather flow, and turbine generators are used to drive the wet weather pumps. If the 440 MGD pumps were run by electricity, a peak demand rate based on the highest power consumption would be applied for the entire year, even though the station operated at 30 MGD for the majority of the time. The difference is staggering.

ENERGY PROSPECTUS

Energy is a most challenging subject for the design, operation and maintenance engineers that must design and operate our buildings, plants and power systems. Its application in the value engineering field is becoming a more important factor as energy becomes scarcer. We envision that in the future, comparisons may soon be done on the basis of the use of energy as opposed to the actual cost. This is, of course, a projection of what may occur in the future. Our investigation of energy for the purpose of writing this book shows some very startling facts. First of all, the implications of our nonrenewable energy sources at our present rate of consumption indicates that our life-styles will be changing drastically. The emphasis on new and different building designs that are directed toward more energy conservation are important. Soon we may be defining value engineering as a method of determining the best functional balance between the cost, performance, the reliability and the energy efficiency of our buildings' systems. The importance of energy consumption and its use are relevant factors in any VE study, and the intention of this chapter is to sensitize the reader to the impact of energy to ensure that, in the analysis of building systems, energy comparisons are evaluated.

AREAS OF POTENTIAL ENERGY SAVINGS IN PLANT DESIGN

Energy consumption and the resulting energy bills may be reduced substantially by improving the design and operation of plant and building facilities. Energy savings of 50 percent have been made in many instances. This checklist is by no means comprehensive, but it is a start toward reviewing plant and building energy use and may help to save energy.

1. Evaluate economical pipeline size to determine impact of increased friction head on power consumption.
2. Recover waste heat from combustion systems. Minimize excess combustion air.
3. Be cognizant of electrical rate structures and reduce demand charges.
   a. Motor load factors
   b. Power factor (capacitors or synchronous motors)
   c. Reduced voltage starters
4. Place several structures or plants under one meter if the high loads are at different times. Load shedding ensures control of peak loads and eventual demand charges.
5. Recover heat from large engines and motors. As an example, use air to air-heat exchangers on equipment exhaust systems as a source of heat for the buildings.
6. Insulate storage tanks in cases where temperature is a determining factor on performance.
7. Preheat combustion air where practical.
8. Evaluate piping sizes and frictional coefficients to reduce pumping horsepower.
9. Be careful about projected flows. Many plants operate with inefficient pumping systems because of low flows at start up.
10. Use waste products as a supplemental fuel.
11. Cogeneration of power using product waste gas and natural gas to trim peak electrical loading.
12. Reduce system pressures where possible.
13. Use water conservative flush valves, showerheads and toilet bowls. These features reduce system demands and eliminate additional pumping and treatment costs.
14. Check existing plant facilities for duct, tank, building and piping insulation. Many old facilities did not insulate because of the cheap energy supply when they were constructed.
15. Reduce losses through vehicular doors.
16. Use double door vestibules for high traffic areas.
17. Control makeup air for heating systems. Minimize where possible.
18. Analyze building and equipment heat losses as a system. Take advantage of available heat where possible.
19. Investigate solar heating as a means of trimming peak electrical demands.
20. Reduce hydraulic heat losses by energy efficient design.
21. Control oxygen to aeration basins. Provide controls to reduce power input when unnecessary. Cut back on speed and horsepower at low flow periods.
22. Optimize sludge solids concentrations before combustion of solids.
23. Prevent leaks, breaks in insulation, system control breakdowns. MAINTAIN EQUIPMENT AND PROCESS TO PEAK EFFICIENCY.

24. Control the operation of the facility to reduce energy consumption. NOTE: Suggestions on building design for energy conservation are appropriate to plant facilities. Refer to the energy model and list of conservation measures for buildings found in this chapter.
25. Recycle scrubber air and water to reduce makeup quantities.
26. Use available heat in sewage, where possible, to heat buildings.

10
Value Engineering Case Study No. 1: Wastewater Treatment Plant

INTRODUCTION

Located near Oklahoma City, the facility serves several municipalities surrounding the city. In 1975 the estimated population of the service area was 391,000 people and an increase to 503,000 by the year 2000 is forecast. The proposed facility, when complete, will provide sewage treatment services to the area until the year 2000 at which time additional treatment capacity may be needed.

TREATMENT PLANT SERVICE AREA

There are two main drainage basins that collect wastewater within the service area of the City of Oklahoma. The treatment plant under study primarily serves the North Canadian basin, which had been served by six smaller facilities and selected parts of the adjacent Deep Fork Basin.

The new facility is planned for an ultimate capacity of 80 million gallons per day (MGD). The Phase I expansion of the facility provided 40 MGD of treatment capacity and was under construction at the time of the study. Phase II of the facility, which was the scope of the value engineering study, included a 20 MGD expansion to the liquid treatment system and construction of the solids handling system for the ultimate 80 MGD capacity of the plant. The estimated construction cost for the proposed expansion was $26,890,000 based on 1978 costs.

The VE study was prepared for the City of Oklahoma City who will own and operate the treatment plant. The VE study is a part of the US/Environmental Protection Agency requirements for projects over $10 million in construction cost that receive federal funding through the Construction Grants Program. The Oklahoma State Department of Health and the City also played a key role in the study.

The VE study was conducted by the firms of Arthur Beard Engineers, Greeley & Hansen, and Cunningham-Judd & Associates and were led by Glen Hart and Larry Zimmerman.

PROJECT REQUIREMENTS

The primary parameters in the design of a wastewater facility are the size (capacity) of the plant and the degree of treatment necessary to meet the discharge requirements. Treatment capacity requirements are established during the planning stage. Effluent limitations are set by the State Department of Health based on assimilation characteristics of the receiving stream and other health factors. Requirements for the effluent limitations are shown in Table 10-1. These requirements influence the process selection used to achieve the required level of treatment.

DESCRIPTION OF PROJECT

The treatment plant was designed with a single stage activated sludge process for the liquid stream and vacuum filtration with incineration for disposal of solids. The unit operations required for treatment are shown in Table 10-2. Many treatment alternatives were analyzed before determining the final treatment process. The Facilities Plan (Planning Report) compared treatment alternatives and their respective costs. Figure 10-1 is the flow diagram of the selected process.

The plant expansion program was divided into three phases. Phase I (40 MGD) was under construction at the time of the study. Phase II (20 MGD liquid and 80 MGD solids handling capacity) comprises the scope of work for the VE study, and Phase III is planned for future expansion to increase the liquid stream capacity to 80 MGD.

ORGANIZATION AND STAFFING OF VE TEAMS

In selecting the number of studies, the number of teams and the team members for a $25 million project it is important to provide the proper mix of talent in the various design disciplines involved in the project. A familiarity with the designer's schedule for completion of plans and specifications is also necessary. The teams are established to ensure adequate time and talent to analyze all aspects of the project.

The first step in organizing the VE study was to determine the proper number and timing of the studies. Two studies were proposed. One at the conceptual stage of design (20–35 percent) and another during the design

Table 10-1. Effluent Limitations: Wastewater Treatment Plant—Case Study 1.

	30-day Average	7-day Average
Biochemical Oxygen Demands, mg/1	20	30
Suspended Solids, mg/1	30	45
Fecal Coliform Bacteria, number per 100 ml	200	400
pH, limits:	6-9	6-9

TABLE 10-2
PROCESS COMPONENTS
NORTH CANADIAN WASTEWATER
TREATMENT PLANT

Liquid Stream**	Sludge Handling*
1. Influent Pumping	1. Primary Sludge Pumping
2. Screening	2. Activated Sludge Holding
3. Grit Removal	3. Activated Sludge Pumping
4. Primary Clarification	4. Gravity Thickeners
5. Activated Sludge Unit	5. Flotation Thickeners
6. Recycle Pumping	6. Chemical Conditioning
7. Final Clarification	7. Vacuum Filters
8. Chlorination	8. Incineration

*For Ultimate Capacity of the Plant
**For 20 MGD Average Flow

development stage when the design was 60–75 percent complete. The two-stage approach was used so that major concept changes could be implemented early in the project without significant impact on the schedule and redesign cost. The first study analyzed the process of design, layout, design criteria, equipment sizing and arrangement and modes of operation. The second study was to analyze hardware, buildings and detailed design aspects of the project. The second study relates to the constructability of the total project. Table 10-3 shows the VE teams for the project. All team members had prior value engineering experience. Consultants for the study were selected through prescribed procurement procedures.

DESCRIPTION OF VE WORKSHOP

During the proposal and contract stages of the study, the consultants outlined the steps necessary for the completion of the studies. A coordination meeting was held to acquaint all parties involved in the study with value engineering techniques and to outline the responsibilities of the designer, the owner and the VE consultant. Glen Hart and Larry Zimmerman conducted the meeting explaining the VE procedure and identifying information needed to conduct the study. Plans, specifications and background information on the project were provided to the team members for review prior to the study. Preliminary construction cost estimates provided by the designer were analyzed and a cost model prepared.

INFORMATION PHASE

The VE workshop (40 hours in this case) began with a presentation by the designer which outlined the project and the constraints to be placed on the

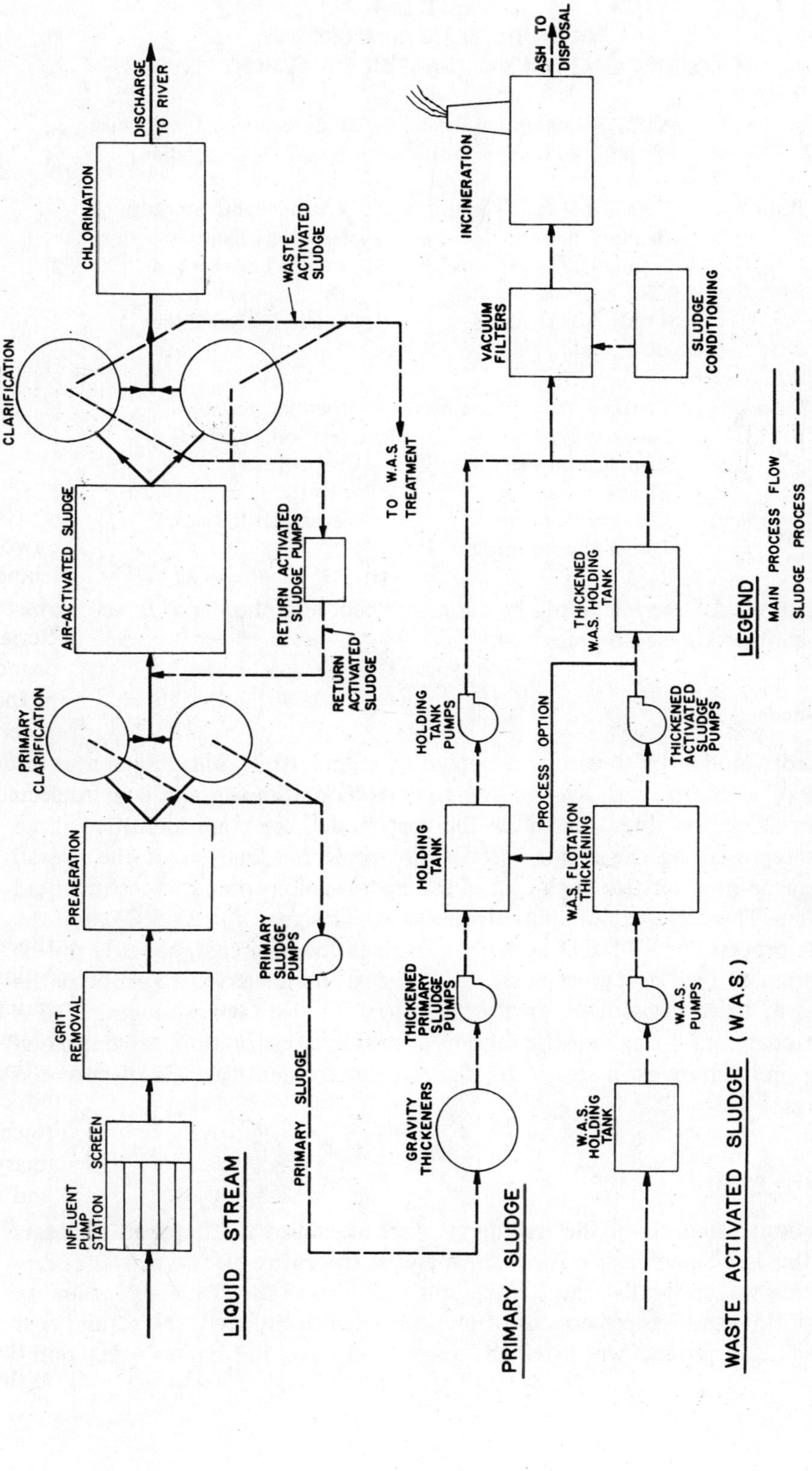

Figure 10-1. Process Flow Diagram—North Canadian Wastewater Treatment Plant.

TABLE 10-3
VE STUDY TEAM COMPOSITION
NORTH CANADIAN WASTEWATER TREATMENT PLANT

	Study A-Conceptual Design (20-35% Completion)	Study B-Design Development (60-75% Completion)
Team 1	Certified Value Specialist	Certified Value Specialist
	Sanitary Engineer	Mechanical Engineer
	Sanitary Engineer	Sanitary Engineer
	Civil Engineer	Cost/Construction
	Landscape Architect	Owners Representative
	Structural Engineer	
Team 2	Certified Value Specialist	Structural Engineer
	Sanitary Engineer	Electrical Engineer
	Chemical Engineer	Civil Engineer
	Electrical Engineer	Architect
	Cost/Construction	Mechanical Engineer
	Owners Representative	

VE study. A description of the design concept and phasing of the construction contracts was also presented.

Cost Model

The cost model for the study is shown in Figure 10-2. This model is in the form of a matrix with system components along the top and construction trades along the side. Based on the cost model, the team identified those areas representing the major costs in the project. Analysis of the overall system pointed out the high cost of solids processing compared to the liquid stream. The fact that the liquid process was designed for 20 MGD and the solids process for 80 MGD partially explained the high cost, however potential areas of high cost were evident. The cost model served to sensitize the teams to the areas with the greatest potential for cost savings. Figure 10-3 is a bar chart indicating the distribution of cost by construction element based upon preliminary estimates. This figure helps to identify areas of potential savings.

Function Analysis

Functional analysis of the treatment plant identified the required elements and the associated costs. The team analyzed the entire plant where the *basic function* was to treat sewage. Each unit process was described in a verb-noun description and basic/secondary functions were deciphered. Next, the cost of each unit process was listed and a worth applied. In Chapter 4 describing

Function Analysis, worth is described as the least cost of performing the required function. Determination of worth aids in the development of creative ideas. These comparison ideas were the beginning of the creative idea listing.

The last step in the functional analysis was the calculation of cost-to-worth ratios. The cost-to-worth ratio (cost divided by worth of the basic function) for the project was 25.5 to 1. This assumed that the solids disposal system was not a basic function. This high ratio indicates considerable potential for cost savings. Figure 10-4 is the function analysis worksheet.

CREATIVE PHASE

During the creative session, team members considered alternate methods of completing the functions required by the design in order to generate ideas to be considered for evaluation. A total of 70 ideas were formulated during the creative session and the functional analysis stage. By using brainstorming as the primary technique, the team generated creative ideas as listed in Figure 10-5. As you can see, the ideas included site arrangements, process changes, material changes and construction-related design alternatives.

JUDGMENT PHASE

The team judged each idea for its technical merit and potential for acceptance. Ideas were rated from one to ten using the following criteria:

1. Potential cost savings
2. Validity of the idea
3. Improvement to the design
4. Impact on project schedule
5. Cost of redesign
6. Likelihood of acceptance

The judgment weightings are shown in Figure 10-6 along with the creative idea listing. Advantages and disadvantages were thrashed out for each idea.

DEVELOPMENT PHASE

A total of 33 ideas were carried forward to the development phase. They were developed into preliminary designs for presentation to the designer and the owner. Table 10-4 is a Summary of Recommended Cost Savings that tallies the ideas recommended. Two examples of recommendations that were implemented by the designer are shown at the end of this chapter as an illustration. Comparison cost information and supporting calculations convey the VE team's concept for each recommended design modification.

No.	System / Unit Process / Description	Site Work	Liquid Process					
			Influent Pumping & Screening	Grit Re-moval	Pre Aera-tion	Primary Clarifica-tion	Aeration	Recycle Pump Station
1.	Excav. & Backfill, Roads	1,275,000	14,700	5,700	15,700	84,300	88,600	8,800
2.	Concrete		199,200	188,000	207,400	352,700	831,000	93,300
3.	Architectural		94,500	18,100	6,000	2,700	16,200	101,600
4.	Misc. Metals		55,000	26,500	8,400	9,500	148,700	51,900
5.	Process Piping		2,300	6,300	9,700	10,300	217,200	59,000
6.	Major Equipment		590,900	164,200	100,800	741,800	1,856,400	62,400
7.	Misc. Equipment		17,400				5,200	
8.	Gates, Weirs, Fibreglas Panels		117,200	42,100	150,100	70,500	130,700	
9.	HVAC		72,000	47,600	9,400	9,500	4,800	85,200
10.	Plumbing		30,800	20,300	4,000	4,100	2,100	36,600
11.	Electrical		44,400	26,200	8,500	5,200	91,000	49,000
12.	Instrumentation		11,600			9,400	13,100	22,200
	Total Cost	1,275,000	1,250,000	545,000	520,000	1,300,000	3,405,000	570,000
	Percent by Process	5.2	5.1	2.2	2.1	5.3	13.8	2.3
	Percent by System						36.9	

Figure 10-2. Matrix Cost Model—North Canadian Wastewater Treatment Plant.

RECOMMENDATION PHASE

To conclude the 40-hour workshop, the VE team summarized their work and organized their presentation of results. On the Tuesday following the workshop, the VE consultants presented the recommendations of the team to the owner, designer, State Department of Health and the US/EPA representatives. The VE Summary Report was submitted shortly thereafter.

Findings of the study revealed the potential for significant savings on initial cost as well as the life-cycle costs of the plant. One recommendation was proposed to change the type of solids dewatering facilities to obtain a dryer

			Solids Process							
Final Clarification	Chlorination	Misc.	Flotation Thickeners	Sludge Pumping	Holding Basins	Gravity Thickeners	Vacuum Filters	Incineration	% of Total	Totals
122,000	23,500		5,400	4,800	24,400	27,200	85,000	36,000	7.4	1,821,100
340,800	65,400		56,500	35,900	336,600	114,000	374,000	475,000	14.9	3,669,800
2,600	2,800		61,500	37,100	24,200	900	595,000	364,000	5.4	1,327,200
66,700	17,300		31,400	15,100	16,700	3,100			1.8	450,300
24,400	25,600		35,700	51,500	42,300	3,300			2.0	487,600
155,200	83,200		632,500	104,900	341,900	254,800	1,651,000	7,350,000	57.2	14,090,000
					23,200		51,000		0.4	96,800
						7,600			2.1	518,200
			51,600	7,900	21,400	3,100	136,000	146,000	2.4	594,500
			22,200	3,500	8,800	1,300	34,000	11,000	0.7	178,700
8,300	21,200		29,800	36,300	21,000	1,700	204,000	218,000	3.2	764,600
	21,000	520,000	13,400		9,500	3,000			2.5	623,200
720,000	260,000	520,000	940,000	297,000	870,000	420,000	3,130,000	8,600,000		24,622,000
2.9	1.1	2.1	3.8	1.2	3.6	1.7	12.7	34.9	100	
			57.9							

Figure 10-2. Matrix Cost Model—North Canadian Wastewater Treatment Plant.

sludge prior to incineration. This recommendation had a potential life-cycle cost savings of $15,928,000, indicating the usefulness of the life-cycle costing approach.

After the owner and designer reviewed and accepted or rejected the VE recommendations, the report was forwarded to the state and federal regulatory agencies. Review comments by the regulatory agencies were also evaluated as a part of the implementation steps in the review process. Those recommendations accepted were then implemented into the design.

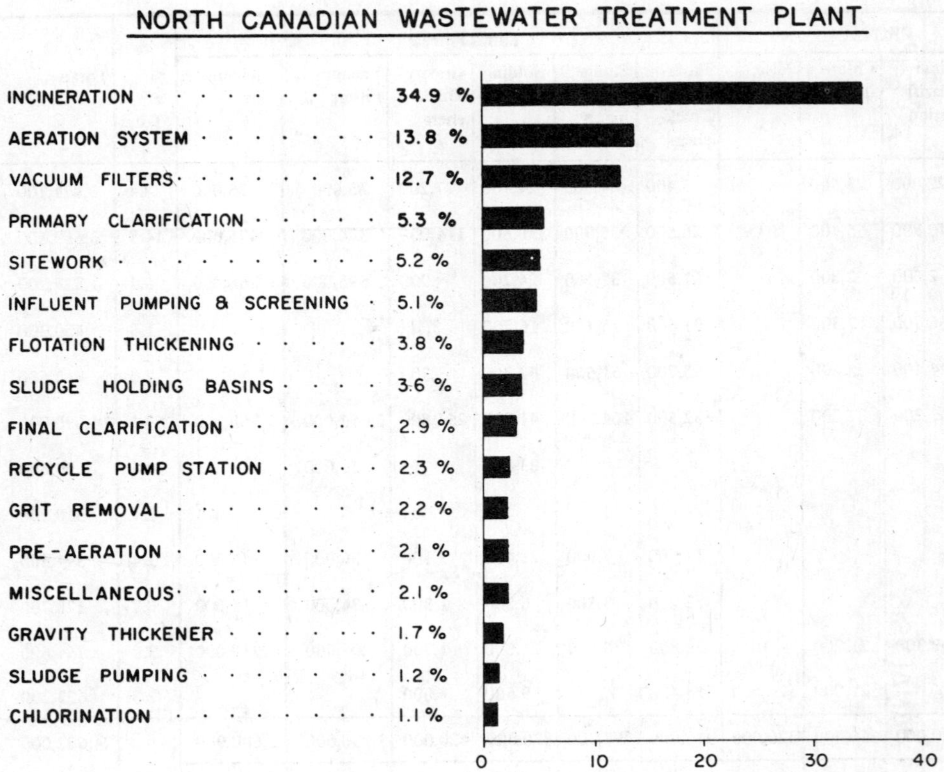

Figure 10-3. Graphical Summary of Costs.

PROJECT ____________

LOCATION ____________

CLIENT ____________

DATE ____________

PAGE ______ OF ______

INFORMATION PHASE

FUNCTION ANALYSIS

ITEM : Entire Plant

FUNCTION : Treat Sewage

FUNCTION ANALYSIS

ITEM #	DESCRIPTION	FUNCTION			COST	WORTH	COMMENTS
		VERB	NOUN	KIND			
	Influent Pump Station	Lifts	Sewage	S			
	Screening	Remove	Trash	S	1,250	1,000	
	Flow Measurement	Measure	Flow	S			
	Grit Removal	Remove	Grit	S	545	50	
	Pre-aeration	Freshen	Sewage	S	520	0	
	Primary Clarifiers	Remove	Solids	B	1,300	750	
	Aeration Basins & Equipment	Remove	BOD	B	3,405	2,000	
	Recycle Pump Station & Secondary Clarifiers	Remove	Solids	B	1,290	1,000	
	Chlorination Facilities	Disinfect	Effluent	B	260	250	
	Instrumentation	Monitor	Process	S	520	0	
	Site Work	Position	Plant	S	1,275	500	

ACTION VERB KIND — B = Basic (Basic Function Only)

MEASURABLE NOUN — S = Secondary Cost/Worth Ratio = ______

Figure 10-4. Function Analysis Worksheet—Entire Plant.

PROJECT ____________
LOCATION ____________
CLIENT ____________
DATE ____________
PAGE ______ OF ______

INFORMATION PHASE

FUNCTION ANALYSIS

ITEM : Entire Plant
FUNCTION : Treat Sewage

FUNCTION ANALYSIS

ITEM #	DESCRIPTION	FUNCTION VERB	FUNCTION NOUN	KIND	COST	WORTH	COMMENTS
	Primary Sludge Pumping Station	Pump	Sludge	S	137	125	
	Activated Sludge Holding & Pumping	Pump	Sludge	S	280	150	
	Flotation Thickening	Thicken	Sludge	S	940	500	
	Gravity Thickeners	Thicken	Sludge	S	420	0	
	Mixed Sludge Holding	Blend	Sludge	S	260	0	
	Vacuum Filtration	Dewater	Sludge	S	2,390	500	
	Incineration	Reduce	Volume	S	7,500	500	
					22,292	7,325	$\frac{\text{COST}}{\text{WORTH}}$ = 3.04
							$\frac{\text{COST}}{\text{WORTH (BASIC)}}$ = 25.57

ACTION VERB
MEASURABLE NOUN
KIND: B = Basic (Basic Function Only); S = Secondary
Cost / Worth Ratio = ______

WORKSHEET No 2

Figure 10-4. Function Analysis Worksheet—Entire Plant.

PROJECT ____________
LOCATION ____________
CLIENT ____________
DATE ____________
PAGE ______ OF ______

CREATIVE PHASE — CREATIVE IDEA LISTING | **JUDGEMENT PHASE** — IDEA EVALUATION

NO (1)	CREATIVE IDEA (2)	ADVANTAGES (3)	DISADVANTAGES (4)	IDEA (5) RATING
1	Reduce air volume in space above pumps	Reduce Energy		7
2	Use screw pumps for return sludge pumps	Lower Energy Cost	Less Flexibility	3
3	Combine influent pump station with Existing station	Less Cost Easier Operation	Work while plant in operation	6
4	Install only 20MGD capacity	Save initial cost		6
5	Check hydraulic head losses	Minimize Head	None	7
6	Relocate grit tanks adjacent to Phase I, Plant	Less intercystor Combine operations	None	10
7	Reduce freeboard - Lower Roof of Grit Building	Initial Costs	None	7
8	Reduce size of Preaeration Tanks	Energy savings	None	10
9	Use Common Wall Construction with Grit Tank	Cost Savings	Minor Savings	7
10	Relocate meters	Save money	Eases Operation	10
11	Use Rectangular Clarifiers	Cost	Redesign	9
12	Reduce Yard Piping - Use Channels		More cost	4

LIST ALL CREATIVE IDEAS BEFORE PROCEEDING TO JUDGEMENT PHASE. 10 MOST DESIRABLE 1 LEAST DESIRABLE

WORKSHEET No 3

Figure 10-5. One Of The Creative Idea Listing Worksheets To Show The Types Of Ideas Generated In The Creative Session.

TABLE 10-4. SUMMARY OF POTENTIAL COST SAVINGS

Item No.	Description	Initial Cost	Proposed Cost
1A,1B, 1C,2,3	OPTION 1 Relocate Phase 11 Structures within the limits of the Phase 1 Roadways	1,385,304	783,304
4	OPTION 2 Utilize Rectangular Structures and Common Wall Construction	1,385,304	395,304
2	Reduce Roadways	38,500	–
10	Relocate Raw Sewerage Pump Station	317,000	243,000
11,12 &16	Eliminate Installation of Equipment for Future Design Flows	328,000	–
22	Omit Preaeration Basin - Use Preaeration Channels	520,000	40,000
24	Use Common Walls on: Infl. P.S., Grit Tanks & Preaeration Basin	28,000	–
26&40	Convert Primary & Secondary Clarifiers from Circular to Rectangular	2,140,000	1,610,000
29D	Cover Tanks with Concrete Domes	588,400	331,300
31	Primary Clarifier Sizing	1,300,000	900,000
38	Combine Return Sludge Systems & Aeration Basins	438,500	299,700
47	Relocate CL_2 Contact Basin: See Alt. Recommendation Item No. 48	330,000	260,000
48	Eliminate Outfall Line: See Alternative Recommendation Item No. 47	70,000	2,000
52	Omit Waste Activated Sludge Holding Tank	120,000	–
53& 58A	Reduce Number of Flotation Thickeners	940,000	607,500
54	Omit Gravity Thickened Sludge Holding Tank & Long Suction Lines; Add Pumps	137,000	162,000
55	Eliminate Gravity Thickeners	1,953,000	1,815,000
57	Shorten Conveyors by Relocating Vacuum Filter Building	13,200	–
58C	Reduce Size of Incinerator Building	1,250,000	849,870
59	Move Bulk Storage Outside	42,000	24,000
64D	Omit Incinerators; Use Composting	8,600,000	5,200,000
65	Use Port. Platform in Flot. Thickener Bldg.	20,000	2,000
66	Delete Wash-Down & Sludge Loading Area	490,000	344,000
68	Alternate Pumps & Sludge Flotation Thickeners	36,800	25,000
69	Primary Clarifier Dewatering Lines	36,000	9,000
70	Reduce Waste Activated Sludge Estimates	12,930,000	10,980,700

TABLE 10-4.

Initial Savings	Annualized Initial Savings	Annual O&M Savings	Total Annual Savings	Present Worth Annual Savings
602,000	55,178	–	55,178	601,998
990,000	90,742	–	90,742	989,993
38,500	3,529	–	3,529	38,500
74,000	6,780	1,020	7,800	85,100
328,000	30,064	–	30,064	328,000
480,000	43,566	8,199	52,196	569,458
28,000	2,566	–	2,566	28,000
530,000	48,580	–	48,580	530,000
257,100	23,566	–	23,566	257,100
400,000	36,660	1,000	37,660	410,870
138,800	12,726	–	12,726	138,840
70,000	6,416	–	6,416	70,000
68,000	6,235	–	6,235	68,025
120,000	11,000	19,384	30,384	331,489
332,500	30,477	–	30,477	332,504
(25,000)	(2,331)	9,248	6,917	75,464
138,000	12,649	–	12,649	138,000
13,200	1,209	400	1,609	17,554
400,130	36,676	–	36,676	400,130
18,000	1,650	–	1,650	18,000
3,400,000	311,640	–	311,640	3,399,992
18,000	1,650	–	1,650	18,000
146,000	13,382	–	13,382	145,998
11,800	1,083	1,000	2,083	22,725
27,000	2,475	–	2,475	27,000
1,949,300	178,671	–	178,671	1,949,300

PROJECT	DEVELOPMENT AND RECOMMENDATION PHASE	WORKSHEET № 4
LOCATION		
CLIENT		
DATE		
PAGE ___ OF ___	ITEM: Eliminate Outfall Line	NO: 48

ORIGINAL CONCEPT: (Attach sketch where applicable)

The original outfall from the chlorine contact basin is contained in a 72" diameter RCP pipeline before discharging into an open channel.

PROPOSED CHANGE: (Attach sketch where applicable)

It is proposed that the length of the enclosed pipe be reduced and 450 linear feet of open channel be constructed in its place.

DISCUSSION:

The proposed channel alignment can be aligned to reserve space for future plant additions. Reduction of the initial cost of this proposal is a definite advantage.

LIFECYCLE COST SUMMARY	CAPITAL	O & M COSTS	TOTAL
INITIAL COST— ORIGINAL	70,000		
— PROPOSED	2,000		
— SAVINGS	68,000		
ANNUAL COST— ORIGINAL	6,420	0	6,420
— PROPOSED	185	0	185
— SAVINGS	6,235	0	6,235
PRESENT WORTH – ANNUAL SAVINGS			68,000

Figure 10-6. Example 1—Modification Of Outfall Line From Chlorination Tank.

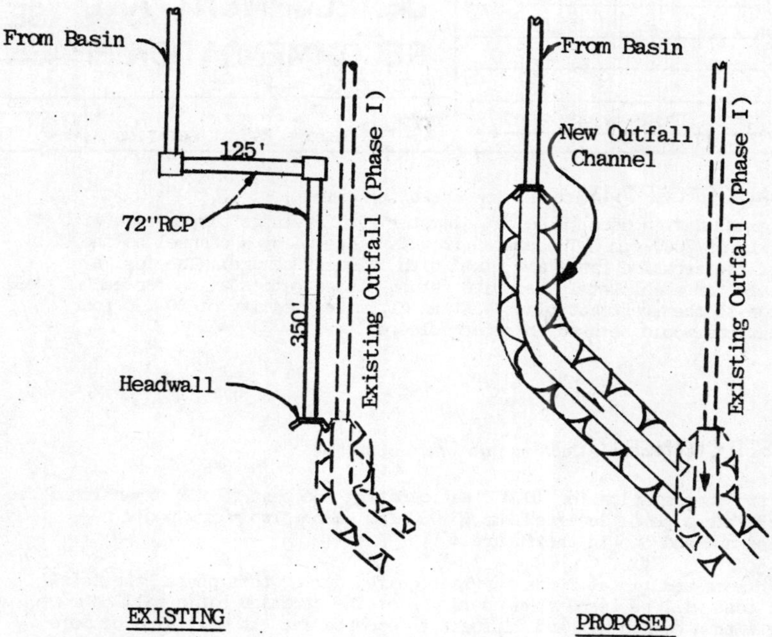

Figure 10-7. Sketch Of Original Outfall Design And Proposed Design.

PROJECT ____	DEVELOPMENT AND RECOMMENDATION PHASE		WORKSHEET No 4
LOCATION ____			
CLIENT ____			
DATE ____			
PAGE ____ OF ____	ITEM: Combine RAS at Aeration	NO: 38	

ORIGINAL CONCEPT: (Attach sketch where applicable)

The original design uses three 54" diameter return sludge pumps each with a capacity of 7000 gpm. The pumped flow is conveyed by a channel to the front of the aeration tanks and mixed with influent sewage. The design concept is for a completely seqerate return sludge pump station for each 20 MGD expansion to the treatment plant. At an ultimate capacity of 80 MGD four pump stations would be used to return sludge.

PROPOSED CHANGE: (Attach sketch where applicable)

Design the pump station for 40 MGD anticipating the next 20 MGD expansion. Use three 72" screw pumps designed for 16,000 gpm each. Two pumps would be installed now and one in the future.

Although some additional funds may be required during this phase, the total capital cost will be less. The operation of the aeration basin will be more uniform with a common mix and influent to each basin. It will also be more convenient to operate one station rather than two.

DISCUSSION: It is also proposed that the return sludge mixers be combined in one basin and configuration modified as shown on the enclosed sketch.

LIFE CYCLE COST SUMMARY	CAPITAL	O & M COSTS	TOTAL
INITIAL COST– ORIGINAL	438,540		
– PROPOSED	299,700		
– SAVINGS	138,840		
ANNUAL COST– ORIGINAL	40,196	0	40,196
– PROPOSED	27,470	0	27,470
– SAVINGS	12,726	0	12,726
PRESENT WORTH – ANNUAL SAVINGS			138,840

Figure 10-8. Example No. 2—Combine Return Activated Sludge Pump Station With The Proposed Station For The Next 20 MGD Expansion. Construct One 40 MGD Station In Lieu Of Two 20 MGD Stations.

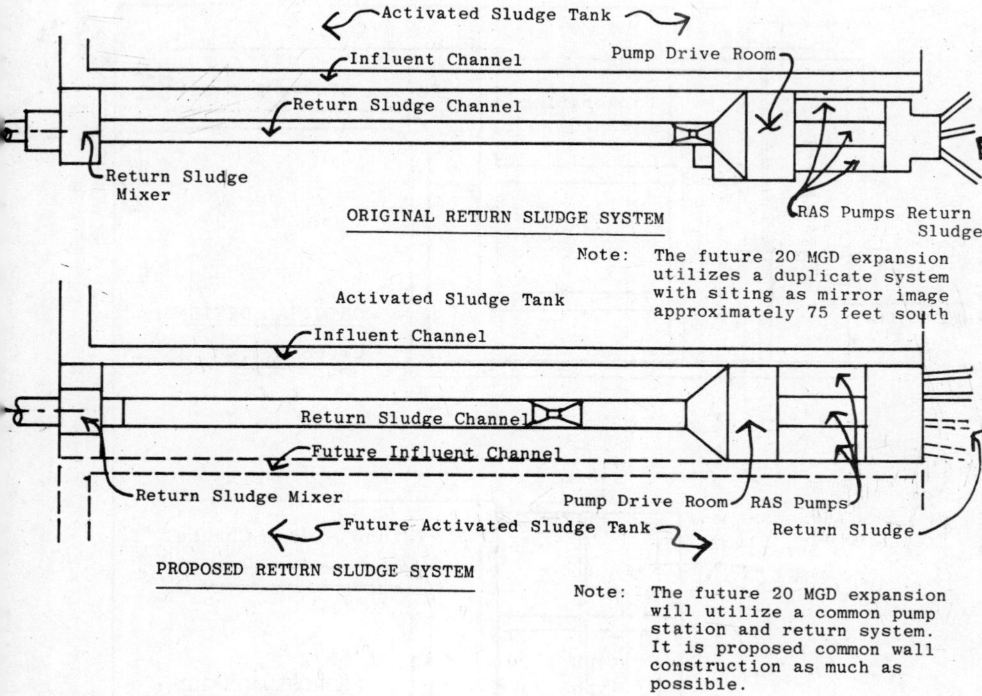

Figure 10-9. Sketch Of Original And Proposed Return Sludge Pump Station And Conveyance System.

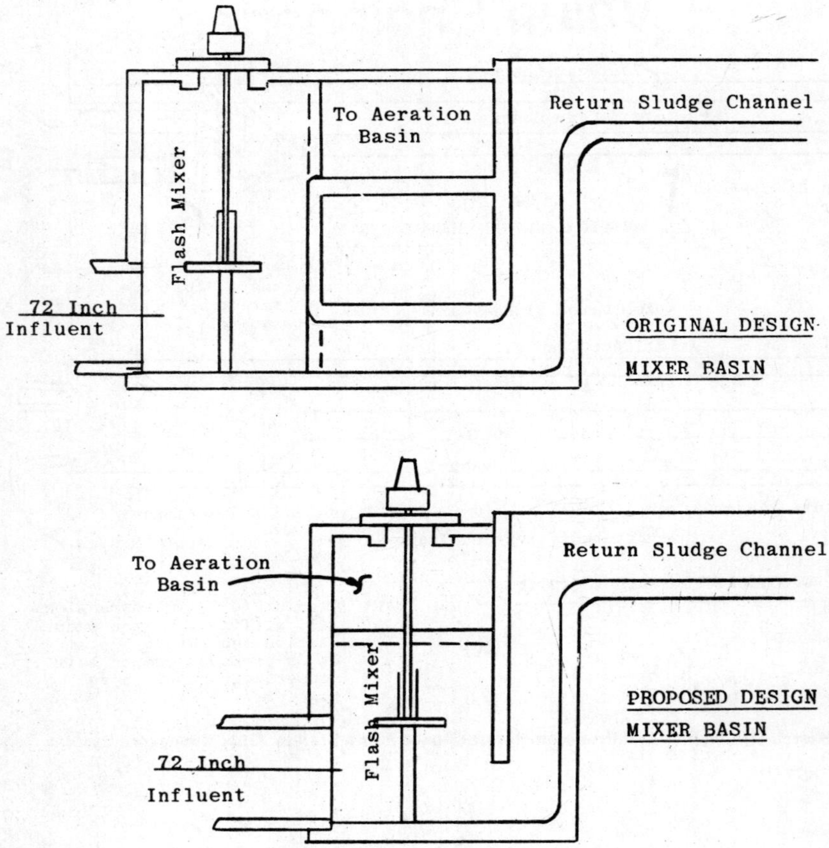

Figure 10-10. Sketch Of Original And Proposed Mixing Channel At Aeration Tank.

11
Value Engineering Case Study No. 2: Wastewater Treatment Plant

Management and coordination have been stressed as a significant factor in a VE study. The success of the study also depends on the thoroughness of design information and objectivity of the designer who is participating in the study and who also is reviewing the VE recommendations. The VE Case Study 2 contained these elements, and their results were a benefit to everyone.

The planning report studied several treatment processes, including land treatment of sewage. Analyses were also conducted during the planning to determine the feasibility of expanding the existing outdated treatment plant. Combined sewers service part of the drainage area in the city. High peak flow requires flow equalization to dampen the impact on the treatment processes. The City predicated the need to move the plant to its selected site.

The Wastewater Treatment Plant is to be designed to treat an average flow of 12.5 million gallons per day (MGD). The estimated construction cost of the treatment plant is $18,763,000. The study is part of the US/EPA requirements for wastewater treatment plants exceeding $10 million in construction cost. Government agencies involved in the review and approval were the Colorado Department of Health and the US/EPA. Value engineering studies for the project were conducted by Arthur Beard Engineers, Inc. In addition, the City Engineer and a sanitary engineer from the design firm were on the study teams. The first study was conducted at the 20 percent completion stage, and the second study at the 60–70 percent stage. The case study information presented here is from the first study conducted in April of 1979.

PROJECT REQUIREMENTS

Design capacity for the dry-weather flows to the treatment plant was 12.5 MGD. Storm-water flows were not firm at the time of the first study, as the design engineer was in the process of computing storm-water runoff flows by using the STORM computer model. It was estimated that the required storage capacity could be as much as 30 million gallons of storm water. Storm-water volume was important because it affected sizing of the flow equalization basin and preliminary treatment units.

Effluent requirements set by the State Department of Health for the Wastewater Treatment Plant are shown in Table 11-1.

Table 11-1. Effluent Limitations Wastewater Treatment Plant.

Biochemical Oxygen Demand	30 mg/l
Suspended Solids	30 mg/l
Chlorine Residual	0.3 mg/l

Final requirements for discharge were not finalized at the time of the study. In addition, there was concern about the salinity requirement from wastewater flow into the Colorado River.

DESCRIPTION OF PROJECT

The proposed treatment plant design includes a liquid stream process with a single stage, diffused air-activated sludge facility with chlorination and dechlorination. Solids handling facilities included anaerobic digestion of primary sludges and aerobic digestion of secondary waste activated sludge. Both sludges are blended together before being dewatered by belt filter presses.

In determining the treatment process, intensive studies of land treatment were made. Land treatment was not the most cost-effective treatment alternative for the wastewater needs for the project.

Figure 11-1 is a diagram of the Process Flow Diagram, and Table 11-2 shows the Process Design Criteria used as the basis of design for the project. The process flow diagram and design criteria summarize many months of planning, calculating, studying and analyzing of alternative designs. This information was provided to the VE team for review.

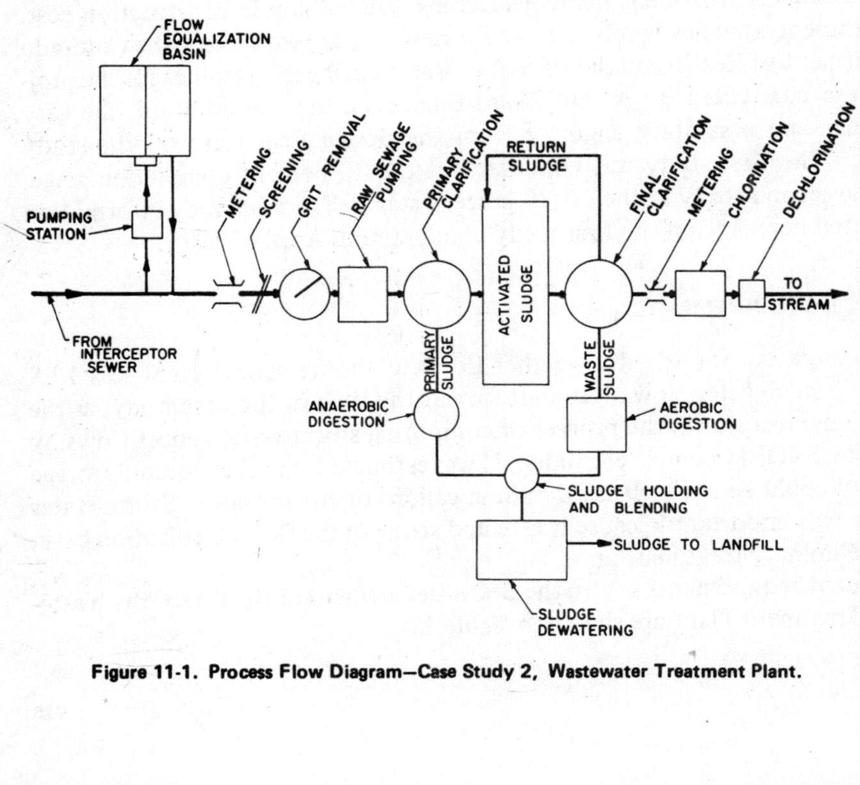

Figure 11-1. Process Flow Diagram—Case Study 2, Wastewater Treatment Plant.

Table 11-2. Process Design Criteria—Liquid Stream Only Wastewater Treatment Plant.

RAW WASTEWATER CHARACTERISTICS	
Flow–Design Avg. Day	12.5 MGD
Flow–Design Max. Day	25.0 MGD
BOD_5	254 mg/l
Total Suspended Solids (TSS)	225 mg/l
PRELIMINARY TREATMENT	
Metering	
Parshall Flume–3′-0″ Throat 0.60 to 33.5 MGD	
Screening	
Mechanical Barscreen (4′-0″ wide)	
Grit Removal	
Grit Collectors (two)	18′ Diameter
Settling Rate	40,000 GPD/SF
Grit Volume	2 CF/MG (Average Flow)
Primary Clarification	
Primary Clarifiers (two)	115′-11 Dia. × 8′ SWD
Surface Settling Rate	653 GPD/SF @ 12.5 MGD
Weir Loading Rate	9600 GPD/LF @ 12.5 MGD
Detention Time	3.11 hrs. @ 12.5 MGD
SECONDARY TREATMENT	
Activated Sludge System	
BOD_5 Applied (35% Removal by Primaries)	168 mg/l
TSS Applied (60% Removal by Primaries)	100 mg/l
Detention Time	6.2 hour @ 12.5 MGD
MLVSS	2100 to 2200 mg/l
Units (4)	120′ × 60′ × 15′ SWD
F/M	0.34
Sludge Retention Time	7–12 days
Oxygen Required	17,602 pounds/day (Average)
Final Clarification	
Final Clarifiers (Two)	125′ diameters × 14 feet SWD
Surface Settling Rate	548 GPD/SF @ 12.5 MGD
Weir Loading Rate	5750 GPD/LF @ 12.5 MGD
Detention Time	5.8 hour @ 12.5 MGD
DISINFECTION	
Chlorination Detention Time	30 min @ 25.0 MGD 60 min @ 12.5 MGD
Dechlorination	Instantaneous

ORGANIZING AND STAFFING OF VE TEAMS

In presenting these case studies, the concept of how to develop and structure a value engineering team has been highlighted. Project descriptions have been presented to show how the team members and their areas of expertise are organized to provide diversity of talent and experience. Selection of the number of studies and the scope of each study are also based on the size, complexity and cost of the project.

Two studies were proposed for the VE of the Wastewater Treatment Plant. The first study served as the basis for the case study presented herein. A study is usually conducted at the 20–35 percent completion of design to analyze the overall process and layout of the project. The savings generated can be more easily implemented without insurmountable impact on redesign cost and scheduling.

The study teams for the Wastewater Treatment Plant are outlined in Figure 11-2. Having a representative from the owner's staff and a member of the design staff on the team added a worthy element to the study. Both participants were interested in helping the designer prepare a better product for the owner.

The expertise and management of a VE study was also enhanced through the leadership of a certified value specialist. All of the team members, with the exception of the owner's representative had prior experience in value engineering.

DESCRIPTION OF VE WORKSHOP

The value engineering studies were a part of the designer's contract for the project. The VE consultant was selected as a subcontractor to ensure that an independent and objective analysis was performed.

The first step of the services provided by the VE consultant was an orientation meeting with the owner, designer and the VE consultant. The VE consultant presented an overview of how a study is conducted, including the information and assistance required from the designer. The most important aspect of the orientation is to bring an understanding of what VE is and how it works. It is also the first opportunity to show the owner that the quality of his project is not in jeopardy. It must be understood that there is unnecessary cost in all designs, and by removing that cost, the VE consultant is reinforcing the integrity of the project. The orientation is also an opportunity to establish a rapport between the designer and the VE team. Remember that both are dependent on each other for achieving benefits useful to the owner. During the orientation, the designer also discussed the history of the project and schedule for the VE study.

Cost estimates, plans, specifications, design reports, discharge requirements, the 201 Facilities Plan, utility rates and other background information were forwarded to the VE team prior to the workshop session. The data were well organized and complete.

Certified Value Specialist	VE Consultant
Civil Engineer	VE Consultant
Sanitary Engineer	VE Consultant
Sanitary Engineer	Design Firm
Structural Engineer	VE Consultant
Estimator	VE Consultant
Civil Engineer	Owner's Representative

Figure 11-2. Value Engineering Team: Wastewater Treatment Plant (Study A).

THE VE WORKSHOP

Constraints to the project design were summarized in advance by the designer. The constraints for the study are outlined in Table 11-3. The constraints describe the needs of the specific design requirements based on physical conditions and specific requirements by the regulatory agencies.

Representatives of the design team, owner, state and US/EPA attended the first and last day of the VE study.

The VE workshop began with an introduction by the VE consultant briefly describing the VE procedure and stressing that it is always easier to analyze an existing design than it is to invent a new one. Presentations by the project manager and project engineers for specific areas of design helped familiarize the VE team with the particulars of the design. Questions about the design were addressed by the team members. In particular, the subject of sizing and design of the flow equalization basins and layout of the plant were discussed. The design staff completed its presentation but remained available for questions throughout the week.

COST MODEL

Preliminary engineering estimates formed the basis for the cost model for the study. Figure 11-3 is a condensed version of the cost model. The team's analysis of the cost model for the entire project provided the following conclusions:

Table 11-3. Project Constraints Wastewater Treatment Plant (Study A).

1. The site of the facility has been identified. Orientation of units within the site boundaries are subject to value engineering review subject to subsequent project constraints.
2. The basic treatment processes and treatment capacities are identified in the Predesign Study.
3. The discharge permit requirements have been identified for secondary treatment. Additional requirements regarding nitrification are unknown until completion of EPA water quality assessment study of receiving stream.
4. An interim treatment study and facility design will precede this project. The interim treatment facility will be located at the new plant site and will incorporate units which will become an integral part of the new plant when completed. The units being considered for the interim treatment facility are:
   (a) The flow equalization basin is being considered in the interim treatment concept as an aerated lagoon.
   (b) The aerobic digesters are being considered in the interim treatment concept as a package activated sludge treatment plant.
5. EPA grant and grant amendment special conditions influence design considerations as they apply to future disposal of plant effluent.
6. The flow equalization/storm-water retention facility will be required. Sizing and siting of this facility is subject to value engineering review.
7. The 100-year flood level at the site determines minimum unit and building floor elevations.
8. A private landing strip is located adjacent to the project site on the western boundary. The County is presently developing restrictions pertaining to the operation of such landing strips. Clearance zones and height restrictions are not known at this time.
9. The State has established salinity discharge standards which allow a 400 mg/l increase in salinity from raw water source to wastewater treatment plant effluent.
10. Building code requirements determine minimum design standards for all disciplines involved.
11. Utility rate structures and supply (electrical, natural gas, potable water and other fuels) affect design requirements.
12. The owner has requested that odor control be given a high priority in the design of the facility.
13. The flexibility in operation of the plant and the operation and maintenance costs of the plant cannot be compromised in the value engineering study.

Item No.	Description (System / Unit Process)	Site Work	Admin. Bldg	Flow Equal. Basin	Pre-Treat Unit	Raw Sewage P.S.	Prim. Clarifier	Aeration Basins
				Liquid Process				
1.	Excavation and Backfill	2,050,000		358,900	32,100	19,300	55,800	123,400
2.	Concrete			1,980,000	164,000	100,000	301,000	710,000
3.	Architectural		312,800		91,100	47,400		158,400
4.	Misc. Metals							
5.	Process Piping			12,500	10,000	85,000	16,500	50,000
6.	Major Equipment			590,000	142,500	291,800	410,000	975,500
7.	Misc. Equipment		141,600					
8.	Gates, Weirs, Troughs			78,500	153,900	47,100	19,300	168,100
9.	HVAC		52,500					
10.	Plumbing		28,800					
11.	Electrical		43,800	75,000	67,100	125,100	15,200	246,600
12.	Instrumentation/Metering	700,000			9,800			34,500
	Total Cost	2,750,000	579,500	3,094,900	670,500	715,700	817,800	2,466,500
	Percent of Total	16.2	3.4	18.2	3.9	4.2	4.8	14.6
	Percent by System			($8,999,400) 52.9%				

Figure 11-3. Matrix Cost Model—Case Study 2, Wastewater Treatment Plant.

1. Excavation, backfill and concrete costs are above average when compared to similar projects.
2. The percentage costs for liquid stream are above normal when compared to the solids system.
3. The flow equalization basin costs (18.2 percent) appear high and the \$1,980,000 of concrete in the basin is 11 percent of the entire project.
4. The aerobic digestion cost of \$1,234,400 is higher than the cost of anaerobic digestion, or contrary to what one might expect.
5. Major equipment for flow equalization, raw sewage pumping, aeration basins, aerobic digesters and sludge dewatering equipment are major expenditures. (High-cost areas—they may be necessary, but are still costly.)

Historical data and the experience of the team members helped to identify the conclusions listed above. Having sensitized the team to the cost of the project, the team leader next led the VE team through the functional analysis.

			Solids Process							
Final Clarifier	CL_2 Cont. Tank	CL_2 Bldg	Primary Sludge PS	Anaerobic Digesters	Aerobic Digesters	Sludge Hold Tank	Supern. Hold Tank	Sludge Dewat Bldg	% of Total	Totals
86,900	22,900	4,400	8,000	33,660	80,100	5,300	4,200	22,000	17.1	2,906,900
378,300	152,500	38,800	49,500	316,500	405,000	71,000	26,500	112,500	28.3	4,805,600
		74,400		73,800	81,000			262,500	6.6	1,101,400
				4,500						4,500
18,700			20,000	204,900	92,600	10,000	3,100	242,000	4.5	765,300
225,000	40,000	62,500	32,500	372,500	425,000	57,500		767,500	25.9	4,392,300
	10,600	10,100	5,000	10,000	10,000			395,000	3.4	582,300
19,400				8,800				700	2.9	495,800
									0.3	52,500
									0.2	28,800
19,400	25,000	20,100	17,000	113,900	123,400	7,200		161,400	6.2	1,060,200
	25,000				17,300				4.6	786,600
747,700	276,000	210,300	132,000	1,138,500	1,234,400	151,000	33,800	1,963,600		16,982,200
4.4	1.6	1.2	0.8	6.7	7.3	0.9	0.2	11.6	100	
			$4,653,300 (27.5%)							

Contingencies @ 5%	849,110
Inflation @ 5% (To First Quarter 1980)	891,560
Preliminary Cost Total	$18,722,870

Figure 11-4. Figure 11-3. Matrix Cost Model—Case Study 2, Wastewater Treatment Plant.

FUNCTION ANALYSIS

Functional analyses are prepared for the entire treatment plant and for several of the higher cost unit processes in the project. Figure 11-4 is the functional analysis of the entire plant. Note that each unit is described in a verb/noun description and the functions are identified as basic or secondary. The basic function is to remove pollutants; therefore, only those items that remove pollutants are basic functions. Costs are taken from the cost model and the worth or least cost of providing the required function is identified. The team originated many ideas when deriving a worth. In coming up with the least cost to perform the function, alternate ways of designing the project were discovered. The cost/worth ratio for the project was 3.41 to 1, which

PROJECT ______
LOCATION ______
CLIENT ______
DATE ______
PAGE ____ OF ____

INFORMATION PHASE

FUNCTION ANALYSIS

ITEM : Treatment Plant
FUNCTION : Remove Pollutants

FUNCTION ANALYSIS

ITEM #	DESCRIPTION	FUNCTION			COST	WORTH	COMMENTS
		VERB	NOUN	KIND			
1	Flow Equalization	Equalize	Flow	S	3,100,000	500,000	
2	Pretreatment Facilities	Remove	Trash & Grit	B	670,000	400,000	
3	Pumping Station	Elevate	Sewage	S	722,000	500,000	
4	Primary Clarifiers	Concentrate	Solids	B	820,000	500,000	
5	Aeration Basins	Grow	Microbes	B	2,470,000	1,500,000	
6	Secondary Clarifiers	Concentrate	Solids	B	750,000	650,000	
7	Chlorine Contact Tank	Disinfect	Sewage	B	276,000	150,000	
8	Chlorine Building	Houses	Equipment	S	210,000	125,000	
9	Aerobic Digestors	Stabilize	Solids	S	1,234,000	600,000	
10	Anaerobic Digestors	Stabilize	Solids	S	1,140,000	900,000	
11	Sludge Dewatering	Removes	Water	S	1,614,000	900,000	
12	Operations Building	Houses	Personnel Control	S	5,724,000	760,000	
13	Site Work	Services	Units	S	2,050,000	1,500,000	
14	Instrumentation	Monitors	Process	S	700,000	700,000	
15	Sludge Drying Beds	Removes	Water	S	300,000	-0-	
16	Primary Sludge Pumping	Move	Sludge	S	169,000	150,000	
17	Sludge Holding & Blending	Store	Sludge	S	151,000	151,000	
18	Supernatant Holding Tank	Store	Supernatant	S	34,000	-0-	
					17,000,000	4,980,000	

ACTION VERB
MEASURABLE NOUN

KIND: B = Basic; S = Secondary

(Basic Function Only) Cost / Worth Ratio = $\frac{17,000,000}{4,980,000} = 3.41$

WORKSHEET № 2

Figure 11-4. Function Analysis Worksheet—Case Study 2, Entire Plant.

indicates that there may be unnecessary cost in the design. The functional analysis of the flow equalization basis is shown in Figure 11-5. It is included to show the functional breakdown of a unit process within the entire plant.

CREATIVE PHASE

Individual and group creative sessions provided a large quantity of ideas to augment the ideas generated while speculating on worth. A total listing of 105 ideas came from the functional analysis and creative phase. The first 12 ideas are shown as an example of the idea listing (Figure 11-6).

JUDGMENT PHASE

The VE team jointly evaluated the ideas in the creative listing. Ideas were assigned a rating from 1–10 with the team's rating of those ideas shown on the Creative Phase/Judgment Phase worksheet. Many of the team members' ideas appeared to have a high potential for savings.

DEVELOPMENT PHASE

During the development phase of the VE study, ideas that were worthy of further analysis were assigned to the team members. A total of 38 recommendations were prepared. Figure 11-7 is a listing of the ideas recommended to the designer and to the owner. Two examples of accepted VE recommendations are included at the end of this chapter to give the reader an understanding of the scope of each recommendation. The design engineer's response to the VE recommendation is also included to show a good example of the required backup.

RECOMMENDATION PHASE

Oral presentation of the VE results was made to the design firm, the County Utilities Commission, the State Department of Health, and the US/EPA. The presentation started with an introduction by the team coordinator. Next, each recommendation was explained by members of the VE team. Copies of all of the VE worksheets were prepared for the designer and the owner to allow them to begin analyzing the VE recommendations. The VE team's report was completed and forwarded to the designer three weeks after the completion of the workshop.

The cost savings for the accepted VE recommendations were estimated at $1,269,694 for initial savings, and $2,184,284 for the present worth of the life-cycle cost savings. In addition, redesign cost necessary to implement the required changes was $42,000. The net savings in initial cost was $1,227,694. A return for investment dollar of over 20:1 was saved in the VE study.

PROJECT ______	**INFORMATION PHASE**
LOCATION ______	**FUNCTION ANALYSIS**
CLIENT ______	ITEM : Flow Equalization
DATE ______ PAGE ____ OF ____	FUNCTION : Equalizes Flow

WORKSHEET No 2

FUNCTION ANALYSIS

ITEM #	DESCRIPTION	FUNCTION VERB	FUNCTION NOUN	FUNCTION KIND	COST	WORTH	COMMENTS
	Excavation	Prepare	Site	S	166,000	166,000	
	Struct. Backfill	Protect Fill	Structure Hole	S	8,000	8,000	
	Select Backfill	Supports	Tank	S	184,000	-0-	$10/yd
	Reinf. Concrete	Contains	Liquid	B	1,980,000	800,000	
	Sluice Gates	Direct	Flow	S	78,000	200,000	
	Process Piping	Convey	Liquid	S	12,500	12,500	
	Pumps	Elevates	Sewage	S	300,000	-0-	
	Aeration Equipment	Suspends	Solids	S	290,000	-0-	
	Electrical	Energize	System	S	75,000	-0-	1,006,500
	TOTALS				3,093,500	800,000	

ACTION VERB
MEASURABLE NOUN

KIND: B = Basic, S = Secondary

(Basic Function Only)
Cost/Worth Ratio = 3.86

Figure 11-5. Function Analysis—Case Study 2, Flow Equalization.

PROJECT ____________
LOCATION ____________
CLIENT ____________
DATE ____________
PAGE ______ OF ______

CREATIVE PHASE — CREATIVE IDEA LISTING | **JUDGEMENT PHASE** — IDEA EVALUATION

NO (1)	CREATIVE IDEA (2)	ADVANTAGES (3)	DISADVANTAGES (4)	IDEA (5) RATING
1	Replace Suction Secondary Clarifiers with STD or Rim Feed Units	Less Cost	Reduced Efficiency	6
2	Flow Equalization after Primaries	Reduced Costs Keep Down Odors		10
3	Flow Equal Impact/Downstream Units			8
4	Aerobic Digester Loadings	Less Cost	None	10
5	Anaerobic Digester Loading	Less Cost	Less Gas Less Flexibility	5
6	Redundant Supernatant Tank	Stand by Unit	Less Units	8
7	Variable Speed R.S. Pumps (2 constant, 2 variable)	Less Cost	Less O&M	9
8	Standby Sludge Drying Beds (Elim.)	Reduces Cost Less O&M	Less Flexibility	9
9	Why Use Electrical Heat instead of Gas	Available at Site		10
10	Is Standby Generator Necessary			9
11	Screw Pumps for R.S. Pumps	(See Item 23)		9
12	Plant Layout	More Compact Even Flow		9

LIST ALL CREATIVE IDEAS BEFORE PROCEEDING TO JUDGEMENT PHASE. 10 MOST DESIRABLE 1 LEAST DESIRABLE

WORKSHEET № 3

Figure 11-6. Creative Idea Listing. Example of VE ideas from the creative session.

Item No.	Description	Initial Cost
2	Flow Equalization after Primaries	5,474,700
4	Loading of Aerobic Digester	895,075
6	Eliminate Anaerobic Digester Supernatant Tank	33,700
7	Variable Speed on Raw Sewage Pumps	238,000
8	Eliminate Standby Sludge Beds	350,000
13	Chlorine Contact Sizing	276,000
14B	Use Enclosed Screw Pumps to Equalization	350,000
25&42	Aeration Tank Influent Flow Meters	67,625
28	Reduce Aeration Basin Pipe Handrail	1,031,580
29	Decrease Freeboard in Aeration Basins	710,000
32	Eliminate Brick Veneer on Anaerobic Digesters	28,040
33	"Shotcrete" Dome top for Anaerobic Digester Primary	135,000
35	Reduce Number of Belt Presses	1,210,539
36&37	Bulk Polymer and Ferric Chloride Storage Outside	26,350
38	Delete Ferric Chloride Conditioning	463,705
43	Deepen Flow Equalization Basin	3,044,300
44	Modify Building Exterior Walls and Roof System	423,356
46	Eliminate Odor Control from Primary Clarifiers	260,000
47	Reduce Number of Bar Screens	528,125
48	Change Sluice Gates to Retangular Butterflies	279,500
53&54	Combine CL_2/SO_2 and Solids Building Make Solids Building	751,760
83	Reduce Stairway on Screw Pump Station	150,000
85	Eliminate Flash Mixer CL_2	280,000
86&88	Discharge Pipeline	13,133
90	Eliminate In-Board Weirs on Primary Clarifiers	33,914
103	Bypass Secondary System with Storm Flow	5,960,900
104	Bypass Plant with Storm Flows Using Existing Plant	5,457,700
105	Reorientation of Aeration Tanks	43,500
14,19 20,21	Combine Grit Unit with Equalization	
23,99	Basin Use Aerated Grit Tank. Combine Screw Pump Station	

Figure 11-7. Summary Of Potential Cost Savings. A Listing Of The VE Recommendations Proposed To The Designer And Owner.

Proposed Cost	Initial Savings	Annualized Initial Savings	Annual O&M Savings	Total Annual Savings	Present Worth Annual Savings
5,059,300	415,400	38,331	28,987	67,318	720,161
474,389	420,686	39,325	26,602	65,927	705,280
-0-	33,700	3,150	6,682	9,832	105,180
175,000	63,000	5,889	-0-	5,889	62,998
-0-	350,000	32,717	-0-	32,717	350,000
220,800	55,200	5,160	-0-	5,160	55,200
328,950	21,050	1,968	-0-	1,968	21,053
33,000	34,625	3,236	10,950	14,186	151,760
978,856	52,724	4,928	-0-	4,928	52,719
667,500	42,500	3,973	-0-	3,973	42,503
16,123	11,917	1,114	-0-	1,114	11,917
46,500	88,500	8,273	-0-	8,273	88,500
967,264	243,275	22,740	4,110	26,850	287,238
26,100	250	23	17,180	17,203	184,036
333,313	130,392	12,189	2,000	14,189	151,793
2,567,130	477,150	46,602	-0-	46,602	477,148
209,299	214,057	20,009	-0-	20,009	214,054
-0-	260,000	24,304	3,300	27,604	295,305
475,000	53,125	4,966	-0-	4,966	53,125
210,000	69,500	6,497	-0-	6,497	69,504
737,253	14,507	1,357	1,000	2,357	25,204
140,500	9,500	888	-0-	888	9,500
256,000	24,000	2,244	46	2,290	24,498
9,023	4,109	384	-0-	384	4,109
26,210	7,704	720	-0-	720	7,704
3,861,550	2,099,350	196,239	12,200	208,439	2,229,860
2,565,100	3,392,600	317,126	28,200	345,326	3,694,263
10,725	32,775	3,063	-0-	3,063	32,768
	143,000	13,367	(-) 3,326	10,041	107,418

Figure 11-7. Summary Of Potential Cost Savings. A Listing Of The VE Recommendations Proposed To The Designer And Owner.

EXAMPLES OF IMPLEMENTED VE RECOMMENDATIONS

Two implemented value engineering proposals are included in this section. The VE team recommendations and the designer's response help the reader to grasp the level of effort needed to develop a proposed idea. Remember to place yourself in the shoes of the designer or the review engineer from the regulatory agency.

Example 1: Flow Equalization Basin After Primaries.

Figure 11-8 is the Development and Recommendation Phase Worksheet explaining the original concept design and the proposed change. A discussion of the VE team's rationale for the proposed change is also given. Figure 11-9 shows the flow scheme of the proposed design, and Figure 11-10 the hydraulic profile.

Comparison cost estimates of the original design and the proposed change show the initial cost savings. A comparison of the power cost for changes in horsepower resulting from hydraulic head and increased number of treatment units reflects a life cycle cost savings. (Table 11-4.)

Not all of the VE recommendations could be accepted. The designer's response explains how part of the idea was implemented.

DESIGNER'S RESPONSE

Original Concept

Install a flow equalization basin ahead of the preliminary treatment system to dampen peak flow rates into the treatment plant.

Proposed Change

Provide preliminary and primary treatment for the entire storm-water flow prior to pumping into the flow equalization basin. Wastewater in the flow equalization basin would then be bled back into the raw sewage pump station at a controlled rate by gravity to continue through the treatment system.

Discussion

The VE team felt that the flow equalization basin should follow the primary treatment system to reduce odors and solids in the basin. This arrangement would only require one pump station instead of the two proposed. Removal of debris, grit and settlable solids would be improved in the bar screens, grit chambers and primary clarifiers. The potential elimination of surface aerators also exists if the basin follows primary treatment. Power consumption of the surface aerators could drastically affect the peak demand charge.

The concept of locating the flow equalization basin after the preliminary and primary treatment facilities is desirable; however, the cost-effectiveness of enlarging these facilities to handle peak storm flows requires further investigation. In either case, aeration of the flow equalization basin will be required to reduce odor control. Should flow equalization follow preliminary and primary treatment, aeration equipment may be sized to maintain a positive dissolved oxygen (D.O.) concentration; whereas, if flow equalization were to precede preliminary and primary treatment, it would be impractical to supply sufficient air for mixing to maintain solids in suspension. At the advice of

PROJECT ______
LOCATION ______
CLIENT ______
DATE ______
PAGE ______ OF ______

DEVELOPMENT AND RECOMMENDATION PHASE

ITEM: Flow Equalization After Primaries **NO:** 2

WORKSHEET № 4

ORIGINAL CONCEPT: (Attach sketch where applicable)

Flow equalization is installed before the preliminary treatment system. The basin is used to dampen peak flow rates into the treatment plant system.

PROPOSED CHANGE: (Attach sketch where applicable)

Provide preliminary and primary treatment for the entire storm water flow and place the equalization basin after the primary system. The flow would be bled back into the system by gravity into the new pump station.

DISCUSSION:

Because of odor considerations and the need to handle solids more readily, it was felt that the equalization basin should be placed after the primary treatment system. This system would utilize one pump station instead of the two proposed. Flow could more easily be stored after the major grit (sand), screenings and primary sludges were removed. We have also shown the bar screens before the screw pumps to remove heavy materials. We believe that the odor problems would be greatly reduced if the basin was after primary treatment. Also, it will be easier to remove debris, grit and settleable solids in the clarifiers, grit chambers and bar screens. Much of this material will end up in the equalization basin. It may also be possible to delete the aerators if the basin is installed after Primary Treatment. Power consumption will lessen the peak demand charge.

LIFECYCLE COST SUMMARY	CAPITAL	O & M COSTS	TOTAL
INITIAL COST— ORIGINAL	5,474,700		
— PROPOSED	5,059,300		
— SAVINGS	415,400		
ANNUAL COST— ORIGINAL	511,263	55,494	566,757
— PROPOSED	472,932	26,507	499,439
— SAVINGS	38,331	28,987	67,318
PRESENT WORTH - ANNUAL SAVINGS			$720,161

Figure 11-8. Example Of VE Recommendation No. 1. Placing Flow Equalization After The Primary Tanks.

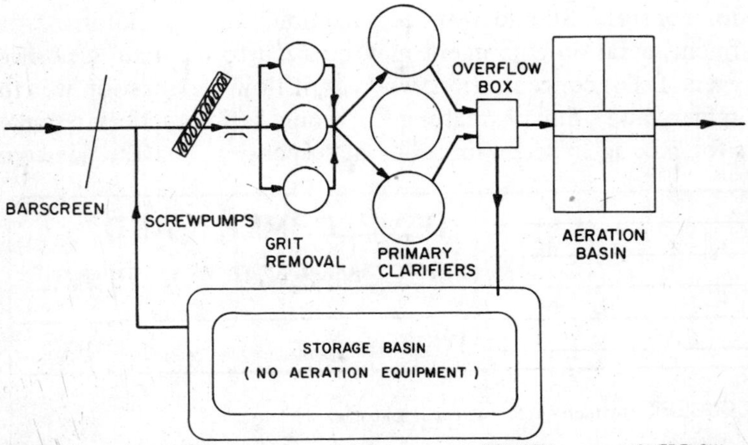

BARSCREENS	SCREW PUMPS	GRIT REMOVAL	PRIMARY CLARIFIERS	OVERFLOW	STORAGE BASIN
3 BARSCREENS 1 UNIT (future) WIDTH 6'-0"	2-72"♦ FLOW (each) 2-96"♦ 12.5 MGD 1-96"♦ 25 MGD DRYWEATHER USE 1-72"♦ PEAK DRYWEATHER 1-72"♦ or 1-96"♦ WET FLOW 2-96"♦ or 2-72"♦+ 1-96"♦	AVE. FLOW 12.5 MGD PEAK 25 MGD WET WEATHER (FLOW TOTAL) 50 MGD (design) 75 MGD (future) 4- BASINS (12.5 MGD AVE.) (25 MGD PEAK) 3 NOW	3-115" DIA. UNITS Q = 50 MGD SOR = 1400 gpd/ft^2 (PEAK) EACH UNIT 13,225 ft^2 1-115" DIAMETER (in future)	12.5 MGD TO AERATION BASIN 25 MGD PEAK	VOLUME 12 MILL. GAL. DEPTH 19' SWD LENGTH 416' WIDTH 208'

Figure 11-9. Proposed Flow Scheme of Recommended Proposal.

the designer's process consultant, aeration for odor control should provide 10CFM/1000CF of basin capacity to maintain a positive D.O. level. Therefore, the cost savings associated with deleting capital costs plus operation and maintenance costs for mechanical aeration equipment are not appropriate.

Recommendation

It is recommended to partially accept the proposed change to follow preliminary and primary treatment units with the flow equalization basin. Aeration of the basin is planned for the reduction of potential odors. (Since sizing criteria for the flow equalization basin is still required from both the State and EPA as of this writing, a final design of this unit is not possible at this time.)

Example 2: Modify Building Exterior Walls and Roof System.

Building construction uses precast concrete double tees for roofing, with case-in-place bearing concrete walls. The VE team's recommendation was to job-cast roof beams for the structure and use tilt up nonbearing walls. Figure 11-11 is the Development and Recommendation Phase worksheet summarizing the recommendation. Figures 11-12 and 11-13 are sketches of the existing and proposed wall and roof systems.

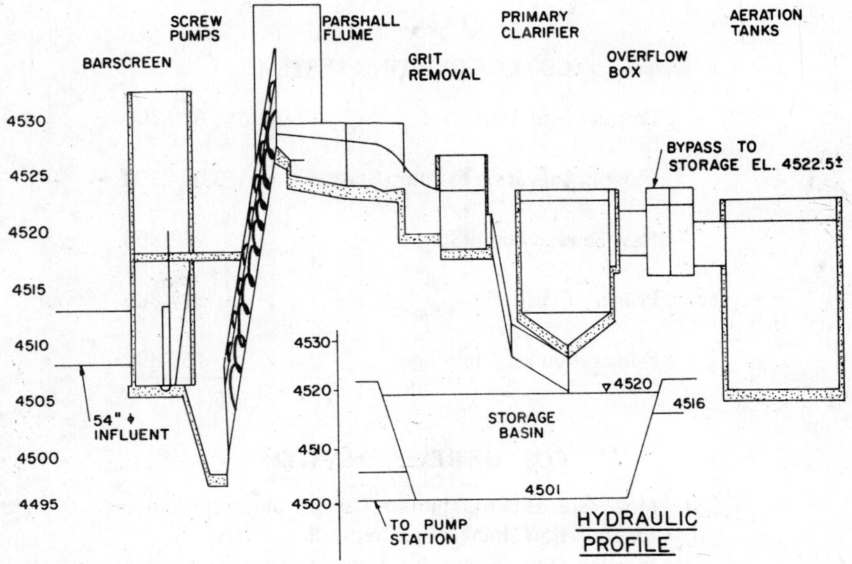

Figure 11-10. Proposed Hydraulic Profile of Recommended Proposal.

Summary of cost savings is as follows:

Cost Summary

	Area	Unit Cost Original	Unit Cost Proposed	Cost Original	Cost Proposed
Roof	24,772 SF	$7.50	$4.10	$185,790	$101,565
Walls	27,624 SF	$8.60	$3.90	$237,566	$107,734
			Subtotal	$423,356	$209,299

Proposed Savings $214,057

DESIGNER'S RESPONSE

The designer's response to the proposed recommendation was as follows:

Original Concept

The exterior walls are cast-in-place concrete with sandwich insulation and are designed as bearing walls with architectural treatment. The roof is precast double tees resting in wall slots with built-up roofing to include insulation; flashing into reglet at the top of wall.

TABLE 11-4.

COST OF EXISTING SYSTEM

Pretreatment Unit	$ 670,300
Flow Equalization & Pump Station	3,094,300
Raw Sewage Pump Station	722,500
Primary Clarifiers	817,800
Primary Sludge Pumping	169,800
	$5,474,700

COST OF REVISED SYSTEM

Move screens before pumps. Use one pump station for total flow. Increase grit removal capacity. Increase primary capacity. Drain stored flow direct to screw pump wet well.

1. Bar Screen Building	$ 335,000
2. Screw Pump Station	654,000
3. Grit Removal	620,000
4. Primary Clarifiers (Increase size to take storm flow)	1,226,700
5. Raw Sludge Pumping	254,700
6. Equalization Basin	1,876,400
7. Overflow Box	80,000
8. Piping	12,500
	$5,059,300

Proposed Change

Use tilt-up concrete nonbearing exterior walls with sandwich insulation. These walls can be given any desired architectural treatment. A cast-beam roof system can be lifted into place. Built-up roofing can be provided with insulation and a full-cap flashing.

Discussion

Cast-in-place walls are very difficult to form, reinforce and place due to sandwich insulation. Double tees could penetrate the insulation and the inside

TABLE 11-4.

COMPARISON OF OPERATING COSTS

Item	Designed			Proposed		
	HP	HRS	Remarks	HP	HRS	Remarks
1. Screens	5	8640	2-6′ Wide	5	8640	2 - Same
2. Pumps	100	720	3 Units	70	8640	1 - 72″ϕ
	70	8640	Lump	125	720	2 - 96″ϕ
3. Grit Removal	5	8640	2 Units	5	8640	2 Units
				5	720	1 Unit
4. Primaries	3	8640	2 Units	3	8640	2 Units
				3	720	1 Unit
5. Aerators	100	720	3 Units			
	100	8640	1 Unit			

HORSEPOWER HOUR COMPARISON

Designed		HP-HRS	Proposed		HP-HRS
1. 5 (8640) (2)	=	86,400	5 (8640) (2)	=	86,400
2. 100 (720) (3)	=	216,000	70 (8640) (1)	=	604,800
70 (8640) (2)	=	604,800	125 (720) (2)	=	180,000
3. 5 (8640) (2)	=	86,400	5 (8640) (2)	=	86,400
			5 (720) (1)	=	3,600
4. 3 (8640) (2)	=	51,840	3 (8640) (2)	=	51,840
			3 (720) (1)	=	2,160
5. 100 (720) (3)	=	216,000	0		
100 (8640) (1)	=	864,000			
HP-HRs	=	2,125,440	HP-HRs	=	1,005,200

COMPARISON OPERATION COSTS

Designed	2,125,400 (0.746) (0.035)	=	55,494
Proposed	1,015,200 (0.746) (0.035)	=	26,507
	Savings		$28,987*

NOTE: POWER DEMAND CHARGE REDUCED SUBSTANTIALLY

PROJECT ______	DEVELOPMENT AND RECOMMENDATION PHASE		WORKSHEET No. 4
LOCATION ______			
CLIENT ______			
DATE ______			
PAGE ______ OF ______	ITEM: Modify Bldg. Ext. Walls & Roof System	NO: 44	

ORIGINAL CONCEPT: (Attach sketch where applicable)

Exterior walls are cast in place concrete with sandwich insulation and are designed as bearing walls with architectural treatment. Roof is precast double tee resting in wall slots. Built up roof with insulation; flashing into reglet at wall top.

PROPOSED CHANGE: (Attach sketch where applicable)

Exterior walls are tilt up concrete with sandwich insulation and are non-bearing. Walls can be given any desired architectural treatment. Roof is beam, slab cast on floor, and lifted into place. Built up roof with insulation; full cap flashing.

DISCUSSION:

Existing ext. C.I.P. walls are very difficult to form, reinforce and place due to sandwich insulation. Double tees penetrate insulation, inside face subject to cracking. Existing double tee roof system will be expensive due to long haul from plant (Denver). New walls are easily formed and finished. Do not require high brg. strength. Roof beams and slab less expensive due to site availability.

LIFECYCLE COST SUMMARY	CAPITAL	O & M COSTS	TOTAL
INITIAL COST – ORIGINAL	423,356		
– PROPOSED	209,299		
– SAVINGS	214,057		
ANNUAL COST – ORIGINAL	39,574	-	39,574
– PROPOSED	19,565	-	19,565
– SAVINGS	20,009	-	20,009
PRESENT WORTH – ANNUAL SAVINGS			214,054 ✓

Figure 11-11. Example VE Recommendation No. 2. Modify Exterior Wall.

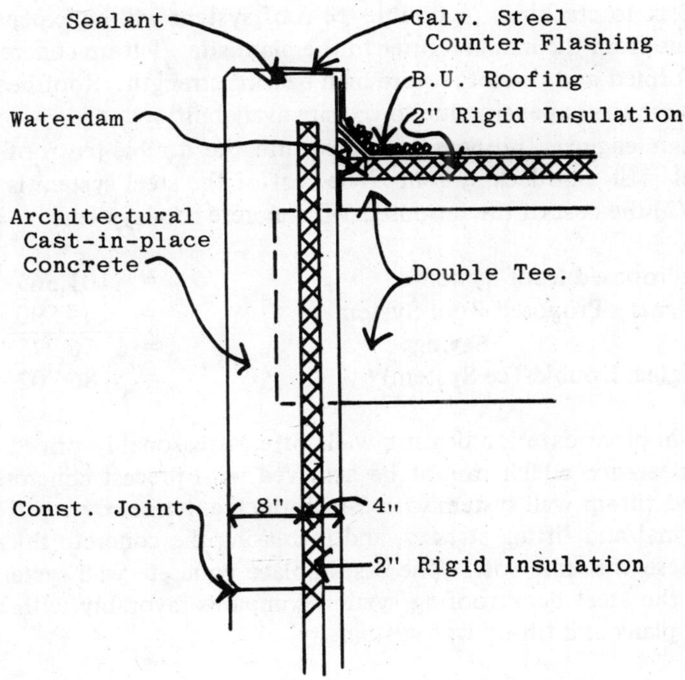

Figure 11-12. Sketch of Original Wall Section.

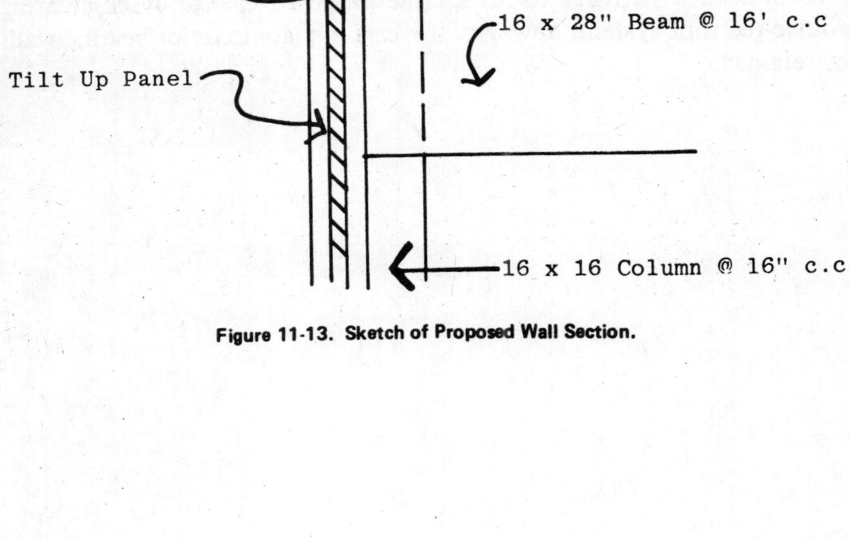

Figure 11-13. Sketch of Proposed Wall Section.

face is subject to cracking. A double-tee roof system will be expensive due to long hauls from the manufacturer to the plant site. Tilt-up concrete walls are easily formed and do not require high bearing strength. Roof beams as a slab system are less expensive due to the site availability.

The design engineer proposes to substitute the double-tee roof system with a steel joist and deck system. The cost of the steel system is around one-half (1/2) the cost of the proposed VE concrete roof system.

VE Proposed Roof System	=	$101,565
Designer's Proposed Roof System	=	44,590
Savings	=	$ 56,975
(Original Double-Tee System)	=	$ 86,702

The cast-in-place exterior bearing walls offer a reasonably priced system with an appearance which cannot be acheived with precast concrete. The VE proposed tilt-up wall system with 2-inch thick exterior cover will be subject to thermal and lifting stresses, and increasing the concrete thicknesses would increase the unit cost. The cast-in-place concrete wall system combined with the steel deck roofing system compares favorably with the VE light-weight plank and tilt-up wall system.

VE Proposed Wall and Roof System L.W. Plank and Tilt-Up Wall	=	$209,299
Proposed Wall and Roof System Steel deck and CIP Wall	=	254,277
Negative Savings	=	$-44,978

Recommendation

It is recommended partially to accept the proposed change by eliminating the double-tee roof system; however, the cast-in-place exterior bearing walls will be retained.

12 Value Engineering Case Study No. 3: Engineering Management Building

The Norfolk Naval Shipyard is one of the U.S. Navy's facilities for construction and repair of large ships. It contains slips and drydock facilities to handle some of the largest naval vessels afloat. Engineering for ship construction are located adjacent to the dockside in a number of facilities scattered in separate buildings throughout the shipyard. The Engineering Management Building (EMB) was designed to combine the engineering functions that are currently located throughout the shipyard in one facility. The first phase of building construction is designed to meet the immediate need for providing office space for approximately 1150 engineers and support staff. The ultimate capacity of the building will be 2826 staff personnel.

Ten million dollars was appropriated to build the 180,000-square-foot facility. The proposed structure will be located on what is now a golf course. The EMB will be located close to the dock and pier area to facilitate access to the ship construction and repair activities. Plans for the first phase of construction (the scope of the VE study) are for a six-story building with approximately 30,000 square feet per floor. The second phase expansion (19,000 additional square feet) is scheduled for construction in the 1990s. A third and final expansion has not been scheduled at this time.

The EMB was being designed by an architectural/engineering firm for the Atlantic Division of the Naval Facilities Engineering Command (NAVFAC). The NAVFAC routinely requires value engineering studies on their construction projects as a tool to keep projects within budget limitations and to ensure the most effective and efficient utilization of taxpayer dollars. The NAVFAC contracts for value engineering services are a part of the architect's overall consulting services contract. The value engineering team may be composed of members of the architect's design firm, provided they have not been involved in the original design. However, the leader of the VE study must be a Certified Value Specialist, or licensed by the Society of American Value Engineers. The A/E firm usually subcontracts for the services of a certified value specialist. The Navy sets the criteria for the number of value engineering studies to be conducted on a project. This criteria is set during the contract negotiation stage for the project.

One value engineering study was conducted for the EMB. The study coincided with the 35 percent preliminary design submission of plans and specifications. The Navy's review of the design and of the VE recommendations is done simultaneously to save valuable time in the project schedule. Because they fund the total cost of the project, the Navy serves as both the owner and the review agency.

BUILDING REQUIREMENTS

Design life-span for the EMB is 25 years. The structure is classified as permanent construction. The structure is to be fireproofed and sprinklered for an ordinary hazard occupancy. A 200-seat auditorium is to be included. Specific requirements regarding layout and space allocation for engineering management and support personnel have been established by the Navy. The building approximates the shape of a square. The shape was chosen as most economical when comparing the cost of exterior walls to the total square footage of the building.

DESCRIPTION OF PROJECT

Site Planning

The location of the EMB is next to Pennock Avenue, as seen in the Site Plan (Figure 12-1). Plans indicate that Pennock Avenue will be relocated to the

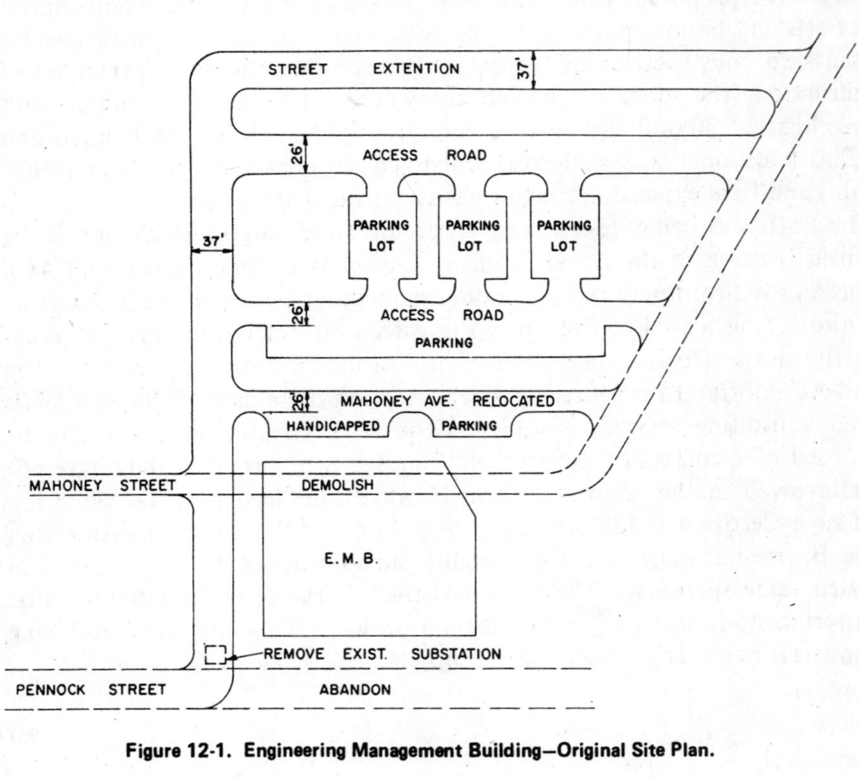

Figure 12-1. Engineering Management Building—Original Site Plan.

west of the proposed EMB. Existing housing must be demolished and site utilities relocated in the area of the structure. Electrical and telephone systems have been designed with new duct banks to provide service to the buildings. Roadways and parking lots are designed with curbing and gutters. Inlets drain the paved area of the parking lot. The proposed parking lot will accommodate 118 vehicles.

Architectural Concept

The building design approximates a square with the entrance lobby at one corner of the structure. The service and utility core is offset to the entrance side. Elevators, lobby corridors, central washroom facilities and mechanical shaft are stacked on the entrance side of the building to allow as much open building space for offices and functional working space as possible. A floor plan of the first floor gives a general layout of the building (Figure 12-2).

Exterior wall construction is a masonry cavity wall arranged in a horizontal line. Fenestrations are fixed panels with reflective, insulated units. The cavity wall is insulated with rigid insulation board. Minimum U value of 0.10 is provided. The roof structure is a flat slab with lightweight concrete topping to obtain the slope required for roof drainage. Rigid insulation and 4-ply built-up roof yields a 0.05 U factor.

Finishes consist of basic construction elements. Ceilings are acoustical tile on a 2 by 4 grid. Bathroom ceilings are in waterproof drywall. Walls are drywall with the exception of stairways and mechanical shafts which are masonry, and toilets which are ceramic tile. Finishes on the floors are ceramic tile in bathrooms, brick pavers in the lobby, carpeting in private offices, and vinyl asbestos tile in corridors, storage and open office areas.

Structural Design

Structural design for the building is reinforced concrete framing using waffle slabs. A two-way beam grid system is incorporated into the waffle construction. Building loads are transferred to the foundation from the framing system by grade beams and pile caps. Piling resists support the building loads of the structure. Building live loads are in Table 12-1.

Mechanical System

Mechanical systems for the building serve to provide a comfortable environment that is conducive to office engineering efforts. Heating systems utilize the existing high pressure steam distribution system available at the shipyard. Heating and hot water is to be provided by fin tube radiation along the perimeter walls of the building. Supplemental heat is provided by hot-water coils in the air-handling units. Ventilation is pressurized to prevent infiltration. Independent exhausts are provided for toilets, electrical closets and the janitor's closet. Return air fans are located in the mechanical room on the roof. These fans exhaust air from each floor individually. Return air is

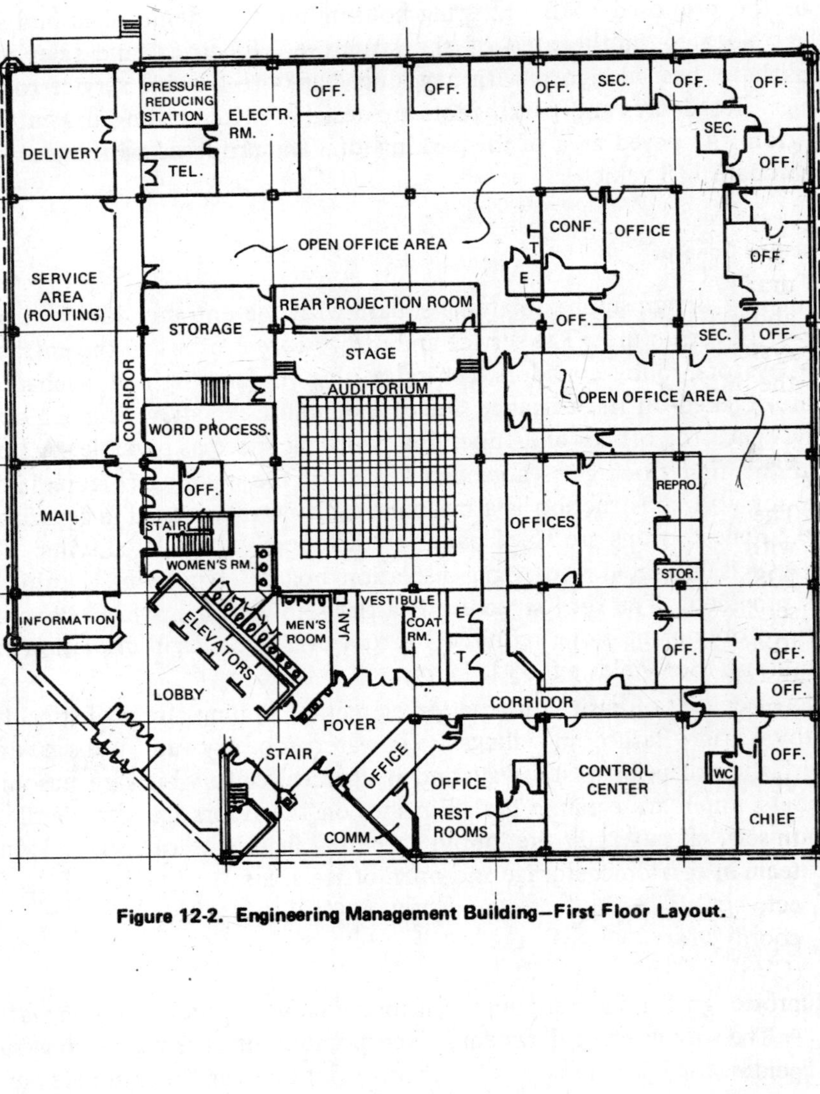

Figure 12-2. Engineering Management Building—First Floor Layout.

Table 12-1. Building Live Loads.

Roof	30 Psf
Typical Floor Loading	80 Psf
Special Service Areas	150 Psf
Wind Loads	30 Psf up to 30 ft.
	36 Psf from 30 to 70 ft.
	43 Psf from 70 to 92 ft.
Seismic Loads	Zone 1

drawn through light fixtures to the plenum between the ceiling and the slab above. Individual airhandling units serve each floor. Variable air-volume systems with an economizer allow up to 100 percent outdoor air for cooling the building.

Electrical

The electrical system is a 480Y/277 volt 3-phase system for equipment with motors over 1/2-horsepower; 277-volt service is used for lighting; and 208Y/120-volt service is provided for service outlets. Electrical and telephone service come from remote locations; duct bank systems are to be constructed to accommodate the new feeders. Lighting for the building is through fluorescent fixtures in to a level of 70-footcandles in office areas. Nonoffice areas have lower illumination levels.

VE PROJECT TEAM

In selecting the VE team, the architectural design firm chose a multidisciplined team. This particular team composition is essential for an architectural project, since changes will impact many aspects of the structure. The team coordinator was the author, Larry Zimmerman, a Certified Value Specialist (CVS). None of the study participants were involved in the design of the project.

The value engineering team for the study was composed of the following persons:

Certified Value Specialist
Structural Engineer
Mechanical Engineer
Architect
Civil Engineer
Electrical Engineer

DESCRIPTION OF VE WORKSHOP

The VE study for the EMB was a 40-hour workshop. Each team member was given 8 hours prior to the workshop to become familiar with the plans, specifications and preliminary design report for the project. The cost estimate was used to develop a cost model for the project.

Information Phase

The VE workshop followed the job plan delineated in this book. Because some of the team members had no prior experience with value engineering, a brief explanation of the job plan was given by the certified value specialist. The architect for the project then explained the scope of the design effort required by the contract and the comparisons that were made in developing the design. In addition, the architect described the constraining factors that influenced the design.

Because there are budget limitations on their projects, the Navy places special emphasis on cost. The VE team is encouraged to find as many ways as possible to reduce costs. The initial review of VE recommendations on Navy jobs selects the savings best suited to the project. When the project bid is over the budget, the Navy often goes back to the VE study to find ways to bring the project within budget limitations. In this case study, the only project constraints were the budget limitation of $10 million and a square-footage area of 180,000 square feet.

Cost Model

The cost model was completed as the first step of the information phase of the job plan. The cost model, shown in Figure 12-3, helped to identify the location of major costs within a project. In this model, costs are expressed in dollars. Costs for the subsystems of the building are organized under the headings of sitework, structural, architectural, mechanical and electrical. Cost from each of the parts of the subsystem are also subdivided to identify the high-cost areas of the design. The worth of each component in the project is also outlined in the cost model. Worth is the VE team's prediction of the least cost to perform the function of the part of system. The cost breakdown for the project by system is shown in Table 12-2. Percentages of the total cost of the building and cost per square foot are indicated. The cost per square foot of the building is approximately $45.6 dollars, excluding cost of sitework.

Function Analysis

The functional analysis benefited the VE team by allowing them to think in terms of function and to consider the cost required to perform each function. Ideas were conceived when the team speculated on the least cost to perform a function, as indicated in functional analysis in Figure 12-4.

The certified value specialist led the team as a group through the functional analysis. First, the team evaluated the entire building to find conceptual changes in the total concept for the project. The *basic function* identi-

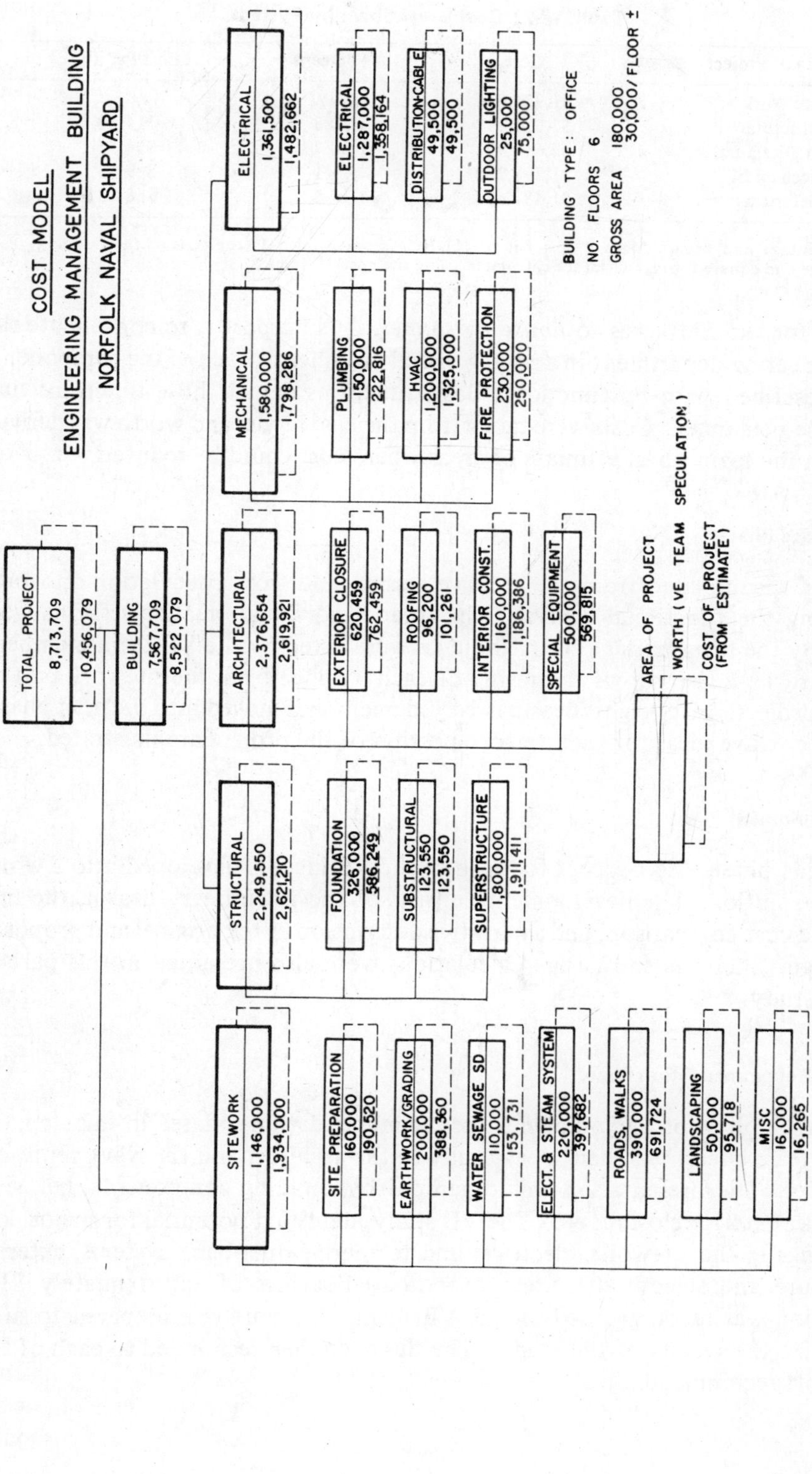

Figure 12-3. Engineering Management Building—Cost Model.

Table 12-2. Cost Breakdown by System.

Area of Project	Cost	*Percent	*Cost Per SF
1. Site Work	$1,934,000		
2. Structural	$2,621,210	30.8	$14.60
3. Architectural	$2,619,921	30.7	$14.55
4. Mechanical	$1,798,286	21.1	$ 9.99
5. Electrical	$1,482,662	17.4	$ 8.23

*Percentage and square footage cost for BUILDING is based on only the cost of the building. Percentage and square footage costs are calculated using the cost of items 2, 3, 4 and 5.

fied for the EMB was to *house personnel.* It's purpose is to consolidate the engineering department in a good work environment. Each of the components is described with its function. Basic functions depict those functions that house personnel. Costs were taken from the cost model and worth was derived from the team's best estimate of areas where cost could be reduced.

Creative Phase

Ideas accumulated from the creative session and from speculation on worth during the functional analysis. Group and individual creative sessions were led by the team leader. Over 100 ideas were listed by the VE team members. Figure 12-5 also shows the rating of each VE idea from the sitework part of the project. Fifty-eight ideas passed judgment and moved into the next phase. The creative ideas for the sitework portion of the project are illustrated.

Development Phase

In this phase, the concept for each of the VE ideas is developed into a workable solution. The development consists of the preliminary design, the life-cycle cost comparison, and a narrative description of the original and proposed design. Sketches and design calculations were also presented in this part of the study.

The Recommendation Phase

The last phase of the job plan is the recommendations phase. In this step, the VE team presented their ideas orally to the architect and the Navy representatives. The presentation was organized by building components, i.e., sitework, exterior closure, etc. The VE study identified potential for major cost savings in the sitework, electrical and telephone duct-bank systems, exterior closure and structural loading. A potential savings of approximately $1.5 million was recommended by the VE team. A report was prepared to summarize the results of the study. The designer then responded to each of the report recommendations.

PROJECT ____________

LOCATION ____________

CLIENT ____________

DATE ____________

PAGE ______ OF ______

INFORMATION PHASE

FUNCTION ANALYSIS

ITEM : Engineering Management Building

FUNCTION : House Personnel
Consolidate Engineering Dept.

FUNCTION ANALYSIS

ITEM #	DESCRIPTION	FUNCTION			COST	WORTH	COMMENTS
		VERB	NOUN	KIND			
1	Foundation	Support	Bldg.	B	586,249	326,000	
2	Substructure	Support	Bldg.	B	123,550	123,550	
3	Superstructure	Support	Bldg.	B	1,911,411	1,800,000	
4	Exterior Closure	Enclose	Bldg.	B	762,459	620,459	
5	Roofing	Protect	Bldg.	B	101,261	96,200	
6	Interior Construction	Create	Envir.	S	1,186,386	1,160,000	
7	Special Equipment	Assist	People	S	569,815	500,000	Elevators
8	Plumbing	Provide	Sanitation	S	222,816	150,000	Original Cost Looks Low
9	HVAC	Control	Envir.	S	1,325,000	1,200,000	
		Light	Bldg.				
10	Electrical	Power	Equip.	B/S	1,358,164	1,287,000	B = 500,000
11	Fire Protection	Protect	People	S	250,000	230,000	
12	Sitework	Provide	Access	S	1,921,000	1,146,000	
13	Electrical Distribution	Service	Bldg.	S	49,500	49,500	
14	Outdoor Lighting	Aids	Security	S	750,000	25,000	
	TOTALS				10,785,869	8,724,233	
	WORTH OF BASIC FUNCTIONS					3,470,000	

ACTION VERB
MEASURABLE NOUN

KIND: B = Basic; S = Secondary

(Basic Function Only) Cost/Worth Ratio = $\frac{10,785,869}{3,470,000}$ = 3.10

WORKSHEET № 2

Figure 12-4. Engineering Management Building—Function Analysis.

PROJECT ____ LOCATION ____ CLIENT ____ DATE ____ PAGE ____ OF ____		CREATIVE PHASE CREATIVE IDEA LISTING	JUDGEMENT PHASE IDEA EVALUATION	
NO (1)	CREATIVE IDEA (2)	ADVANTAGES (3)	DISADVANTAGES (4)	IDEA (5) RATING
	SITE WORK			
1.	Delete Berrien Street Relocation	Less Pumping, Drainage, Fill, Seeding	Possible Security Problem Possible Traffic Hazard	7
2.	Reduce Parking	Save on Pump, Drainage, Fill, Etc.	Parking Already Inadequate for Bldg.	4
3.	Provide Parking Under Raised Building	Eliminates Most Fill, Drainage Problems	Greatly Increase Bldg, Costs	5
4.	Reduce Access Roads & Parking Islands	Save on Paving, Some Fill and Seeding	Reduce Esthetics of Lot - Possible Code Conflict	9
5.	Reduce Fill Under Parking Area	Large Savings on Borrow	Will Cause Drainage Problems for Parking Lot	3
6.	Relocate Building to Avoid Utilities (exist.)	Saves on Paving & Demolition Costs - Keep Ex. Substa.	Possible Conflict w/esthetics. Requires Pkg. Lot Redes.	8
7.	New C2D Communications Duct Overhead	Save $200,000.00 in Ductwork and Trenching	No Overhead Lines @ Shipyard	5
8.	Reduce Pennock Road Relocation Pump Section	Less Expensive Section	Inadequate fcr Loads Over H-20 Hwy. Loading	9
9.	Lower Building First Floor to 104.5	Drainage Still Works Lessen Str. Fill		10
10.	Reduce Demolition - Leave M-8, 29 & 30	Lessen Demolition Costs	Lessens Aesthetics of Site	7

LIST ALL CREATIVE IDEAS BEFORE PROCEEDING TO JUDGEMENT PHASE. 10 MOST DESIRABLE 1 LEAST DESIRABLE

WORKSHEET Nº 3

Figure 12-5. Engineering Management Building—Creative Idea Listing, Example of Ideas for Sitework.

EXAMPLES OF VE RECOMMENDATIONS

The two examples provided here illustrate the types of VE proposals recommended by the VE team. Example 1 deals with a high-cost area in the project, and Example 2 illustrates the point that specifications and criteria of design often offer opportunities for cost savings.

Example 1—Reduce Access Road and Parking Islands

Site work represented a significant part of the total cost of the project. A cost of $1,934,000 was estimated for site preparation, earthwork, roads, walks and utility services. This represented 18.5 percent of the total estimated project cost. One of the VE team ideas was to revise the parking lot layout. Worksheets from the Value Engineering Report (Figures 12-6 and 12-7) explain the recommendation and illustrate the before-and-after design.

Cost comparisons of the VE recommendations are always necessary in order to make a value judgment of the merit of the recommendations. A detailed unit cost breakdown (Table 12-3) indicates a potential cost savings of $302,459 with the proposed change. In addition, more parking spaces are provided with the new design.

Often recommendations are made that challenge the specifications and requirements of the owner. This is the case of Example 2. The Navy specification indicates live loads of approximately 40 pounds per square foot. In multispan open office buildings, a live-load reduction is allowed by many codes. The VE team recommended that the live-load reduction be taken into consideration. The resultant savings in reinforcing steel was $44,497. The VE worksheets explain the recommendation in greater detail (Figure 12-8).

PROJECT EMB	DEVELOPMENT AND RECOMMENDATION PHASE		WORKSHEET Nº 4
LOCATION Norfolk, Va.			
CLIENT NAVFAC			
DATE August 1979			
PAGE ____ OF ____	ITEM: Reduce Access Roads and Parking Islands	NO: S-4	

ORIGINAL CONCEPT: (Attach sketch where applicable)

The original concept was to reroute Pennock Street (used for main traffic flow and heavy traffic) around the perimeter of a large parking complex. Mahoney Avenue would also have to be rerouted due to EMB location, and three separate and parallel access roads were created to accomplish the relocation and to give access to the parking complex. The parking complex was to have a large amount of green landscaped area. Original parking allowed for 118 spaces.

PROPOSED CHANGE: (Attach sketch where applicable)

Proposed change would reorient and redesign parking area to eliminate two access roads and much green area. Pennock Street would be used for main traffic route and for heavy vehicular traffic. Proposed parking lot would be one long rectangular lot with several islands to provide green areas and to break up the group of parked cars. Redesigned along more space efficient lines, the lot would provide space for 144 cars.

DISCUSSION:

Original concept design had four parallel roads to serve functions which require at most two roads: one for heavy traffic (Pennock Street) and one for Mahoney Avenue relocation. Redesign eliminates two roads while preserving easy access to parking lot and allowing for both Pennock and Mahoney Streets to be relocated. More efficient design of parking lot uses less area to provide more spaces (144 vs 118). Smaller area offers easier drainage and less required fill.

LIFECYCLE COST SUMMARY	CAPITAL	O & M COSTS	TOTAL
INITIAL COST— ORIGINAL	$984,066		
— PROPOSED	681,607		
— SAVINGS	302,459		
ANNUAL COST— ORIGINAL	108,345	-0-	$108,345
— PROPOSED	75,045	-0-	75,045
— SAVINGS	33,300	-0-	33,300
PRESENT WORTH - ANNUAL SAVINGS			$302,459

Figure 12-6. Development and Recommendation Worksheet—Parking Lot Redesign.

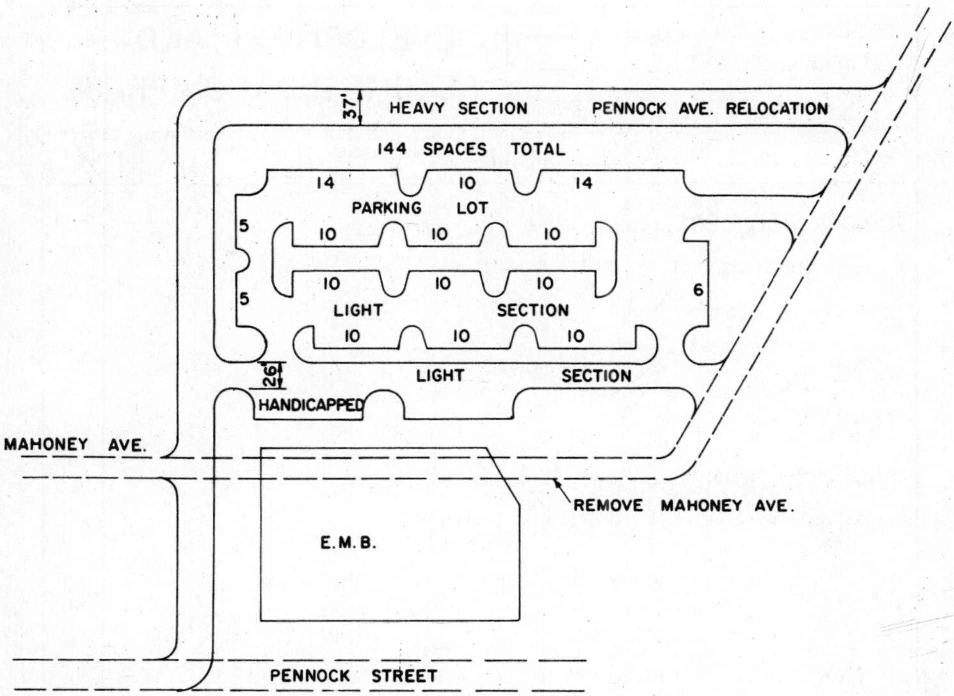

Figure 12-7. Sketch of Proposed Parking Lot Redesign.

Table 12-3. Engineering Management Building.

Example 1—Reduce Access Roads and Parking Islands

COST ESTIMATE

COST OF PROPOSED SYSTEM

Description	Quantity	Unit	Unit Price	Total Cost
Fill	9,500	C.Y.	$10.21	$96,995
Earthwork	14,500	C.Y.	4.85	70,296
Clearing	3	Ac	25.50	7,650
Paving: Heavy Section	4,152	S.Y.	53.33	221,418
Light Section	6,260	S.Y.	33.89	212,144
Storm Drainage				
Curb Inlets	19	Ea.	12.76	24,244
Pipe	1,250	L.F.	39.09	48,860
		Total Cost		$681,607
Cost of Original System (From Estimate)				984,066
		Proposed Savings		$302,459

PROJECT: EMB LOCATION: Norfolk, Va. CLIENT: NAVFAC DATE: August 1979 PAGE ____ OF ____	DEVELOPMENT AND RECOMMENDATION PHASE	
	ITEM: Reduction of Floor Live Load	NO: ST-8

WORKSHEET Nº 4

ORIGINAL CONCEPT: (Attach sketch where applicable)

Navy Standards call for 80 PSF with live load reduction factor.

PROPOSED CHANGE: (Attach sketch where applicable)

BOCA allows live load reduction on 2-unit slabs

$$R = 23 \left(1 + \frac{150}{80}\right) = 23\ (1 + 1.875) = 66\%$$

28.5 x 28.5 x .08 = 64%

Minimum 60%

DISCUSSION:

Assume a reduction of 60%:

Results in a loading of live load = 32 PSF

Ratio $\frac{\text{Total load as proposed}}{\text{Total load as designed}} = \frac{182}{230}$

Concrete not affected, formwork not affected

Reinforcement reduced by ratio $\frac{182}{230} =$ 79%, or a 21% REDUCTION

Recommend use of live load reduction, especially with such a DL/LL ratio

LIFECYCLE COST SUMMARY	CAPITAL	O & M COSTS	TOTAL
INITIAL COST— ORIGINAL	$44,497		
— PROPOSED	-0-		
— SAVINGS	44,497		
ANNUAL COST— ORIGINAL	4,900	-0-	$4,900
— PROPOSED	-0-	-0-	-0-
— SAVINGS	4,900	-0-	4,900
PRESENT WORTH - ANNUAL SAVINGS			$44,497

Figure 12-8. Development and Recommendation Worksheet. Reduction of Live Load.

13
40-hour VE Workshop Seminars

Value engineering workshops are conducted to acquaint people with a proven technique that produces results. Value engineering principles are taught, using a combination of lecture and project time. The seminars last 40 hours, and the participants receive a certificate of completion. The seminars are taught by a certified value specialist, assisted by individuals with a knowledge of value engineering and technical experience in construction and related fields. The methodology of value engineering is fascinating to learn, and even more challenging to apply to actual projects.

There is a definite need for VE training for people that are interested in using VE in their program, or for people working on actual value studies. The list of people that would benefit from a 40-hour VE workshop might include the following:

Administrators of large construction budgets.
Municipal governments with capital programs.
State and federal governments that administer construction grants or actual construction projects.
Persons participating on VE teams.
Persons having their designs value-engineered.
Managers responsible for design of construction projects.
Persons that own and operate plant facilities.
Contractors with contractor-incentive clauses in their projects.
Private developers.
Maintenance personnel.
Operations personnel.
Manufacturers.
Software designers.
ANYONE INTERESTED IN IMPROVING A PROJECT, PRODUCT, PROCESS OR PROCEDURE

The list of people that can benefit from a VE study is virtually all inclusive, since the VE methodology can be applied universally. Seminars can be tailored to fit the area of study. Because actual projects are used in the training process, the area of study can be changed by changing the project used.

Members of engineering and architectural firms, managers, planners and engineers in government and industry would personally benefit from attending a VE workshop. The ultimate benefit will be to the owner in the savings

WORKSHOP AGENDA

MONDAY

8:00	Introduction
8:45	Goals, Background, Explanation of Program Content and VE Examples
9:40	Definition of Four Kinds of Value
10:10	Break
15:15	Major Reasons Poor Value Occurs
10:25	Evaluating the Basic Function
11:00	Job Plan of Value Engineering
11:05	Explanation of Worksheets (EPA, GSA, FHWA)
11:0	Functions of cost model and how it is constructed. (WWTP's, highways, power plants and buildings)
12:00	Lunch
1:00	Project Briefing
1:30	Project Time–INFORMATION PHASE–Familiarize yourself with project design, cost information and functions. Make a cost model. Select an area of study, Set goals. Note questionable specifications and design criteria for challenging. Identify and evaluate functions. Determine required functions. Separate cost by functions. Judge the minimum worth of required functions. Prepare energy and life cycle models. Use worksheets 1 and 2.
6:00	Close

TUESDAY

8:00	Creative Thinking – Part I
8:30	F.A.S.T. Diagramming (handout)
9:20	Project Time – Complete Functional and Cost Analysis Worksheets 1 and 2 as part of INFORMATION PHASE
12:00	Lunch
1:00	Creative Thinking – Part II and Creative Practice Session
1:30	Application to Construction Areas
1:40	Project Time–Complete INFORMATION PHASE and commence CREATIVE PHASE, Worksheet 3
6:00	Close

Figure 13-1. 40-Hour Value Engineering Workshop Agenda.

he will accrue through VE. The importance of management participation must be emphasized. Often managers feel they have no need to attend a workshop seminar. The program is a distinctive step in the improvement of the management capability of people. Many times, managers will not believe the results that their subordinates claim when they return from a seminar. To succeed, a value program must have the support of management.

The 40-hour workshop seminar is divided between presentation (lecture) time and project time. Presentation time deals with the teaching of VE methodology, and the tools used. During project time, the team members apply the VE techniques to an actual project. The participants are divided into teams of five to six people. Depending on the backgrounds of the attendees,

WORKSHOP AGENDA–Continued

WEDNESDAY

8:00 Habits, Roadblocks and Attitudes – Part I
8:30 Life Cycle Costing Techniques, Energy and Resource Budgeting
8:55 Two-minute presentation by each team leader on areas being investigated
9:30 Project Time – Complete CREATIVE PHASE, Worksheet 3. Commence JUDGMENT PHASE or select ideas that warrant further investigation and development.
12:00 Lunch
1:00 Habits, Roadblocks and Attitudes – Part II
1:20 Alternatives in functional design, construction methods and materials.
1:50 Project Time – Complete ANALYSIS PHASE, Worksheet 3. Begin investigating ideas worthy of further development.
5:30 Attitude Adjustment Hour

THURSDAY

8:00 Why the Program Works
8:30 Evaluate by Comparison
8:50 GSA, EPA and FHWA Value Engineering Programs
10:00 Managing and Administering your VE Program
10:05 Project Time – Continue DEVELOPMENT PHASE, Worksheets 4, 5, and 6
11:45 Specifics, Not Generalities
12:00 Lunch
1:00 Human Relations – How to make a sales presentation; negotiating
2:15 Project Time – Conclude DEVELOPMENT PHASE and prepare presentation of your proposals.
6:00 Close

FRIDAY

8:00 Project Time – Conclude preparation of your PRESENTATION
9:30 Team Presentations
12:00 Lunch
1:00 Summary Discussions and Distribution of Certificates

Figure 13-1. 40-Hour Value Engineering Workshop Agenda.

we attempt to have a multidisciplined team composition. Instructors lead the team participants through the study process, in a similar fashion to the way an actual study would be conducted.

Program Contents of 40-Hour VE Workshop.

A workshop's function is to teach the principles and techniques of VE that the participants will need to apply on their projects. As a minimum, lectures on the following subjects are covered:

History of the VE Program
Definition of Value and Function

Reasons Poor Value Occurs
Function Analysis
Job Plan
Cost Modeling
Creative Thinking
Habits, Roadblocks and Attitudes
Life-cycle Costing Techniques
Energy Models
Life-cycle Costing Models
F.A.S.T. Diagraming
Managing Your VE Program
Conducting a VE Study
How to Give an Effective Presentation

In addition, instructors assist the participants as they follow through the VE methodology during project time. The team works on projects that are provided by government agencies, or projects from the participating firms. Private companies often ask us to use their projects in the hope that unnecessary cost might be removed.

Value engineering seminars must meet the minimum criteria established by the Society of American Value Engineers (SAVE). Many government agencies may also require approval of the contents of a 40-hour workshop seminar before accrediting the course. Seminars are taught by a certified value specialist registered with SAVE.

WHAT DO PARTICIPANTS NEED TO BRING TO A 40-HOUR WORKSHOP SEMINAR?

The primary requirement is an open mind and a willingness to grow in an atmosphere of sharing with fellow professionals in their field of study. Other useful tools are estimating guides, references in the field of study, calculators, engineering and architectural scales, triangles and interest tables.

The agenda followed in workshops is shown in Figure 13-1, pp. 272–273.

Bibliography

Boyd, T. A. *Professional Amateur–The Biography of Charles Franklin Kettering*, New York: E. P. Dutton & Co., Inc., 1957.

The Building Estimator's Reference Book, Chicago: Frank R. Walker Company, Eighteenth Edition, 1973.

Cost Control and CPM in Construction. A Manual for General Contractors, Washington, D. C., The Associated General Contractors of America, 1968.

DeGarmo, E. Paul, Canada, John R., and Sullivan, William G. *Engineering Economy*, New York: Macmillan Publishing Co., Inc., Sixth Edition, 1979.

Dell'Isola, Alphonse J. *Value Engineering in the Construction Industry*, New York: Construction Publishing Company, Inc., Second Edition, 1974.

Dubin, Fred S. and Long, Chalmers, G. *Energy Conservation Standards–For Building Design, Construction and Operation*, New York: McGraw-Hill Book Company, 1978.

George, Claude S. Jr. *The History of Management Thought*, Englewood Cliffs, NJ: Prentice-Hall Inc., Second Edition, 1972.

Giblin, Les. *How You Can Have Confidence and Power,* Hollywood, Calif., Wilshire Book Company, 1956.

Haviland, David S. *Life Cycle Cost Analysis 2–Using it In Practice*, Washington, D. C., The American Institute of Architects, 1978.

Kettering, Charles F. "How Can We Develop Inventors?" The American Society of Mechanical Engineers, Annual Meeting Presentation, New York, 1943.

Life Cycle Cost Analysis–A Guide for Architects, Washington, D. C., The American Institute of Architects, 1977.

Life-Cycle Costing–A Guide for Selecting Energy Conservation Projects for Public Buildings, NBS Building Science Series 113, Washington D.C.: U. S. Department of Commerce, Government Printing Office, 1978.

Koontz, Harold and O'Donnell, Cyril. *Principles of Management: An Analysis of Managerial Functions*, New York: McGraw-Hill Book Company, Fifth Edition, 1972.

Lentz, Craig. "Initial Vs. Life Cycle Cost: The Economics of Conservation," *Consulting Engineer*, October 1976, Vol. 46, No. 4.

Loftness, Robert L. *Energy Handbook*, New York: Van Nostrand Reinhold Company, 1978.

Macedo, Manuel C., Jr. Dobrow, Paul V., and O'Rourke, Joseph J. *Value Management for Construction,* New York: John Wiley & Sons, 1978.

Mandelkorn, Richard S. *Value Engineering* Vol. 2, Elizabeth, N. J.: Electronic Industries Association, Engineering Publishers, 1961.

Miles, Lawrence D. *Techniques of Value Analysis and Engineering*, New York: McGraw-Hill Book Company, Second Edition, 1972.

Newman, W. H., and Summer, C. E. Jr., *The Process of Management*, Englewood Cliffs, NJ.: Prentice-Hall, Inc., 1961.

O'Brien, James J. *Value Analysis in Design and Construction* New York: McGraw-Hill Book Company, 1976.

Olson, Robert W. *The Art of Creative Thinking–A Practical Guide,* New York: Barnes & Noble Books, 1976.

Peurifoy, R. L. *Estimating Construction Costs*, New York: McGraw-Hill Book Company, Third Edition, 1975.

Public Building Service (GSA) Handbook P8000.1-Value Engineering, January 12, 1972, Washington DC: U. S. Government Printing Office.

Roose, Robert W. *Handbook of Energy–Conservation for Mechanical Systems in Buildings*, New York: Van Nostrand Reinhold Company, 1978.

Schwartz, David J., *The Magic of Thinking Big*, New York: Cornerstone Library, (Prentice-Hall), 1965.

Smith, Craig, *Efficient Electrical Use–A Practical Handbook for the Energy Strained World*, New York: Pergamon Press, Inc., 1976.

Smith Hinchman & Grylls Associates. Value Engineering–Life Cycle Costing Application Workshop, 1979.

Smith Hinchman & Grylls Associates. Value Engineering Workbook, 1978.

Society of American Value Engineers Proceedings, 1979, Vol. **XIV**, May 1979.

Society of American Value Engineers Proceedings, 1980, Vol. **XV**, May 1980.

Stainton, Bernard W. "Value Engineered Energy, A Preplanned Approach to Energy Conservation," *Plant Engineering*, March 22, 1979.

Thumann, Albert. *Plant Engineers and Managers Guide to Energy Conservation*, New York: Van Nostrand Reinhold Company, 1977.

Value Engineering Program, Progress Record, Washington, DC: Department of the Army Office of the Chief of Engineers, May 1979.

Value Engineering Workbook for Construction Grant Projects, Washington, DC: U. S. Environmental Protection Agency, July 1976, EPA-430/9-76-008.

Watson, Donald. *Energy Conservation Through Building Design*, New York: McGraw-Hill Book Company, 1979.

Index

Analysis procedure, 115
ASHRAE, 207
ASPR Regulation, 14
Association, 98, 138
Attitudes, 23, 126
  attitude screen, 27
  examples, 25, 26, 29
  failing, 96
  human relations, 58
  positive attitude, 30
  roadblocks, 24
Attribute listing, 101

Brainstorming, 100
Building envelope, 200
Building project, 257–270
  cost model, 262, 263
  creative idea listing, 266
  function analysis, 262, 265
  VE recommendations, 267–270
Bytheway, Charles, 74

Case studies:
  No. 1 – Oklahoma City Wastewater Treatment plant, 216–234
  No. 2 – Wastewater Treatment Plant, 236–256
  No. 3 – Engineering Management Building, 257–270
Change, progressive, 107
Checklists, 78, 82, 101, 137
Coefficient of transmission, 200
Communication, 125, 127
Comparisons, 73, 84, 89, 107
Conductance, 200
Conductivity, 200
Contractors, 111
Constraints, project, 35, 36, 132, 239
Construction cost index, 3
Convection, 200
Coordinator, 131
Cost, 141–149
  cost benefit, 113
  cost matrix, 38
  cost model, 38, 141
  cost worth, 67, 68, 145, 221
  index, 3
  initial cost, 34, 53
  life cycle cost, 38, 53
  unnecessary costs, 104
  validation, 38, 132, 142
  who influences, 109, 121
Cost benefit ratio, 113
Cost estimate, 141, 142
Cost model, 38, 131, 132, 141, 144
  functional cost model, 145
  health care facility, 148
  matrix cost model, 144
  wastewater treatment plant, 146, 149, 222
Creative phase, 44, 83–102, 137, 221, 243
  analysis and synthesis, 46
  creative session, 97
Creative session, 97, 137
  guidelines, 98, 102
Creative thinking, 1, 2
  association and quantity of ideas, 98
  benefits, 83
  brainstorming, 100
  characteristics, 87
  creative people, 84
  creative process, 89
  creative session, 97
  crux of creativity, 98
  definition, 84
  guidelines, 102
  psychological basis, 91
  stifling effects, 94
  stimulants, 93, 106
  techniques, 100
Criteria to evaluate value, 62

Demand changes, 212
Designer presentation, 131, 135
    outline, 136
Designers, 111
Development phase, 48, 221, 243
    life cycle costing, 51
    matrix evaluation, 54
    rules for evaluation, 49
    specifics vs. generalities, 51
    steps included, 49
    worksheet, 50
Discounting, 152
    formulas, 153

Efficacy, 204
Embodied energy, 179
Energy, 112, 173–215
    building designs, 188
    checklist, 213–215
    consumption, 173–178, 207
    cost of, 176
    effect of maintenance, 212
    end uses, 179, 182
    energy model, 131, 195
    intensiveness, 182
    non-renewable, 173
    renewable, 173
    sources, 178
    transportation, 182
    WWTPs, 183, 187
Energy consumption, 173–178, 207
    factors affecting, 208–212
Energy model, 131, 132, 146, 185–188, 195
Environmental Protection Agency, 1, 18
Escalation, 153

Fast, 44, 74–79, 137
    applications, 77
    critical path functions, 75
    definition, 74
    higher level functions, 75
    rules for use, 75
    scope line, 75
    types of functions, 75
Fenestrations, 202, 203
Function, 2, 39, 60–82, 137, 220, 265
    advantages, 73, 74
    basic, 39, 43, 64
    bridge, 69
    building, 265
    cost/worth ratio, 43
    definition, 39, 43, 63
    FAST, 74–79
    functional questions, 78–82
    graphical function analysis, 71
    scope of analysis (parts vs. system), 67
    secondary, 39, 43, 65
    types of value, 60
        cost, 61
        esteem value, 62
        exchange, 61
        use, 61
    typical function questions, 72
    wastewater treatment plant, 225
    worksheet, 42
    worth, 43, 64

General Electric Company, 10–13
Gordon Technique, 101
GSA, 1, 16

Habits, 19, 44
    benefits, 21
    guidelines, 95
    habit ruts, 20
    importance, 20
HVAC, 206, 209–212
    control of, 209
    enthalpy control, 211

Illumination, 90
Imagination, 89
Infiltration, 200
Information phase, 35, 137, 218
Inspiration, 89
Insulation, 201, 202

Job plan, 1
    comparisons, 51
    cost model, 38
    creative phase, 35, 44, 83–102, 137
    definition, 34
    development phase, 48, 138
    function analysis, 39–43
    information needed from designer and owner, 36, 37
    inventive process, 32
    judgment phase, 48, 137
    life cycle costing, 53
    matrix evaluation, 54
    project constraints, 35
    reasons for using job plan, 32
    recommendation phase, 139
Judgment phase, 47, 221, 243
    criteria for screening ideas, 47, 86
    matrix evaluation, 54

Kettering, Charles, 93, 95

Life cycle costing, 51, 146, 150
    definition, 150
    discounting, 151
    economic formulas, 153
    facility LCC process, 112–121
    initial costs, 53
    O&M costs, 112–121
    replacement cost, 53
    salvage value, 53
    types of cost, 151
    use of, 160
Lighting, 203–205

Management of study, 103
influences on cost, 109–112
job plan, 104
organization, 108
owner/designer/VE, 107
post VE study procedure phase, 146
prestudy phase, 131
project life cycle process, 112
project study workshop phase, 134
selecting a VE consultant, 123
task flow diagram, 130
VE team, 124
when to apply, 121
who influences cost, 121
why VE works, 104
Matrix evaluation, 54
parameters, 54
weighted evaluation, 54
worksheet, 55
Miles, Lawrence, 10, 63, 72, 84, 126
Morphological analysis, 101
Motivation, 87, 93, 105
Multidisciplined teams, 47, 48, 105, 127

NAVFAC, 257
Negotiation, 139

Objectivity, 109
Operation and maintenance, 111
Owner/user, 110

Pareto's Law, 133
Planning, 114
Prestudy phase, 131
coordination, 131

Recommendation phase, 57, 222, 243
human relations, 58
negotiation, 140
rules for presentation, 57
salesmanship, 59
Resistance, 201
Roadblocks, 24, 44
obstacles to inventors, 29
to creativity, 94

Salesmanship, 59, 126
SAVE, formation, 14, 125, 127, 257, 272
Schedule, 135
Stainton, B. W., 85

Unnecessary costs, 104

Value
criteria for evaluation, 62
definition, 60
evaluation of, 73, 141
reasons poor value occurs, 6–10
types of value, 60
Value analysis, 4, 11
Value engineered energy, 185
Value engineering
creativity, 83–102
definition, 2
elements, 4
function analysis, 60–82
history, 10
incentive clauses, 13
job plan, 32–59
multidisciplined team, 47, 48
Value management, 4
Variable air volume, 208
VE team, 124, 217, 237, 261
coordinators, 126
selecting team, 125
training, 124
VE team coordinator, 126, 132, 134
VE workshop, 271

Wastewater treatment plants
Case Study No. 1, 216–234
Case Study No. 2, 235–256
cost model, 41, 222, 240
creative idea listing, 227, 245
energy model, 188
example recommendations, 229–234, 249–256
function analysis, 225, 242
summary of potential cost savings, 228, 246